THOMAS FARNOLLS PRITCHARD
OF
SHREWSBURY

ARCHITECT AND 'INVENTOR
OF
CAST IRON BRIDGES'

Portrait of Thomas Farnolls Pritchard

THOMAS FARNOLLS PRITCHARD OF SHREWSBURY

ARCHITECT AND 'INVENTOR OF CAST IRON BRIDGES'

by

Julia Ionides

THE DOG ROSE PRESS
LUDLOW
ENGLAND
1999

THOMAS FARNOLLS PRITCHARD OF SHREWSBURY
ARCHITECT AND
'INVENTOR OF CAST IRON BRIDGES'

The Dog Rose Press
26 Bell Lane
Ludlow
Shropshire SY8 1BN

tel. 01584 874848/01584 874567

Designed and set by the Dog Rose Press
in Baskerville BE Regular
Printed and bound by
Biddles Limited
Published and printed in the United Kingdom
date of publication 1999

ISBN 0-9528367-1-8

PUBLISHER'S NOTE

The title 'Inventor of Cast Iron Bridges' comes from a rather crude portrait of Thomas Farnolls Pritchard. The whereabouts of this portrait is not known.

The Dog Rose Press was formed in 1981 to provide support for an 'early music' festival and concerts and other community activities. The facilities of the press have been used extensively for the production of publicity material and brochures to support events in the calendar of the Georgian Group Shropshire and Marches Regional Branch. It seemed logical, therefore, to publish this book through the Press. All the pre-press work for this publication was done in-house in order to bring the project within budget. In view of the changes in the publishing world fewer academic books are being published. However, in the printing world greater specialist development is producing greater economy. Quite independently of the above there is a growing need for specific specialist publications, in particular within the academic world, which are economic and will be printed in limited numbers. The Dog Rose Press seems to be fitting naturally into this new scene. This is the second book produced by the Press and more are planned.

John Baskerville designed the original of the type face used in this book in 1759 and is one the first truly Modern Faces. The face used here is a particularly fine version by Berthold AG established in 1858. Baskerville was born in 1706 in Wolverley, Worcestershire which is about thirty-five miles from Shrewsbury. Although he moved to Birmingham in 1725 where he worked and died in 1775, it seems likely that he would have returned to Wolverley and would have known Wolverley House built in 1746 by David and William Hiorn for Edward Knight . (See Chapter 1) Baskerville established his own type foundry and was printer to the University of Cambridge and published many superb books and several very fine, but popular editions of *The Book of Common Prayer.*

Peter Howell, R.I.B.A.

Julia Ionides and the Dog Rose Press
would like to thank
the following organisations for making this publication possible by their financial support for both research and publication .

The Paul Mellon Centre for Studies in British Art

The Marc Fitch Fund

The Walker Trust

The Scouloudi Foundation
in association with the
Institute of Historical Research

PREFACE & ACKNOWLEDGEMENTS

Thomas Farnolls Pritchard and I owe a great deal to the late Robin Chaplin. Unfortunately I never met him, but I have read many of his letters and his notes with great interest and in many cases amusement at his forthright style. His notes led me in all sorts of directions, most significantly to the Misses Wrigley, formerly of Gaines in Worcestershire and later of Sherborne in Dorset. Through them I was able to trace a chimney piece included in the drawing book and Edith Wrigley presented me with a water colour of Gaines that she painted while living there.

Robin Chaplin carried out much initial research on Pritchard but regrettably died before he assembled it into a book. He was ably assisted by James Lawson, librarian of Shrewsbury School, a great archive researcher and source of information about Shrewsbury and the surrounding area. Another assistant researcher was the late Dr. Stote of Swan Hill Court House, whose daughter Sally has supplied me with much valuable material.

J. L. Hobbs, librarian and archivist of the Shropshire Record Office, (as it then was) also pointed the way towards work by Pritchard and his excellent book, *The Street Names of Shrewsbury*, helped me to identify places where the streets had changed their names. The series, written by Hobbs for the *Shropshire Magazine* on Shropshire architects provides a very useful reference source. Tony Carr and all the staff at Shropshire Records and Research Centre have been most helpful in my researches and I am pleased to say that many of the documents relating to Pritchard are in Shrewsbury and not some far-flung record office as often happens.

I would like to thank all the owners of the houses that Pritchard worked on. They have been interested, hospitable and allowed us to look over their houses and take photographs. The houses are loved and well cared for and together they make up some of the most desirable smaller mid-Georgian domestic architecture: houses that most of us would like to live in. They are the sort of house that a child draws as an ideal.

Unfortunately there were a few houses that I was not able to look at, one of them being Hill Court, in Herefordshire. This is particularly regrettable as it is a house attributed to Pritchard by John Harris and I have given my reasons for not agreeing with this attribution in the first chapter, although stylistically there may be some basis for thinking that Pritchard could have been connected with the work. I looked at the house some years ago, before my 'Pritchardian eye' was developed and another look might have convinced me one way or the other, but this did not happen.

Through my search for Pritchard we have made many new friends. I also joined the Georgian Group and subsequently started the Shropshire and Marches Regional Branch. The events we have organised have been very enjoyable as well as being useful for spreading the 'P' word – P standing for Pritchard. The regular members of the Branch have also lived with Pritchard for some years; one member remarked that I had been writing about Pritchard as long as he has known me. Our thanks to all of them for their support, interest and enthusiasm.

Another pleasure has been getting to know about members of the Pritchard family. Descendants of Samuel Pritchard have contacted me or I have written to ask them for information. Some are in this country, but many are in Canada, descended from John Pritchard (1777-1856) who is described in The Dictionary of Biography, as a 'fur trader, politician, farmer, author, businessman and teacher.

As all architectural historians know, the real cost of writing a book of this type is very high. Many years of research ensue, as, chasing up information and following often tenuous leads takes a great deal of time. It is a pleasurable pursuit though and finding that 'nugget' tucked away in a record office is very rewarding. The staff at the various record offices I have visited have been most helpful and it is not their fault that accessing material is a confusing business. No two record offices seem to work on the same system and I am sure I am not the only person to have filled in many forms the wrong way. Over the years I have ended up with a wallet full of library and record office cards. While the 'blue' card scheme is a great step forward, unfortunately not every record office subscribes to it.

A worrying trend is the ever-increasing charges for photographs from libraries and museums. Architectural books are a good way to lose money and the high fees asked cannot often be met by the author, let alone the publisher. My husband, Peter, has been my photographer and has patiently waited for the right light or the sun to come out while the impatient author, and inadequate photographer's assistant, has paced around wanting to get on to the next place. Photography takes as long as primary research when done thoroughly.

I believe that primary research is of great importance which is one of the reasons why this book has taken me so long to write. Another eye going through papers and documents is often looking at the information from another perspective and not taking in the clue that might be vital to your work. I am sure that there are things that I have missed but in the huge archives of Wynnstay, Attingham and Powis Castle this is not difficult. I have tried to 'read on' and not confuse the Pritchards as happened at Shobdon and could have happened at Powis Castle.

This is not a definitive book as no work can ever be considered definitive and a line had to be drawn somewhere otherwise it would never get published. As soon as we have gone to press, someone will contact me and say 'if only I had known you were writing about Pritchard.' However, we hope that the publication will put Pritchard into people's minds and bring new work forward for consideration.

I am most grateful to my colleagues and friends who have patiently read what I have written and proofed chapters for me, especially Dr. Timothy Mowl, Dr. Terry Friedman and Terry Stone, but as researcher, author, and co-publisher the final responsibility rests with me and errors and omissions are, in the end, all mine. We have also had to make all the editororial decisions such as who or what to include in the index, which photographs to use and so on.

In my quest for Thomas Farnolls Pritchard the man I have not been altogether successful. Primary material relating to his life is almost non-existent and during the time I have been researching for this book I always hoped that some letters might turn up. In the final stages of research I wrote to the Shropshire Star and Shrewsbury Chronicle asking if anyone had any information that might be helpful. I received two interesting letters and some phone calls, but little about the man himself.

Pritchard has been like the 'third person' in our house for several years and has gradually taken over the filing cabinets and several filing boxes. Completing this book was like parting with an old friend, but we feel that the research into his work will never be completely finished and that more information will keep coming to light in the future.

I have already acknowledged our gratitude to those organisations who have funded this publication. Their grants gave fresh impetus to it, but there are many people I need to thank, in particular:

Mrs. M. Afia, Malcolm Airs, Nat Alcock, Andrew Arrol, Peter Bartlett for the supply of film and photographic paper, Sue Bate and her family for the use of The Sheiling where so much work was done, Roger Brown, Neil Burton, Sir Howard Colvin, James Conlan, Belinda Cousens, John Cornforth, John Davies, Brigid Dougal, George and Ruth Freeman, Professor Andor Gomme, Michael Hall, John Harris, Jeffrey Haworth, Roger Keely, Tim Knox, John van Laun, Ludlow Library staff, Maggie McKean, Madge Moran, Caroline Morris, Susan Nakhla, Ian Pritchard, T. W. Pritchard, Ayub Qureshi, Michael Sayer, Jan Siegieda, Tom Wall, Mr. and Mrs. Ward, Sue and John Wheeler, Mr. and Mrs. Wiggin, Gareth Williams, Mr. and Mrs. Wood and Tony Wrenn.

CONTENTS

LIST OF ILLUSTRATIONS

NOTE: Where a reference is given in brackets, for example (AIA 29), this refers to the drawing in the facsimile of Pritchard's Drawing Book printed at the end of this book.

LIST OF ILLUSTRATIONS

Chapter 6

Chapter 12

In the *Introduction to The Drawing Book* the detail photograph is of the chimney piece in the flat of the late Edward Croft Murray at Croft Castle. Before the facsimile of the drawing are some comparisons of the designs and the actual pieces.

Some pages from schedules, specifications and valuations and drawings and actual works have been included in the book but are not on this list.

Hosier's Almshouses

INTRODUCTION

Over the past ten years I have often been asked how I became involved with Thomas Farnolls Pritchard. The answer is rather prosaic. When I had completed the first part of the M.A. in art history, I needed a subject for the dissertation. I had neither the time nor the money to travel abroad or the language skills to tackle anything that required translating. Something in English and close at hand was what was needed. In my filing cabinet I found a thin file marked T. F. Pritchard and knew that I had discovered my subject. Two filing cabinets and many large files later, the book on his work is completed.

Unfortunately, no personal letters to or from him survive and there are few details about his private life apart from the bare, and often sad, facts recorded in the Parish records. His specification for his home, Eyton Turret at Eyton on Severn and his will are the only two documents that reveal a little of the man himself.

The identification of Pritchard's work has proved more successful through numerous visits to houses and buildings. *The Drawing Book* and subsequent attributions of buildings have provided clues to his style such as the use of Venetian windows and doors, Gothick windows with 'y' tracery, Rococo carving on the chimney pieces and low-relief Rococo plasterwork. Further drawings, together with specifications for alterations, additions and renovations have come to light and it has become obvious that he had a very extensive practice within a relatively well-defined area of the Welsh Border Marches. These documents reveal that he was working on several major jobs at the same time as well as carrying out surveys of churches and designs for monuments.

Positive identification of Pritchard's work is not always simple although it is tempting to point to every ogee arch and lugged window in the area and label it 'Pritchard'. Often there is a specification but no drawings or drawings and no specification. Sometimes there is neither but there are strong links with the owners or the stylistic clues cannot be ignored. Driving around the Welsh Border Marches, we see many typical Georgian houses of five or seven bays with the centre bays stepped forward slightly and often crowned by a pediment. They are not all by Pritchard but some, with no evidence, might be and some might have been inspired by his work. Others were built by men as competent in the building trade as he was, but without that something extra, that expertise, which makes his interior work special in the field of provincial architecture. This expertise is especially shown in his work on older houses which is covered in Chapter 9. In this respect he showed a sensitivity to the old fabric of the house while blending in the work that he was required to do.

When I had almost completed the text of this book, I was making marmalade and listening to Radio Three and I heard a style of playing 18th century music described as 'freedom based on order.' Immediately it occurred to me that that was a good way to describe Pritchard's work; he knew the orders, in this case the Classical orders, and the rules of architecture so well that he could create a sound and solid structure, but he was also confident enough to feel free to use this as a basis to create his own style.

How can Pritchard's style be defined? High-quality workmanship must be the first characteristic followed by a sympathetic attitude to older fabric, the whole then embellished with an eclectic mix of Classical, Gothick, Rococo and sometimes Chinoiserie. He often did this by 'mixing and matching' as we would call it today; in other words using different styles in the same room, or even on the same chimney piece. In this he was a true child of the mid-eighteenth century when the rules were relaxed and no one style was prevailing.

It is this eclectic mix that makes his work so distinctive in his home area; we know that he carried out most of his work there and the chances are that if it looks like Pritchard it is. On the other hand, it also makes it hard to identify outside his home 'territory' as there is no real single distinguishing mark. In addition, the contribution the client may have made has to be considered and this is often the unknown factor. No direct communication between Pritchard and his clients has survived and so all the existing specifications and proposals are one-sided.

The publication of Pritchard's drawing book may help to identify the Pritchard style, but this was not the sole purpose in taking the decision to reproduce it. The book is considered as a valuable record of the working methods of a provincial architect who specialised in decorative interior details. The drawings, with the details of the motifs and styles to be used, tables of time taken, the craftsmen involved and in some cases prices, all help to add to our knowledge of how a small practice worked. In the text I have referred to this album, which is owned by the American Institute of Architects, as *The Drawing Book*. There was no consecutive original numbering on it and since it was conserved and bound the pages have been numbered lightly in pencil. These do not show in the photographs and we have therefore added a unique number to each page that will show adequately. These are the numbers that are referred to in the text. The introduction to *The Drawing Book* gives further information about it.

The range of Pritchard's work covers important public buildings such as the Guildhall in Ludlow, private town and country houses like Swan Hill Court House and Hatton Grange, modernising commercial buildings such as the Red Lion Inn at Wolverhampton, castles as ancient as Powis, and several churches and monuments. From the middle of the 1750s, Pritchard showed himself to be a capable architect who was rapidly building up a busy practice around his home town of Shrewsbury. Although he does not appear to have been active in the business of the town, he would have been a well-known and respected figure there. The central position of his yard and house would, inevitably, have involved him in town affairs and he would have been well aware of the events taking place around him; after all, many of his clients were part of the political life of Shropshire.

In Chapter 2 I have discussed Pritchard as 'the Shrewsbury Goth' and examined the reasons for his connection with the 18th century style of Gothick architecture and design. While he did not work exclusively in that style there is no doubt that he produced some very effective decorative Gothick schemes, Croft Castle being a good example. Arbury Hall is a contemporary Midlands building in Gothick style, but here the work was not by a single provincial architect, but by a succession of eminent ones with a strong contribution from the owner, Sir Roger Newdegate. The total effect of the interior of Arbury is fantastic compared with Croft, where the decoration is on a much more pleasing scale. Thomas Malton in 1775 wrote a book illustrating how all the elements of a Georgian house related in size to each other as well as to the human figure. In this respect houses like Arbury Hall and Kedleston Hall are not representative as the homes of the rapidly rising middle class who had money to spend on building projects in the second half of the 18th century. Houses like High Hatton created by provincial architects such as Pritchard were what many of them wanted. As far as I can tell, unlike Roger Newdegate, Pritchard's clients did not contribute to the design of the buildings, but were confident that they could leave the work to him. He gives every appearance of having carried out his work efficiently and as I will demonstrate in Chapter 10, the instances where he seemed incompetent are either mistaken or 'not proven.'

I hope that I have also shed some light on the elusive character, the Georgian provincial architect, who has enriched our towns but in many cases has left little information about himself – perhaps the information was not considered worth keeping. In his essay on William Baker, Richard Morrice stresses the importance of Baker's 'Payment Book' which allows 'detailed consideration of the general practice of an eighteenth century provincial architect.'[1]

The most eloquent testimony to the character of Pritchard comes from his obituary in the *Shrewsbury Chronicle* of 27 December 1777.[2] He is praised for his 'exquisite skill and profound judgement in his profession' and for bearing his illness 'with the fortitude of a good man and the patient resignation of a Christian.'

The Drawing Book was shown in the exhibition 'Rococo Art and Design in Hogarth's England' at the Victoria and Albert Museum in 1984. The entry in the catalogue referred to Pritchard as 'the leading architect working in Shropshire and neighbouring counties in the 1760s.'[3] I hope that this book demonstrates that he deserves that description.

1 Richard Morrice, 'The Payment Book of William Baker of Audlem', *English Architecture, Public and Private*, Essays for Kerry Downes, edited by John Bold and Edward Chaney, London, 1993, p. 233.

2 *Shrewsbury Chronicle*, 27 December 1777, Volume VI, No. 200.

3 *Rococo Art and Design in Hogarth's England*, Exhibition Catalogue, Victoria & Albert Museum, 1984, p. 207.

CHAPTER 1

'Mr Pritchard of Shrewsbury'. Early Life & Influences.

On Saturday last died, Mr Pritchard of Eyton in this county, architect; endured with exquisite skill and profound judgement in his profession, which he supported through life, with that nice sense of honour and integrity, as enabled him to bear a tedious and painfull illness of twelve months and upwards with the fortitude of a good man and the patient resignation of a Christian.[1]

1-1: 6 Quarry Place, Shrewsbury.

This obituary of Thomas Farnolls Pritchard comes from the *Shrewsbury Chronicle* of 27 December 1777 and contrasts sharply with his simple brass memorial tablet in St. Julian's Church in Shrewsbury. It sounds like the 18th century flattery which is so often found on memorial tablets and monuments, but a look through the other contemporary notices of deaths shows that there are few others with such sincere praise.

During his working life Pritchard was the most prolific and successful mid-eighteenth century architect in the English counties that border Wales, known today as the Welsh Border Marches. He worked successfully with both country landowners and town dwellers in a career which was particularly busy during the 1760s and early 1770s.

For many years the amount of work carried out by Pritchard was underestimated because of lack of positive documentation which led to difficulty in recognising the buildings he worked on. The knowledge gained from *The Drawing Book*, identified in the 1960s, has helped to connect him with many more buildings so that he is now considered as Shropshire's leading 18th century architect. Together with his very skilled team he was able to create interiors and monuments that make a valuable

contribution to provincial architecture and design and demonstrate that much was happening outside London.

Pritchard's use of stepped forward central bays with pediments, central windows with luggs, Venetian windows and doors all had an influence that can be seen around Shrewsbury and Shropshire today, indicating that builders, craftsmen and architects followed his style after his death, especially those who had worked closely with him, such as Joseph Bromfield. The similarities, involving some of these characteristics, of the Mansion House at Ford, 6 Quarry Place, Shrewsbury and Wem Hall, Wem has led this group of important buildings to be classified as the 'results of the fall-out of Pritchard's influence'.[2]

This influence places him in the forefront of the many architects and craftsmen of the period who have helped to shape our towns and cities where their work is still visible today. Often we have no idea who these men were, and they were all men, although some of the trades were run by the widows of the owners; Martha Walford of the Grinshill Quarry was one. Who built the wonderful Speedwell Castle in Brewood, Staffordshire, for instance? We can guess at the answers but we cannot always be sure. What we can be certain of is that our townscapes would look very different without their work.

2-1: Wem Hall, Wem.

The Drawing Book has provided valuable details about Pritchard's style for interior work, his use of Rococo and Gothick and the mixing of styles, the materials he used and time taken on a job, as well as the places where he worked. Much of Pritchard's work is fitted neatly into an existing older building so the most useful clue is often the date it was carried out. If it is known to fall between 1758 and 1772, then other indicators such as the family involved and stylistic details take on a new perspective.

3-1: The Mansion House, Ford.

The design for Mr Good's house is a good example of work by Pritchard as it is a typical medium-size house of the period. It demonstrates that his buildings had a clarity of form and simple uncluttered elevations which expressed the function of the building rather than the social status of the occupant as was the case earlier in the century. The house, bounded by a farmyard on one side and the churchyard on the other, had the common parlour and the best parlour on either side of the vestibule at the front of the house. The common parlour was probably used for dining as the kitchen is behind it and next to the kitchen is the servants' 'dineing place and laundry'. The best parlour would have been little used and kept for entertaining company, just as it was until the middle years of this century. At the back of the building are the working parts of the house – the dairy, brewhouse and pantry. Upstairs there are four bedrooms, a cheese chamber and a men's room for the male servants. The house is 45ft. 8 inches wide and 40 ft. 2 inches deep which is not very large in comparison with others that Pritchard designed such as Hatton Grange and Swan Hill Court House, but nevertheless it was a generous size for a town centre and indicates that Mr. Good could afford to be comfortable.

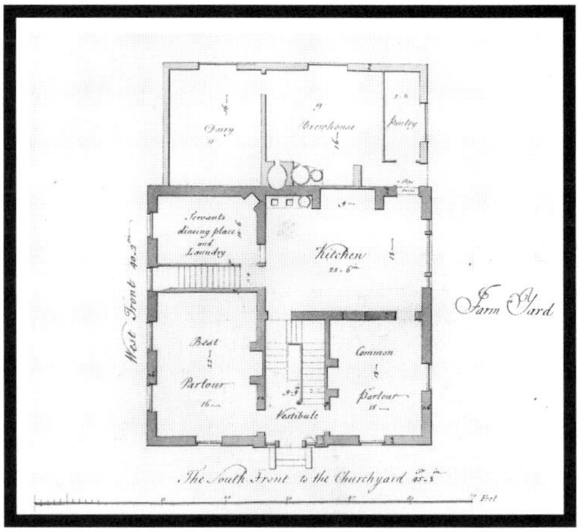

Pritchard designed two chimney pieces for the house; no rooms are given on the designs, but these must have been for the two parlours. One of them (AIA 65) has 'laurell leafe and Ribon' while the other, dated February 1769, (AIA 78) is Rococo in style, its 'C' scrolls enclosing trailing flowers. Pritchard liked to use contrasting styles within a building as he showed at Croft Castle and Hatton Grange, two very different projects. As with Mr. Good's house, Hatton Grange has an unadorned exterior which shows off and emphasises the Rococo designs of the interior.

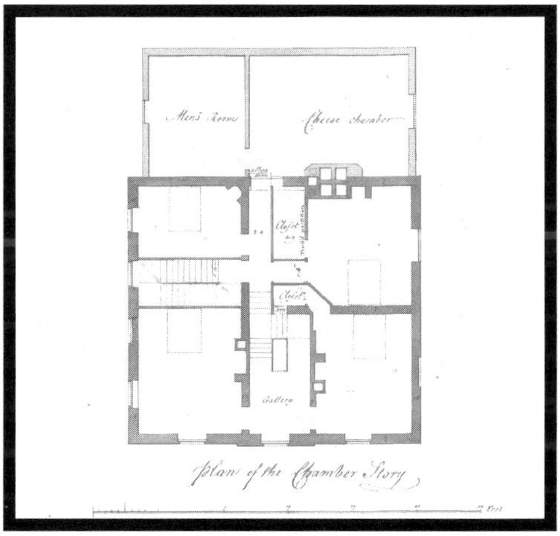

4-1 & 5-1: Plans for Mr. Good's House, 1766.

Other distinctive features that can be connected with Pritchard's interior work are the elegant but simple staircases, usually with three balusters to a tread; depressed arches, often around a staircase area to fit into the existing fabric of a building and low relief Rococo plasterwork, likely to have been executed by the plasterer, Joseph Bromfield. High standard workmanship is Pritchard's hallmark, especially the carving of the chimney pieces, which is of the best quality to show off his designs, particularly Rococo of which he became a master. Often we have been asked to look at a chimney piece with carving that is thought to be by Pritchard's craftsmen. Paradoxically, it is easier to be sure that it is not Pritchard's than to be sure it is. His chimney pieces have a lively exuberance that is almost Baroque in character and while some we have seen have used the same motifs, the carving has been flat and lifeless.

EIGHTEENTH CENTURY SHREWSBURY.

What was Shrewsbury like in the first quarter of the 18th century when Pritchard was born? The town was contained within the old walls and the skyline was punctuated, as it is today, by the spires of the churches of St. Alkmund and St. Mary and the tower of

6-1: Shrewsbury in the 18th century.

St. Julian's; there was also the tower of St. Chad's Church, which collapsed later in the century. Beyond the walls the ground slopes down towards the River Severn which curves around to make the town almost an island. The two river crossings are the English Bridge – then the Stone Bridge – and the Welsh Bridge. At the beginning of the century, Shrewsbury was changing from a town of 'good houses, mostly old buildings, timber' as noted by Celia Fiennes in 1698, to one of brick buildings. Newport House in Dogpole was built in brick in 1696 as the town residence of the Earls of Bradford, followed by the Judge's Lodgings in Belmont in about 1701. Towards the middle of the century the areas around Belmont, Swan Hill Court and St. John's Hill were developed for the increasing number of gentry moving into the town.

Shrewsbury could be considered as representative of provincial 18th century England and by the middle of the period it had become a popular place of residence. When Celia Fiennes visited the town she had written that 'an abundance of people of quality live in Shrewsbury ... its true that there are noe fine houses but there are many old large houses that are convenient and stately, its a pleasant place to live in ... and great plenty, which makes it very cheap living.'[3] Daniel Defoe was also impressed with Shrewsbury when he visited it nearly thirty years after Celia Fiennes. He said it was a 'beautiful, large, pleasant, populous and rich town; full of gentry and yet full of trade too.'[4] The town was so popular that by 1759 the Reverend Job Orton complained that 'a number of gentlemen have taken houses in the town' and this had considerably pushed up prices. 'It was formerly a cheaper place to live in than almost any large town in England,' he grumbled.[5] One of the attractions might have been that 'the inhabitants are in general very polite and much esteemed for their affability to strangers'.[6] Cheap living, combined with good company, was an important factor in the choice of town for 'good families';[7] York is also commended by Defoe for the same qualities.

Echoing these opinions, the newly-established *Shrewsbury Chronicle* ran a series of articles in 1772 about the towns and villages of Shropshire and described Shrewsbury as an 'ancient and flourishing town, pleasantly situated on the banks of the Severn which encompasses it on all sides ... The buildings in this town are in general very good and many genteel families reside in it. The five churches are very handsome structures; and the streets are broad, open and well paved.'[8] The *Chronicle* carried a mixture of international, national and local news, much as the *Shropshire Star* does today. For instance, Pritchard's obituary is tucked into the column on Shrewsbury news with such items as 'a few days since the prisoners in the dungeon of this county gaol were discovered attempting to make their escape through the wall' and a report on attacks by footpads.

Pritchard's Shrewsbury was lively, varied and cultured, and for a provincial town an interesting and, at times, exciting place. In its first issues, the *Shrewsbury Chronicle* gave details of a Circulating Library with a 'Valuable Collection of Books ... calculated for the Instruction and Amusement of readers in General.' The cost of membership was twelve shillings year and the books would 'be constantly added to'. Other reading matter such as the *Lady's Magazine, The Universal Cook* and the *Town and Country Magazine* was advertised every week, together with such diverse events as the arrival of 'a collection of Macaroni and other humorous prints just received from London' and lectures on 'General Chemistry and Experimental Philosophy'.[9] The 'Siege of Damascus', with 'Harlequin's Vagaria' as an interlude, was given at the theatre. The show of the Annual Meeting of Florists included auriculas and polyanthus one year, and for lighter entertainment Mr. Astley and his pupils came to the town to demonstrate feats of horsemanship. During his week there, he cleared 'upwards of 100 guineas from the generosity of the nobility and gentry of the place.' He also put on display 'the Little Learned Military horse whose abilities surpass human conception.'[10] Schools offered classes in French, writing, drawing, music and dancing. The famous dancing master,

John Weaver, after making his name in London had returned to his native Shrewsbury where he gave lessons. In 1750, he staged a performance of *The Judgement of Paris*, his 'Dramatic Entertainment in Dancing and Singing' in the room over the Market Hall.[11]

Events such as parliamentary elections, the quarter sessions and the assizes attracted people to the town; the gentry sat on the jury and came to consult the attorneys who served the courts. Horse racing was another popular pursuit and a first race course was laid out at Kingsland, south of the River Severn and then another at Bicton Heath, north of the town. Prizes were donated by Lord Clive and Noel Hill and the stewards were such gentlemen as the Hon. Edward Clive and Richard Morhall. Race meetings were big social occasions as Mrs Lybbe Powys recounted in her visit to Ludlow in 1771 when she 'flew' breathlessly from race course, to dinner, the theatre and a ball over the two-day meeting.[12]

Accompanying all these events were assemblies, balls, plays, concerts and less cultural activities such as cock-fighting. Religious gatherings were also held in Shrewsbury; the Quakers hired a room for four days for their national conference in 1727 and again in 1748.[13] Abiah Darby, of the Quaker family, disapproved of the town's 'frivolous pursuits' and in 1752 wrote a 'Serious Warning to the Inhabitants of Shrewsbury' about their drinking, rioting and 'wantonness.'[14] Things evidently did not improve as she wrote again in 1765 against 'the Card Assembly'.[15]

Shrewsbury continued to be a social centre even after transport improved and other larger towns and cities came within easier reach. The roads improved, the turnpike tolls were let to the 'best bidder' and the competition for passengers, especially to London, increased during the 1770s. The *London and Shrewsbury Machine* began in April, 1773 and ran three times a week during the summer from the Red Lion Inn, now the Lion Hotel, in Wyle Cop. This was rivalled by the *London and Salop New Machine* which left from the Raven Inn and later by the *Original London Machine* which boasted a time of two and a half days to London in the winter season. Soon the *New Fly*, which was steel sprung, was claiming to do the journey in one and a half days. The average cost of the trip was £1. 10s. for inside passengers and 17s. for those outside. A weekly wherry took passengers from Wyle Cop to Gloucester, so as the century progressed Shrewsbury was building up good communications with other towns and cities.

The *Shrewsbury Chronicle* carried both national and international news, so the people of the town would have been aware of events around the world, albeit somewhat later than we receive them today. The colonial struggle between the powers was taking place in both North America and in India; news from North America was widely reported in the paper but the exploits of Robert Clive in India would have been of more personal interest to his fellow Salopians. Also nearer home, Samuel Johnson of Lichfield had just published his *Dictionary of the English Language* so there may have been curiosity to see the great man when he visited the town with his friend, the Salopian-born architect John Gwynn. The advent of provincial newspapers brought the outside world closer and Pritchard would have been as aware as anyone of the fashions and trends taking place in London and beyond.

THE FAMILY OF THOMAS FARNOLLS PRITCHARD.

This was the town that Thomas Farnolls Pritchard was born in on 11 May 1723, this busy bustling market town, serving a large area of the Welsh Border Marches, much as it does today. He was the eldest son of John and Hannah Pritchard and was baptised in St. Julian's Church where the Parish Register record of his christening gives the occupation of the father as 'joyner'.[16] John Pritchard is also listed as 'joyner' when he was churchwarden for St. Julian's Church in 1743, but when he served the church in that office again in 1747, he is put down as 'inholder'.[17] This confirms the fact that he retired to keep an inn at Meole Brace; Pritchard's maternal grandfather had been the Parish Clerk of Meole Brace so there was already a connection with the village. Today, Meole Brace is almost part of suburban Shrewsbury, but is still a charming little area with a self-contained village atmosphere. In the 18th century the parish of Meole Brace stretched over the present A5 main road to include the area now occupied by Shrewsbury School and much of the land on the south side of the River Severn. John Pritchard died in 1747, aged fifty, without leaving a will and the letter of administration gives no information about what he left.[18]

Thomas was named after his maternal grandfather, Thomas Farnolls from Hanwood, a small village a few miles south of Shrewsbury. The name is variously spelt Farnoll, Farnalls and Farnolds. His grandmother was Anne Farnolls, née Corfield. Thomas was left her silver tankard when she died in 1748; she also bequeathed the sum of £120 to be invested for the benefit of her daughter Hannah and her husband John Pritchard and after their deaths to Thomas and his two surviving brothers in 'equall shares and proportions and share and share alike'.[19] Anne Farnolls also directed that her 'six messuages or tenements in Coleham one of the Suburbs of Shrewsbury ...' should descend 'according to a Deed of Entail by me made ...' in 1734. These are the messuages that passed to Thomas and in his will he left them to Samuel who was already in 'possession' of them 'in Trust'.[20]

Anne Farnolls was relatively prosperous as she left other small sums of money to several relatives. In 1700 Francis, Earl of Bradford, then Lord Lieutenant of Shropshire, commissioned Thomas Farnolls as quartermaster 'of a troop of horse'. The citation reads 'Thomas Farnolls, gent'.[21] Fifteen years later there is another similar document, probably at the time of the Jacobite uprising in the north. This citation subtly changes Pritchard's status on his mother's side and may help to explain his ability to work successfully with the landowners of the

county. Thomas's younger brother, John, served as secretary to the Governor of the West Indies, a post that demanded a reasonable level of education, although there is no information about the schooling of the Pritchard children. Another brother, William, lived until 1792, dying aged 66, but the only sister, Mary, died aged four. The youngest brother Samuel lived in Shrewsbury and became a prosperous hatter, supplying hats to the local gentry such as the Hills of Tern Hall and also to the Foundling Hospital.[22] Samuel and his wife, Mary Harries, had a large family;[23] Mary was related to the Reverend Edward Harries of Cruckton, a small village near Shrewsbury. Harries was one of the shareholders of the Iron Bridge Company, Samuel Pritchard another and when Pritchard died his shares passed to Samuel.

7-1: Eleanor Pritchard.

On New Year's Day 1751 Pritchard married Elinor, or Eleanor, Russell in St. Julian's Church, Shrewsbury. There is no information about her before her marriage and little afterwards, but the couple had four children, three of whom died in infancy: Thomas died in 1757, Elizabeth in 1760 and Priscilla in 1766, two years before her mother. Their only surviving child, Anne, died in 1813. The impression is that it was a contented marriage with only the mortality of their children to mar their lives, although the only known portrait of Eleanor gives her a determined look. After their marriage, the Pritchards lived in Shrewsbury in a house at the top of Pride Hill, while the workshop and yard were in nearby Ox Lane, the address given on the list of voters in 1772; Ox Lane is now St Mary's Street. The earlier name came from the annual cattle fair held there and was changed in 1825. The area of the yard would have been quite large as during the mid-1760s there was a considerable amount of work being carried out on such sizeable items as the chimney pieces for houses like Hatton Grange and making the packing cases for transporting them.

Before Eleanor died Pritchard was preparing a country home for them both at Eyton-on-Severn, near Shrewsbury. At that time his interest in cast iron was growing and, combined with his farming activities at Eyton, he was moving away from conventional architecture. The Minutes of the Iron Bridge Company indicate that he was ill for the last year of his life.

Pritchard's father is always referred to as a 'joyner' but it is possible that he was also involved in building and acted as an architect on some projects. The entries in the parish registers record Pritchard as a 'joyner' at the same time as he was working as an architect and putting this on the monuments he designed. The almost synonymous nature of the words at that time could indicate that John Pritchard was of higher status than a craftsman.

During the 18th century the form of commissioning or contracting for a building was changing, with the employer becoming a client rather than a patron. This, in theory, raised the professional status of the architect who became increasingly concerned with protecting that client's interests, supervising the financial arrangements for the building work as well as carrying out the designs. The architect was therefore taking over the rôle of the master-craftsman whose importance had diminished over the century.

Few 18th century architects received any formal training and the dividing line between joiner and architect was narrow, especially in the provinces. Pritchard's contemporaries in Shrewsbury, the Haycocks, Haywards, Carlines and Scoltocks were families who had been carpenters and builders and later became architects.[24] If John Pritchard was more of an architect than a craftsman, then it is also possible that Thomas learnt his architectural skills from his father, together with a sound training in the craft side of the business. Fellow Salopian John Gwynn (1713-1786) started his career as a carpenter.[25]

The Carpenters and Bricklayers Company Roll for Shrewsbury contains no records of any Pritchards, although other familiar names appear there such as the Haycocks, Richard Lee, the carpenter, William Cooper, the bricklayer and Tobias Coffee, the plasterer and over the years at least five Scoltocks.[26] If Thomas's father was a joiner then he should have been on the Company Roll and Thomas, like all the Scoltocks, should have followed in his footsteps. If the Pritchards were considered as architects more than 'joyners' and Thomas Farnolls Pritchard was of a different status he may not have needed to join the company. This higher status might explain why John Nelson (1726-1812) and Joseph Bromfield (c1743-1824), both experienced men who worked with Pritchard, waited until almost the end of his life before applying for admission, in all likelihood with Pritchard's blessing.

As neither of the Pritchards is mentioned in the Shrewsbury Carpenters and Bricklayers Company Roll, the same applies to the Register of Freedom Admissions of the Joiners Company in London. A Thomas Pritchard was admitted in January 1712:[27] he was the son of Thomas Pritchard, 'joyner' of London and there is also a Richard Pritchard listed for the same date. It is just possible that these men could have been members of the Shrewsbury family and this could help to explain the high quality of work that Pritchard carried out during his career, which in many respects is superior to that of the average provincial builder-architect.

THE EIGHTEENTH CENTURY ARCHITECT.

How did a provincial craftsman like Pritchard begin to learn about the new styles that were so essential for gaining work from people who had the money and leisure to spend on their houses? Training in an architect's office and travel to Italy were obviously desirable, but not obtainable for most people. The many pattern books being printed during the 18th century were designed so that any ambitious craftsman could learn 'the Orders'. These were the Classical orders which formed the basis of much 18th century architectural work. From these pattern books craftsmen could learn to make the mouldings and ornament so necessary for the vocabulary of Georgian architecture. Lord Chesterfield, like many of his contemporaries, laid great emphasis on knowledge of the orders and writing to his son in August 1749, he urged him to learn

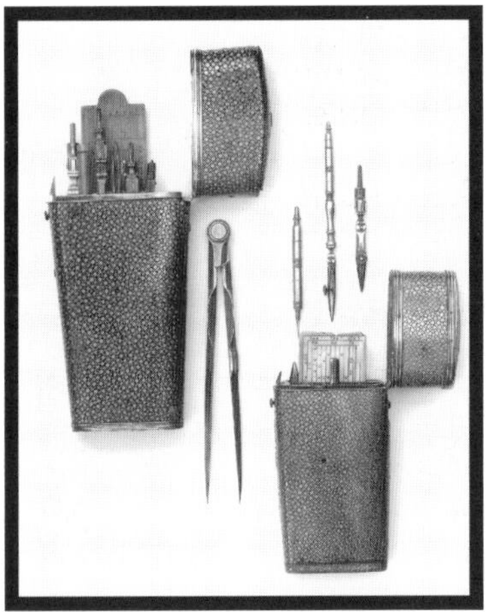

8-1: Pritchard's pocket instruments.

> the five Orders of Architecture, with their general proportions; and you may know all that you need to know of them in that time. Palladio's own book of Architecture is the best you can make use of for that purpose, skipping over the lowest mechanical parts of it, such as the materials, the cement, &c.[28]

From his father and from the pattern books Pritchard would have obtained a firm grounding both in practical building and in 'the Orders'. Examples included the many popular books by Batty Langley and the more scholarly volumes by James Gibbs as well as Isaac Ware's *A Complete Body of Architecture* which not only covered the architectural styles but gave information so that the gentleman 'could instruct the practical builder in not only what he ought to do but how he should execute it.'[29] This book would have been particularly useful to the amateur gentleman architect who, with some education and the grand tour behind him, considered that he knew about building a house of Palladian proportions. In another letter to his son Lord Chesterfield wrote: '... you may soon be acquainted with the considerable parts of civil architecture; and for the minute and mechanical parts of it, leave them to masons, bricklayers, and Lord Burlington; who has, to a certain degree, lessened himself by knowing them too well ...'[30]

The advice of Lord Chesterfield, therefore, was to know what you wanted to achieve but to leave the 'mechanical parts' to someone like Pritchard. Most of Pritchard's known patrons seemed happy to leave it all to him and not play the rôle of architect themselves. The exception was Richard Payne Knight of Downton Castle and his relations with Pritchard will be discussed later.

CHAPTER 1

WILLIAM BAKER OF AUDLEM.

There is little definite information about Pritchard's early work, but he may have gained further architectural experience with William Baker (1705-71) of Audlem in Cheshire. Baker, who lived in Leominster in Herefordshire and Bridgnorth in Shropshire before moving to his wife's estate in Cheshire, had a widespread practice in the West Midlands and the Welsh Borders. When Pritchard's *Drawing Book* came to light in Washington, there was no positive identification for it and for some time it was thought to have belonged to Baker. Baker's payment book records his activities for 1748-59 and helps to provide information about his possible connections with Pritchard, although he is not mentioned directly.[31] The work of Arthur Oswald and Richard Morrice has helped to show the extent of Baker's work through analysis of this payment book, which indicates that he was a very busy and successful architect and surveyor.[32] Not many of Baker's buildings survive in their original form; some of his work was not executed or cannot be identified, so it is not always easy to distinguish his style.

The influence of James Gibbs can be seen in Baker's work, the Butter Cross in Ludlow for example. Baker is known to have worked at Ditchley House in Oxfordshire in 1727, a house Gibbs designed for the Earl of Lichfield, where Francis Smith of Warwick was the mason and contractor. Baker is also connected with other houses built by the Smiths, such as Mawley Hall in Shropshire, Swynnerton Hall in Staffordshire and Wingerworth Hall in Derbyshire. Baker must have learnt much from these master builders, as well as absorbing the style of Gibbs from his direct contact with the architect.

Both Baker and Pritchard are linked with the Infirmary in Shrewsbury, originally built as Broom Hall by Corbet Kynaston and

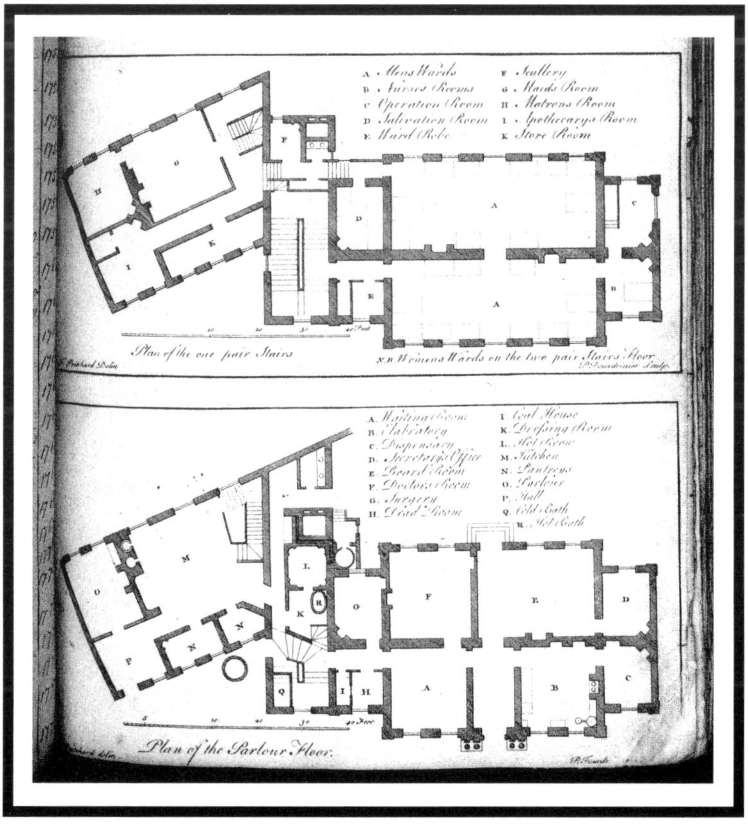

9-1: Plan of Shropshire Infirmary.

opened as an Infirmary in 1747.[33] Shrewsbury was ahead of many of its rival provincial towns in providing a public hospital;[34] once built, it was then partly funded by the annual hunt ball, one of Shrewsbury's great social events.[35] Baker's payment book and the Minutes of the Infirmary show that in August 1746 he received a total of twelve guineas, ten for the plans and two for expenses for his journey. Existing

10-1: Shropshire Infirmary.

copies of the plans and elevation have Pritchard's name on them and the Minutes record that on 10 January 1746 it was 'ordered that Mr Prichard [sic] draw a plan & elevation of the building.'[36] The sum paid to Baker seems to correspond with other payments for comparable plans, but not for supervising the work. Pritchard's rôle here is not clear as there is no payment made to him in the Minutes.

The top central window of the Infirmary has the lugged surrounds which James Gibbs illustrates in his *Rules for Drawing the Several Parts of Architecture*, first published in 1732.[37] Pritchard was to use the same feature around the windows in later buildings such as the house for Mr. Good, so he was learning from buildings like the Infirmary. In addition, that work brought him into contact with future clients; Thomas Hill of Tern Hall was a Trustee and Bartholomew Barnaby of Brockhampton, near Bromyard in Herefordshire, gave an annual subscription of ten guineas to the fund for the Infirmary.

The stylistic connections between Baker and Pritchard include the use of thermal windows and Venetian windows and doorways; thermal windows are on Baker's Butter Cross in Ludlow. Both thermal and Venetian windows were almost a 'trademark' of William and David Hiorn, the master-builders of Warwick and appear on many of their buildings, notably Kyre Park, near Bromyard in Worcestershire and Edward Knight's Wolverley House near Kidderminster, Worcestershire. Baker put a Venetian doorway on the house that he designed in 1743 for the Salwey family in Broad Street, Ludlow; Pritchard included one on Mr. Good's house as well as Swan Hill Court House, both in Shrewsbury and 27 Broad Street, Ludlow.

Gothick was not habitually used by Baker but he showed a sense of humour and certain eccentricity in the battlements he created, which is unexpected as he usually employed a straightforward Palladian style. His battlements, or gables, are usually grouped in the middle of the building on a parapet and added in a token way.[38] Sibdon Castle, near Craven Arms, Shropshire, where Baker worked in the 1740s and 1750s[39] is an example where eccentric battlements, a central thermal window and small round windows are much in evidence, recalling Pritchard's use of some of these elements on the Gazebo in Ludlow.

11-1: Sibdon Castle Shropshire.

On 2 March 1743-4 Pritchard put forward a plan, which has not survived, for the rebuilding of the Butter Cross in Ludlow, but the job went to Baker,[40] who designed what the *Shrewsbury Chronicle* called a 'stately modern building'.[41]

Both architects submitted plans to Ludlow Corporation for work on Hosier's Almshouses and Gaolford Tower. Baker presented his plans for rebuilding Hosier's in 1756, but it was not until 1758 that the Corporation asked 'Mr. Pritchard of Shrewsbury' for advice on this project. Baker's payment book recorded that he was paid two guineas in 1756 by Mr. Somerset Davies of Ludlow for a plan for 'the Almeshouses & Gaol' but there is no indication in the Corporation minutes for the reasons for the postponement of the work or the suitability of the plan.[42] The gaol, in Upper Gaolford, Ludlow, was subsequently rebuilt by Pritchard in 1764-5. These public works are described in more detail in Chapter 3.

Baker also worked at Powis Castle between 1748 and 1754

for the Earl of Powis, carrying out alterations to the north range as well as general improvements and repairs and 'made numerous journeys' to the Castle.[43]

One of Baker's influential clients was Sir John Astley of Patshull Hall, or House as Baker called it, in Staffordshire and he recorded many visits there and refers to work on a parlour, library, stables and a chapel; these are located in the buildings around the forecourt. The exterior work that Baker carried out at Patshull is Palladian in style, square, sturdy and symmetrical, with a strong influence of James Gibbs. Other work at Patshull was varied: he designed the entrance gateway as well as supplying Sir John with 'Chocolate and Glass'.[44] They were obviously on friendly terms as Baker wrote in August 1756, 'that Sr. Jon. told me he will leave me a Legacy in his Will which he must now make.'[45] Baker noted that Sir John was making a will as in '1756, August Died Mr. Prince Astley (only son of Sr John Astley) at Boloon in France, he being obliged to fly from England for wishing ill to his Majesty King George - he died by the effect of drinking - was brought over & buried at Kensington.'[46] Sir John was MP for Shrewsbury from 1727-34 and for Shropshire from 1734 until his death in 1772. It is perhaps not surprising that his son fled to France as the Astley family may have had Jacobite sympathies, like Sir John's fellow Tory M.P. Sir Richard Lyster. Sir John was the patron of St. Julian's Church in Shrewsbury and gave £100 towards its rebuilding. Contact with William Baker would have brought some rewarding patrons to a young architect like Pritchard.

As Baker retired to spend more time on his estate at Audlem in the 1760s, Pritchard appeared to have taken over some of his clients. By this time Baker was nearly sixty and probably wanted to reduce the time spent travelling and working away from home as he had the farm, a dairy and a brick kiln at his house, Highfields, to keep him busy. Jane Dod, his second wife, inherited the house which had been in her family since 1585.

Caution needs to be exercised in reading too much into these links as Pritchard's name does not appear in Baker's surviving documentation, but a clue may lie in Richard Morrice's comment that there is 'a general lack of knowledge on Baker's fitting out of interiors.'[47] Interior work was a field in which Pritchard excelled so he could have carried out this work for Baker and at the same time learnt his architectural skills from him.[48]

FURTHER EARLY WORK.

The Drapers' Company gave a contribution to the rebuilding of St. Julian's Church and this may have led to more work for Pritchard.[49] The accounts of the Drapers' Company record payments of £170 to 'Cooper and Pritchard' in 1749, but the place of the work is not specified. By 1758 he was working at the Kan Office, variously spelt Can or Cann, at Kingsland, on the south bank of the River

Severn.[50] The Drapers' Company purchased the Kan Office in May 1758 for £160 and in October Pritchard was paid £6 'for part of the mason's work' there with a further bill of £2. 17s. paid the following April. Some years later he was still working for the Drapers' Company as he received £20. 18s. in July 1762.

The Kan Office, now called Kingsland Bank, has long been attributed to Pritchard but the house there today gives little indication of what work he might have done, although there are remains of a thermal window. The interesting three-storey house, which shows evidence of 17th or early 18th century origins in the roof timbers and kitchen area, has been extended several times so its history is hard to determine. The only carved chimney piece, very much in Pritchard's style, was brought in recently from Shavington in Shropshire. The Kan Office and Boat House were recorded in the Meole Brace parish records in 1750 for assessment for highway repairs.

An early work that has been attributed to Pritchard is Hill Court at Ross on Wye, Herefordshire, then owned by the Clarke family.[51] The basis for the attribution is Pritchard's plan for the house for Mr. Good in Shrewsbury. This was compared with a drawing of Hill Court in an unknown hand, thus providing what appeared to be a clue to Pritchard's participation in the work there. The drawings have similarities in their pediments and fenestration patterns, although the sizes are very different. The writing on both plans and elevations is also alike, but there was really only one way of using a nibbed pen legibly in the 18th century, which could account for the similarity in handwriting.

The work at Hill Court has been dated to 1745-50 and if this is correct, it does not seem likely that Pritchard would have been working so far from Shrewsbury at that early stage of his career. His reputation had not spread further than Ludlow nor had he, as far as is known, yet been involved in building a country house. The exterior of Hill Court today, with its pedimented and stepped forward central bays, undoubtedly has many features which can be compared to Pritchard's later work such as Hatton Grange

12-1: Mr Good's House, 1766.

at Shifnal, Swan Hill Court House in Shrewsbury and Brockhampton House near Bromyard, but it also resembles many other houses of the mid-eighteenth century.

The Clarke papers in Hereford Record Office give no information about the architect involved, but John Cornforth considered that it might be William Baker. Perhaps this is the link with Pritchard, who could have been the draughtsman for Hill Court, as he had been for the Infirmary in Shrewsbury and might have drawn up the plans for Baker. If the early date is correct, then this might be another instance of Pritchard learning from the work on the building rather than being the architect.

Another early job by Pritchard was the Foundling Hospital in Shrewsbury which is described in more detail in Chapter 4. The building, as Shrewsbury School, was remodelled in 1878-82 by Sir Arthur Blomfield but the framework of the original building remains. Shrewsbury School was still in the centre of the town in the 18th century and Pritchard worked there over a number of years. '1757 Thomas Farnolls Pritchard his bill in full £16.18.0.'[52] is recorded by the Bailiff's Accounts which refer to Pritchard as a joiner, even in 1765 when he was working on such prestigious projects as Hatton Grange and Croft Castle. These payments to Pritchard are comparable to the thirty guineas he received for the extensive survey of Powis Castle and all the drawings, at a time when the annual income of over a quarter of the population was in the range of £50-200.[53]

During the 18th century many architects made a reasonable living. Robert Campbell had remarked in 1747 in *The London Tradesman* that architecture is the 'Art of Building Houses, Palaces and other Edifices ...' and '... is reckoned one of the Liberal Arts: Its use is universal, and the Profits arising from it are very considerable.' Pritchard was able to expend a considerable sum on his house and farm at Eyton, although this was repaid by the Newport estate and the rent increased accordingly. For most jobs where the information exists, Pritchard worked for a fixed fee rather than a percentage which was normally 5%. For the work at the Foundling Hospital, he asked for the sum to be made up to more if it was satisfactory. There are few records of any travelling expenses paid to Pritchard or his workmen, except one payment to 'his man', Jonathan Reynolds. When work was going on at Kyre Park in Worcestershire, the Hiorn brothers recorded expenses of 5s. 6d. for sending a man to Warwick for cash and for going to Worcester 'for deals' on an overnight trip; this cost 6s. 6d.[54] The distances Pritchard travelled were not as great as those covered by Robert Mylne in the same period who seemed to be almost commuting from London to Scotland. Pritchard would not have stayed away from home often and therefore the expenses, and discomfort, of inns would have been avoided on a regular basis.

Pritchard's social status was one of a freeman and as such he voted in the Shrewsbury elections; in 1774 he cast his vote for Lord Clive and Mr Pulteney. The importance of large landowners in the country, such as Clive and Pulteney, was significant. Since the succession of the Hanoverian kings the centre of authority had shifted from the court to the country, and the houses and estates of the great landowners became the centres of influence. The acquisition of land conferred power on the owner and the more land owned the greater that power. Control of parliamentary seats reinforced the supremacy of the great landowner as well as enriching him. The country houses and their owners and occupants dictated politics, patronage, fashion, taste and the success of social events; their approval and granting of commissions was of great importance to anyone wishing to succeed. Sir Richard Lyster of Rowton Castle, Shropshire, described in Chapter 11, is an example of an old-style country landowner and his arrivals and departures from the county reflect the respect with which he was regarded.

At the same time, new money was mingling with old lineage to bring fresh impetus to building projects. Thomas Johnes was able to modernise Croft Castle with money from the iron-founding family of his wife, Elizabeth Knight. Times were changing and a new stratum of society with industrial wealth was entering the patronage field. Ambitious young architects such as Pritchard were able to take advantage of this new source of money.

1 27 December 1777, Volume VI, No. 200. Usually the death is announced with the addition of 'much lamented' or a short piece of information about the person such as 'Mr Jones of Abbey-Foregate in this town.'

2 This very apt phrase was used by Andrew Arrol of the Shrewsbury Architects, Arrol and Snell. Andrew has been a Pritchard-watcher for many years.

3 Celia Fiennes, *The Illustrated Journeys of Celia Fiennes*, edited by Christopher Morris, London, 1982, pp. 185-6.

4 Daniel Defoe, *A Tour Through the Whole Island of Great Britain*, edited by Pat Rogers, London, 1992, p. 143.

5 Angus McInnes, 'The Emergence of a Leisure Town: Shrewsbury 1660-1760.' *Past and Present*, No. 120, 1988, p. 64.

6 *Shrewsbury Chronicle*, 28 November 1772, Volume I, No, 2.

7 It is estimated that out of a town of around 8000 people, 600 of these were 'good families.' Peter Borsay, editor, *The Eighteenth Century Town 1688-1820* London, 1995, pp. 100-1; McInnes, pp. 53-87.

8 *Shrewsbury Chronicle*, 5 December, 1772, Volume I, No. 3.

9 Macaronis were 18th century dandies who were much ridiculed for their extravagant clothes and hair styles.

10 *Shrewsbury Chronicle*, 30 January, 1773, Volume II, No. 4.

11 For further information see Richard Ralph, *The life and works of John Weaver*, Dance Books, London 1985. Weaver had a very long life; he died in 1760 aged 84.

12 *Passages from the Diary of Mrs. Philip Lybbe Powys*, edited by E. J. Cleminson, London, 1899, pp. 133-136.

13 McInnes, p. 81.

14 Rachel Labouchere, *Abiah Darby of Coalbrookdale*, York, 1988, pp. 56-8 and p. 142.

15 Labouchere, p. 142.

16 Shropshire Records and Research Centre, (hereinafter cited as SRRC), Parish Registers for St. Julian's Church, Shrewsbury for 1723.

17 *Transactions of the Shropshire Archaeological and Natural History Society*, Volume X, 1887, p. 246.

18 Lichfield Joint Records Office, 1748 John Pritchard.

19 Anne Farnolls' will, dated September 1745 in Lichfield Joint Record Office.

20 Public Record Office, (hereinafter cited as PRO), Pritchard's will, PROB11/1043 f.138.

21 SRRC, 6001/299, f. 167 and f. 244.

22 The pocket book of Edward Knight of Wolverley records the purchase of 'Hats, &c £2.12.6' from Pritchard in April 1760 and it seems very likely that this was Samuel Pritchard. Worcester Records Office, (hereinafter cited as WRO), BA10470, 899:310, 000283.

23 See *Canadian Dictionary of Biography*, Volume VIII, p. 713-715 for information on John Pritchard and publications about his life as a fur trader, especially in relation to the Red River Settlement, now Winnipeg.

24 Samuel Scoltock further increased his status when he married, in the Abbey Church, a Miss Bailey, 'an agreeable lady with a genteel fortune.' *Shrewsbury Chronicle*, 28 November 1772, Volume I, No. 2.

25 Other examples are John Wood (1704-1754) who was the son of a local builder in Bath and little is known of his early training, while Joseph Pickford of

Derby (1734-1782) was the son of a mason and went to London to work as a sculptor and monumental mason in his uncle's yard.

26 The Carpenters and Bricklayers Company Roll, Shrewsbury, SRRC 6000/13487. When William Cooper died in 1773, the *Shrewsbury Chronicle* called him 'an architect of this town.' 24 July 1773, Volume II, No. 29.

27 Joiners Company Register of Freedom Admissions, Ref: 8051-3, f.16. Guildhall Library. Manuscripts. William Buckland, a contemporary of Pritchard's, who trained in England but later went to America, is entered there. There is further information about William Buckland in Appendix 2.

28 *The Letters of Philip Dormer Stanhope Lord Chesterfield*, edited by Lord Mahon, London, 1845, Volume 1, p. 294.

29 Isaac Ware, *A Complete Body of Architecture*, London, 1756, Preface.

30 Chesterfield, pp. 334-5.

31 Mr. J. B. Baker, owner of the payment book, has confirmed that there is no mention of Pritchard.

32 Arthur Oswald, 'William Baker of Audlem,' *Collections for a History of Staffordshire 1950 and 1951*, The Staffordshire Record Society, Kendal, 1954, pp. 109-135. Richard Morrice, 'The Payment Book of William Baker of Audlem', *English Architecture, Public and Private*, Essays for Kerry Downes, edited by John Bold and Edward Chaney, London, 1993, pp. 231-246.

33 For information about the Infirmary see SRRC, 3909/6/2, Minutes. It was replaced in 1827-30 to a design of Edward Haycock.

34 Winchester had only built an infirmary nine years earlier.

35 'Some one suggested the happy thought that the day of the annual hunt ball should be utilised in the morning for the annual service on behalf of the infirmary, and this idea was adopted, with the result that some very characteristic arrangements were made. Those interested in the institution met at the board-room and in company with the treasurer for the year, who was always chosen for his wealth and position in the county, walked in procession to St. Chad's Church, where a sermon was preached by some clergyman nominated by the treasurer. At the conclusion of the service the collection was made at the door, the places being held by two young ladies previously chosen for the purpose ...' These ladies were from the county ranks and were dressed in their ball gowns - 'a trying process on a cold November morning.' Quoted in T. Auden, *A Historical and Topographical Account of the Town of Shrewsbury*, London, 1923, pp. 234-5.

36 SRRC, Infirmary minutes, Ref: 3903/1/1 No. 47, 10 January 1746.

37 James Gibbs, *Rules for Drawing the Several Parts of Architecture*, London, 1753, Plate XLV.

38 Richard Morrice thought that 'Baker was thinking in terms of these gables as particular features' and 'enjoyed' adding them. Morrice also pointed out that at Powis Castle Baker 'used an identical gable' to those that he put onto several buildings on the borders of Staffordshire and Shropshire; the form of these battlements is five merlons, two set lower than the three central ones. Perhaps Baker considered that an ancient castle had to have battlements.

39 Although there are no direct payments to Baker for Sibdon, there are payments from 'a Mr. Stubbs'. One of these, dated 1753, states that it was 'on acct Mr Fleming' the owner of Sibdon Castle so there seems to be strong evidence for his work there. Morrice, p. 239, n.18.

40 Howard Colvin, *A Biographical Dictionary of British Architects, 1600-1840*, Yale, 1995, p. 94. The Butter Cross is described as 'a robust but unpolished classical building.' SRRC, LB/2/1/52, f.353, 2 March 1743.

41 *Shrewsbury Chronicle*, 28 November, 1772, Volume I, No. 2.

42 SRRC, 356/2, Box 462, f.47.

43 Oswald, p. 113.

44 Oswald, p. 113.

45 Oswald, p. 113.

46 Oswald, p. 113.

47 Morrice, p. 234.

48 Baker worked at Enville in Staffordshire; the large angle pilasters on the stable block seem characteristic of his work, but he was probably not the Shrewsbury man who committed such 'an Horrid Massacre of a fine Gothick design of yours' as J. Talbot wrote to Sanderson Miller in 1754 after a visit there. Miller designed the Gothick summer house which was built in 1750 and it has been assumed that the 'Horrid Massacre' was committed after the building was completed, but the letter could refer to the way it was built to Miller's designs. Talbot, from Lacock Abbey, Wiltshire, where Sanderson Miller also provided Gothick designs, could have been comparing the design with the executed building. In view of his sympathy with the Gothick style, it seems unlikely to have been Pritchard who committed this 'crime', as some writers have thought and could have been one of the building families such as the Scoltocks or Haycocks working as the contractors. It is often not clear what a client has asked for and what Talbot considered a 'Horrid Massacre' could have been something that had been requested.

49 SRRC, MS1831. Accounts: 2/2-3.

50 'Heath House, No. 19, Gaskell Avenue, was formerly known as the Cann Office, where weights and measures were officially tested.' From *A Historic Guide to Knutsford in Cheshire*, 1993: p. 16.

51 For attribution see John Harris, 'Pritchard Redivivus,' *Architectural History,* ii, 1968, p. 17-24. See also John Cornforth, 'Hill Court, Herefordshire I , II and III,' *Country Life,* 1966, 27 January, 3 February, 10 February, pp. 180-183, 228-231, 286-289.

52 Information from James Lawson from the Shrewsbury School Bailiff's Accounts for 1664-1798.

53 John Rule, *The Vital Century*, London, 1992, p. 25.

54 WRO, Baldwyn Childe Papers 4707/4. Ref: b899:396.

CHAPTER 2

'The Shrewsbury Goth'. The Rage of Building.

During the middle years of the 18th century there was a great flurry of building activity as a result of the stable political and economic state of the country, but the century as a whole was one of ups and downs as far as the building trades were concerned. The fluctuations year by year can be measured by output of bricks, tax on glass and imports of deals and fir timber. Timber imports rose dramatically in the years 1763-1769, which are the most important as far as Pritchard's work is concerned. The main reasons for these fluctuations are interest rates and war which led to 'the imposition of taxes on building materials, to a shortage of shipping and cutting off of supplies of timber.'[1] With the end of the Seven Years' War in 1763, 'the rage or at least hurry of building is so great at present, that the bricks are often brought to the bricklayers before they are cold enough to be handled.'[2]

As the century progressed, the need for skilled craftsmen and people to oversee them increased. There was a building revolution in many parts of the country, and as early as 1747, as we have seen, Robert Campbell was able to write that 'the profits from it [Architecture] are very considerable.'[3] This 'rage of building' produced plenty of work for architects like Pritchard, both for the renovation of existing houses and for newly-built ones.

The 1760s are Pritchard's best documented years when he was carrying out major work at the Deanery and the Red Lyon in Wolverhampton; work was just starting on the new house at Hatton Grange, the Gaolford Tower at Ludlow was being altered and restored and the new Foundling Hospital was nearing completion. This period also includes interior details for important jobs such as 27 Broad Street, Ludlow, Shipton Hall and Tern Hall, both in Shropshire and Croft Castle, Herefordshire.

With so much work going on at the same time, how was it organised? A contemporary architect-builder was John Platt of Rotherham (1728-1810) and extracts from his journal of 1763 show that he was working on a wide variety of projects.[4] He was surveying and making drawings for bridges, designing chimney pieces, erecting a glasshouse, discussing the paving of footpaths as well as deliberating on plans for building Wortley Hall with Edward Wortley. He was, of course, involved in even more projects but this brief list indicates the scope of his activities.

Men such as Pritchard and Platt were already skilled craftsmen and acted as their own architect, who 'either undertakes the whole work for a certain Sum, or is paid for superintending the work only,' as Robert Campbell wrote.[5] In some cases, each trade confined itself to its own skills and 'sublet' work to others which was often 'accomplished by a species of barter whereby one tradesman aided another in the performance of his appropriate task, thus reducing cash payments to the minimum ...'[6] In 1747 Shrewsbury had four glaziers, five joiners, as well as bricklayers, a timber merchant, paviors and a stone cutter; these must have been some of the men employed by Pritchard.[7] Where full accounts exist for work he carried out, payments to such tradesmen are often recorded and for his own house at Eyton, where a barter system might have been expected, sums are paid to Dale, a carpenter, Croft, a brickmaker, Thomas Colley, a mason and so on.

Pritchard, together with Edward Smith, a carpenter and Robert Braybrook, a mason, surveyed the Old Manor House at Sudborough and the schedule of work is set out under the various trades: 'Mason's Work, Carpenters and Joiners, Plaisterer, Glazier, Slater, Plumber and Painting'. The estimates for the work in Wolverhampton, such as the Red Lyon and the Deanery, are also set out under the trades. From the disputes over these two accounts that followed, the documents show that Pritchard was paid the full sum for the work and then paid the other tradesmen. The accounts also show that work was done in his yard in Shrewsbury as amounts are included for making packing cases to transport chimney pieces and his own team was used to carry lime, stone and other materials during the work at Eyton. The accounts for Hatton Grange for Kenyon Slaney, while detailed, do not enumerate the different trades; instead the valuation is itemised room by room.

In modern terms, the rôle of the architect can be defined as one of design and supervision, but Pritchard was also responsible for hiring and paying the sub-contractors. He does not appear to have had a large permanent workforce but contracted with tradesmen and labour as necessary, such as Halley and Danders who make occasional appearances in *The Drawing Book* while John Nelson, John van der Hagen and Swift are a regular part of the team. The situation was somewhat different for the Foundling Hospital job. Here the gentlemen of the Committee were their own contractors with Pritchard acting in a general supervisory capacity as architect, surveyor for valuations and purchaser of materials. In the somewhat undefined situation prevailing in the 18th century, there was no single way of doing things.

THE SHREWSBURY GOTH.

Pritchard has been called 'The Shrewsbury Goth'[8] implying that he specialised in this form of architectural design. Pritchard himself referred to the style as 'Gothick'[9] and his skill as a designer of Rococo-Gothick has now been recognised. In 1968, John Harris wrote that

Pritchard 'merited a respectable footnote in the history of the Gothic Revival'[10] and Howard Colvin considered that Pritchard 'was a competent designer of decorative features in the Rococo style and he also made Gothic design in the manner of Batty Langley.'[11] 'Among provincial masters, the work of T. F. ('Ironbridge') Pritchard of Shrewsbury is outstanding,' wrote J. Mordaunt Crook.[12]

How did writers in the 18th century view Gothick? In 1703 *The City and Country Purchaser* and *The Builders Dictionary* disapprovingly called Gothic 'massive, cumbersome and unwieldy.' This is more likely to be a reference to the original Gothic style, which at the time was confused with Saxon or Norman architecture and therefore could be considered as 'massive'. By 1726 the *Dictionary* entry for 'Gothick or Modern Architecture' said it 'is far removed from the Manner and Proportions of the Ancients' and is 'wild and chimerical ... it is oftentimes found very strong and appears very rich and pompous.' It added that it had come from the North and then it was 'brought by the Goths into Germany, and has since been introduced into other Countries.'[13] By 1736, the *Dictionary* had had a complete about-turn when it wrote that 'modern Gothic ... runs into the contrary Extreme, and is known by its Disposition, and by its affected Lightness, Delicacy, and over-rich, even whimsical Decorations.'[14] John Evelyn referred to 'Gothic' as 'Modern' in the 17th century so by the time that Pritchard was working on his best Rococo-Gothick designs in the 1760s, the style could be considered as almost out of date. The influence of the Neo-Classical style was already being felt; James Stuart built the Greek Doric temple at Hagley in Worcestershire in 1758-9 and *The Antiquities of Athens* by James Stuart and Nicholas Revett appeared in 1762. Fashion was turning away from the 'whimsical' Rococo-Gothick.

The first quarter of the century had been dominated by the Palladian style, championed by Lord Burlington, described as 'the Apollo of the Arts', an amateur, but very competent, gentleman architect who had enough money to indulge his passion for building. He was assisted in his work by capable professional architects such as Henry Flitcroft and his most notable associate was William Kent, Burlington's 'proper priest' as Horace Walpole, who made pungent pronouncements upon most subjects, called him. Kent had a whimsical and creative mind and is credited with introducing Rococo-Gothick. This is a paradox considering Burlington's strict adherence to Palladianism, but Kent was too much of an inspired designer and an individual character to be constrained by one style. Most of his Gothick was used in a contextual way with a reference to existing buildings; Esher Place in Surrey, for instance, had a 15th century gatehouse. There is no doubt that Kent's works such as the Royal Barge and the illustrations to John Gay's poems are all Rococo in style, while his schemes of furnishings for Gloucester Cathedral and York Minster show him as a very Gothick designer. He could well be, perhaps indirectly, the architect of the Strawberry Hill-style Shobdon Church, in Herefordshire. The work at Gloucester Cathedral disappeared in the 19th century and the furnishings at York Minster were burnt in the fire of 1829. Even garden design came within Kent's scope: Walpole said that Kent 'leapt the fence, and saw that all nature was a garden.' Kent, while not the actual inventor of the ha-ha, used it effectively and brought the house, garden and park together as one. This idea affected the outlook from the house and perhaps the level of the windows to view the outside scene and had repercussions for Pritchard at Tern Hall; when he worked at Powis Castle in 1772 he acknowledged the fashion of the day.

Times were changing fast: Lady Mary Wortly Montagu sighed in 1740 that they were 'sick of Grecian eloquence and symmetry or Gothic grandeur; we must all seek the barbarous gaudy gout of the Chinese.'[15] In 1754 *The World* noted 'it has not escaped your notice how much of late we are improved in architecture; not merely by the adoption of what we call Chinese, nor by the restoration of what we call Gothic; but by a happy mixture of both. From Hyde Park to Shoreditch scarce a chandler's shop or an oyster stall but has embellishments of this kind.'[16]

Pritchard used all these styles in an eclectic way, often without reference to their context as Kent had done. There was no attempt at archaeological recreation because few people were knowledgeable about medieval Gothic and most were not interested. It was not until 1817 that the periods and styles of Gothic were classified by Thomas Rickman (1776-1841).

By the 1760s, many of the houses in Shropshire and the neighbouring counties needed bringing up to date. The reason why Rococo-Gothick found favour in Shropshire may have been because some of Pritchard's clients were Tory squires of the old school, such as Sir Richard Lyster and the Kynaston family, perhaps with Jacobite tendencies, far enough away from London and its direct influences to do what they wanted with their houses. Gothick could give their buildings an appearance of age and ancestry they did not always possess and thereby raise the status of the occupants. The whimsy of ogee arches, crockets and finials and other decorative features of the period appealed in the mid-eighteenth century, as it does today. Even in the 1780s, when Horace Walpole was becoming more conscious of the archaeological correctness of the work he was carrying out at Strawberry Hill, he could write that Lee Priory as 'a child of Strawberry' was 'prettier than the parent.' 'Pretty' is a word that can therefore be added to 'whimsical'.

THE INFLUENCE OF THE PATTERN BOOKS.

From the late 1720s pattern books were circulating that would make the latest styles available to all. The most prolific producer was Batty Langley, whose publications were very influential in his day. Eileen Harris, writing in 1990, said that 'Langley emerges as Hogarth's equivalent in architecture: a pioneer of the Rococo, a leading spokesman of the opposition to the Burlington establishment, a champion of English craftsmen, and, above all, an avid freemason, passionately devoted to the education of his brethren.'[20]

1-2: Windows of the Guildhall, Ludlow.

Of all Langley's many books the most important was *Ancient Architecture Restored, and Improved*, published in 1741-2, or *Gothic Architecture* as a later edition was called.[21] The book attempted to apply the principles of the Classical orders to Gothic forms and in addition, it championed Gothic for being English. It was dedicated to two dukes who were prominent freemasons and promoted the cause of freemasonry. On a more practical and useful level to his fellow masons, Langley produced such works as *The Builder's Bench-Mate or Inestimable Pocket Companion* (1747), *The Measurer's Jewel* (1742) and *The Young Builder's Rudiments* (1730). These books were literally designed to go in the pocket and be carried around the workplace and on site. They were sold widely and over 500 people from all the building trades around the country subscribed to *The Builder's Complete Assistant* (1738).

Over the past years Eileen Harris has helped to rescue Langley from the position of ridicule into which Walpole and the 19th century Gothic Revival had placed him. Walpole at first admired the work of Langley, but in 1755 he wrote to Richard Bentley that Latimers, an old house in Buckinghamshire 'had undergone Batty Langley discipline: half the ornaments are of his bastard Gothic and half of Hallet's mongrel Chinese. I want to write over the door of most modern edifices, "Repaired and Beautified: Langley and Hallet, Churchwardens."'[22] Walpole had been very sympathetic to the Gothick style and in the early stages of his enthusiasm said, 'One must have taste to be sensible to the beauties of Grecian architecture; one only wants passion to feel Gothic.'[23] The implication is that Gothick, and therefore old buildings, were more impressive for their emotive qualities and were not to be taken seriously. Many other leading architects, such as William Chambers, showed no interest in Gothic, with or without a 'k', while others were eclectic designers; Roger Morris built the castellated Clearwell Castle as early as 1728, at the same time as he was working on the Palladian Marble Hill at Twickenham.

If builders from many parts of the country were consulting Langley's books as examples of fashionable design, it is not surprising to find Pritchard's use of them on such buildings as the Guildhall in Ludlow where the doorway closely resembles Plate XXII and the windows from Plate XL in Batty Langley's *Gothic Architecture*.[24] These arched windows with 'y' tracery could be considered as one of the hallmarks of 18th century provincial Gothick.

Another feature of Gothick architecture is battlements, again to give an ancient appearance to a building and these appear on some of Langley's 'Temples and Pavilions'.[26] The battlements which Pritchard added to Croft Castle are not those we see today. Photographs of Croft Castle before the early 20th century alterations show tall thin battlements on the east side and a pencil drawing of the

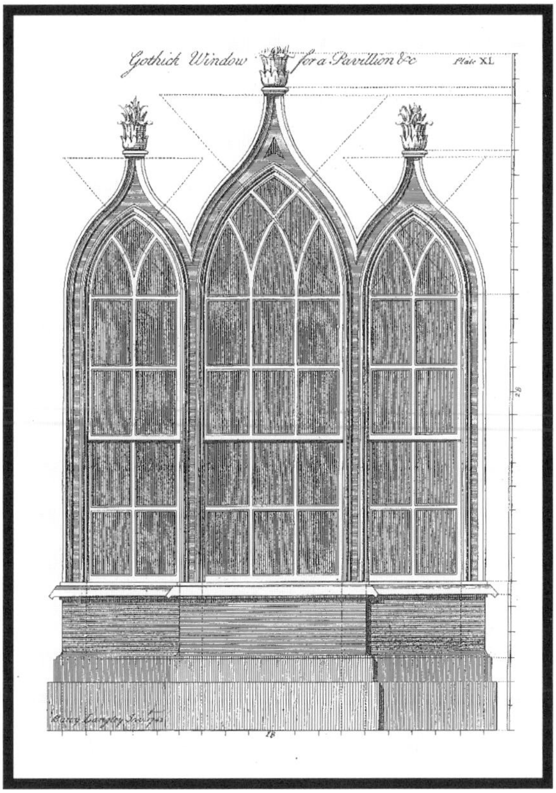

2-2: Batty Langley, Plate XL.

south side in 1834 also shows similar ones with stepped gables rising up high in the centre. The token stepped mock battlements at Croft Castle resemble those on the Broadgate House in Ludlow where Pritchard almost certainly worked.

Abraham Swan's *The British Architect*, first published in 1745, was another popular book which provided practical details and fashionable Rococo-style ornaments derived from French examples.[28] Unfortunately there was no inventory of Pritchard's possessions after his death, so it is not possible to know which publications he owned, but he must have been familiar with the book as the carved 'stair case brackets' at Hatton Grange follow an example by Swan. However, the name of 'Mr. Tho. Farnols Pritchard, Salop' appears in a 'List of Subscribers' to the second edition of William Enfield's *An Essay Towards the History of Leverpool*, published in London in 1774. This book contained engravings drawn by Michael Angelo Rooker, who made one of the famous views of the Iron Bridge a few years later.[29] This one publication, which does not have a direct link to Shropshire or the work he was currently carrying out, does indicate that Pritchard subscribed to others. John Summerson rightly pointed to the influence of James Gibbs through *A Book of Architecture* published in 1728. Many later books derived from Gibbs so it succeeded in its purpose of producing clear designs 'for country gentlemen in districts remote from architectural advice' that could be 'executed by any workman who understands lines.'[30]

To find Pritchard's sources for his Rococo-Gothick chimney pieces, it is necessary to look at the pattern book of furniture-makers such as William Ince and John Mayhew. In *Universal System of Household Furniture*, published in 1762-3, the 'Gothic Chimney Pieces' show many of the elements employed by Pritchard. The book contains '300 designs in the most elegant taste, both useful and ornamental' and is 'made convenient to the nobility and gentry, in their choice, and comprehensive to the workman.'[31] The book's witty and eclectic combination of motifs certainly fulfil Horace Walpole's 'pretty' description and would be 'pleasing to the ladies' as Rococo was considered suitable for their bedrooms and boudoirs: it was furniture made to dally and gossip by, not to be taken too seriously.

Matthias Lock and Thomas Johnson were other furniture

makers and designers who showed an inventive turn of mind. Johnson's *Collection of Designs*, dated 1758, shows chimney pieces which are similar to the Croft Castle chimney frame. (AIA 5) These designs are more Rococo than Gothick but somewhere among the flowers and leaves are motifs which might just be recognisable to a medieval stonemason.

While the library chimney frame at Croft Castle is Pritchard's best piece of Rococo-Gothick, his most popular design is the type of chimney piece designed for Samuel Egerton of Tatton Park with large water-leaf decoration along the frieze, two columns each side with stiff leaf capitals, shaft rings and water-holding bases. (AIA 40) The part of the design which makes this more than Gothick, and turns it into Rococo-Gothick, are the flowers twined around the cluster columns.

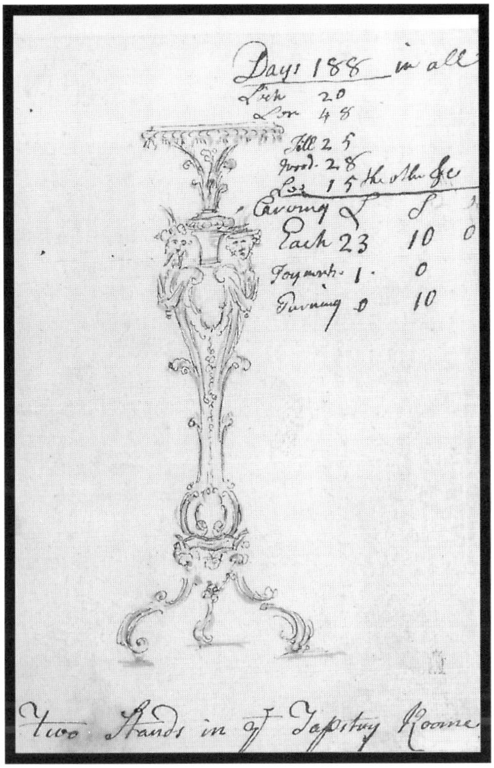

3-2: Drawing by Matthias Lock.

Batty Langley's 'Umbrellos, Gothic Temples and Pavilions' are a delight and there is one to suit almost any situation in his *Gothic Architecture.* Pepper-pot turrets, corner turrets, finials and crockets abound and umbrellos are provided for all positions in the landscape, for the intersection of walks in woods and wildernesses and to terminate a view. Pritchard's only authenticated garden temple at Broseley Hall (AIA 71) pales into insignificance beside the wonders of Langley, but is simple and elegant with cluster columns, shaft rings and stiff leaf capitals supporting cusped ogee arches topped with finials. The Gazebo at 27 Broad Street in Ludlow has a more robust and substantial form than a mere garden building; its high solid profile and stepped battlements can be seen from any points around the town.

HENRY CHEERE, JOHN GWYNN AND ROCOCO.

Rupert Gunnis, writing in 1951, considered that some of Pritchard's monuments were 'of the school of Henry Cheere' (1703-1781) and it has been suggested that early in his career Pritchard might have worked with the sculptor.[32] There is no evidence to link the two men, but there is a third party, the architect John Gwynn, who could have been instrumental in bringing them together. Gwynn was born in Shrewsbury and maintained contact with his home town so it comes as no surprise that he was consulted on the Shrewsbury Foundling Hospital in 1762, but wisely decided not to become involved. Gwynn's father lived in Coleham in Shrewsbury where Pritchard's grandmother owned the tenements.[33] Gwynn called himself a native of Shrewsbury[34] and at the first exhibition of the new Royal Academy, he entered a drawing entitled 'Alterations of an old Room in Shropshire'.[35]

There is an account of Gwynn in the 1828 publication, *Nollekens and His Times*:

> John Gwynn resided in Little-court, Castle-Street, Leicesterfields. He was an Architect, and he built among other works, the bridge at Shrewsbury; with which the inhabitants were so much pleased, that a portrait of him was voted to put up in the Town-hall. He was supported by his steady friend, Doctor Johnson, who wrote several powerful letters concerning his talent and integrity; particularly when Gwynn held a long and serious competition with Milne [sic] for the designing and building of Blackfriars-Bridge. Gwynn was the professed author of that most ingenious and entertaining work, entitled, "*London and Westminster Improved*". His friend, the Doctor, wrote the preface, and, in many instances corrected the book; and, to the credit of this production, the public have availed themselves of his suggestions and very copiously too, in the late extensive and liberal improvements of New London, for so it must now be considered.[36]

Gwynn was '... lively, quick and sarcastic; of quaint appearance, and odd manners ... Dr Johnson was fond of his lively humour, and odd, and sometimes keen, sallies ... He was ... poor, but high-spirited and of unimpeachable integrity.'[37] He was just the right person to show his friend, Dr. Johnson around Shrewsbury on a visit in 1774.[38] It would be fascinating to know if they met up with Pritchard.

> In London, Gwynn moved to 77, St Martin's Lane, a house built by old Payne, the architect, who designed Salisbury Street, and also the original Lyceum, &c. and here he resided. Payne was very friendly to Gwynn, the Architect and also to Samuel Wale, Lecturer on Perspective in the Royal Academy, who was the designer of an immense number of subjects for books, which were mostly engraved by Grignon. Mr Payne built two small houses, at the end of his garden, purposely to accommodate Gwynn and Wale.[39]

In addition to his circle of talented and useful contacts, Gwynn had a good working knowledge of classical history and French philosophy as he demonstrated in his *Essay on Design* and *London and Westminster Improved.* These wide-ranging interests are comparable with another Salopian, the dancing master John Weaver, who was educated at Shrewsbury School. There is no record of Gwynn's attendance there but his writing indicates a high standard of education.

Gwynn was a member of the group called the 'Slaughter's

Coffee-House' or 'St. Martin's Lane set' by Mark Girouard in his important articles on the subject [40] and was on the committee of artists set up to discuss the formation of an academy of arts.[41] Gwynn had noted that 'the establishment of the [London] Foundling Hospital, which was a national concern, and attracted the notice of the publick in a very particular manner, gave the opportunity, when finished, for displaying a scene entirely new to this nation.'[42] He referred with some satisfaction to the 'annual exhibition at the Hospital' and to the chartering of the Society of Artists of Great Britain on 26 January 1765.

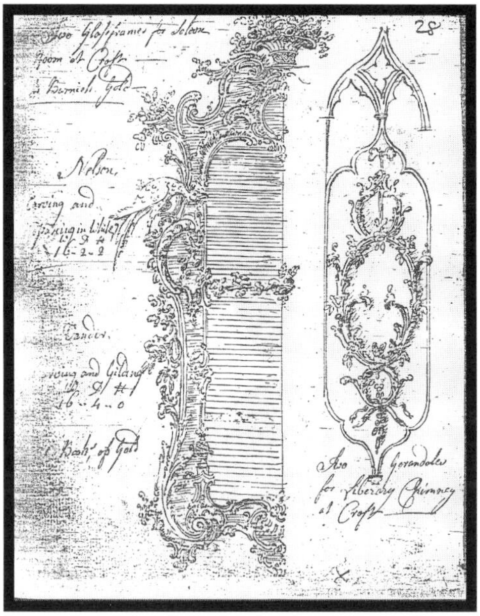

From Gwynn's writing it is clear that he had a sound knowledge of architecture; his example of light in rooms shows that he was conversant with the design of buildings, but there is no indication of where he obtained his architectural knowledge and little known work by him survives. It is possible that this knowledge was passed on to Pritchard and influenced his use of Rococo, especially as Gwynn was keen to promote the reputation of English artists and craftsmen. Girouard considered the style was spread and encouraged through the 'Slaughter's Coffee-House' group, as an anti-Palladian gesture and as a new and exciting decorative form, albeit from France, that could be usefully employed in the work of English artists and designers. Also in the group were Cheere and his son Charles and on the periphery were craftsmen such as Johnson, Lock and John Linnell, who all worked in the Rococo style which they made more applicable to English tastes. Gwynn's encouragement, together with information from Henry Cheere and other London craftsmen, could have given Pritchard the expertise to carry out such high-quality work as 'Glass Border Pier Frame' for Croft Castle.

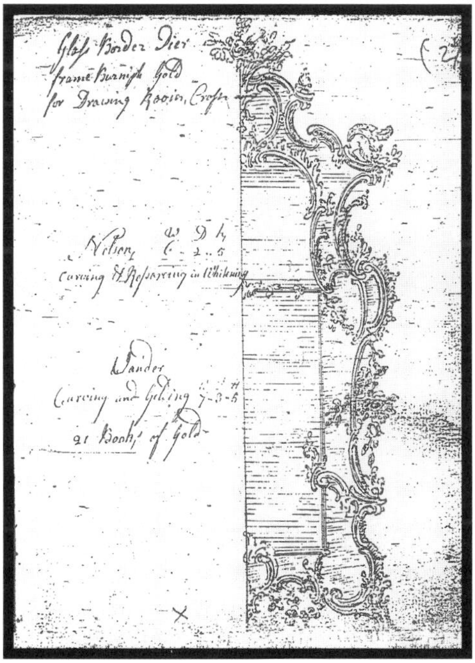

4-2 & 5-2: Two drawings by Pritchard.

During his working life Cheere ran a large yard employing many people. His work slowed down in the 1760s and it is conceivable that both Nelson and van der Hagen could have been with Cheere at some point as their work shows his influence.[43] They arrived in Shrewsbury skilled and well trained in a craft that they must have learnt from a master.

Many 18th century pattern books and similar publications were designed to appeal to a wide readership by including 'Gentlemen and Builders' in the title and the speed of producing some of these publications was in response to the upsurge in popularity for the new 'French' style as it was called.[44] Rococo was widely used in France from about 1700, but its origins went back into the 17th century. After the death of Louis XIV it dominated as a style in France during the *Regence*, when the strictly laid down architectural regime of the previous reign was relaxed. It gained popularity in England between the years 1713 and 1744 when France and England were at peace. The style was also spread by the Huguenot craftsmen who settled in London, in particular the silversmiths, but despite all this activity, the earliest dated piece of Rococo carving in England is thought to be a picture frame of 1742. Anti-French feeling persisted throughout the century and popular sentiments were expressed in a novel published in 1757:

> Far be it from me to condemn my Countrymen for adopting any Invention of Arts or Sciences, which owes its Birth to the fertile Genius of our bitterest Enemies. No – let us endeavour at raising ourselves to an equal, if not superior Pitch of Excellence, in every Science and Profession, to all the Nations of the Globe.[45]

Gwynn echoed this:

> Happy would it be for this country if we imitated the French in that patriotic prejudice for their own productions, which has rendered them the arbiters of taste in Europe; the rewards and honours paid to the artists of their own nation, have been the great incitement of every work of genius for which they are distinguished.[46]

6-2: Chimney piece at Loton Park, Shropshire.

Linda Colley, writing in 1984, commented on the expediency that helped craftsmen and artists overcome 'the contradiction between their patriotism and their work; it was indeed very much in their interest to deny any such conflict. Rococo art and craftsmanship was labour intensive. It employed more workers and, when fashionable, often fetched higher prices than less ornate work.'[47] This neatly sums up the commercial attitude towards the style and the fact that English craftsmen were adapting the French style to their own designs. Pritchard's chimney pieces and other designs, such as 'Two Glass Frames for Croft' and 'Glass Border Pier frame' could be considered as some of the best examples of provincial 'English Rococo' but they are somewhat removed from their original French ancestry.

PROBLEMS OF IDENTIFICATION.

Lack of documentary evidence poses problems when looking at some of Pritchard's work. Even when there are designs for interior features such as chimney pieces and doorcases, it does not always follow that the rest of the contemporary work in the house was done by him. The architect, Robert Mylne, may have carried out the modernisation work at Condover Hall, near Shrewsbury, while Pritchard designed and produced the interior details. Unlike Pritchard, Mylne kept a diary of his work and on 22 May 1766 noted 'internal alterations' for Condover. Pritchard's designs of chimney pieces and a doorcase for Miss Leighton (AIA 44 and 45) can be dated to around this time. On 26 June 1766 Mylne recorded that he sent to 'Miss Leighton a drawing for a chimney piece and another for doors' so this could indicate that Pritchard did this work for him.[48] Pritchard also worked for Miss Leighton's father, Charlton, at Loton Park as there are two very similar chimney pieces in *The Drawing Book* (AIA 40 and 52) for him. The latter, still at the house in a large upstairs room, is one of the designs most often used by Pritchard with flower-

7-2: The Tree House at Pitchford Hall, Shropshire.

entwined columns, shaft rings and stiff leaf capitals.[49] Mylne was involved at Loton Park in Shropshire in 1773 and he may have commissioned Pritchard to supply more chimney pieces as there is another one in the house with a Rococo frieze. This could be an example of a craftsman, who was also an architect, working for another architect.

Only about a quarter of the designs in *The Drawing Book* can be definitely identified as still existing in a recognisable form, if not in the original place in the building. Many, such as 27 Broad Street Ludlow, almost exactly follow their design, but Noel Hill's house, Tern Hall, has been enveloped in a new building and Gaines and Condover have had all their chimney pieces and doorcases removed either during 19th century renovations or in this century during change of ownership.

Some writers see the ogee arch as Pritchard's 'signature' because it was used on the Iron Bridge and link it with the ogee arches over the door and windows of the Gazebo behind 27 Broad Street. The bridge was built two years after Pritchard's death and his early design differs from the one eventually built. The later design, and the model Pritchard made, have not survived.

There is an ogee arch on the front entrance of Croft Castle as old photographs reveal and a large one at the top of the stairs at the Guildhall in Ludlow. Overall, Pritchard tended to use the ogee arch, with or without cusps, for structures of a lightweight character such as the garden temple for Broseley Hall (AIA 71) and the Gazebo in Ludlow.

Some notable Gothick plasterwork is attributed to Pritchard but there are no extant designs. The work at Shipton Hall and Croft Castle took place in 1765 judging from their proximity in *The Drawing Book* and in both buildings spectacular Gothick plasterwork can be found on the stairs. He may also have been responsible for the 'pretty' plasterwork decoration and Gothick windows of the Tree House at Pitchford, just as the interior of the White Castle at Hawkstone Hall could well have been carried out by Pritchard and his 'Gothick' team.

The reference to Pritchard as the 'Shrewsbury Goth' is apt; this type of work was not being carried out by any of his contemporaries in the area with the same flair and he took advantage of the inventive Rococo motifs and wove them into his Gothick work to create some notable pieces such as the delicately sinuous chimney frame at Croft Castle and the spectacular staircases at Croft and Shipton Hall. All these pieces and many others add up to a collection of Rococo-Gothick designs which are probably unparalleled in provincial 18th century architecture.

The Drawing Book.

The most important evidence that exists for Pritchard's work is *The Drawing Book* which contains designs for interior features for many of the important houses in Shropshire, as well as Herefordshire,

Worcestershire and Cheshire. Many of the clients and buildings are identifiable, but it is difficult to know where some of the clients lived in Shrewsbury. For instance, although there is an elevation, three plans and two chimney piece designs for Mr. Good's house, the location of the proposed house, which was adjacent to a churchyard with a farmyard at one side, is not known. Similarly, there is a design for Mr. Lloyd of Raven Street but this house has not been identified.

Most of the chimney pieces in *The Drawing Book* were made of wood, with the exception of three in stone and another, no longer in existence, for Miss Leighton at Condover; this was made partly of marble with elegant fluting and diaper work with 'marble ornaments polished'. Various coloured marbles were used for the surrounds of the chimney pieces. The grey marbles, the most common group, included Dove, Darby and Derbyshire as well as the dark grey Hoptonwood stone with its characteristic fossils. Some of the specified marbles were more exotic such as the 'Italian white and vein'd, French, Purple, Jasper', black and yellow marble and 'Sienna' marble. These surrounds were not solid marble but facing slips. Existing documents for work at Kyre Park, near Tenbury Wells, Worcestershire, carried out by William and David Hiorn in 1753-5 for Edmund Pytts, show that they, like Pritchard, used a variety of marbles including 'white & Viend' and Dove.[50]

JOHN NELSON, JOHN VAN DER HAGEN AND OTHER CRAFTSMEN.

Working with 'the Shrewsbury Goth' were John van der Hagen, John Nelson and Swift, known only by his surname, who were the principal carvers over a long period. In *The Drawing Book* their time is recorded on most of the carvings, so it would appear that they were working as 'sub-contractors' for Pritchard, at the same time as carrying out jobs on their own behalf.

John van der Hagen was born about 1732 and moved to Shrewsbury in the 1760s.[51] He followed the trade of his father, Alexander, who was a stone carver and may have worked for John Michael Rysbrack. A 'Mr ... Hunderhagen' is listed as a subscriber to Palladio's *The Four Books of Architecture*, published by Isaac Ware in 1738; this could have been Alexander van der Hagen. Little is known about John's early working life but he probably came to Shrewsbury to work with Pritchard. It was a prestigious thing to bring in a London craftsman: Ann Ridding, in the 'business of a Carpenter and Joiner' proudly announced in Berrow's *Worcester Journal* of 14 May 1774 that she had 'engaged a person from London.' Van der Hagen's arrival in Shrewsbury can probably be dated to 1763 when the fine work was carried out on the monument to Sir Whitmore Acton in Acton Round Church.

The Drawing Book gives the names of all the carvers involved on a piece and the time taken by them for the chimney pieces and other interior work. There are no craftsmen's names by the designs for two of the monuments which indicates that these might have been van der Hagen's work which he specialised in. This was a lucrative business as Robert Campbell pointed out in *The London Tradesman*; 'they [masons] are idle about four Months of the Year, unless they have some skill in sculpture in which they may be employed all the Year.'[52]

Van der Hagen continued his work with monuments after Pritchard's death and in 1778, as a statuary and carver of Mardol, Shrewsbury, he advertised in the *Shrewsbury Chronicle* 'that he had just finished a large monument which can be viewed at his house; he will do ornaments, marble and wood chimney pieces glass frames etc. with the utmost exactness and on the most reasonable terms. NB. Marble mortars and alabasters to be sold at the above place.'[53]

John Nelson was Pritchard's near-contemporary and his name, along with van der Hagen's, runs throughout *The Drawing Book*. The three men formed a highly skilled team during the 1760s. Nothing is known of Nelson's early career but it is thought that he came to Shrewsbury about 1760. The form and grouping of the cherubs' heads, especially those originally on the monument of Richard Lyster in

8-2: The Lion Hotel, Shrewsbury.

Alberbury Church, are similar to those used by Cheere and from Pritchard's account for the monument in *The Drawing Book* we know that Nelson carved them. (AIA 83 and 84)

When Pritchard moved out to Eyton in 1769 or 1770, Nelson probably took over the yard in St. Mary's Street, as well as his house at the top of Pride Hill in Shrewsbury; neither place exists today. A month before Pritchard's death in 1777, Nelson as a 'statuary carver and stone mason' applied for freedom of the 'Guild of Bricklayers, Carpenters and Tylers and Plasterers'. He paid the £10 fee and as an experienced craftsman, it was immediately 'agreed that Mr Nelson shall make a drawing of a frontispiece with an estimate thereto annexed to put up in front of the Company's arbour.'[54] The Guild and Company Arbours were across the River Severn from the Quarry on the site which is now part of Shrewsbury School.

The fact that Nelson was in business for himself before 1777, although not a member of the Guild, is reinforced by a brief item in the *Shrewsbury Chronicle* in 1772 referring to Richard Winney, 'Late Journeyman to Mr Nelson, carver'.[55] By the middle of the century the strong position of the Guilds to control the apprentice system and work done by non-members was being eroded everywhere and regulations ignored.[56]

In 1773 the *Shrewsbury Chronicle* had reported that 'Mr. Nelson,

9-2: The White House Suckley, Worcestershire.

carver of this town, was putting up some pictures at Nicholas Smith's esq. at Cundover when one of the rounds of the ladder on which he stood broke by which accident he unfortunately broke his right thigh.'[56] Presumably he recovered as he continued to make monuments after Pritchard's death and these can be found in churches along the Welsh borders, while his most prominent works are the two lions at the Lion Hotel in Shrewsbury, one at the front and one at the back. Pritchard may have specified the work for the Lion before his death and it was then carried out under the supervision of Nelson and Joseph Bromfield. When Nelson died in 1812, *The Gentleman's Magazine* wrote that 'his eminent abilities as a statuary will be long remembered in Shropshire and the neighbouring counties ... having had a liberal education and possessing a fund of lively anecdotes, was a pleasant companion,' while *The Salopian Journal* wrote that his 'moral worth excited the esteem of all acquainted with him.'[57]

The other constant name in the design book is Swift about whom nothing is known. There is also no information about Halley and Danders, the other craftsmen who appear for a short time.

Joseph Bromfield, who applied for the freedom of the Guild at the same time as Nelson as an 'ornament plasterer' had a distinctive style that can be seen in many of the houses connected with Pritchard; his low-relief Rococo plasterwork wall panels and ceilings can be found in The White House and Gaines, both in Worcestershire, Croft Castle, Herefordshire and Bitterley Court, Shropshire. Other plasterwork showing the influence of Bromfield's time with Pritchard is in Sham Castle, Acton Burnell and the ballroom at the Lion Hotel. Bromfield became a burgess of Shrewsbury in 1792 and then Mayor. He died a man of property, described in his will as an architect. His architectural projects included work at Styche Hall and Walcot Hall, homes of the Clive family. He is thought to have built the houses in The Crescent, Shrewsbury and owned them at the time of his death. He lived in a very pleasant house in St. Julian Friars, Shrewsbury which has a plasterwork ceiling much like the one at the Lion Hotel, but on a smaller scale.

In this chapter I have looked at Pritchard's work in relation to the contemporary Rococo and Rococo-Gothick styles and have endeavoured to justify the title of the 'Shrewsbury Goth' for him. I have also established that his position as an architect and designer was pre-eminent in Shropshire during the 1760s and early 1770s. In the next chapters the specific buildings on which he worked will be looked at in detail.

1 For further information, see T. S. Ashton, *Economic Fluctuations in the 18th Century*, Oxford, 1959.

2 From *The Annual Register*, 17 July 1765, quoted in Ashton, p. 98.

3 Robert Campbell, *The London Tradesman*, London, 1747, p. 155.

4 J. D. Potts, *Platt of Rotherham, Mason-Architects 1700-1810*, Sheffield, 1959, pp. 10-20.

5 Campbell, p. 24.

6 Colvin, p. 24.

7 Figures from research on the Shrewsbury Poll Book by Professor Angus McInnes, History Department, University of Keele.

8 This description of Pritchard was given by Roger White in his essay, 'John Vardy' in *The Architectural Outsiders*, London, 1985, p. 74.

9 For example, as in 'Eight Gothick Colloums for Mr. Freeman'. (AIA 52)

10 Harris, pp. 17-24.

11 Colvin, p. 662.

12 Charles Eastlake, *The Gothic Revival*, ed. J. Mordaunt Crook, Leicester, 1970, p. 37.

13 Richard Neve, *The City and Country Purchaser's and Builder's Dictionary: or the Complete Builder's Guide, London*, 1726, p. 155.

14 Richard Neve, 1736 edition.

15 Quoted in *Dictionary of Ornament*, Philippa Lewis and Gillian Darley, London, 1986, p. 79.

16 Quoted in Kenneth Clark, *The Gothic Revival*, London, third edition 1962, p. 54. It is interesting to note that there is Rococo-style decoration on traditional fairground items such as caravans, roundabouts and organs. A case of survival here perhaps.

17 Eileen Harris and Nicholas Savage, *British Architectural Books and Writers 1556-1785*, Cambridge, 1990, p. 262.

21 It was called *Gothic Architecture, Improved by Rules and Proportions* in the 1747 edition and this is the edition that I had access to and all references are to it.

22 Letter to Richard Bentley, *Horace Walpole, Letters*. Volume III, 5 July 1775. William Hallett was a London cabinet maker, known for his Chinoiserie.

23 Horace Walpole and George Vertue, *Anecdotes of Painting in England*, published in four volumes 1762-80, Volume I, p. 200.

24 Batty Langley, *Gothic Architecture, Improved by Rules, and Proportions*, London, 1747, Plate XL.

25 Batty Langley, XXIIL.

26 Batty Langley, Gothick Temples, Plates LVIII and LIX, Gothic Pavilions, Plates LX and LXI.

27 Richard Morrice, p. 238.

28 Plate XXXIII, Abraham Swan, *The British Architect*, London, 1747. The inventory of William Buckland, the English architect working in Virginia and Maryland showed that this book was in his library; his use of it can be found in the houses he worked on in Annapolis, Maryland such as the Hammond-Harwood and the Chase Lloyd Houses.

29 This interesting information was given to me by Dr. Terry Friedman.

30 The wording is almost identical to that used by Isaac Ware in *A Complete Body of Architecture.*

31 William Ince and John Mayhew, *The Universal System of Household Furniture*, originally published 1759-62, reprinted London, 1960. See especially Plate LXXXVL.

32 Letter from Dr. John Physick, 28 August, 1997.

33 Further information about John Gwynn in Colvin, pp. 440-441 and J. L. Hobbs, *Shropshire Notes and Queries*, January 1962, pp. 22-24.

34 J. L. Hobbs, p. 22.

35 Wyatt Papworth, 'John Gwynn, R.A.', *The Builder,* xxi, 1863, f.22.

36 John Thomas Smith, *Nollekens and his times*, 2 Volumes, London 1828, Volume II, p. 109.

37 Papworth, f.34.

38 T. Auden, *A Historical and Topographical Account of the Town of Shrewsbury*, London, 1923, p. 208.

39 Smith, p. 223. Wale carried out the engraving for Gwynn's plans for *London and Westminster Improved.*

40 Mark Girouard, *Town and Country*, Yale, 1992, p. 16.

41 For further information, see Girouard.

42 John Gwynn, *London and Westminster Improved*, London, 1766, p. 23.

43 M. I Webb, 'Henry Cheere, Sculptor', *Burlington Magazine*, Volume 100, 1958, 232-400, 274-9.

44 Other probable sources for these designs included William Jones, *The Gentlemen's or Builders' Companion*, the earliest published designs for furniture by an English author. The edition of 1739, the year Langley's plates were engraved, contained twenty-eight designs for Rococo tables. These were derived from Nicholas Pineau's *Nouveau Desseins de Pieds de Tables*, published in France the same year. This work included chimney pieces and mirror frames.

45 Quoted in Linda Colley, 'The English Rococo', essay in *Rococo: Art and Design in Hogarth's England*, V&A Exhibition Catalogue, London, 1984, 106. The novel is *The Anti-Gallican: or, the History and Adventures of Harry Cobham, Esq.*, 1757.

46 Gwynn, p. 32.

47 Colley, p.16.

48 *The Mylne Diaries*, 10 June 1765, R.I.B.A. Library.

49 The chimney piece has been fire-damaged and expertly restored.

50 In 1755, their workman, Robert Greensmith, went to Kyre from Warwick to set up the chimney pieces 'with coves & hearth' and at the same time repaired an old red marble chimney piece. This included piecing it together, 'Rubing & Polishing... Cutting it less to fitt ye place, Putting it in place.' This work took Greensmith seven days at 2s. 6d. a day. Eleven packing cases, made to transport these chimney pieces, cost £1. 8s. 6d. (Details of work at Kyre from WRO, Baldwyn Childe Collection: BA4575, and BA4707, b:899:396, parcel 4.)

51 Gunnis, p. 406.

52 Campbell, p. 159.

53 *Shrewsbury Chronicle,* 20 June, 1778, Volume V11, No. 285. Crushed alabaster and marble was used as an aggregate for building.

54 The Carpenters and Bricklayers Company Roll, Shrewsbury, SRRC, 6000/13487.

55 *Shrewsbury Chronicle*, 12 December 1772, No. 4.

56 For further information see Stella Kramer, *The English Craft Guilds*, New York, 1927. My thanks to Sir Keith Thomas for this information.

57 *Shrewsbury Chronicle*, 17 July 1773, Volume II, No. 28. Monuments by Nelson and van der Hagen are at Overton on Dee in the Wrexham area.

58 Gunnis, p. 270.

'An Experienced Workman'. Public Buildings In Ludlow.

1-3: Typical doorway in Ludlow

During his career Pritchard carried out work for public organisations such as the Corporation of Ludlow. His contacts with members of the Committee and governing bodies brought him commissions over many years in Ludlow, a thriving town thirty miles south of Shrewsbury.

As the headquarters of the Council of the Marches, which in effect ruled the Welsh Border from the 15th to 17th centuries, Ludlow had grown from a settlement around the Castle in early medieval times to a town with many fine timber-framed and brick buildings. As well as being an administrative centre and market town for the area, it was also a social centre for the winter season and many of the gentry had their town houses there. We have already seen Mrs. Lybbe Powys rushing from one event to another and when she arrived at the ball she found the families of two lords and six baronets there, a satisfying collection even if 'it seem'd a mortifying thing that Lord Clive's family were at Spaw [in Germany] and Lady Powis ill in London.'[1] She thought that Ludlow was 'esteem'd the prettiest town in England ... every street as remarkable for neatness as they are for the goodness of the houses.'[2] According to the *Shrewsbury Chronicle*, Ludlow was 'a large populous town, the homes are well built, the streets exceeding clean and many people of fashion reside in it. Upon the whole, it is one of the most elegant towns in England perhaps, the most agreeable for such as having but small estates ...'[3] The paper also commented on the annual horse races and the 'most noble gothic structure' of the church. Altogether a satisfactory place to reside as well as visit and one which would provide work for an able architect such as Pritchard.

Ludlow is still admired today for its architecture so it is therefore satisfying that Pritchard, as a local man, played a significant part there. Ludlow still retains many splendid buildings from a range of periods and two of its public buildings, Hosier's Almshouses and The Guildhall, contain work by Pritchard. He also worked on Gaolford Tower and is connected with at least two major domestic buildings in the town.

There are many Ludlow houses dating from around the middle of the 18th century which have the characteristic detailing used by Pritchard and Baker on public and domestic buildings. These include the large keystones on 13 Corve Street, rebuilt 1750 and 14-15 Corve Street, built in the 1770s. There are houses with doorcases similar to the Salwey's House in Broad Street, such as 13 Corve Street and the present Ludlow College, once the town house of the Coltman-Rogers family of Stanage.[4] In Broad Street, there is a Venetian doorway at 27 and a Venetian window at 38, the home of the London attorney, Mr. Toldervy. There is a strong possibility that Pritchard was involved with this fashionable updating as he had been connected with Ludlow since 1743, when he was only twenty years of age.

THE BUTTER CROSS, LUDLOW, 1743.

2-3: The Butter Cross Ludlow.

The Bailiff's accounts for 1743 record that plans and estimates had been sought 'for pulling down and rebuilding the cross in the town.' It was 'ordered that the town ... pay to Mr Prichard [sic] of his trouble one guinea.'[5] The same entry ordered 'that Mr Baker be employed by this corporation in pulling down the cross ... and rebuilding the same according to the plan ... given into this corporation.' The Corporation members included Richard Knight of Croft Castle, Richard Salwey of The Moor, Richard's Castle, Lord Herbert of Powis Castle and the Charltons of Ludford House, all useful connections for a young architect.

We do not know what the old Cross looked like and neither Baker's nor Pritchard's plans for the new one survive. What is certain is that the cream stone Butter Cross, with its cupola and clock, dominates the top of Broad Street. It is still used as a market hall and meeting place. The pedimented portico has a thermal window above and the other windows have large keystones, heavy lugged surrounds and supporting brackets.

HOSIER'S ALMSHOUSES, 1758-9.

If the work on St. Julian's Church in 1748-9 marked the first recorded major architectural work by Pritchard, then the work on Hosier's Almshouses in Ludlow in 1758 spread his reputation more widely around Shropshire and the Welsh Border Marches. Hosier's Almshouses, like all the former property of the Palmers' Guild, was taken over by the Corporation of Ludlow after the Reformation.[6] The Guild had been founded in Ludlow in about 1250 and by the end of the 14th century its membership, numbering over 4000, was all over the country. Members paid fees or made donations so that priests could be employed by the Guild to say masses in the Parish Church both before and after the death of the member.

John Leland, who visited the town in about 1540, noted that 'there was a very rich merchant in Ludlowe not long synce called Hosier, buried in the parish church.'[7] John Hosier died in 1463 and in 1486 his executors gave the Almshouses to the Palmers' Guild 'as a permanent endowment'.[8] Before the Reformation, only brethren of the Guild were admitted to the Almshouses, which in 1551 had '33 chambers, each with a chimney'. In 1552 the Almshouses, together with all the property of the Palmers' Guild, became the property of the Corporation, who administered it until 1806 when the duty was passed to a small committee.

By 1732, the Almshouses appear to have become rather dilapidated; nine of the residents complained that they were 'in manifest danger of their lives owing to the collapse of partitions between the chambers, and the poor conditions of floors.'[9] Eight years later the residents were still just as concerned about their safety as nothing had been done and the inmates were ordered 'to reside [there] under threat of stopping their pay.'[10] It was not until 1756 that the Corporation decided that they could no longer put off the work and in January the Corporation asked Somerset

3-3: Hosier's Almshouses

Davies to 'produce an estimate and plan in order for the building of the almshouses.'[11] The minute for the following month gave 'An estimate of expense of rebuilding of almes House at Ludlow according to a plan del. by William Baker.'[12] Baker proposed to

> pull down the old buildings and lay off materials in the churchyard or some other convenient place and carry off rubbish into or near the road way; to dig a foundation and lay of same with old stone - to build all of back wall and north end with old stone - to build all of rest of walls with brick, to cover the whole building with old and new tiles to lay brick floors ...[13]

Unfortunately the remainder of Baker's estimate is missing so there is no indication of the cost. Perhaps it was rather high, or what the Corporation considered high, because it took them another two years to revive the project. The Corporation then set up a committee and in February 1758 the rebuilding was finally approved, with Pritchard now in charge of the job.

The work on the Almshouses was a significant turning point in Pritchard's career as well as bringing him further important connections with the members of the Corporation who now included Thomas Johnes of Croft Castle, Somerset Davies who lived at 27 Broad Street, Ludlow and Edward Harley whose family owned much property on the Herefordshire and Welsh border. [14]

No plans or estimates by Pritchard exist for this work on the Almshouses, but as the Corporation had asked Baker to prepare plans, and paid him, they probably used them when the rebuilding actually did take place. Therefore the work that Pritchard surveyed and supervised was almost certainly designed by Baker; the windows, with their rather overlarge keystones, have a certain similarity to the house he built for the Salweys in Broad Street.

Today the external appearance of Hosier's Almshouses, next to the Parish Church, is little changed. Just as the Butter Cross acts as a foil to the adjacent timber-framed building, so the brick Hosier's Almshouses, with its almost domestic scale, is a counter to the grandeur of the Perpendicular St. Laurence's Church and its exceedingly tall tower. In the 18th century, Hosier's Almshouses would have seemed a large building and Ludlow must have been very proud of its handsome new addition which consisted of a three-storey brick block of seven bays, the centre bay stepped forward under a pediment. There are two cross wings of two bays each. The keystones, included in Pritchard's survey of December 1758, are still above the windows, but the sashes have been replaced by modern casement windows.

John Yates, a mason who worked regularly with Pritchard, made the steps and worked on the flagstones. He also assisted the carver to 'get out the ground of the arms'. This was the Corporation's coat of arms over the front entrance and for this work Yates submitted a bill for '19 days myself 1.18.0; 13 days my sun 0.17.4'.[15]

The cartouche, containing the Corporation coat of arms, made by Yates and his 'sun',[16] is still on the pediment. Below the pediment is a Latin inscription recording the rebuilding and below that is a round-headed niche.

By the end of 1758 work was progressing well. At the beginning of December Pritchard 'Measur'd and abstracted' the work and signed a valuation of £27. 2s. 5d. The valuation was for both stone and woodwork as well as keystones and trusses.

In March 1759 payment was recorded to 'master workmen and labourer pulling down for a week - £8.17.2.' A week later payment of £8. 13s. 9d 'to the same' was recorded. A larger sum of £14. 16s. 3½d. was paid on 1 April for 'the same and to a supervisor of the work.'

All must have proceeded well; on 24 July £2. 2s. was recorded as a further payment to the 'supervisor for extraordinary diligence and other things not charged.'[17] The supervisor could have been Jonathan Reynolds, described in one entry as 'A person sent to look over the work'. The accounts record 'pd. Mr. Pritchard's man, Jonathan Reynolds £2.1s.'[18] Reynolds's name is also mentioned in the Bailiff's accounts for Shrewsbury School as well as the Foundling Hospital so he must have worked with Pritchard for some years. His name occurs throughout the accounts for the rebuilding of the Almshouses; he signed the day work sheets presented to him on small scraps of paper, painstakingly written by the workmen. The minutes include a payment to him for expenses and five shillings for a journey from 'Wolverhampton to Ludlow 29 June' but no reason is given for it.

Reynolds acknowledged receipt of payment from the Corporation of Ludlow for '29 days and a half work and ale demands.'[19] Ale was traditionally provided for the workmen at significant stages of building and when the laying of the foundation was completed, the Corporation paid five shillings and ten pence. Mr. James Wilde also surveyed the Almshouses and was paid for this work in December 1758 and May 1759; on both occasions that payment was £10. 10s. He could have been another foreman or clerk of works employed by Pritchard as Ludlow is a good day's ride from Shrewsbury and he would have needed responsible people on the site. At the same time as work on the Almshouses was progressing, he was involved with Tern Hall, near Shrewsbury. An undated entry in the accounts recorded that a payment of £21 was made to 'mr. Richard [sic] Farnolls Pritchard for planning and surveying the work from time to time.'[20]

Costs were cut at the rear of the building and 'the materials' which Baker had been instructed to set aside in the churchyard were used to make the back walls of rubble stone, but as the site is tightly packed this is not very visible. Some old mullion and transom windows with lead glazing were also retained and used where they would not be seen.

Internally the building has been completely modernised and the cornices that Pritchard valued have disappeared. Handsome iron railings and a gate with a lantern over it were erected in the early nineteenth century but unfortunately removed in 1968; a photograph of 1959 shows them still in place. The Almshouses still serve the same purpose over 500 years after John Hosier first endowed them. The residents no longer have the strict regime of doors being locked at nine in the evening, but they have secure and comfortable accommodation, as the endowment intended.

GAOLFORD'S TOWER, 1764-5.

The Gaol, on the site of Gaolford's Tower, was demolished in the 20th century. It was part of the medieval defensive system of towers, gates and walls that once enclosed Ludlow. The Record of Public Works states that 'this building was erected at the charge of the Corporation ... for the common prison of this town in the place of Gaolford Tower an ancient gate and prison become ruinous by length of time.'[21] The only known photograph of it, taken in the 1890s, shows a tall, plain three-bay building with a central pedimented bay that is slightly stepped forward. There is an arched window under the pediment and below this is a string course and a stone tablet for an inscription, perhaps with the wording quoted above. The window on the right of the stone entrance is round-headed, perhaps remaining from the original tower.

4-3: Gaolford, Ludlow, 1895.

During the time Pritchard was working on the Foundling Hospital he was also working in Ludlow on Gaolford's Tower, a job which is typical of small towns, then and now: uncertainty about which course of action to take, builders putting forward estimates with additions, not agreeing with the architect's proposals and the building partnerships appearing to change during the course of the work.

The 'Scheme for repairing Ludlow Gaol' was originally drawn up by William Baker in an undated document.[22] In the same bundle of documents, there is also an estimate to the value of £90 from Walter Hattam, who later worked with Pritchard at the Guildhall. In March 1763, 'Mr Baker's plan was delivered to Mr Pritchard' and a minute of June recorded that he had done a survey and delivered a plan for the repairs to be done to the tower. Davies and Watkiss then put in their estimates to 'repair and alter Gaolfords Tower in the manner intended by Mr Pritchard with the following additional work which is not mentioned by him although absolutely necessary.'[23]

Pritchard's proposals included, among other items, building a 'partition two bricks thick across the North tower to make a dungeon ... a new window with iron barrs ... to open an old doorway in the north tower ... to make a strong door to fit into it.'[24] All the rooms 'described on the plan' were to have 'necessary places'[25] which would be plastered and whitewashed. At this date the battlements on the tower must have been surviving as one item instructs that the 'bad parts' of these should be taken down and the 'whole' to be repaired with a 'broad stone copeing' put on. Additional items entailed removing the 'decay'd roof' which was beyond repair as it had been mended so often and to recast sheets of lead that were faulty. The documents noted that many of the sheets of lead were 'much too short for their places; others cract and torn in a bad matter so as not to be made sound by soldering.' The estimate of Davies and Watkiss came to £212. 14s.

Another team of builders, Goodwyn and Sheward, also put in an estimate according to Pritchard's proposals and this came to £183. The carpenter, Edwin Goodwin, gave a separate estimate of £63, which included 'one strong double door bound with iron by the constables prison.' Goodwyn and Sheward planned to use Clay (Clee) Hill free stone for all the new windows 'with good substantial iron work in all the several windows likewise whatsoever iron work shall be wanted for the splicing and scarfing on the timbers upon the roof.'[26]

In the end it may have been decided that the tower was 'too ruinous by length of time' to be fully repaired. An agreement was made with Watkiss and Sheward in May 1764, who by this time seemed to have joined forces, to 'pull down the westward front of Gaolford Tower from the buttrices on the northside to the chimney place on the south side and to rebuild the same in a good and workmanlike manner with stone face and laid in courses.' The builders had to provide all the materials and the first £35 would be paid as work started with completion by 1 September. Walter Hattam proposed to 'put down the front and rebuild up same ... with one large arch for a gateway with stone 4 windows in front ... and the walls on the front and back towers to be coped and finished battlement

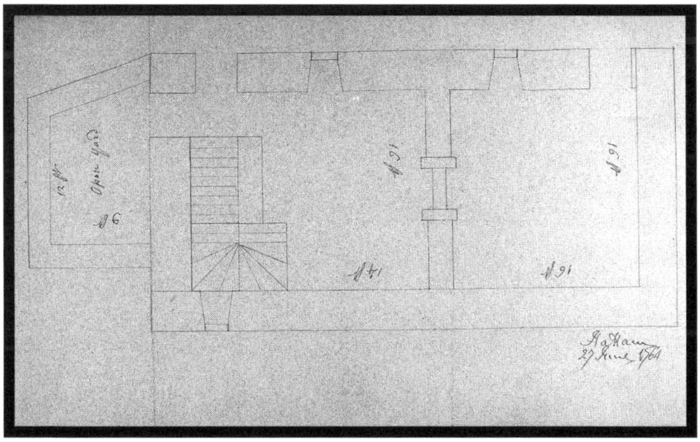

5-3: Plan of Goalford Tower, 1764.

fashion ...'[27] A simple drawing, labelled 'Walter Hattam's plan 27 June 1764' shows a building 20ft. long and 9ft. deep with thick stone walls and a central partition with a staircase in one corner.[28] This scheme does not appear to have been the one built, although there is no record of who carried out the building work.

In the photograph, compared with the brick buildings around it, the 'Clay Hill' stone looks rough so perhaps true to its character it had weathered badly. There are no indications of any battlements and the steeply-pitched roof could date from the 19th century. Only one stone wall remains today in the position of Gaolford's Tower, but the building opposite the site of the Gaol, until recently a public house, looks very similar to the Gaol as it was in the 18th century. It has a small pediment above a slightly stepped forward central bay and could once have been part of the complex of Gaol buildings.

THE GUILDHALL LUDLOW, 1774-6.

6-3: The Guildhall, Ludlow.

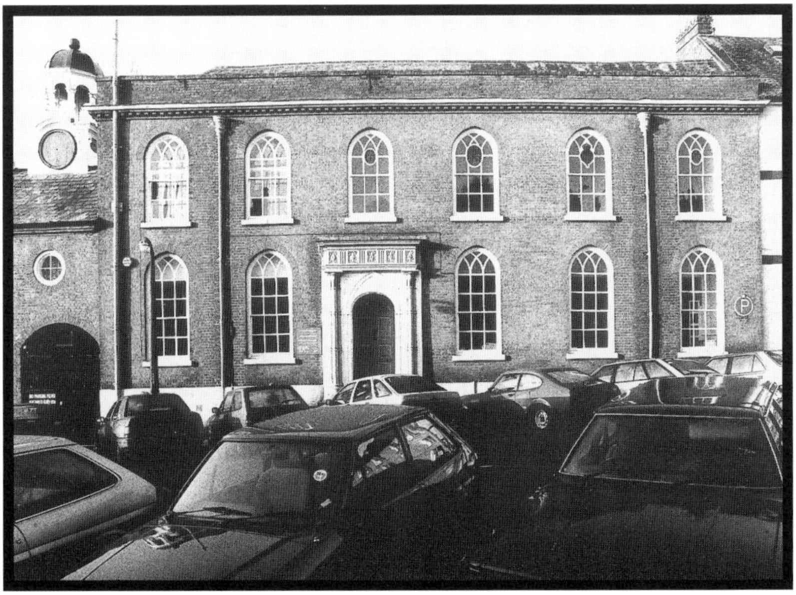

The work on the medieval Guildhall in 1774 was another important later commission for the Ludlow Corporation. The Guildhall had also been a Palmers' Guild building and in 1552, after the Reformation, it became the property of the Corporation. The splendid timber roof, now mainly concealed under the 18th century ceiling, testifies to the wealth of the Guild. The Court of the Council of the Welsh Marches also sat at the Guildhall before it was abolished at the end of the 17th century.

Today the brick building presents an elegant front elevation of six bays onto Mill Street, one of Ludlow's main streets, which slopes down to the River Teme where there were once water-powered mills. A cross section of the street shows the road rising upwards by the Guildhall, which is surrounded by houses that were also modernised in the 18th century. The true medieval nature of these houses lies in their roof timbers and timber-framed structures.

Pritchard did not alter the basic form of the Guildhall

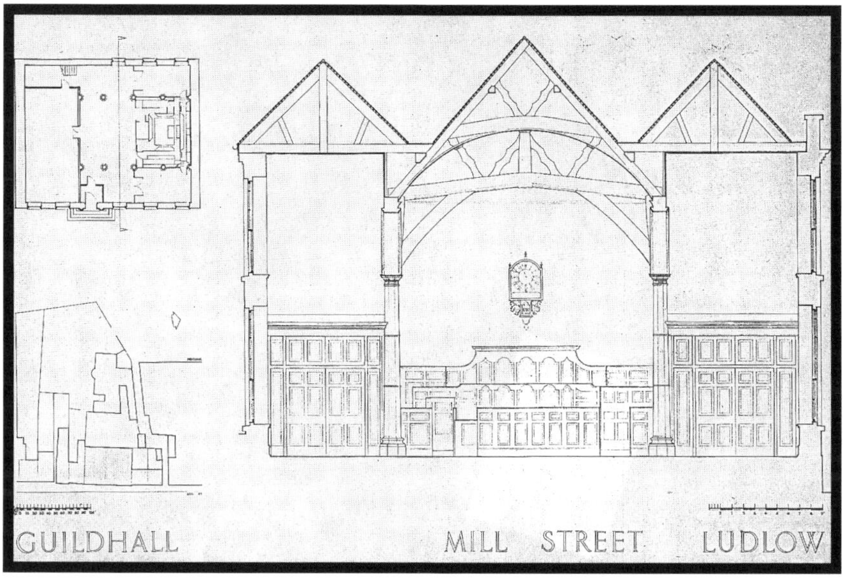

7-3: Drawing of the Guildhall.

externally and retained its rectangular shape while changing the layout of the spaces internally. The central space was occupied by the aisled hall which ran from north to south and may originally have been larger and extended further to the north. This space is now divided into the court room and offices. After the Reformation the south part was used for the storage of grain. The front, or east, elevation has eleven round-headed windows with 'y' tracery and the main doorway is placed asymmetrically with three bays on one side and two on the other, a form dictated by the timber framing behind.

8-3: Doorway of the Guildhall.

By the time that Pritchard was asked to work on the property it was probably somewhat run down and so the walls were rebuilt in brick, concealing the timber framing beneath. Internally 'the timber uprights of its hall [were] prettily encased in Gothic columns'[29] and a false ceiling put over the great hall. This obscures most of the fine timber roof but some of the cusped wind braces can still be seen. The courtroom fittings, now painted pale blue and grey, seem more suited to a theatre, but they do present a very good example of an 18th century courtroom which is still in use today. The original 18th century ironwork and oak floor have been retained.

The accounts for the Guildhall have survived and show that the main contractor was Walter Hattam, who had worked with Pritchard on Gaolford's Tower. The main stage of the work, costing £233. 17s. 6d., was 'Measured & Valued by Mr Pritchard' in 1774 and included 'turning out column posts, stopping the joints and Grooving pieces in the

9-3: Interior of the Guildhall.

Old Beams Casing and Moulding the Braces above the Beams.'[30] The 'deal shafts to Octagon Pillars' came to a total of £21. 0s. 10d. Three hundred and fifty two foot of oak for sash frames and astragal sashes were used; four chimney pieces were put in and both square and turned balusters used on the stairs. A new oak table 'framed for the Barr' cost £4. 4s. and 'one pair of mortice dovetail hinges and putting on the locks' was 5s. 6d. At one stage Walter Hattam forgot to charge for 21ft. of 'ovolo deal wainscot' although it had been measured by Pritchard and the 16s. 3d involved would have been quite a loss to the builder.

The names of the craftsmen are given in the accounts; Edward Jones supplied the ironwork, while the mason's work was carried out by Thomas Wathies. Workers such as William Davies, Thomas Burgess, Thomas Woodale, James Weston, John White and John Harris were paid by the day. From the daily rates paid it is clear that the work continued during the winter of 1774-5 as day work payments are recorded for January and February. There is no record of payment to Pritchard for this job which he completed in 1776 when he 'measured & abstracted' the work for, among other items, '24 yds. of bricks and half walling in windows' and 'lime and sand to chimney pieces'.

The Guildhall is notable for its Gothic doorway on the front elevation; the arch around the doorway, the quatrefoil above and the frieze bear a close resemblance to Plate XXII, Sixth Frontispiece,[31] from Batty Langley's *Gothic Architecture* of 1747. As noted, the Guildhall's windows are similar to Plate XL in the same book.

It is not clear why Pritchard chose Gothick for the Guildhall. The 1770s are late for work in this style and he might have been expected to put on a Classical façade and update the building internally in a more modern fashion. Mindful of the ancient history of the building, he probably used what he considered a suitable style. The Ludlow Corporation were not opposed to 'modern' building as they had demonstrated when the Butter Cross was rebuilt nearly thirty years earlier. The conclusion has to be that Pritchard, by now a very experienced and respected architect, made the decision to choose Gothick out of respect for the age of the Guildhall. This idea is reinforced by the splendid ogee that spans the width of the staircase on the top landing at the back of the building. There is a depressed cusped ogee arch at the bottom of the stairs, in an area now made secure, leading to the courtroom; this arch is very similar to the arch dividing two of the rooms at Gaines in Worcestershire.

The Guildhall was admired: ' ... is a very elegant building ...

the Hall, in which sundry meetings of the Corporation, Quarter Sessions etc are holden, is large and commodiously adapted to the purpose ...'[32] John Price wrote in *The Ludlow Guide* of about 1795.

The final valuation took place a year before Pritchard's death and it would be interesting to know how often he had to come to Ludlow. Some of the valuations could have been done from the accounts submitted by the workmen, but the work needed to be measured to check the accuracy of their claims. There is no mention of Jonathan Reynolds or anyone else acting as 'Mr Pritchard's man'. Often this necessitated remaining there overnight. Was Pritchard invited to stay with Somerset Davies at 27 Broad Street? It would be pleasant to think that he did as Mrs Lybbe Powys said that the hospitality of the Davies household was 'in the Highest elegance.'[33]

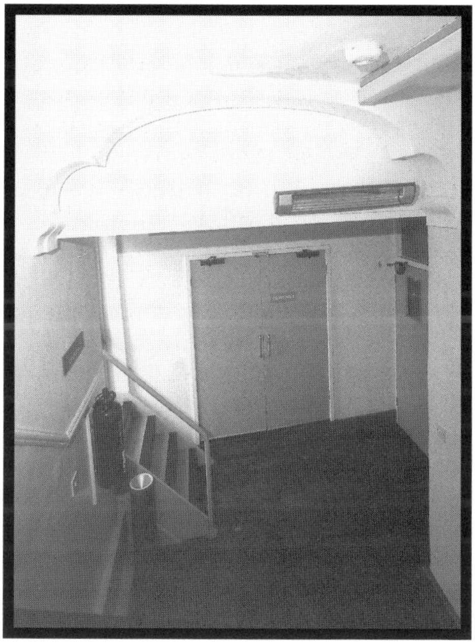

10-3: Arch under stairs, Guildhall.

11-3: Arch over stair, Guildhall.

1 Mrs. Lybbe Powys, p. 134.

2 Mrs. Lybbe Powys, p. 135.

3 *The Shrewsbury Chronicle*, 23 November, 1772, Volume 1, No. 1, f. 6 and 28 November, 1772, Volume 1, No. 2, f.14.

4 They were the owners of Stanage after Pritchard's time.

5 SRRC, 441/1 Ludlow Corporation Bailiff's, Chamberlain's and Renter's Accounts. Folio 333, 2nd March, 1743.

6 Palmers were pilgrims who had returned from the Holy Land with palm branches or a leaf. Although there is no connection with Edward the Confessor and the Guild, the Palmers' Window in Ludlow Parish Church shows the king giving a ring to St. John disguised as a beggar and then the ring being given by St. John to the Ludlow Palmers, who were then given the Guild Charter by King Edward.

7 Quoted in David Lloyd and Peter Klein, *Ludlow: A Historic Town in Words and Pictures*, Chichester, 1984, p. 36.

8 Victoria County History of Shropshire, *A History of Shropshire*, Volume II, p. 108.

9 VCH., p. 109.

10 VCH., p. 109.

11 SRRC, Ludlow Corporation minute Book 1746-87, 356/2/6, f.47.

12 SRRC, 356/32, Box 447.

13 SRRC, 356/32, Box 447.

14 Somerset Davies loaned £300 for the work to be completed.

15 SRRC, 356/32, Box 447, bundle headed 'Bills and Receipts for materials and workmanship by measure at the Almshouses 1758/9.'

16 SRRC, 356/32, Box 447, bundle headed 'Bills and Receipts for materials and worksmanship by measure at the Almshouses 1758/9.' These titles have been written on the outside of some of the bundles.

17 Payments in this section from SRRC 356/32, Box 447, Bailiff's accounts made up on 24 October 1760.

18 SRRC, 356/32, Box 447, bundle headed 'Bills and Receipts for materials and worksmanship by measure at the Almshouses 1758/9.'

19 SRRC, 356/32, Box 447.

20 These were made up on 24 October 1760. SRRC, 356/32. Box 447, 'Mr. Pritchard's Survey of Almshouse.'

21 LB7/1133/34.

22 Information about the work on Gaolford's Tower is from SRRC, Ludlow Bailiff's Account, Records of Administration. LB/7/1121-1134, Gaolford's Tower 1763-64.

23 SRRC, LB7/1129.

24 LB7/1122.

25 A necessary place seems to be an 18th century euphemism for a lavatory.

26 Thomas Sheward was the builder and owner of the Broad Street house which has eight Venetian windows, memorably described by Alec Clifton-Taylor as 'over-egging the pudding.'Alec Clifton-Taylor, on 'Ludlow', in the *Six English Towns* series, London, 1978, p. 22 and information from Mark Girouard, *The English Town*, London, 1990, p. 107.

27 SSRC, LB7/1131.

28 SRRC, LB7/1132.

29 Girouard, p. 22.

30 SRRC, Ludlow Borough 356 Box 462.

31 Although this 'Sixth Frontispiece' is included in *Gothic Architecture* which was published in 1747 the plate states 'Batty and Thos. Langley, Invent and Sculp. 1741.'

32 Quoted in Lloyd and Klein, p. 76.

33 Mrs Lybbe Powys, p. 135.

CHAPTER 4

'Mr Pritchard the Surveyor'. The Shrewsbury Foundling Hospital.

1-4: The Foundling Hospital, Shrewsbury.

In 1772 the *Shrewsbury Chronicle* described the Foundling Hospital as '... lately erected – situated on an eminence from whence there is such a delightful prospect over Shrewsbury, the Severn and the neighbouring counties, as is not exceeded by any in England.'[1] A visitor said it was 'a fine brick building with thirteen windows in front and two small wings.'[2] The building of a major public institution, commissioned by an important London organisation, would have attracted a great amount of attention in the town. The people of Shrewsbury must have watched its progress with interest.

An undated print of the Foundling Hospital before its 19th century refurbishment shows its south elevation and position above the Severn. The dormers were added after the original plan was drawn up. In front is a two-storey, three-bay boathouse close to the river. To the right of the picture is a small building which could be the housing for a spring or well. Another undated print of the 'North East' elevation shows that both sides of the building are the same in form.

Pritchard's rôle in the building of the Shrewsbury Foundling Hospital was a crucial one as sub-contractor, as well as architect. The building process is set out below chronologically from 1758 following a brief summary of events leading up to that date and a summary of the later history.

The documentation gives a detailed account of how a major public institution was constructed in the provinces and of how a provincial architect worked on a big contract with local gentry as members of the Committee, together with the building materials and methods used. The extensive correspondence and minute books meticulously recorded every step taken and practical points about the care of the orphans are interspersed with instructions for the building work. Fortunately the documentation for this work has been preserved and is now in the Greater London Record Office.[3] The letters of Taylor White, Treasurer of the Foundling Hospital in London, express in a forceful manner his impatience and annoyance with problems and delays.

The London Hospital was set up by Captain Thomas Coram to house poor children who were the victims of murder, exposure and exploitation. Building commenced in 1742, on what is now known as Coram's Fields in north London. In an uncharacteristic moment of generosity, Parliament granted financial aid on condition all children were accepted. By 1756 the Hospital became overwhelmed as children poured in from the provinces and the scheme for building a Hospital in Shrewsbury was in response to this.

This work puts Pritchard into a wider context and links him with a fashionable London institution which was set up for the public good and attracted the attention of the aristocracy. It became a smart place to visit and society flocked there for concerts by Handel and for the christenings of the orphans who were often called after those subscribing funds. They were also named after important historical people and the Shrewsbury orphans included Oliver Cromwell, Geoffrey Chaucer and Isaac Newton.

William Hogarth, the artist, was a supporter and several of his works were given to the Hospital which still owns them. Hogarth was not only acting in a charitable manner but was looking for his own advancement among the people who patronised the Hospital. Pritchard could equally have regarded the project in Shrewsbury in the same way.

A suitable and satisfactory design had already been produced for Ackworth Hall, so the Governors decided to repeat it. An engraving of Ackworth was sent down for the Committee and Pritchard to see and designs drawn up along the same lines. Pritchard's elevation and plan of the Shrewsbury 'Orphan Hospital' is blackened with soot from being stored for many years in the attic at Ackworth Hall.[4] This shows a building of nine bays wide with the central three bays projecting forward under a pediment containing a round window; there are two cross wings of two bays wide linked to pavilions by arcades with arched doorways in the centre. These pavilions, with thermal and Venetian windows, contained the stables, cow house, kitchen and matron's room. The servants' hall, Court Room, School Room and secretary's office were placed in the cross wings. The dining room was on the ground floor of the main block. The main doorway and the windows over it were similar to those at the Shrewsbury Infirmary.

Although this is not confirmed by the minutes, it is possible that Pritchard went to London to see the Foundling Hospital as by

1758 transport from Shrewsbury to London was easier. The only possible clue to this trip being undertaken is the plasterwork at Shipton Hall. When the old London Foundling Hospital was taken down in 1926, the Court Room was carefully preserved and rebuilt in the new building. This room has some splendid plasterwork dating from about 1745 which resembles the plasterwork in the entrance hall at Shipton,[5] so it is possible that the plasterwork at the London Hospital influenced the design of the work that Pritchard carried out at Shipton.

In 1758 the General Committee of the Orphan Hospital was given the power to purchase or rent land in Shrewsbury for the purpose of building an Orphan Hospital and a Committee of local gentlemen was appointed to put this plan into action. Building was in progress when Parliament started to cut back on the funding and stopped it completely in 1770, so the financial viability of the Hospital was always in question and its life was short. The Treasurer, Taylor White, outlined the problems to Roger Kynaston, chairman of the local Committee, when he explained that before 1756, the Foundling Hospital was a private charity and that they only took the number of children they could support. When it became a public charity in June 1756, all children had to be accepted until the number was more than 2000 children under five years old. In addition, as Parliament had voted money to the Hospital, possible donors thought that funds were not needed and this was compounded by the fact that Parliament did not pay. The building was completed in 1765 and with dwindling numbers of children was closed by 1772. It remained empty until the Shrewsbury Parishes purchased it for a 'House of Industry' in 1773. The buildings and land were sold at a massive loss and in the late 19th century Shrewsbury School took over the site and updated the existing building and added further accommodation and a chapel.

1758.

It was, however, with a spirit of optimism that the project was started and an impressive list of governors was assembled which included the Lords Bath and Powis and 'Knights of the Shire' Sir John Astley, Sir Richard Corbett and Sir Richard Lyster, together with Thomas Hill, M.P., Roger Kynaston and Francis Turner Blythe. They read like Pritchard's own client list and although many had become acquainted with his work at St. Julian's Church, it was the job at the Foundling Hospital that firmly established him.

The importance of contacts is emphasised in a letter from London to Kynaston in 1760. 'I hope that your building is carryed on with spirit and that it will make a good figure at your races and that you will show it to Genll Clive who has I don't doubt both power and inclination to assist us in so good work.'[6] The Committee considered that they were 'doing mankind the greatest benefits' and that all means of obtaining assistance should be employed.

A Grand Committee meeting was held on 16 August to 'approve of the Plans and Elevations of the building proposed' and

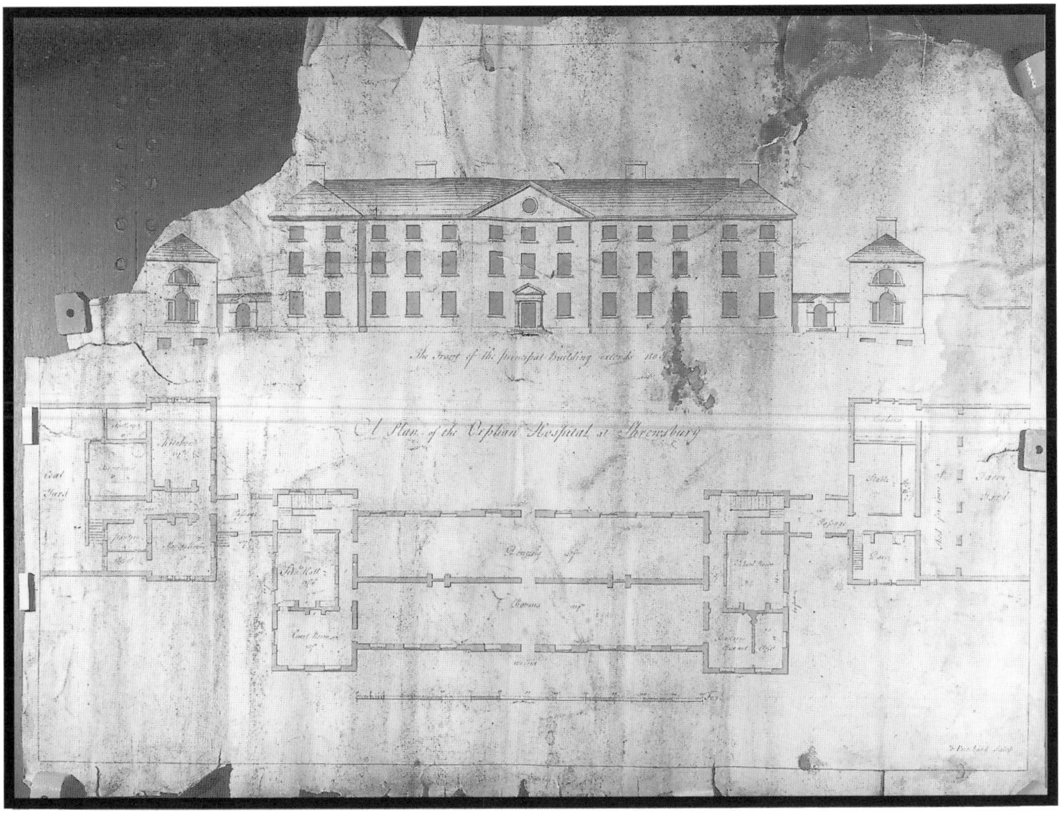

2-4: Pritchard's drawing, 1759.

the order to begin was given in October.[7] Once the Committee was formed letters flowed from Shrewsbury in a steady stream to Roger Kynaston in London. At the beginning, the main correspondence was between Thomas Collingwood, assistant to the secretary who was representing the Foundling Hospital in London and Roger Kynaston, with later correspondence from Taylor White, appointed by London to oversee matters in Shrewsbury. White, a lawyer and one-time second Justice of Chester, was Treasurer from 1745-1771 and is described as doing 'arduous and patient work during a time of financial problems.'[8] White urged caution and economy all the time. 'I cant see how you can contract for the building timber till a plan is fixed on by which lengths, dimensions of the timbers wanted may be known. Timbers seem to be dear with you and it seems cheaper to buy the timber rough than square sawn for the slabs cut off will I think pay for the sawing,' he wrote on 25 November.[9]

Initially a house was leased in Dog's Lane, Shrewsbury for the children but the first group did not arrive until 1759. During this period of negotiations '2 closes of land' were purchased, after some delays, at Kingsland, south of the River Severn. White received a 'plan of the ground which is prettily drawn and shows the person employed to be an artist'[10] and in April he wrote to Kynaston that he hoped the purchase would be completed as soon as possible 'because the season for building advances fast.'[11]

As the Hospital at Ackworth was already built White sent down a plan and later obtained a copper plate engraving.[12] He involved himself in every aspect of the project including drawing a sketch for the proposed kitchen grate.

When the purchase of the land was complete, Taylor White

> ... ordered your workman to draw a plan and estimate after my Direction of our Hospital to be built on Congreve's land. I gave him strict charge not to make any valuation which was not to be depended on. His estimate was I think £3800 or thereabout. Our surveyor says such a building would cost £5500. I hope the surveyor is mistaken ...[13]

The finances are not easy to work out; in the same bundle of letters is an estimate from Richard Lee, carpenter, and William Cooper, bricklayer, for a 'building lofty 36 feet to wall plate' for a total of £4,992. Bricks, stones, lead, tiles etc. added another £2,487 and carpentry £2,505.[14] William Cooper was Pritchard's partner in the work for the Drapers' Company in 1749.

1759.

The attitude of the Committee towards the builders became apparent at an early stage. Taylor White wrote to Roger Kynaston in January:

> In obedience to your commands I ordered the articles with Mr Fowler to be sent to you as to the Bricklayer it seems to be a very unusual and unnecessary thing for us under our zeal with workmen. We think if we employ them it is a favour to them which we may discontinue whenever we find it necessary and therefore tho we have always expected articles from our workmen signed by them we have executed any counter parts of such articles there being nothing more to be done on our part but paying for the work they do according to the rates agreed for which the law obliges us to do.[15]

Pritchard's rôle does not start to become clear until July when White wrote to Kynaston that he had 'received Mr. Pritchard's draughts, also a letter from him.' The minutes noted that 'Mr. Pritchard delivered to the Board the plan referred to him with an estimate of the charge of executing the same. Ordered that the said plan and estimate lie on the table for further consideration.'[16] Before work started, Mr Kynaston 'expressed his sentiment that this Committee are the properest Judges when to begin building and that surely in this weather no time ought to be lost.'[17] Had Pritchard advised otherwise or were the Committee just showing that they knew best? There is no comment from Pritchard and there had been no mention of his involvement since the plans were put on the table, but over dinner in October it was

> agreed with Mr Thomas Pritchard to act as surveyor to the building now erecting; to overlook the workmen, to draw plans to purchase materials if required to procure workmen if directed; at the rate of 80 guineas for the whole job, Mr Pritchard referring it to the Committee to make that sum up to £100 if they think he deserves it.[18]

This would indicate that Pritchard was present at the dinner when this appointment was being discussed and that he was accepted socially among the Shropshire gentry, at least as far as the Foundling Hospital work was concerned,. In one letter he is referred to as 'our friend, Mr Pritchard'.[19]

After they had seen the plans, the Committee decided to keep matters in their own hands. Taylor White wrote regarding Pritchard's draft and letter:

> which should have been addressed to this Committee as the proper judges of the workmen to be imployed here and the prices of the materials here and expressed that it would be unadvisable to contract for the whole building at once without a large security for the performance according to articles and mentioning the inconvenience of such contracts above the contractor generally setting out the work and taking 2 or 3 shillings in the pound for doing nothing.[20]

Taylor White did not have a high opinion of builders either; 'I have been forced to wait on the workmen myself, often to make them pull down their work,' and he cautioned against the damaging practice of rubbing the face of bricks which left them vulnerable to weather, before going into further details:

> As for the surveyors being empowered to make controls for you, I am sure you never approve of any such thing. Nor do I think it would be right to contract for the whole work at a time but only for so much as is to be done immediately for them if you find any part of the work ill done you will immediately turn of the workman or if you find any unnecessary delay in carrying on the work. For nothing is more common here than for workmen to undertake large works more than they can finish in a season's proper for building and if they build after the frost has set in the work is good for nothing. Besides workmen are apt to do little jobs for their customers in summer and carry on their great works in autumn when

> they have no other business. This has been a damage to this hospital which can never be made amends for and therefore I most earnestly intreat you not to be persuaded by any workman to go on with any building after the frost sets in. They pretend methods of mixing the lime to set in bad weather but I have by fatal experiences found all these methods good for nothing.[21]

At this stage of Pritchard's career it was important that he carried off this prestigious job well, but the Committee in London was not easy to deal with and kept a sharp eye on proceedings in Shrewsbury. They considered 'that timber must be bought this winter or the carpenter will not be able to keep pace with the bricklayers and provision must be made for scaffold poles on the best terms.'[22] Later in October, a tin box with the plans was sent down, together with an estimate for the timber.

By September the work had begun and on 3 October the order was given for the digging of the foundations under the direction of gentry-playing-architect. Sir Richard Corbett, Mr. Birkbeck and Colonel Congreve, probably the former owner of the land, supervised a new road which was to run up from the River Severn. A pump was erected near the river to bring up water for the bricklayers and a well was sunk where the borers had found 'running sand'. Mrs Henley made a contract to ferry people across the river for two shillings a week, while a shed was erected for the 'three [recently purchased] melch cows'. During the next year there are records of amounts paid to Pritchard: 100 of deals from Bristol for £19.14s. with carriage, £29.12s for a further 200 and £30 for freight of slates to Chepstow.

Local knowledge was important and a sharp look-out was kept for sources of materials or reusable items. The Committee heard that a timber house was to be sold and Lee, the carpenter, was 'directed to visit the house and contract for it if he find the timber good and of a reasonable price' as this would be suitable for 'windows cills and caps'.[23] In November Pritchard reported that the 100 fir trees now growing at Woodhall could be used for scaffold at a cost of 4s. a tree which he thought was a good price. He was ordered to buy them and in January, 106 trees arrived. The rope makers had been asked for proposals for making 'scaffold cording according to Pattern left at the hospital for that purpose', but it was too expensive and they settled for second-hand cordage instead.

1760.

Work stopped during the worst of the winter months and restarted in April with an order for another 600,000 bricks 'at the same price' as last year from Abraham Davies. There must have been some delays as it was feared 'that the best moulders may be engaged if not employed immediately in our service.'[24]

On 5 May Pritchard was ordered to contract for stone for

the window sills and for the masons' work to prepare them. Word had come to the Committee about a 'fall of young oak for poles for ledgers and putlocks' and Pritchard was instructed to contract for as many of them as he needed. It was agreed with Edward Haycock, of the Shrewsbury building family, to do the sawing at 2s. 4d. per hundred for as 'long as he does it well or so long as the Committee think proper.'[25] He must have been satisfactory as payments to him occur throughout the minute book.

Pritchard had been told about a 'parcel of fir poles to make large ladders' that were being sold at Hardwick, north of Shrewsbury and he bought a wagon-load of them at a reasonable rate. Timber was purchased in quantities; 120 tons of oak in May for delivery at the beginning of August at 40s. per ton. Fifty of these trees were twenty three feet long and four inches square in the scantlings and the remainder as the surveyor 'shall think proper for the building.' Best Grinshill stone was ordered in May from George Walford at 14s. per ton 'to be well sized and scabbald' to Pritchard's directions; the 'frontice piece' and twenty windows to be delivered within a month. John Yates was undertaking the mason's work at 10s. per foot for the 'frontice pieces' and 5s. for the window sills. In September '100 tons of stone of large scantlings for the cornice' was ordered, 50 tons each from George Walford and John Glover. The direction was for stone 'free from sand holes and of such scantling as the surveyor shall direct.'[26] Two years later George Walford was dead and his widow Martha had taken over the quarry. She was still in charge when stone was supplied from Grinshill for Shrewsbury's English Bridge in 1766.

Pritchard was certainly earning his fee and the gentlemen, who might think themselves qualified to supervise foundations and drains, relied on him to make sure that the materials were the right quality. A further thirty tons of fine oak timber 'such as the cleft has not been taken off the scantlings' was to be ready by late August. Pritchard reported that soft clay had been found in the grounds near the river 'fit for making arch bricks' and it was ordered that a quantity of this should be taken to the brick kilns for this purpose.[27]

Work was progressing so well that the Committee thought that an inspector should be appointed 'to attend the building constantly' and Jonathan Reynolds was given the job 'to inspect the buildings ... to measure all materials to prevent fraud in workmen and others and to all other business as the board shall direct at the rate of 2s. per day.'[28] Jonathan Reynolds was Pritchard's 'man' for the work on Hosier's Almshouses in Ludlow.

In August Pritchard was requested to 'make estimates of the expence of materials for covering in the principal buildings next year.' As this minute is dated 12 August and the entry for the estimate is dated 13 August, either the order was given earlier or Pritchard must have worked fast. In any case the estimate 'for carcassing in the Orphan Hospital ... where it is intended to be covered up at the end of the year 1760' came to nearly £1000.[29] This sum included 'iron stirrups etc. to the roof' which came to £33, as well as 4,464 feet of lead gutters, 70 tons of slates at £3 per ton delivered and all the labour involved. Pritchard was asked to find 'proper masons to work the stone cornices and report their terms to the board.'[30] Richard Lee carried out the carpenter's work and was paid £30 on 20 October. It was agreed to pay him 6d. per foot to make sash frames in the 'best manner', but in case it 'should appear to the Committee that 6d. is too small a price he is to be allowed half a penny a foot more.' Lee and Pritchard were associated over many years on such projects as Tern and Wynnstay.[31]

In October the building of a stove to dry the sash and other timber was approved together with the addition of a room for workmen to lodge in to protect the stones against theft. At the same time the ferryman's hut was to be made warmer and 'more convenient'. At the next meeting it was reported that the ferryman's hut, built 'only of clods' was ready to fall down and not able to be repaired, so it was decided that another should be erected immediately with a room eight foot square with a fireplace and 'loft for a bed'.[32]

After attending to the ferryman, it was time to make sure that the roof of the Hospital was waterproof and Pritchard was 'empowered to contract for 70 tons of Westmoreland or Lancashire slate to be delivered here by water carriage.'[33] In early December Pritchard reported to the Committee that he had been to the slate quarries in Westmorland and ordered the finest slates. These were to be delivered to Chepstow at a cost of 43s. per ton. The amount would fill two tubs and for his travelling expenses Pritchard was repaid £4. 19s.

This is one of the few pieces of information about Pritchard travelling outside his usual area of work. He may have gone to Bristol and it is probable that he travelled more often, but there are no details. The same letter also records that Pritchard 'is going tomorrow to the North of Cheshire on Business' on his way to Westmorland; this may have been to visit the Egertons of Tatton Park. The minutes also recorded that he was away from home in July 1763.

The slate quarries in Coniston were on the land of the le Fleming family and in 1750 they signed a lease giving permission to William Rigg of Hawkshead to work 'all the quarries within the Manor of Coniston.'[34]

1761.

It was Rigg who wrote to Pritchard concerning the shipping of slate in 'the Happy Returne Cleminson' who had sailed on the first spring tide. Rigg also wrote that he had 'taken on another ship for Chepstow burthern 70 tons in which I intend to ship the remainder of the slate you ordered and 40 tons for Mr Hiorn of Warwick.' He wanted to know as soon as possible if he

> should ... load this ship all with slates and as 17 tons would make up the first order of 70 tons as I have shipped 53 by

> Cleminson and whether it will suite you to take 30 tons fine and second slates to make up the loading for the vessel or I must take in pig iron to load her out. I think the ironmasters will not be willing to send a less quantity than 10 tons in which case I could only send you 20 tons.[35]

The slates and their carriage proved expensive; in August Mr Beard was paid £42. 8s. for carriage from Chepstow, with another payment of £31. 19s. in October and Pritchard was paid a further £21. 15s. for slates in October 1762. During 1761, Rigg was paid a total of £133 and a further £48. 8s. in December, 1762. Meanwhile Taylor White was keeping a cautious eye on things as he was concerned that building work was continuing late into the year and anxious that Cooper, who was acting as main contractor, would take 'proper care to secure it from the frosts.'[36]

The Committee still kept Pritchard hard at work; in January he sent to Bristol for 100 of the best Christina deals and he was to enquire about the cost of the best 'Bristol Crown Glass' for the sashes. In December he had been given orders for framing the roof and in February he was asked to prepare a model of the roof of the main building 'for the inspection of the board'.[37] Richard Lee made a model of the roof of the 'center of the building' while Jonathan Reynolds made one of the roof of the wings and three weeks later these were viewed and approved. Orders were given in the same month for the bricklayer to proceed immediately on the inside walls as they were sheltered enough to allow work to continue during the winter.[38]

In March, to prevent damage to timber by steam, washing and brewing was not allowed in any part of the main building. The same entry also instructed Jonathan Reynolds to design a brewhouse and washhouse for the next meeting and to include a bakehouse, scullery, pantry and cellar. Reynolds was ordered to do this because of the 'absence of the surveyor'[39] which not only shows that he could be a deputy capable of carrying out designs but that Pritchard was probably away again on other business. In the next month Reynolds was ordered to go to Ellesmere to measure boards. It was then decided that instead of temporary buildings, the brewhouse and washhouse would be the permanent ones proposed by Reynolds working under Pritchard's direction. The ground for 'the said sketch' would be staked out for the Committee to see.

By May progress was being made to the extent that Mr Kynaston was allowed to 'give drinks to the workmen ... as he shall think proper.'[40] In September a guinea was given so that the workmen could drink the health of their Majesties for the coronation and all the orphans were to have roast beef and pudding for dinner. Every Christmas 10s. was given to the clerk sexton at St. Julian's Church 'as a Christmas box in cleaning the church where part of the children attend divine service'.

Lead had been ordered in March and was now being laid. By June they were ready to obtain prices for the garret ceiling and walls to be plastered and whitewashed with two coats at 2½d. per square yard from William Cooper and the 'attick story' with three coats at 3d. by the splendidly named plasterer, Tobias Coffee. Richard Lee was in charge of all the doors and architraves 'according to the patterns exhibited to the board.'[41]

The next entry for 29 June explains why the plan was changed from the drawing which was put before the Committee in 1759. A later undated print of the completed Hospital shows dormer windows all along the elevation facing the river. Despite having seen a model of the roof, the Committee thought that the garrets at the east and west ends 'could not be lighted from the dormers on the inside as was proposed for the center of the building, and that the center part would be better lighted on the outside and for uniformity sake.' It was therefore resolved that all dormers should be made on the outside of the building.[42]

After settling this question, the Committee returned to ordering timbers –'5000 quarter oak boards and 7000 bastard boards as per the patterns' and the minute severely notes 'the inspector to go to the wood and measure the same and receive none worse than the patterns.'[43] Pritchard was paid £50 on 9 November and regular payments over the months were made to Tobias Coffee. Richard Lee was turning the balusters for the stairs, according to the approved pattern, at a rate of 3¼d. per baluster.

1762.

At the beginning of 1762 the Committee was being attacked for the amount of money they were spending on the building and an anxious Taylor White wrote to Roger Kynaston complaining that:

> I dont find any parliamentary assistance from the members of Salop or those in the county which I thought we had great reason to expect if they either understood the interest of the kingdom in general or of their own country. I expected your rich representative would have thought it both for his honour and interest to have assisted us in these difficult times, but have heard nothing from him.[44]

White had found Pritchard's schemes too expensive for the funds available and considered they were 'calculated for the benefit rather of the workmen than the charity' as 'they contain many useless parts and their divisions make the expence too great for us to undertake.' White had hoped for the assistance of John Gwynn but this had not materialised. It is interesting to learn that John Gwynn had been consulted and either out of loyalty to Pritchard or because he sensed trouble, declined to get involved.

White then proceeded to set out his ideas for improving the plans and completing the work to prevent the inconvenience of 'having workmen among the children.' He appeared to have acquired a further knowledge of building and in March aired this with a long letter explaining the ventilation necessary for the washhouse and brewhouse and warning about the steam melting the lime.[45] At the same time a sample shutter was shown for the lower rooms and it was ordered that a pattern should be made of 'shutters that are to open in two heights.'[46] Pritchard was ordered to produce a plan for a dye house to be built near the river for the next meeting. In the same minute it was recorded that Mr. Godolphin Edwards presented two pieces of painted glass to the new building.

In the spring the Committee were negotiating with the Drapers' Company for a small piece of land to complete the terrace so White next turned his attention to landscaping. He asked for 'ten or a dozen' workmen to be available for his next visit with 'garden lines and stakes always in readiness' as this work needed to be completed before the children moved in.[47] White was not impressed with the work when he did see it:

> I cant say whether the Gardener you employed did understand my directions or not they were to let the Terras descent regularly at each end so as to humour the ground and not to raise it to the level of the middle. Also in the slope of the hill to consult nature and not regularity and to remove as little earth as possible otherwise than with the cast of the spade. ... I also desired your gardiner to turn off all bad workmen of which there were a great number when I was there.[48]

White considered that 'a dozen good hands' could complete the work in a fortnight and then the 'new ground might be sowed as soon as possible with hay seeds that it might gain a turf before michaelmas ... Hayseeds may I hope now be got as well as Dutch clover.' In the same letter White urged Kynaston to speed up the plastering by hiring extra hands, otherwise the plaster would not be dry enough that summer and this would delay the project for a whole year as after 'March plaister will not dry as to be fit to be inhabited in many months.'

White repeated his concern that the workmen should not be in the building when the children moved in. As he considered himself an amateur architect as well as guardian of the finances, he had had time to consider in more detail the plans for the outbuildings and wrote at length on his ideas for changes; an annotated plan was enclosed with his letter, which included practical proposals for digging a sewer for the brew and bake house 'which will keep the vaults dry and carry off all the wort water and that should run through the privys to wash them' as well as the route for the drains; storage of coal purchased for the washhouse and brew house and division of the back kitchen to let in more light were other matters that he fussed over. He was concerned that 'the girls privy is too near the edge of the terrace which ought to be free from all annoyances' and the milk room should be placed far from the house so that 'it might not be in the way of the children for if it is ... they will be always begging for milk.'[49] White characteristically but perceptively ended his letter by writing that 'you will perhaps wish I was not so much attentive to building but observe the necessity I am under to be a good husband. You must needs see that the utmost frugality is become necessary.'[50]

1763-5.

Pritchard was in charge of ordering fire stoves and perhaps he also cautiously over-ordered alabaster as in May 1763 there was more than was required and the surplus was sold off.[51] In February 1764 he was paid another £50[52] and as the time was approaching for the final reckoning he was asked to make a plan and estimates of the outhouses still needed and to see how far the unused materials on the site would go towards them. Each of the workmen had to deliver 'a bill of the work done ... by Michaelmas and that the same be signed by the Surveyor and compared with the estimate.' Economy was now becoming urgent and the Committee decided to take down the house built for Jonathan Reynolds and all the buildings in front of the hospital and re-use the materials elsewhere. The small house by the river in the print of the hospital is probably of a later date.

3-4: Shrewsbury School today.

Richard Lee was replaced as carpenter by Owen Edwards. The peremptory minute 'Ordered that the said Mr. Lee be no longer Carpenter to this Hospital' so something had gone wrong there. In April a further payment of £43. 3s. was made to Pritchard. Roger Kynaston called the meeting to approve it in the coffee house in London; this could have been the Salopian Coffee House, near Trafalgar Square which is first mentioned about 1749.[53] There are no payments in the minutes to Jonathan Reynolds so he must have been paid directly by Pritchard.

The whole building cost a total of £16,960 and was not completed until 1765. It could arguably be considered as one of

Pritchard's most important jobs when it began but by the time it was completed he was busy working in many different parts of the county as well as Herefordshire and Worcestershire.

As we have seen, the form and style of the Foundling Hospital, which was a very large building by Shropshire standards, were dictated by the precedent of London and Ackworth. The function for them had already been worked out, so it would appear from the minutes and the correspondence that Pritchard's contribution in terms of the actual design was limited to the architectural expression of this function. His main role was to interpret the plans of the other buildings and the instructions of the Committee as well as making up working drawings for the builders and craftsmen. He also procured materials and carried out the valuations at appropriate times.

4-4 & 5-4: Chimney pieces at Shrewsbury School.

Miss Florry from Cleobury Mortimer, when she visited Shrewsbury in the 1760s, noted there were 'five churches and the Foundling Hospital a beautiful building.'[54]

Six years after Pritchard's death, his own parish of St. Julian's joined with the other Shrewsbury parishes to buy the 'Hospital Houses, Buildings and Lands' of the Foundling Hospital for the 'Lodging of the Poor.' The parishioners agreed to pay £314 3s. 8d. annually for the 'maintenance of the poor.'[55]

Today the Foundling Hospital forms the basis of Shrewsbury School on Kingsland Bank. Although Arthur Blomfield carried out alterations and additions in 1878, the elevation, viewed from the Quarry in Shrewsbury, is still very similar to the original building.

1 *Shrewsbury Chronicle*, 12 December, 1772, Volume I, No. 4, f.30.

2 Thomas Pennant, *Tours in Wales*, 3 Volumes, Caernarvon, 1883, Volume III, p. 234.

3 All the letters and papers relating to the Shrewsbury Foundling Hospital are in the London Metropolitan Archives, (hereinafter cited as LMA) Northampton Street, London, EC1R 0HB. General Reference A/FH/D02. I am grateful to Tim Harris of the London Metropolitan Archives and to Rhian Harris, Curator of The Thomas Coram Foundation for Children for their assistance. The material and letters used in the section belong to The Thomas Coram Foundation for Children, who have given me permission to use them for this book.

4 LMA, Shrewsbury Committee minutes (minutes), A/FH/D02/1/1.

5 There are no surviving designs by Pritchard for plasterwork but as he carried out designs for an overmantel and grate at Shipton Hall, it is assumed that all the other work was done by him. The hall plasterwork is however quite unlike the plasterwork on the staircase at Shipton or in other houses in the area such as Bitterley Court. It could, therefore, have been done at an earlier date than the staircase, which is contained in the extension built onto the back of the house around 1764.

6 LMA, Mostyn to Kynaston, 30 August 1760.

7 Reference for plan and picture A/FH/031/4/4.

8 R. H. Nichols and F. A. Wray, *The History of the Foundling Hospital*, Oxford, 1935.

9 LMA, White to Kynaston, 25 November 1758.

10 LMA, White to Kynaston, 25 November 1758.

11 LMA, White to Kynaston, 1 April 1759.

12 LMA, White to Kynaston, 12 March 1759.

13 LMA, White to Kynaston 31 May 1759.

14 LMA, minutes, 29 May 1759.

15 LMA, White to Kynaston, 8 January 1759.

16 LMA, minutes, 2 July 1759.

17 LMA, minutes, 22 September 1759.

18 LMA, minutes, 15 October 1759.

19 LMA, White to Kynaston, 12 October 1760.

20 LMA, minutes, 21 July 1759.

21 LMA, White to Kynaston, 20 July 1759. Taylor White was not alone in his opinions. James Paine warned that unless an architect was skilled in valuing work 'he must necessarily call in the aid of workmen, and in that case unavoidably submit to the gratification of their avarice, which in some of them is hardly to be satisfied...' (James Paine, *Plans, Elevations and Sections of Noblemen and Gentlemen's Houses*, London, 1767, iii.)

22 LMA, Morgan to Collingwood, 1 October 1759.

23 LMA, minutes, 5 October 1759.

24 LMA, Thomas Morgan to Collingwood, 26 and 28 April 1760.

25 LMA, minutes, 12 May 1760.

26 LMA, minutes 12 May, 25 August and 5 September 1760.

27 The minutes record that Pritchard's brother Samuel was paid £1. 13s. for 33 boys' hats and the widow Henley paid two guineas to land passengers in the Hospital field on the show day. Shrewsbury Show dated back to the celebration of Corpus Christi by the Trade Companies. After the Reformation the processions were still kept up, ending at Kingsland, but over the years the show became rowdy and when Shrewsbury School took over the site in 1875, it was abolished.

28 LMA, minutes, 2 June 1760.

29 The 'Timber-work (as it were the Skeleton) of a House, before it is Lath'd and Plaistered.' Neve, *Builder's Dictionary*, p. 96.

30 LMA, minutes, 25 August 1760.

31 *The Shrewsbury Chronicle* yields 'nuggets' of information about these people. 'Mr. Lee, carpenter' is advertising a 'new built brick house' for auction in Abbey Foregate (26 June 1773, Volume II, No. 25) and 'a servant of Mr. Haycock, carpenter, cut his leg so badly with an axe it must be taken off.' (12 December 1772, Volume 1, No. 4).

32 LMA, minutes, 27 October 1760.

33 LMA, minutes, 10 November, 10, 5 & 15 December.

34 Alastair Cameron, *Slate from Coniston*, Cumbria Amenity Trust Mining History Society, 1996, pp.10-12.

35 LMA, William Rigg to Pritchard, Hawkshead, 25 May 1761.

36 LMA, White to Kynaston, 12 October 1760.

37 LMA, minutes, 2 February 1761.

38 All the time the building work was taking place, the minutes give details about the orphans. For instance, it was discovered that the sleeves of the girls' coats would not allow them enough room to stretch forward for spinning.

39 LMA, minutes, 28 March 1761.

40 LMA, minutes, 12 May 1761.

41 LMA, minutes, 29 June 1761. The 'attick' was the uppermost storey of a building while the garrets were the spaces created immediately beneath the roof.

42 LMA, minutes, 29 June 1761.

43 LMA, minutes, 13 July 1761.

44 LMA, White to Kynaston, 28 January 1762.

45 LMA, White to Kynaston, 15 March 1762.

46 LMA, minutes, 15 March 1762.

47 LMA, White to Kynaston, 15 March 1762.

48 LMA, White to Kynaston, 9 April 1762 from Ruthin.

49 LMA, White to Kynaston 9 April 1762.

50 In these papers, Pritchard's brother Samuel becomes more than just someone who took over Thomas's shares in the Iron Bridge Company. The Foundling Hospital records showed that he supplied hats to the children and that he also took some of the boys as apprentice hatters. He also had a woollen manufactory at Meole Brace which at that time was in the same parish as the Foundling Hospital. Apart from the building work, there were other pressing matters for the Committee to attend to. Schoolmasters resigned frequently and new and often unsatisfactory ones were appointed; one was dismissed for 'irregular behaviour and another for abusive language.' At the end of the minutes the Committee had decided that the children should be corrected only with birch rods and the use of sticks would lead to expulsion. Unsatisfactory boatmen probably led to a hawser being stretched across the river for use by the ferry. This can be seen in the picture of 18th century Shrewsbury in Chapter 1.

51 Alabaster was used as the aggregate in the mortar.

52 LMA, minutes, 3 February 1764.

53 See Bryant Lilleywhite, *London Coffee Houses*, London, 1963.

54 MSS Diary of Miss Florry (1744-1832), Birmingham Reference Library Ref: 259854/226613

55 *Transactions of the Shropshire Archaeology and Natural History Society*, Volume X, 1897, 211.

CHAPTER 5

'Elegant and compleat'. Houses in Herefordshire & Worcestershire.

The name of Pritchard as an architect is mainly connected with Shropshire but he also carried out some major projects further afield in Herefordshire and Worcestershire. For instance, Perrott House, Pershore, of about 1760, is one house that has been attributed to him wiht no hard evidence. Much of his work in these counties still exists but for many of the buildings there is no documentation other than Pritchard's designs in *The Drawing Book.*

There are no plans, accounts or receipts for Croft Castle in Herefordshire which represents one of Pritchard's most important interior decorative schemes, or for Gaines, on the Herefordshire-Worcestershire borders, which is the furthest south of the area that he covered, as far as we know. There are designs in *The Drawing Book* for both Gaines and also for nearby Brockhampton House, near Bromyard, but no other surviving documentation and there are no drawings at all for The White House at Suckley near Worcester, but these three buildings can be linked together as they were all in the ownership of the same family during the mid-eighteenth century. Together they could provide the strongest illustration of family patronage for Pritchard. The work for all these houses was carried out in the 1760s, Pritchard's busiest years, and he must have spent much time on the road visiting them.

Pritchard is thought to have worked on the first four buildings in this section during the same period of time and if *The Drawing Book* is in the correct, or almost correct, chronological order, then designs for Croft come first, followed by Brockhampton, Gaines and then Kinsham. Kyre, with its dated survey, comes last. Stanage Park, although it is in Powys, has been included here because of its close connection with Croft Castle and the Johnes family.

CROFT CASTLE.

Pritchard had come into contact with Thomas Johnes of Croft Castle when he worked for the Ludlow Corporation in 1758. The Johnes archive in the National Library of Wales has no references to work carried out at Croft and the only evidence for Pritchard's involvement there are his designs and the style of the Castle's extensive mid-eighteenth century refurbishment.

1-5: East front of Croft Castle, late 19th century.

Croft Castle is one of the most attractive buildings in this part of the Marches. Situated on rising ground it overlooks the valley of the River Lugg and although the defensive aspects of the building have been softened over the years, it still manages to conjure up an image of knights and ladies, with Pritchard's inventive and charming interiors adding to this illusion.

Arthur Oswald, writing in 1950, remarked that the 'seeds of the Gothic Revival took root and flowered early' in the Marches.[1] He went on to say, with reference to the curtain wall and mock towers at the entrance, that Croft seemed to have been one of 'the first houses in the county to be consciously Gothicised.'

Croft is a stone building of two storeys with an attic and cellars and as it still retains much of its earlier medieval form, the rooms are arranged around the central courtyard. The round towers remain at the four corners and the walls on the south and west sides are thicker and probably the oldest. John Leyland in the 16th century described the building as 'dyched and waullyd castle-like.'[2] The castle is thought to have been considerably damaged in the Civil War and restored in the 17th century.

The Castle had been owned by the Croft family from the time of the Domesday Book, but in the middle of the 18th century it was mortgaged and in 1746 became the property of the wealthy iron master, Richard Knight of Downton. In 1746 Knight's daughter, Elizabeth, married Thomas Johnes, from a family of Welsh squires. Johnes was not a rich man so the main work on the Castle was probably paid for by Elizabeth's dowry and her inheritance from her father who died in 1765.[3] 'Mr. Knight made considerable alterations after it [Croft] came into his hands and by Mr. Johnes the eastern side was rebuilt and the whole fabric greatly modernised.'[4] The extent of Knight's work is uncertain as it is considered that Thomas and Elizabeth Johnes carried out the main alterations and decorative schemes.

The plan of Croft relates to the building as it was before further alterations were made in the 20th century. The heavier lines denote the old fabric and the lighter ones the 18th century work. It demonstrates how Pritchard created a domestic house within an ancient structure.

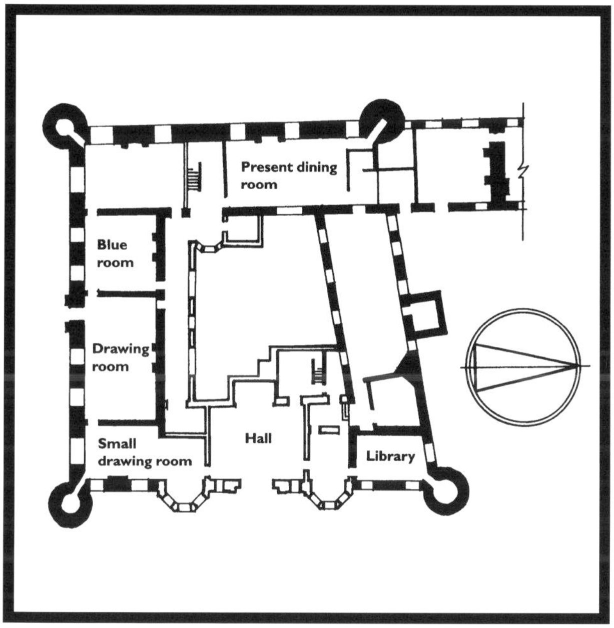

2-5: *Plan of Croft Castle before 19th century alterations.*

The plans show how the east side was filled in to form a hall. Other work included the creation of a passage on the south side of the central courtyard and the present ante-room, with the canted bay, formerly part of the small drawing room, was probably originally open to this passage. The arch between the ante-room and the passage has now been blocked up and the chimney frame moved into the space. The library containing Pritchard's chimney frame was then in the north-east corner.[5] The roof was raised to provide attics, which were fitted up with both Gothick and Rococo cornices, plasterwork and chimney pieces.

Externally, Pritchard added the two canted bays to the east front, designed perhaps to echo the round towers on each corner. While the oriel window in the centre of this front could be of an earlier date, he certainly was responsible for the pointed ogee arches over the main doorway. These arches are now covered by the porch, but they are visible in the photograph of the tenant of the Castle, Mr. Kevill-Davies, being presented with a silver salver.[6] The tradesmen of Leominster stand formally on each side thus allowing for an excellent view of the main doorway and the arches; the lower one is topped with a finial and there are four slender supporting columns.

3-5: Main entrance of Croft. Presentation to Mr Kevill-Davies.

When the porch was added in the early 1900s, the tall arched windows were changed to a rectangular form, presumably to match those on either side of the canted bays. The symmetry of Pritchard's elevation has been affected as the two canted bays and the section between them made up a uniform unit. The battlements have also been altered and now only remain on the canted bays and towers and the central gable which appears in photographs has gone just as the crow-stepped battlements no longer exist on the south side.

Internally, the entrance hall behind the main doorway may have been decorated in the same fashion as the rest of the house, but covered in the 20th century by the present re-used 17th century panelling. Anne Rushout, from nearby Burford House, visited Croft in 1805 and found 'the house very comfortable ...

4-5: Croft Castle today.

the House is partly Gothic and partly modernised, the Hall very pretty, there are towers at each end to give it the appearance of a Castle.'[7] The hall, as it is now, could not be called pretty, so there must have been another scheme there. Unfortunately, the usually loquacious Mrs. Lybbe Powys did not leave any information. 'The next day we had an invitation to Croft Castle, Mr. John's, and for the day after to Burford,' she recorded laconically on her Shropshire visit in 1771.

There are at least ten chimney pieces surviving throughout Croft that can be attributed to Pritchard, but unfortunately only one of them, for 'the Bishop's Room' in the south-east corner, appears in *The Drawing Book.* (AIA 10c) This is a design of leaves with a wreath in the centre. Five of Croft's chimney pieces are Rococo, with 'C' scrolls, 'S' scrolls and cabriole sides. Another illustration (6-5) shows one of these chimney pieces in a room with 17th century panelling on the first floor of the east side. The wooden carving overlaps the veined marble in a fashionable style, while the fire surround has Sadler and Green tiles, like many of the fireplaces in the Castle. When Arthur Oswald wrote his article in 1950 for *Country Life*, Croft's 18th century architect was unknown, but Oswald believed that the work, particularly the Blue Room chimney piece, was 'clearly by a leading London firm, one, too, in which the designer showed a considerable degree of freedom and invention.'[8] A pleasing thought that Pritchard's skills were so well recognised, even if his name was not widely known at the date.

5-5: Chimney piece in Bishop's room. (AIA 10c)

6-5: Chimney piece at Croft.

If the small chimney piece (7-5) in the south-east attic bedroom, which looks back to earlier forms, is also by him then he was carrying out another example of the historicism which is noted elsewhere and was to be central to architectural thought in the later 19th century. Could he have noticed a similar early design while working in the castle and copied it here?

The number of chimney pieces at Croft, together with the cornices and plasterwork, reinforce the conviction that his work was more extensive in other houses he is connected with, but that it has not survived. Throughout the Castle he used both Classical and Gothick styles, the latter splendidly demonstrated by the first design in *The Drawing Book* for Croft, the chimney

frame for 'the Liberary' dateable to September, 1765. (AIA 5) This piece is Pritchard at his best and is so self-assured in its Rococo-Gothick form that it is apparent that he already knew exactly what was required. The chimney frame combines all the best features of Rococo-Gothick style: lightness of touch, curvaceous lines, leaves, flowers, bows and medieval Gothic motifs in the form of cluster columns with stiff leaf capitals, cusped ogee arches with crockets and finials with crockets.

In Pritchard's design the side panels inside the cusped ogee arches are empty but in the actual finished work the design for 'Two gerandoles' has been inserted. Did Thomas and Elizabeth Johnes find the original design too plain, or was extra light needed for the 'liberary'?[9] Girandoles, to hold candles, were fashionable then as similar designs in Thomas Chippendale's 1754 *The Gentleman and Cabinet-Maker's Director* show. Another contemporary, Thomas Johnson, included many designs in his books for these elaborate sconces.

7-5: Chimney piece at Croft, south east attic.
8-5: Chimney frame by Pritchard. (AIA 5).

Two other works by Pritchard, no longer at Croft, 'Glass border pier frame' and 'Glass frames' also used the Rococo pattern books of Thomas Johnson and Ince and Mayhew as well as Chippendale. The 'Glass Frames' for the Drawing Room took van der Hagen over forty five days to carve and gild and twenty one books of gold were used; in the mid-eighteenth century these cost around 3s. each. Nelson was also involved for thirty eight days with carving and preparing the gesso ground to receive the gold leaf.[10] (Illustrated in Chapter 2: 4-2 and 5-2) No gold leaf is specified from the chimney frame so the gilding on it now may not be correct.

By 1765, Rococo-Gothick was becoming old-fashioned but there was a time-lag before London styles reached the rural areas, despite the increasing availability of pattern books and improved mobility for craftsmen. Some years earlier, in *A Complete Body of Architecture*, Isaac Ware had advised that before using the Rococo style 'the fancy of the proprietor' should be sought.[11] He reluctantly recognised the eclectic nature of the time and the importance of the various styles and advised the craftsman 'first to establish in his own mind the great superiority there is in the true and noble ornaments over these petty wildnesses; but we must advise him also to understand the construction of both: for, unless he can conform himself to fancy, as well as work with judgment, he will do little in an age like this.'[12] Pritchard seemed to have heeded these words well.

In sequence, the Saloon, now the drawing room, the Blue Room and the Oak Room are all on the south side and take advantage of the light and the view over the Herefordshire countryside. During the 20th century tenancy, interior alterations were made and Pritchard's chimney pieces and doorcases moved around. So '2 door friezes to Mr. Johnes Dressing Room', once on the north side of the Castle, are now in the Saloon together with the door 'freezes' (AIA 10a) which were designed for that room.

These door friezes, like the two 'Chimney Freezes' on the same page, (AIA 10c and d) have Classical motifs such as the lion, oak leaves, acorns, all put together with the indispensable raffle leaf.[13] The ceiling of the Saloon, with its octagonal 'raised coffers', is in the Balbec-Palmyra style illustrated in Robert Wood's *The Ruins of Palmyra* of 1753 and *The Ruins of Balbec* of 1757.

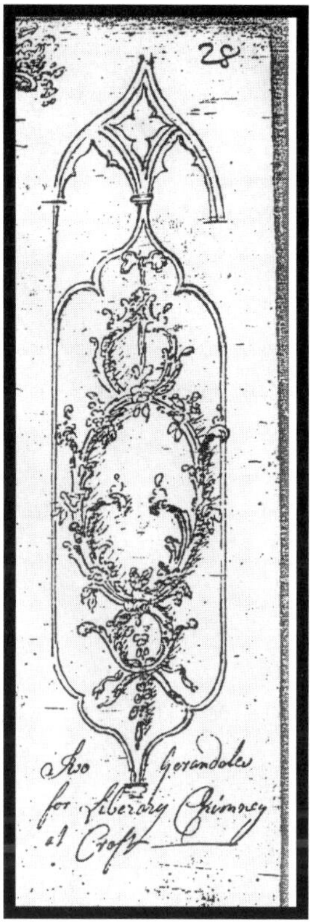

9-5:'Two Gerandoles' by Pritchard, c.1765.

The Blue Room, with a delicately scrolling Rococo plasterwork ceiling in the style of Bitterley Court, takes its name from the colour of the panelling which is believed to have been decorated with its gold roundels, or bosses, by Pritchard. A similar form of decoration was seen by Mrs. Lybbe Powys when she visited the Vyne in Hampshire in 1780.[14] The Blue Room chimney piece and overmantel are the most elaborate in the castle and include many motifs used by Pritchard elsewhere, such as musical instruments, Ionic capitals above therm-shaped pilasters with a cartouche and a lion's head at the top, but unfortunately no design for it exists; the closest comparison is the overmantel at Shipton Hall. (AIA 3) The limewood carving is very finely detailed, especially the heads of the dogs, which look like real dogs and were possibly the Johnes's hunting hounds. It was originally in the adjacent former dining room, now the Oak Room, and in its present position it is slightly too large for the space and underlines the warning by Sir William Chambers that 'in designing these, regard must be had to the nature of the place where they are to be employed.'[15] The ceiling in the Oak Room has a

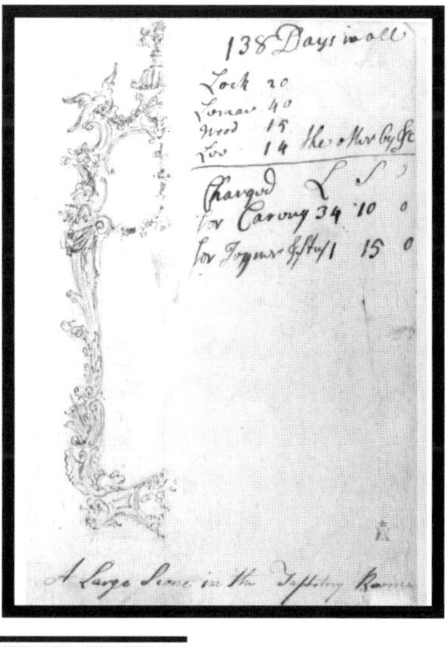

10-5: Design by Matthias Lock, c.1745

11-5: Door frieze at Croft. (AIA 10b).

plasterwork design incorporating musical instruments to complement those on its former chimney piece.

Throughout his article, Oswald pointed to the Gothick theme of the castle[16] and when he came to the grand staircase created on the south west side, conceded that it 'was all quite pleasant and harmless, and one does not feel that there is any discordance with the classical detail of the dining-room doorcase or the arches in the corridor above.'[17] A comparison between the Gothick stairs and staircase at Croft with the work at Shipton Hall indicates that the same plasterers and wood carvers could have carried out this work as there is the same exuberance of decoration. Fulsome Gothick motifs – cusped ogee arches with finials, quatrefoil frieze, waterleaf cornice – blend into the more delicate carving of the newel posts and tread ends.

Next to the Gothick staircase is the present dining room, created in this century on the west side. Pritchard's 'flower pots', once over the doors of the library, now decorate the walls. (AIA 31b) The existing structure of the castle probably did not permit a grand central staircase, so a second, more modest one was put in a newly-created space behind the hall to serve the north and east sides.

Why did Pritchard use Rococo, Gothick and Rococo-Gothick for Croft? The inevitable question arises regarding Pritchard's involvement at the Strawberry Hill-style Shobdon Church. The Batemans at Shobdon Court were near neighbours and no doubt Thomas Johnes would have watched the rebuilding of the church with interest. It is, of course, very possible that Pritchard had also visited the church, either on his own account or with Thomas Johnes. The overall design at Shobdon has a similarity of motifs and use of the Gothick vocabulary, but Croft shows the lightness of touch that we have come to expect from Pritchard's work. It might be possible that Pritchard was influenced by Shobdon but did not have any hand in creating it. He was not well known in the area in the 1750s when the work was done and it was probably too early in his career to be participating in such a scheme. Work at Lord Bateman's house, Shobdon Court, is discussed in Chapter 10.

The use of Gothick at Croft can therefore be indirectly linked with the exciting work at Shobdon Church, but perhaps the need to reflect the older fabric of the Castle might have been important to Richard Knight and his daughter, Elizabeth. Their status came from their industrial wealth rather than ancient lineage, unlike the Johnes whose ancestry could be traced back for many centuries.[18] Knight, having gained the castle from the Croft family, would have been conscious of this and reminded of it by the monument in Croft church of Richard Croft, who died in 1509. In addition, the use of Rococo, sometimes with Gothick, could have been a deliberate attempt to lighten the interior of the castle and create a contrast to the fortified appearance of the exterior.

12-5: Plasterwork detail, Blue Room.

In the mid-eighteenth century liberation from the strict Palladian rules and its connections with the Whig aristocracy led to the form of patronage changing from upper-class to middle-class.[19] Richard Knight's widow lived with her daughter at Croft: both women were known to have strong characters and their money may have been a deciding factor in the choice of decorative styles at Croft.[20] If so, this makes an interesting connection between Rococo and the Industrial Revolution.[21]

13-5: Blue Room at Croft.

This was a busy period in Pritchard's career and Croft Castle was an important commission but it was not the only one. The design for the 'flowers pots' over the library doors at Croft shares the page with the 'Pedement' for Hatton Grange, Shropshire, (AIA 31a) indicating that Pritchard was working on these two major projects at the same time.

Croft Castle is a medieval castle with a Georgian interior

14-5: The Gothick staircase at Croft.

containing some of Pritchard's most ambitious, and probably most successful, decorative schemes. They are successful because they are attractive and interesting to look at, without being overwhelming in scale and the eye is drawn to the finely carved chimney pieces and then to the varying patterns of the plasterwork ceiling. The rooms of the old castle have been given increased comfort, combined with a variety of styles like theatrical sets, which was perhaps one of the aims.[22]

15-5: 'Flower pot' now in Dining Room.

Croft Castle and The Stanage Connection.

The Blue Room panelling came from Stanage, a Radnorshire estate given to Elizabeth Knight by her father on her marriage. The tale of how Stanage came into the possession of the Knights and then the Johnes is a complex one. Elizabeth Knight's mother, who married Richard Knight of Downton in 1717, was Elizabeth Powell, daughter of Samuel Powell of Stanage. The Stanage estate passed to Elizabeth's nephew, Richard Powell.

As the boy was a minor Richard Knight was appointed one of his guardians. The story is told in *Recollections* by Mr. Price, M.P:

> Mr Price's father was negotiating to buy Stanage from the Powells but was outbid by Mr. Knight. Mr. Knight settled the estate on his daughter (Elizabeth) on her marriage to Mr. Johnes, before he purchased Croft Castle and intended to make this the family residence. After that, they pulled down the house that remained at Stanage to repair Croft. And I have now been told that some curious wainscoting painted light blue and gold, now in the room adjoining the dining room at Croft, was taken from the dining parlour at Stanage. I have heard also that a wagon, loaded with window frames, was upset in the way, and all the glass and timber broken into pieces.[23]

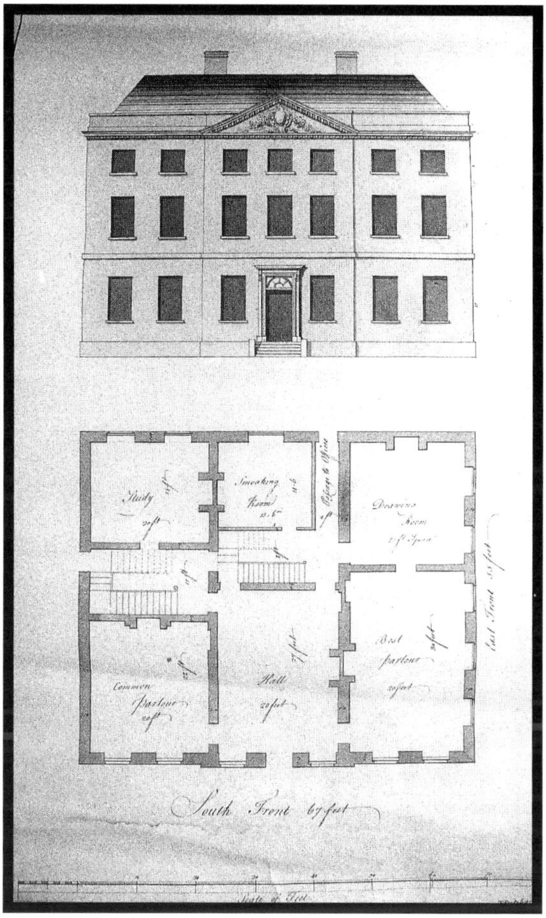

16-5: Plan and elevation for Stanage.

Among the Stanage papers is 'Mr Johnes plan for Building at Stanage' with Pritchard's name on it; it is addressed to 'Tho. Johnes esq. Ludlow'. The Stanage estate was sold again in 1799 to Mr. Rogers and the old house, by then apparently somewhat denuded, was pulled down and a 'noble Gothic mansion' built in its place.

The unexecuted plan by Pritchard is for an almost square house of seven bays, the three centre bays almost imperceptibly stepped forward. The elevation of the south front shows an elaborate pediment over the centre bays; with its Rococo cartouche and floral swags it looks remarkably like the 'Pedement' Pritchard designed for Mr. Slaney at Hatton.

There are two staircases, a smaller servants' one towards the back of the centre of the house and a larger main one on the west side. On either side of the hall are the common and best parlours with the drawing room towards the back on the west side. Tucked under the servants' stair is a smoking room and next to that a study. A passage leads to 'offices' in the old house.

As Stanage stands in a romantic situation on the Welsh borders, it is possible that young Thomas Johnes considered building a house there before he discovered the Welsh site where he built Hafod.

BROCKHAMPTON HOUSE, HEREFORDSHIRE.

17-5: Brockhampton House.

Brockhampton House, a handsome typical mid-Georgian red-brick house of almost square appearance, stands up high above the Bromyard Downs. The house is seven bays across, the centre three bays stepped forward and topped with a small plain pediment. The exterior is unadorned and contrasts with the rich decorative scheme of the interior.

Pritchard had already encountered Bartholomew Barnaby when he was working on the Shrewsbury Infirmary. Barnaby married Betty Freeman, granddaughter of Bellingham Freeman of Gaines, in 1756 and her dowry may have permitted some building work, or perhaps rebuilding of the house on the high point of the Brockhampton estate where there was already a farm. Betty's father died in 1764 which may have released further money and the major work on the house could begin.

As the Barnaby papers were destroyed this century it is

As the Barnaby papers were destroyed this century it is impossible to know exactly what happened, but we do know that Pritchard designed two chimney pieces for 'Esq. Barnaby'. No house is given for these designs (AIA 14 and 46) but it is assumed that they were for Brockhampton and the architecture of the house is attributed to Pritchard.

The front elevation of the house is so similar to Hatton Grange that it provoked correspondence in *Country Life*.[24] The seven bays with central pediment, central window details and pedimented doorway make these houses almost identical. During the 19th century the windows at Brockhampton were given heavier stone surrounds, but these have been removed as the lighter replacement brick now around the windows shows.

The main block of the house has an entrance hall running from front to back with reception rooms on either side; the drawing room and music room are on the right and the dining room and present kitchens on the left. Originally the kitchen would probably have been in buildings at the back and it would appear that both Hatton Grange and Brockhampton had an older house behind them that was used later as a service area. Behind the main block at Brockhampton are an assortment of two-storey buildings of various dates and amongst these buildings are flues and ovens of considerable dimensions that clearly predate the main 18th century house.

18-5: Entrance hall at Brockhampton.

The interior layout resembles Hatton Grange in the general disposition of the main rooms, but the decoration of the interiors at Hatton is virtually unaltered and has an elegant, neat but unpretentious appearance, while at Brockhampton it is grander with its spacious entrance hall leading up to the screen of columns and the single staircase with two returns. The date of this screen and the heavy marble chimney piece in the hall are in doubt; they have been dated to 1870 when alterations were made to the house, both inside and out.[25] The other example of a screen by Pritchard is the plainer one at Bitterley Court, which has an essential structural part to play in supporting the floor above after alterations. The screen at Brockhampton, while more decorative, could be supporting the return of the stair and therefore could date from the 1760s.

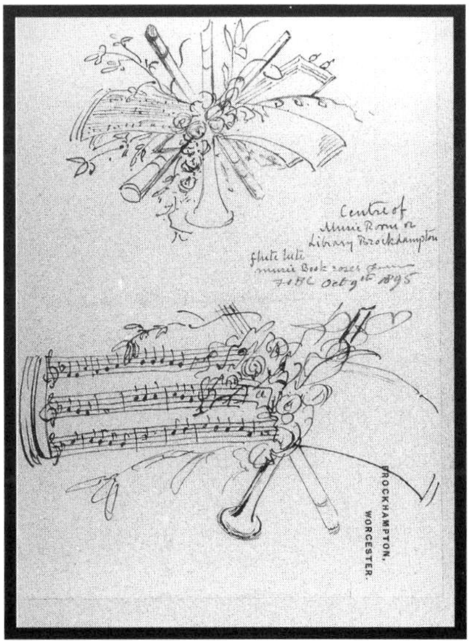

19-5: Sketch of plasterwork at Brockhampton.

20-5: Watercolour of Brockhampton.

The elegant stairs are of a standard mid-Georgian type, with carved tread ends like those at nearby Gaines. There is a fine Venetian window on the stairs. The similarities between the stairs and hall at Brockhampton and the contemporary Chase-Lloyd House by William Buckland in Annapolis, Maryland, are notable and indicate that forms and styles were being taken across the Atlantic with relative ease.

The fireplace in the hall of Brockhampton, on the other hand, is not at all in Pritchard's style and is more likely to be of a later date. The two chimney pieces, no longer in the house, which were designed for Mr. Barnaby by Pritchard are separated by at least two years. They are both for the 'Drawing Room', but none of the rooms at Brockhampton is big enough for two fireplaces so perhaps there was a change of mind. The earlier design has a dog's head in the frieze; again a very definite dog, perhaps owned by Mr. Barnaby.

Brockhampton has some interesting plasterwork, especially in the music room with the renowned central motif of the music for *God Save the King.*[26] If Pritchard is connected with the building of the house, then this plasterwork would almost certainly be his. The flowing lines and low relief are typical and Mr. Barnaby may have requested that particular piece of music. The plasterwork of the other rooms is more questionable. The cornice in the present dining room shows similarities to the dining room at Mawley Hall, while the plasterwork in the present drawing room is altogether heavier and may date from the 19th century.[27]

One person who was interested in the music was Miss Baldwyn Childe who visited Brockhampton in 1985 and made the pen, ink and wash pictures of the house which capture its elegant character.

SHERFORD HOUSE.

21-5: Sherford House.

The delightful Sherford House in Bromyard is thought to have been a dower house for nearby Brockhampton but like its larger neighbour no documentation survives for it. The exterior is red brick with a pronounced stone cornice that does not extend right around the building. The interior has been little altered over the years and still contains the high quality of the work that we have come to expect from Pritchard.

There are two finely carved chimney pieces, one with ho-ho birds perched on rocks. A depressed arch in the hall, carved tread ends to the stairs and Gothick plasterwork pendants around some of the cornices all indicate that Pritchard could have worked on the house at the same time as he was working on the other houses in the area.

The high quality of work in the upper storey suggests that the occupants were not short of money and were used to comfort while the rooms on the top storey are not of a type usually provided for servants so are more likely to be for companions of a former lady of Brockhampton.

22-5: Chimney piece at Sherford House.

23-5: Hall at Sherford House.

24-5: *Watercolour of Gaines by Edith Wrigley, 1952.*

GAINES, WORCESTERSHIRE.

The only link with Pritchard and Gaines are five drawings in *The Drawing Book* for Mr. Freeman. No other evidence exists, but it is fairly certain that Pritchard modernised and extended the house in the 1760s. Attempts to find documentation have failed and the fact that it stands on the Herefordshire-Worcestershire border has made this even more of a problem as the various local authorities have either claimed or denied ownership. It is also one of the few Pritchard houses that I have looked at in detail that has changed hands many times and the interior has been altered in some places.

It is also one of the most interesting houses to be connected with Pritchard as I will show but there are still many areas that remain unresolved. At the time of writing, Gaines is a Christian Youth Centre, in good hands and full of life with young people coming and going. As an entity, the building now lacks form, but its underlying structure and interior details make it very interesting in architectural historical terms but not satisfying in aesthetic ones. A late 19th century photograph of the house shows that it was either stuccoed or painted white. This was cleaned off during restoration work in the 1920s, which is a loss as visually it pulled the house and its various additions together

25-5: Plan of Gaines.

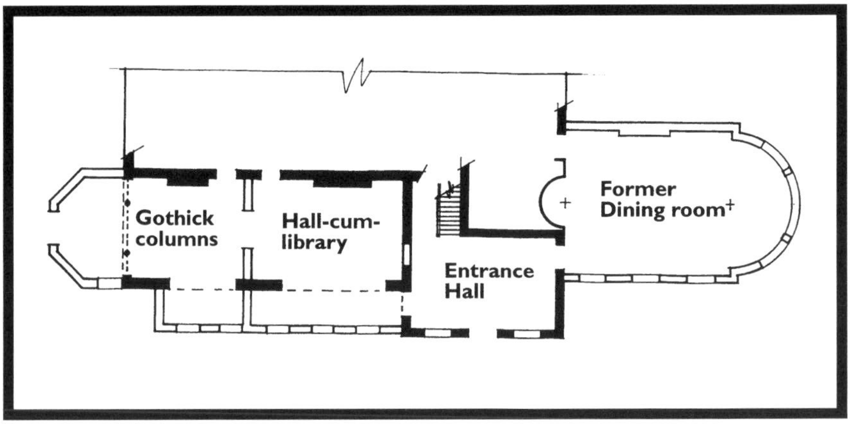

giving it a coherence which it lacks today. Essentially the house is a square red-brick block with a large addition on the north end and a smaller one on the south end and extensions on the east front. The plan shows the east side of the building with the darker lines indicating the older house and the lighter ones the additions by Pritchard.

There may have been a house already on the site when the Freeman family bought the estate in 1683. Bellingham Freeman, already a large landowner, acquired Old Gaines at the time of his marriage to Elizabeth Gower of Suckley, a village nearby. He died in 1689 after the birth of their fourth child, but during their short marriage they 'planned and embarked on the grand new house known as New Gaines.'[28] Old Gaines, a timber-framed house, can still be seen nearby.

This 'grand new house' is probably the one in a late 17th century or early 18th century painting which shows it in a hollow between the surrounding hills. This house is five bays wide and four bays deep with three storeys and an attic with dormer windows. There are two-storey cottages on each side, linked to the main building and on the other side of the house is a walled garden. There are two chimneys at either end of the hipped roof which has a flat central section and balustrade around it.

26-5: Detail from 'Gaines Manor', c.1720.

This was the house which was raised and reroofed, perhaps early in the 18th century when Bellingham's son John married Abigail Jones in 1727. The painting does not indicate the slope that the house stands on. This creates problems with levels and today, there are four storeys at the back and three at the front on the external elevation of the house, with large cellars underneath. The cottages shown in the painting on each side of the main block appear to have been demolished and rebuilt as extensions to the main block. The north end now rises to the same roof level as the main block while the extension on the south is slightly lower.

27-5, 28-5, 29-5: Rear and front elevations of Gaines and front entrance.

The grandson of the first Bellingham, another John, is thought to have employed Pritchard to modernise and extend the house after his marriage to Ann Harris of Leominster. These additions consisted of a two-storey extension ending in a semi-circular bay on the north side and another terminating in a five-sided canted bay on the south end, as well as a single storey extension on the east front.

This extension was butted onto the original east front of the building and at the same time the original entrance was probably rebuilt. The circular and oval shaped ornament over the front door, which leads into the present entrance hall, echoes the motifs found around the walls of the downstairs rooms.

The single-storey extension on the east front would appear to have been created to provide extra space for the room behind. The lower ceiling of this extended section has shallow ribbed 'vaulting', similar to the entrance passage at Ludford House in Ludlow. A 19th century photograph of the room behind shows Pritchard's 'Hall Chimney for Mr Freeman at Gaines' (AIA 57) with Rococo plasterwork above, which is very similar to the White House at Suckley and the Powis Castle Ballroom. Like all the chimney pieces that Pritchard designed for Gaines this one

is no longer in the house but survives, by chance, in a house in Sussex.[29] The room is fitted with bookcases which appear to be 18th century, so it could have had a dual use as a 'Hall-cum-Library'; Gaines is not a deep house and there is not as much space as would appear from the exterior. There was once a doorway, shown on the plan, which led back to the small entrance hall and stairs but this was blocked up and a cupboard put in its place.

From the 'Hall-cum-Library' sliding double doors lead into the extended room with the canted bay. The cusped ogee arch over these doors resembles the arch on the Whitmore Acton monument at Acton Round and the Guildhall, Ludlow.[30]

Above 30-5: Entrance passage at Gaines.

31-5: 'Hall-cum-Library' at Gaines in the 19th century. Pritchard's chimney piece is on the right. (AIA 57)

33-5: Details of Gothick columns. (AIA 54)

Below 32-5: AIA 57

34-5: Room with the Gothick columns in the 19th century.

Throughout these two rooms, apart from the Rococo plasterwork, there is a consistent Gothick style which includes the slim panels on the walls, the panels on shutters and the waterleaf moulding around the cornice.

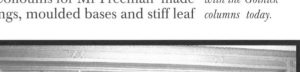

Pritchard's 'Eight Gothick Colloums for Mr Freeman' made up of clustered columns with shaft rings, moulded bases and stiff leaf capitals are the most intriguing designs he made for the house. (AIA 54) He specified '2 whole Collums' together with '4¾' and '2½' columns. The two whole free-standing columns were made up in cast iron, while the part columns were made in wood. The reason for using cast iron in this situation is not clear as the columns are only iron up to the capitals and from thereon are wooden. This would not make them sufficiently strong to be loadbearing unless they have iron cores and this has not been determined.

35-5: The same room with the Gothick columns today.

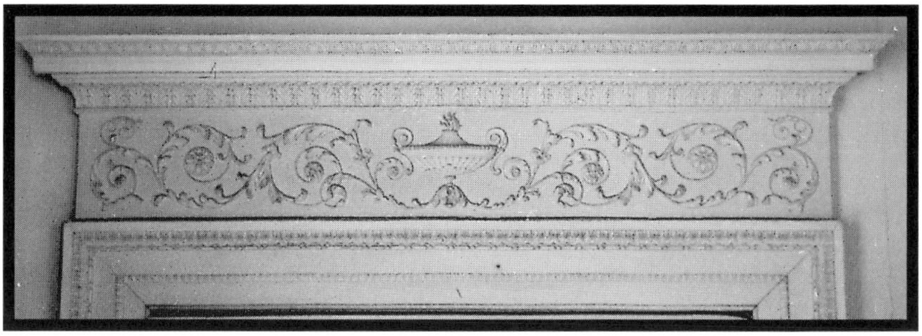

36-5: Frieze of a doorcase at Gaines.

The early use of cast iron for architectural purposes is a debatable point on which few people seem to agree and evidence for it is slight.[31] The drawing for the Gaines columns is datable to late 1768 or early 1769 and if this is correct these columns would appear to predate other use of cast iron in domestic buildings. As Pritchard had connections with John Wilkinson, the iron master, he cannot have failed to have been interested in the work at Coalbrookdale and to have looked for ideas for the use of iron.

37-5: The dining room at Gaines in the 1940s.

At the south end of Gaines is a well-crafted wooden staircase which has three balusters to a tread, carved tread ends and the handrail curving around the newel post at the base; a style similar to other staircases that Pritchard designed.

The extension at the north end is curved and the large downstairs room, once a dining room, has three tall windows; original sashes and crown glass remain in two of them, some of it curved, indicating that expense was not spared to create the desired effect. *The Builder's Price Book* of 1776 quotes a price of 3s. 6d. per foot for 'best Crown Glass bent circular for shop windows.' This was against a price of 'Neat Ratcliff Best Crown Glass' at 1s. 3d.

At the north end the mood changes; the oval serving niche in the former dining room is supported by plain pilasters with Corinthian-type capitals and plasterwork with sprays of husks radiating out from the centre; this resembles the work at Kyre Park where the oval ceiling of the boudoir had trailing hop vines on it, very suitable for a hop-growing county such as Worcestershire. The doorcases of the dining room had friezes over them but these were removed, probably at the same time as some of the chimney pieces. The upper room of this extension still retains its Neo-Classical door case and also has a fine but damaged low-relief Rococo plaster ceiling. Externally, the supporting 'buttress' for the chimney stack has the same curved detailing as one at Brockhampton House, thereby providing a link between the two houses.

The house was refurbished in the 1920s by the firm of Waring and Gillow, but no records for the work survive.[32] Internally, Gaines has two contrasting styles of decoration at its opposite ends; Gothick at one and Neo-Classical at the other. This again shows that an overall scheme was not Pritchard's method of decorating a house.

38-5: The north extension at Gaines.

39-5: The former dining room at Gaines today.

40-5: South elevation of Kinsham Court.

KINSHAM COURT.

After he had visited Presteigne in September 1756, Bishop Pococke wrote that he went 'near Kenson, another seat of Lady Oxford's, which with an estate of about £700 a year was left to the family by a relation.'[33]

Kinsham Court, a tall red-brick house, stands high above a valley on the Herefordshire side of the Welsh borders. It was once the dower house of Brampton Bryan, Herefordshire, seat of the Harley family and a favourite house of Bishop Harley who died in 1788. In the 20th century it was bought by the Arkwrights, of the textile family, who also owned Hampton Court, near Leominster.

The house is possibly 17th century and was extended and remodelled in the 18th century. Originally it appears to have been an L-shaped house and the older fabric is still apparent. The entrance in the 18th century was probably on the west side leading into what is now a study. The main alterations of that time seem to have involved raising the south wing to three storeys and adding a bay window to the east wing, thus providing three substantial reception rooms on the ground floor where the new chimney pieces were installed.

There are drawings in *The Drawing Book* for chimney pieces for the 'Honourable Mr Harley' and three are still at Kinsham. (AIA 27, 35, 40 and 41) The chimney piece designed for the 'Best Parlour' has a shell pattern on the frieze with a lion's head and grapes on the tablet in the centre. (AIA 35) At the side of the fireplace are wall panels topped by an espagnolette, a female head with a ruff around it; below is scrolling foliage and ribbons.[34]

Another chimney piece was designed for the common parlour which is now probably the kitchen. (AIA 27) Much of this one remains as part of the chimney piece and overmantel in the present dining room where it has been combined with the design containing waterleaf coving and frond-like branches. (AIA 41) This design was for Mr. Harley 'for Hall' – a slight puzzle as the only space for a hall never appears to have had a chimney piece. It is just possible that this was originally made for the Harley's other house, nearby

Above
41-5: Chimney piece at Kinsham. (AIA 35)

Left
42-5: Chimney piece at Kinsham. (AIA 41)

Brampton Bryan Hall. The carving surrounding the Derbyshire marble is made up of bead and space and twisted ribbon and flower from the 'Common Parlour' chimney piece. Pritchard also used this design for Samuel Egerton of Tatton. Another chimney piece in an upstairs room reflects Pritchard's style with its scrolling foliage and pineapple or pine cone in the centre.

Another design, shared with Loton Park, Shropshire and Tatton Park no longer exists at Kinsham or was never executed. (AIA 40) It is one of Pritchard's popular Rococo-Gothick designs with a water-leaf frieze and flowers twisted around the cluster columns on the sides. The Kinsham chimney pieces are interesting instances of the same design being used for different clients which was probably quite usual.

Kinsham was modified several times in the 19th century, when the present roof, with wide overhanging eaves with an unusual deep coving, may have been put on. While these eaves appear to have more in common with C. A. Voysey's work at such houses as Perry Croft at Malvern, Worcestershire, and owe more to the Arts and Crafts movement than the 18th century, it is also necessary to look at Rudhall House, Brampton Abbots, in Herefordshire. Here the early 16th century, partly timber-framed building has deep coving above the jetty which was perhaps the inspiration for Kinsham's eaves.[35]

43-5: Kyre Park.

KYRE PARK, WORCESTERSHIRE.

Kyre Park, near Bromyard, is a house of several building periods. Pritchard carried out a survey for alterations for Jonathan Pytts at Kyre Park in May 1776. The present handsome red-brick house is described as L-shaped in plan, the foot of the 'L' being formed by a 'thick-walled building'[36] which may be the remains of the 14th century fortified house. In the late 16th or early 17th century a hall was added on the north-east side when the house came into the possession of the Pytts family.[37]

Further work was carried out on the house in the 1750s by the Hiorn brothers of Warwick for Edmund Pytts; this included filling in the recessed west side of the house to form the drawing room and the rooms above and adding canted bays on the north and south ends. Thermal and Venetian windows, almost their hallmark, are still prominent on that end of the building.[38] This stage of the work, completed in 1756, came to £1,855. 2s. 4d., plus their fee for drawings and supervising the contract, but the account was not settled until 1761 and the state of the Pytts finances may have been the reason for the work not being completed.

The darker areas on the plan define the old house and the light areas the 18th century work.

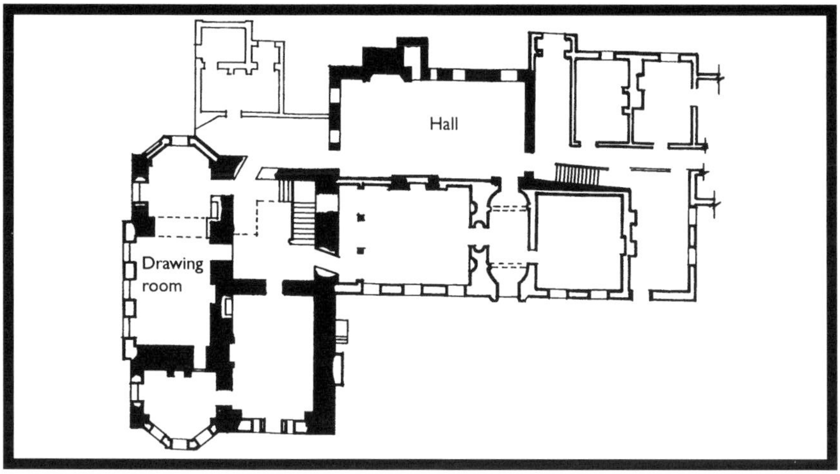

43-5: Plan of Kyre Park.

Pritchard made his survey and estimate twenty years after the first stages were carried out, but in the interim some work was done, not very satisfactorily, by a Mr. Bromfield. The lead gutters were too narrow and Pritchard reported that they had so 'little fall that they are not sufficient to carry off the rain water from the roof.' Bromfield has also built on to the east end to provide the servants' hall and laundry but this was in such a bad condition that it 'must be totally taken down and when rebuilt may be much improved in point of light and convenience.' There is no indication of who Mr Bromfield was, but Robert Bromfield, a builder of Stourbridge, had been called in to make a valuation of the disputed work at the Red Lion Inn, Wolverhampton. Was this the same Bromfield? Joseph Bromfield, Pritchard's plasterer, did not become involved in building work until after Pritchard's death.

It was probably because of the Pytts' finances that Pritchard wrote cautiously: 'You will be pleased to observe that I have not at this time been so particular as to make plans and an exact estimate - these are general ideas for your inspection and approbation.'[39] His plans for Kyre amounted to £2000; he proposed that the end of the old house on the east side should be 'entirely taken away' and the south front 'carried on a straight line with another bow as far as the end of the present hall.' This new front would include 'a very large handsome dining parlour' and the present hall would become a common parlour and a good back staircase would be put in next to the best staircase. Pritchard put his 'general ideas' forward as three proposals:

> to do the immediate necessary repairs and fitt up the hall and chamber, to raise the attic story on the south front and to have the fronts made regular, the rooms to be constructed on a new plan and the whole made elegant and compleat.[40]

It is tempting to think that some of the work carried out at a later date was designed or at least influenced by Pritchard. Some work was done in the 1780s, under the supervision of Jonathan Pytts, who had taken over the estate from his brother Edmund. Jonathan inherited money from his grandfather and it was after this that he was able to get the work restarted. Unfortunately, the splendid plasterwork done at that time by George Roberts has gone but photographs show his skill especially in the boudoir ceiling. The elaborate chimney piece and overmantel in the former drawing room are very similar to the one at Shipton Hall; both look back to the Baroque style. The only Pritchardian clue is upstairs where there is an arched 'vaulted' connection between the two main blocks, which has shallow ribs in a similar fashion to the 'vaulting' at Ludford House and Gaines.

As the house has undergone so much alteration in the 20th century it is hard to tell what did take place. The 1917 *Country Life* photograph of the south elevation reveals that the attic storey has been added since that date. A drawing from around the same date shows that much of the medieval structure of the house still existed, including the 'ancient chamber' on the north side, but was later demolished.[41] On the south side, the west end has been stuccoed and painted in cream, throwing the Venetian and Thermal windows into sharper relief and contrasting sharply with the red brick of the rest of this elevation. Pritchard was correct when he said that the house needed to be 'made elegant and compleat' and given a coherent appearance.

Herefordshire and Worcestershire contain some of Pritchard's most important work. Croft Castle was one of his principal commissions of the period and here he was able to show what he could do to modernise an old structure and yet retain its character and dignity. He demonstrated his ability to provide exciting designs with the Gothick staircase and the chimney frame for 'the Liberary' while at the same time creating elegant Rococo plasterwork ceilings. At Gaines, Pritchard's southernmost project, his use of new materials for the Gothick columns is notable and has yet to be explored in more detail. As with Croft, he mixed the styles, mingling Gothick with Classical. Pritchard's work on the projects in these counties extends his range both geographically and as a designer and architect.

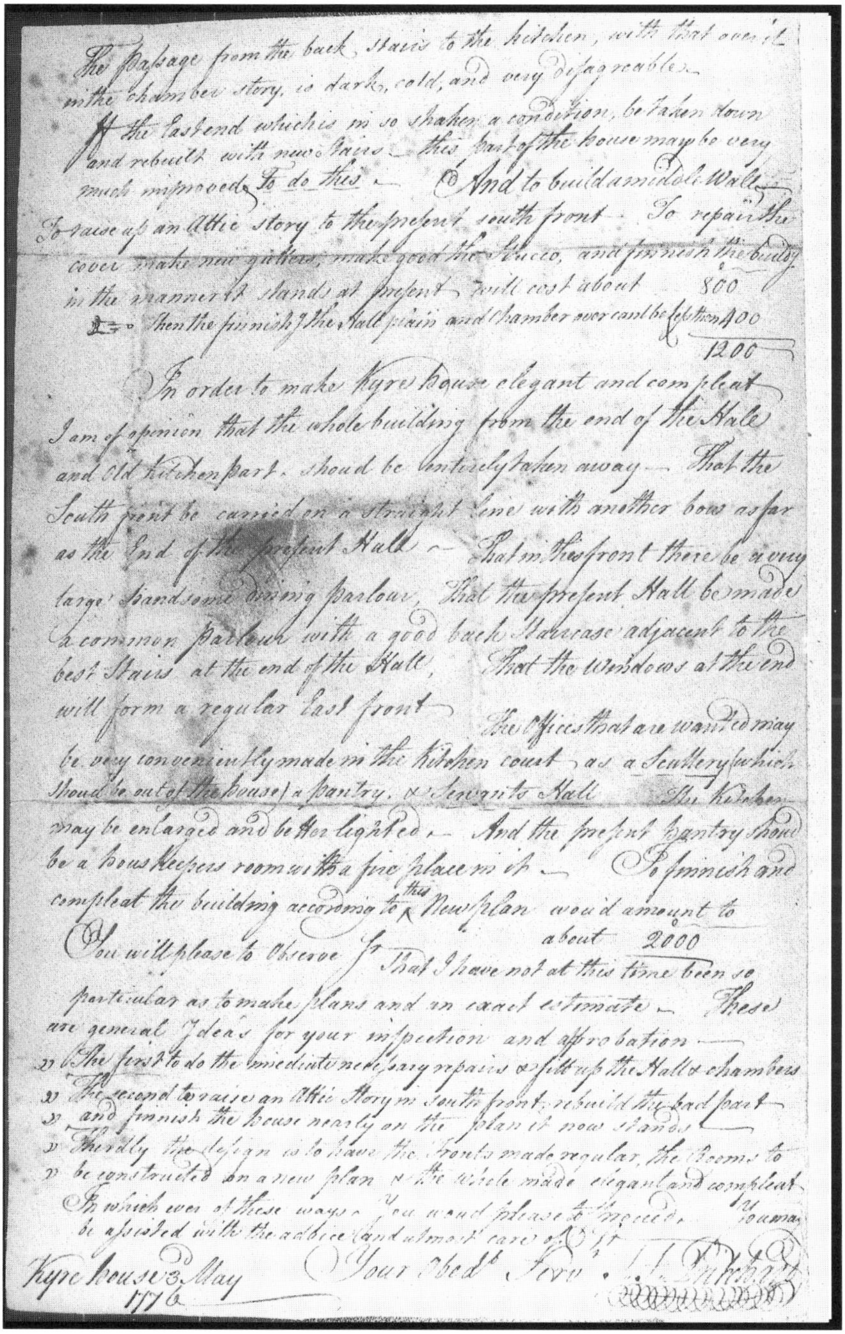

The Passage from the back Stairs to the kitchen, with that over it
in the chamber story, is dark, cold, and very disagreeable

If the East end which is in so shaken a condition, be taken down
and rebuilt with new Stairs — this part of the house may be very
much improved To do this — And to build a middle Wall

To raise up an Attic story to the present south front — To repair the
cover make new gutters, make good the Stucco, and finnish the body
in the manner it stands at present — will cost about 800
Then the finnish of the Hall plain and Chamber over canl be less then 400
1200

In order to make Kyre House elegant and compleat
I am of opinion that the whole building from the end of the Hall
and Old Kitchen part, shoud be intirely taken away — That the
South front be carried on a straight line with another bow as far
as the End of the present Hall — That in this front there be a very
large handsome dining parlour, That the present Hall be made
a common Parlour with a good back Staircase adjacent to the
best Stairs at the end of the Hall, That the windows at the end
will form a regular East front — The Offices that are wanted may
be very conveniently made in the kitchen court as a Scullery (which
shoud be out of the house) a Pantry, & Servants Hall — The kitchen
may be enlarged and better lighted — And the present Pantry shoud
be a Houskeepers room with a fire place in it — To finnish and
compleat the building according to this New plan woud amount to
about 2000

You will please to Observe Sr That I have not at this time been so
particular as to make plans and an exact estimate — These
are general Ideas for your inspection and approbation —
The first to do the immediate necessary repairs & fill up the Hall & chambers
The second to raise an Attic Story in South front, rebuild the bad part
and finnish the house nearly on the plan it now stands
Thirdly the design is to have the Fronts made regular, the Rooms to
be constructed on a new plan & the whole made elegant and compleat
In which ever of these ways — You woud please to proceed, You may
be assisted with the advice and utmost care of Sr

Kyre House 3 May 1776 — Your Obedt Servt T. F. Pritchard

45-5: Extract from Pritchard's survey of Kyre Park, 1776.

1 Arthur Oswald, Croft Castle, *Country Life*, 5 May, 1950, p. 1292.

2 Royal Commission on Historic Monuments, 1931-34, Volume III, 35-36.

3 For further information on the Johnes family, see Elizabeth Inglis-Jones, *Peacocks in Paradise*, London, 1950.

4 Rev. C. J. Robinson, *The Castles of Herefordshire*, Hereford, 1869, p. 38.

5 The photograph in the 1950 *Country Life* article appears to show it in its original position. Oswald, p. 1294. This room subsequently became the 'little dining room'.

6 Descendant of Somerset Davies of 27, Broad Street, Ludlow.

7 Diary of Anne Rushout. Manuscript privately owned. Around 1783, Croft Castle was sold to Somerset Davies, owner of 27 Broad Street, Ludlow and in 1805 the family were the owners. I am grateful to The Hon. Mrs. Diana Uhlman for this quotation and all the other help and information she has given me on Croft Castle, her family home.

8 Oswald, p. 1295.

9 Isaac Ware, *A Complete Body of Architecture*, London, 1757, p. 189. This was important as Isaac Ware pointed out the number of candles needed to light a room taking into account the different types of wall coverings. A painted wainscoted room would take only six, whereas one with hangings, such as tapestry, would take ten. This was a consideration when good candles were expensive. An illustration in Dan Cruickshank and Neil Burton, *Life in the Georgian City*, (London, 1990, p. 44) of a family being read to shows them grouped around the table which has two tall candles on it. The sconces on the wall are empty which suggests that for informal gatherings candles were carried from room to room and the sconces only lit when company was present.

10 An account for August 1763 for Petworth House lists '2 books gold at 0. 3. 0.' and at these rates 21 books cost £3. 3s. Information from *Of Gilding* by Pippa Mason and Michael Gregory, London, 1989, unpaginated. Taking the daily rates of a craftsman at about 3s., this amounts to £12. 9s. for labour, making a total, without materials other than the gold, of £15. 12s. It is possible that Nelson and van der Hagen, being skilful craftsmen, were paid slightly more than the average journeyman who had an annual income of around £50 at this time. These figures can be compared with a sketch for a pier glass c.1745 by Matthias Lock, who was one of the first furniture designers in England to adopt the Rococo style. Like Pritchard's work, only half the design is shown and similarly there is an account beside it. Lock's pier glass took a total of 138 days, which compares with 83 for Pritchard's, and the carving cost £34. 10s. and 'For Joyners and stuf £1. 15s. 0d.' However, these are London figures.

11 Ware, p. 501.

12 Ware, p. 501.

13 From its ancient classical origins, raffle leaf, rinceau or scrolling foliage progressed through the Renaissance to be adopted by the craftsmen using Rococo decoration. It then came full circle to be used by Adam in his Neo-Classical work. The importance of raffle leaf in 18th century decorative work is emphasised by Ince and Mayhew's inclusion of 3 plates of examples of it for 'young beginners in their first practice of drawing.'

14 In 1789, *The Topographer* wrote of 'a large room' at the Vyne 'with wainscot painted blue, studded with gold.' The panelling at the Vyne has since then been stripped back to plain wood. 'History and Description of the Vine.' *The Topographer*, London, MDCCLXXIX, p. 58. (Mrs. Philip Lybbe Powys, p. 204.)

15 William Chambers, *A Treatise on Civil Architecture*, London, 1759, p. 77.

16 Oswald does not spell it with a 'k' but I have included one for the sake of consistency when referring to the 18th century variety.

17 Oswald, p. 1295.

18 Inglis-Jones, p. 35.

19 Girouard points to 'English Rococo ' as working in a 'liberated atmosphere'. Mark Girouard, *Town and Country*, Yale, 1992, pp. 32-33.

20 Inglis-Jones, pp. 54-5.

21 This was suggested regarding the 'machine grate' designed by Pritchard for Shipton Hall by Gervase Jackson-Stops, in *Rococo, Art and Design in Hogarth's England*, V&A Exhibition Catalogue, 1984, p. 207.

22 Robert Taylor had been one of the first English architects to introduce the French innovation of different shaped rooms arranged in a sequence and he carried this out to great effect at Harleyford Manor in Buckinghamshire in 1755. The idea was taken up by Adam for his grand houses.

23 *Recollections* from Mr. Price, M.P., written down by Edward Rogers in 1845. Information from David Coltman-Roger and Mrs Diana Uhlman. It was considered that Richard Knight defrauded his nephew and paid a low price for the estate.

24 Michael Hall, 'Brockhampton, Herefordshire', *Country Life*, 4 January, 1990, pp. 46-51; also Correspondence in *Country Life*, 4 April, 1968, p. 815 and 22 February, p. 1990.

25 Hall, p. 49.

26 This tune has a long and complex history and can be found in America and Germany. See *The Oxford Companion to Music*, Percy Scholes, tenth edition, 1970, pp. 408-413.

27 Interestingly, the late Robin Chaplin in his notes on Pritchard has pointed to the possible involvement of Henry Holland in 1770 or 1780, referring to his work at Claremont. There is no mention of Holland having worked at Brockhampton but as he was at Berrington Hall, which is not that far away, then it is not wildly implausible.

28 For further information on Gaines and the Freemans, see Phyllis Williams, *Whitbourne*, Herefordshire, 1979.

29 It was found in an outhouse and given to a friend in Sussex who installed it in her house. The 18th century chimney pieces seem to have been removed either before or during the 20th century refurbishment. The late Robin Chaplin had done some amazing detective work concerning the 20th century occupants of Gaines; his information was very useful in tracking down this chimney piece.

30 The influence of the designs of Batty Langley is evident, especially in the cusped arch illustrated in *Gothic Architecture*, Plate XLIII.

31 Nikolaus Pevsner cites the use of it in Portugal for a chimney support in 1752. (Nikolaus Pevsner, *Pioneers of Modern Design*, London, 1986 edition, p. 118.) John Harris put forward the theory that Wren had used cast iron supports for a gallery that was added to the House of Commons in 1706. (John Harris, 'Cast Iron Columns 1706', *Architectural History*, CXXX, 1961, pp. 60-61.) His theory is based upon evidence in an engraving of 1749 and a painting of 1833 which show the extreme thinness of these supports. Wren had worked with the great blacksmith, Jean Tijou, at St. Paul's Cathedral and Hampton Court Palace and Tijou published *A Newe Booke of Drawing* in 1693 in which a thin column and base with a Corinthian capital were illustrated; this looks very much like the Wren columns in Parliament. The design was copied by Batty Langley as 'A Capital for an Iron

Support to Galleries &c.' Langley, *The City and Country Builders and Workman's Treasury of Designs*, London, 1741, plate CLXXX11. Harris considered that Wren made the columns of cast iron and the capitals of wood and that there was no practical reason why columns twelve feet in length could not have been cast then. While this was possible, it seems strange that no further use was made of cast iron in this way. Both Wren and the House of Commons should have attracted attention to its usage and spread the idea, but this does not seem to have happened. The capital seems more likely to have been made of wrought iron.

32 The late Lindsay Boynton was very helpful in this respect but no records for the house have been found. The Waring and Gillow chimney pieces in their turn were removed in the 1950s and one is now down in Somerset.

33 Richard Pococke, Bishop of Ossory and of Meath, *The Travels Through England of Dr. R. Pococke*, 2 Volumes, London, 1888, Volume I, p. 221.

34 Batty Langley gives examples of these in *The City and Country Builder's and Workman's Treasury of Designs*, 1741, Plate LXIV, LXVII and LXXXIV.

35 In Knighton, Powys, not far from Kinsham, a house in the main street has deep eaves supported on curved brackets imitating coving. These are definitely 20th century. Other examples can also be seen around the Herefordshire/Powys border.

36 Victoria County History, (VCH) *Worcestershire*, Volume III, 1901-1924, p. 279.

37 VCH, *Worcestershire*, Volume III, pp. 279-80.

38 Broadward Hall, near Leominster, has the same features, but nothing as yet is known of its history.

39 The information is taken from Pritchard's survey at Worcester Record Office in St. Helen's Church, Worcester. Baldwyn Childe Papers, 4707/4; Ref: b899:396, Parcel No. 4. Other papers relating to Kyre are under the same reference. These include the albums *Herefordshire* by Frances Baldwyn Childe, *Building of Kyre 1588, 1754, 1880* and *Kyre Bills 1752-1783.*

40 WRO, Kyre survey.

41 VCH, p. 280.

CHAPTER 6

'Neat Capitals and Wreaths of flowers'. Houses in Shropshire.

This chapter covers the work that Pritchard carried out in Shropshire and demonstrates that much of his most important work was in his home county. His influence can also be found on many other properties dotted around this large inland county, often in the form of Rococo-Gothick, the style he made his own. By the middle of the 18th century many Shropshire country houses needed modernising, such as Tong Castle, Lutwyche Hall and Shipton Hall, or others were newly built like Hatton Grange and High Hatton Hall. Buildings in Shropshire and the neighbouring countie, with even older origins, are included in Chapter 9. Tern Hall, near Shrewsbury, which had its own particular problems, has not been included here but can be found in Chapter 10.

The 'fall-out' buildings have already been mentioned, but there are others which do not come into any particular category, such as Delbury Hall in the Corvedale, between Craven Arms and Bridgnorth, which was built by the Hiorn brothers. The carved chimney piece in the drawing room is so similar to Pritchard's style that these Warwickshire master craftsmen could have been very influential in all aspects of his work. There is also Meole Brace Hall, owned by the Bather family later in the 18th century but perhaps rented by them at an earlier date. Several designs exist in *The Drawing Book* for Mr. Bather, one of them noting 'in Mardol', a street in central Shrewsbury, but it is not certain which house he actually owned. Ashford Hall, near Ludlow, looks as if Pritchard should have worked there while nearer to Shrewsbury are Great Ness Hall, The Old Hall, Cressage, Hardwick Hall, Hardwick Grange and Eaton Mascott. Slightly further out, Whitton Hall at Westbury and Woodlands Hall, near Bridgnorth, both have Pritchardian characteristics. No evidence exists at present for work on these buildings, but as *The Drawing Book* was only identified thirty years ago, there is reason to hope that further information might come to light in the future.

The large amount of building work during the 18th century in the county indicates that it was going through a prosperous period and that country landowners were taking an interest in their estates and were prepared to spend time there. There was an injection of money into the country from the East India Company, principally through Lord Clive; his purchase of the Walcot estate permitted the

Walcot family to carry out the work on Bitterley Court. Rentals from iron masters funded the rebuilding of Hatton Grange, so that by the middle of the century money from industry was starting to take effect in Shropshire and the neighbouring counties.[1]

The first four houses in this chapter all appear in *The Drawing Book* so the designs can be dated to around the same period. The outsider is Downton Hall and its undated designs and I have left it to the end, although theoretically it could predate the other four buildings.

1-6: Shipton Hall

SHIPTON HALL.

2-6: Plan of Shipton

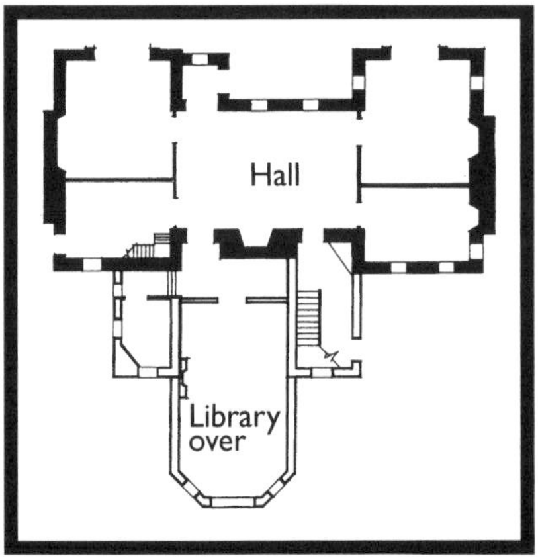

Shipton Hall, in the Corvedale, is a building outstanding for its size and presence in the area and the small cottages and modest farmhouses in the immediate vicinity make it even more conspicuous. However, it has rival contemporary near neighbours in Wilderhope Manor and Lutwyche Hall; all three houses were probably built between 1583 and 1587 indicating the richness of the area in the late 16th century. There is also a notable similarity of form between Shipton and Benthall Hall, in particular the two-storey porch and large entrance hall with principal rooms at either end.

Shipton Manor had belonged to Wenlock Priory until the Dissolution and the present stone

3-6: *Hall at Shipton.*

house was built in 1587, replacing an earlier timber-framed one which was destroyed by fire. The village in front of the hall was cleared away to give an uninterrupted view of the Clee Hills from the new house, thus further emphasising its prominent position.

When Pritchard carried out work there in the 1760s, Shipton Hall was in the ownership of Mr. Mitton, or Mytton. The Myttons were an old and extensive Shropshire family who owned property in many parts of the county and they had probably been at Shipton, as tenants of the Priory, since about 1456. In 1922, H. E. Forrest wrote that 'the Hall was well restored in the time of George II; the plaster decorations,

4-6: *Staircase at Shipton.*

fireplaces etc., are excellent. The Library and unfinished room under, now the main drawing room, appear (from bills remaining in the library) to have been built between 1760 and 1767.'[2] Unfortunately the bills are no longer there and there is no explanation as to why the room was not finished.

The front elevation of the house is formed by three bays with high pitched gables and a taller entrance tower. These gabled bays and the tower retain their original mullion and transom windows which give the house its characteristic appearance. The rear elevation of the house presents a very different picture with its sash windows and 'y' tracery and shows how the Gothick windows and interior decoration blend unobtrusively with the older work and demonstrate that a 'modern' extension could be sympathetically added on to an existing earlier building.

The plan shows the main body of the old house with the 18th century extension at the back. The porch at the base of the tall tower leads into the entrance hall. The Baroque and three-dimensional plasterwork above the hall fireplace could either be of an earlier date or was old-fashioned by the 1760s and cannot with certainty be attributed to Pritchard. The plasterwork ceiling, which shows the influence of the French designs by Nicholas Pineau from his *Nouveau desseins de Plafonds invente par Pineau*, has already been discussed in relation to the Foundling Hospital in London. Over the hall are bedrooms, some of which retain their 16th century panelling, but two were updated when the house was extended.

5-6: Library overmantle .(AIA 3)
6-6: 'machine grate'. (AIA 15c)

Doorways with broken pediments lead from the hall to the back of the house, the 'new' staircase and the extended section. The somewhat narrow stairwell is a riot of Gothick plasterwork, almost overwhelming in the confined space where crockets, cusped ogees, finials and pendants splendidly compete with each other for attention. In keeping with the Gothick scheme, on the side of each tread and riser of the stair are small cusped interlaced ogee arches with 'y' tracery neatly contained within scrolls. The staircase, lit by a tall round-headed window, leads up to the library, the main room in the extension.[3] This spacious room, lined with Classical style book cases,[4] has a canted bay window overlooking the garden and hills behind.

The fireplace overmantel (AIA 3) in the library is the first design in *The Drawing Book* which dates it to about September 1765. Its similarities, especially in the Ionic capitals and pilasters decorated with musical instruments, with the overmantel and chimney piece in the Blue Room at Croft Castle suggests that they both might have been designed around the same time. At Shipton, a female head and basket of flowers is at the top instead of the lion's head at Croft. The overmantel in the library does not resemble other work by Pritchard in *The Drawing Book*; it is more Palladian in style and closer to the work of James Gibbs some years earlier.[5] The interior of Shipton Hall has other carved chimney pieces that could be by Pritchard although they are not documented in *The Drawing Book*.

The interesting connection between Rococo and the Industrial Revolution has already been made in relation to Croft Castle, and as Shipton Hall is near Coalbrookdale it is not surprising to find a 'Modele for a machine grate for Colbrook Dale ...' (AIA 15c). A wooden pattern for the iron casting was carved by Nelson. Perhaps this stove was intended as a new revolutionary design; improved forms of heating were developing such as the many-tiered cast iron stoves by Abraham Buzaglo, although the Shipton stove is nearer in appearance to the Venetian Stoves as illustrated in, among other publications, W. and J. Welldon's *The Smith's Right Hand Man*, of 1765. They are described as 'very useful in preventing smoak' which was a persistent problem then.[6] Close examination of the construction of the Buzaglo stove at Williamsburg, Virginia, revealed that the form of it is similar to Pritchard's 'grate' but the functional design is different. The latter appears to be a restricted grate whereas the Buzaglo is a crude controlled combustion stove.

7-6: Stables at Shipton

It is almost certain that Pritchard also designed the stable block at Shipton and some stylistic features, such as the circular window above the main door, could help to establish his connection with the stables at Peover Hall in Cheshire.

BITTERLEY COURT.

Bitterley Court, situated under the Clee Hills not far from Ludlow, was modernised when ownership changed in the mid-eighteenth century. Today the drive leads up the entrance created on the south side while the original drive went to the older west front which still shows its earlier 17th century form. The house had belonged

8-6: Bitterley Court

to the Walcot family from the middle of the 17th century, but in the 1760s was sold for financial reasons. The purchaser was Charles Walcot, a cousin from the elder line, who had sold the family estate of Walcot Hall to Lord Clive.

The sale details for Bitterley included a plan of the house which shows that it was H-shaped with a central hall and a main entrance on the west side; on the north side of the hall was a screens passage. The house is described on the sale details as:

> a large building of stone and slate cover, consisting of a large hall, 2 parlours and a drawing room, wainscotted; a study, a smoaking room, a good kitchen ... etc. on the ground floor ... Over the whole are 6 good Lodging Rooms, Wainscotted, ... and a laundry, with many closets; and over them 5 garrets.

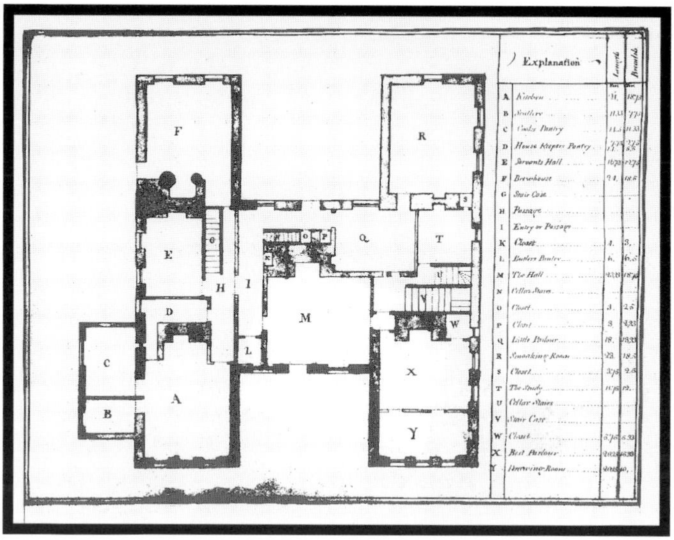

9-6: Plan of Bitterley.

With the medieval central hall out of fashion it was time to modernise the building. The south front was given a symmetrical appearance with a central pedimented bay, so with the focus now being on this side, it was necessary to update the interior. A new entrance hall was created out of the study and the staircase (T and V on the plan). The wainscot was retained, but when the staircase had been removed support was required for the upper floor, so scagliola columns were inserted to prop up the beams in a manner that is decorative, but compatible with the old house.

Owing to the constraints of the existing building and its plan form, it was not possible to have a staircase rising out of the new hall similar to the elegant ones at 27, Broad Street, Ludlow and Brockhampton House, so a new staircase was formed behind the hall in the room marked little parlour (Q on the plan). To compensate for the lack of an effective staircase, Pritchard concentrated on the first floor landing. To add interest to the space around it, he put in depressed, or semi-elliptical, arches which lead into the passageway to the 'good' bedrooms on the south side of the house. He cleverly arranged the arches around the landing to give a feeling of space, again within the form of the original structure. The corridor leading off the landing has arches with pilasters similar to those at Ludford House and Croft Castle.

10-6: Entrance hall.

In my *Country Life* article,[7] I referred to the

possibility of deliberate historicism being used at Bitterley as Pritchard has respected its older fabric and retained much of the wainscot from other rooms for re-use in the hall. The rather naive plaster motifs on the frieze around the landing look back to the earlier plasterwork in the bedrooms which are called the 'good Lodgeing Rooms' on the sale details.

One of these bedrooms, on the south-west corner, has a Rococo chimney piece with cabriole legs (AIA 47).[8] *The Drawing Book* indicates that Pritchard often used this lighter form for chimney pieces and varied the pattern on either side for the different commissions, with a leaf or feather motif in the centre of the frieze. A similar chimney piece is still at Hatton Grange (AIA 30), but two for Miss Leighton at

11-6: Dining room. (AIA 63)

12-6: Drawing room. (AIA 34)

Condover (AIA 13a and 13b)and one for Mr. Bather in Mardol (AIA 12a) do not survive.

The present dining room, on the right or east side of the entrance hall, is arguably the finest room in the house. The arrangement of the rooms has now been reversed and the chimney piece now in this room (AIA 63) is entitled 'Drawing Room'; it is made up of Gothick motifs and dated 1769 'Feby the 4th'. There are cluster columns at the sides and the inner moulding is in the shape of an ogee arch and above this are diaper 'pannells'. This chimney piece is probably one of the most important ones that Pritchard designed and the only one that is almost completely Gothick, with only the gadrooning around the ogee arch not in the same style.[9] The finely carved ornament has such a thin coat of paint that the chimney piece looks as if it is made of marble. Pritchard has written '£6. 7. 7' on the side of the design. Did the carving really cost that little? Little perhaps in our terms, but comparable with other similar chimney pieces such as the one for the 'dressing room over Drawing Room' (AIA 72) for Tern Hall which cost £6. 1s. 5½d. By comparison, Henry Cheere's admittedly more elaborate chimney pieces had cost upwards of £54 twenty years earlier. [10] The diaper work, together with the cluster columns, waterleaf and 'Gothick openings' contrast with the plasterwork ceiling in this room which is a fine and elegant example of the low relief Rococo plasterwork that has become associated with Pritchard in such houses as Croft Castle and Gaines.

On the other side of the hall is the present drawing room, where the best parlour and the dining room (X and Y on the plan) had originally been; originally it was the 'Dineing Parlour' as it was nearer to the existing kitchen (A); later, perhaps in the 19th century, when a kitchen was built on to the east side, the dining room was moved there. The design for this chimney piece is quite different from the other two in the house with its 'Raffle leaf, Egg and Toung, Fluting, Waterleaf and Husk'. (AIA 34) The same design was also used for the common parlour at Hatton Grange. The former dining room at Bitterley was probably intended as a modern room with its restrained panels of plasterwork and motifs as used by the fashionable Robert Adam.

Again different styles have been used for the chimney pieces throughout the house; Rococo was usually put in a minor room such as a bedroom or dressing room, but the use of Gothick was more random, although it was then towards the end of its early revival and had to wait until the next century for a more serious study. Even Horace Walpole was turning to more accurate reconstructions of the Gothick he had helped to popularise. Were the styles used at Bitterley what the client had asked for? Perhaps, as at Croft Castle, they were done deliberately to create different atmospheres for each room; this would have fitted with the romantic feeling that was becoming popular at that time.

HATTON GRANGE.

Hatton Grange, near Shifnal, is important as the only extant house definitely built by Pritchard on a country estate. In addition it is well documented, but no elevations or plans survive. The house was built for Plowden Slaney, the 'Esq. Slaney' in *The Drawing Book* and it is still owned by his descendants, the Kenyon-Slaney family. Hatton represents the typical country house of a Shropshire landowner of the 18th century – impressive but comfortable, modern yet dignified, set within its own landscaped gardens and surrounding farmland. Houses like Hatton formed the background for those prominent in the county such as the Slaneys who have served on committees and councils for generations.

13-6: Hatton Grange.

Plowden Slaney was born in 1724 to a family who could trace their ancestry back to the 16th century. From about 1650 they had owned the Hatton estate, once the grange for Buildwas Abbey. The family came from Yardley in Worcestershire where they were iron masters. This connection with iron continued as Robert Slaney, who was High Sheriff of Shropshire in 1701, owned blast furnaces and slitting mills which he let out and this involvement continued into the next generation when Abraham Darby II leased a farm at Horsehay from the Slaneys in 1754.[11]

In 1722 Robert Aglionby Slaney married Frances Theresa Plowden of Plowden Hall, near Bishop's Castle, one of the oldest families in Shropshire. The money for the new house, therefore, came from both old estate money and new industrial interests. Their son, Plowden Slaney, married Martha Pitt of Priorslee Hall, near Shifnal, in 1752 and inherited the Hatton estate on the death of his father in 1757. After the birth of his sons in 1763 and 1764 he decided to build a new house on the other side of the Dingle, a ravine that was used as fish pools by the monks. Plowden Slaney called the new house Hatton Grange and his old house was known as Grange Farm until recently when it was renamed Plowden House.

Hatton Grange is built of red brick, mostly made on the site at a cost of 7 shillings per 1000, but the better-quality bricks on the front came from nearby Albrighton and were more evenly fired which produced a consistent light red colour. Cream-coloured stone from

14-6: Hatton Grange in the 19th century.

Cosford in Shropshire was used for the small stone parapet, the stone pediment and the surrounds to the windows. There is a stone plinth around the base of the house. The principal elevation of the building is divided by a stone string course at chamber level in the three centre bays. This was later continued around the canted bay windows when they were added in the 19th century. The slate for the roof came from Westmorland.

Externally, Hatton Grange is a simple block plan of seven bays, the centre three bays projecting slightly forward and crowned by a pediment; the same form was used for Hosier's Almshouses in Ludlow and comparisons have also been made with Brockhampton House which has an almost identical front elevation. The pediments of both the buildings as well as the form of the central windows indicate that they may both be by the same person.[12] At Hatton the width of the centre bays is smaller than the width of the two side ones and therefore the pediment seems to be visually too small for the house. The Rococo design (AIA 31a) which shows Plowden Slaney's coat of arms, is the first design by Pritchard for Hatton and took Nelson and Danders over seven weeks to carve in freestone and nine days 'from the lime to painting'. John Yates, a stonemason who worked regularly with Pritchard, was involved at both Hatton and Hosier's Almshouses. The proportions of Hatton appear to be totally functional, reflecting the necessary heights of the various storeys.

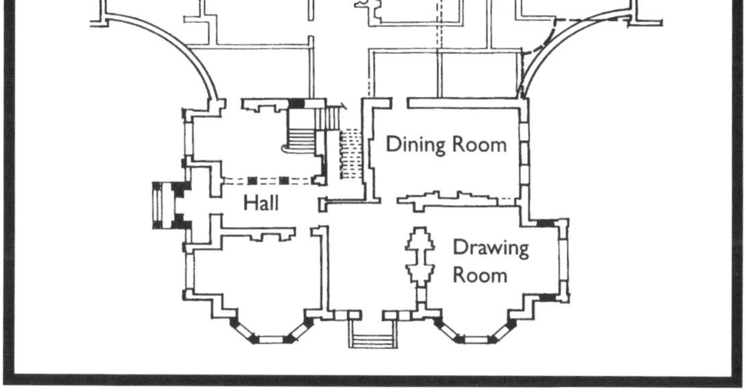

15-6: Plan of Hatton.

It is by no means certain that there was not some sort of structure on the site that Plowden Slaney chose; like Swan Hill Court House and Brockhampton House, there may have been an older, timber-

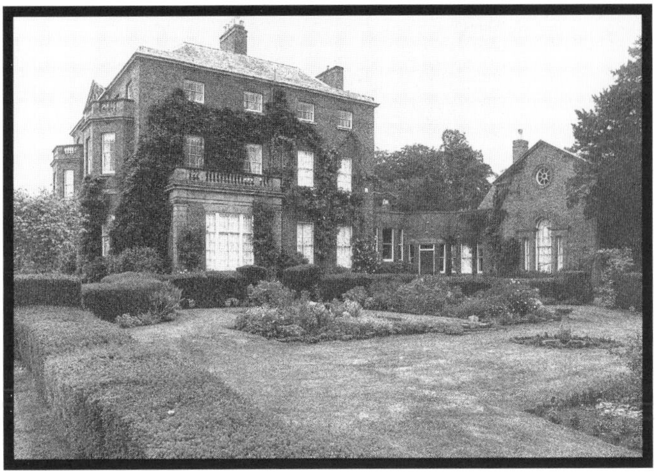

framed building already there and this would have been used as kitchens and sculleries.[13] In his valuation Pritchard included the item 'Laying a New Floor' for the Housekeeper's Room. This implies that an older floor needed to be replaced in an existing building; all other references are just to 'Floors' or 'preparing old Boards to lay the Floors'; these had been brought from another old house.

As the plan shows the form of the main block of Hatton has a resemblance to Brockhampton. From paintings and photographs it is apparent that there was a main entrance on the west side. Now this entrance leads from the garden into the present morning room.[14] The rooms on the west, on both floors, take advantage of the view. The park and gardens were becoming important by the 1760s and at Powis Castle a few years later Pritchard, as we shall see, was anxious to give the garden entrance 'a more open and graceful appearance from the Park.'

16-6: Altered Pavilion.
17-6: Dining room. (AIA 62).

The plan is an abstract of the proposed alterations and additions for bye-law application made by Colonel Kenyon-Slaney in 1897. The alterations are marked in black and include two bay windows on the garden front and a porch to the front door on the north side. Later a large domestic block was added at the back. The addition, and subsequent demolition of this block, has made it even more difficult to know what was there before building work started in 1764.

The arcades are designed to curve backwards from the main pedimented elevation, to pedimented pavilions in a way that has been called 'quite sophisticated'.[15] This is the reverse of examples shown by Gibbs or designed by Adam in the 1760s for

Kedleston Hall, a much larger and grander contemporary. These wings could have been specifically designed to hide the older building behind, but as they have been altered over the years they no longer retain the simple elegance that Pritchard intended. A lobby and 'Colonel Kenyon-Slaney's Room' have been built into the arcade on the south side. In addition, the two-storey canted bays have destroyed the clear-cut lines of the 'simple block plan' and give the house a fussier appearance, but fortunately most of the interior decoration has been left almost untouched.

A contract was drawn up in 1763 and work started a year later with completion due at Michaelmas 1768. The total amount for the job is not clear as originally it was thought to be £1,518 from the amounts paid by Plowden Slaney to Pritchard, but a note written in about 1808 by Plowden's son, Robert, stated that the total, including landscaping and stables, came to £6,630,[16] which sounds more realistic, considering the marble for the chimney pieces surrounds came to over £100.

18-6: Dining room.

19-6: Drawing room (AIA 29).

Pritchard's detailed valuation for Hatton is considered as 'an excellent idea of the range, quality and cost of English provincial work.'[17] For instance, a chimney piece for the hall was to be made out of Painswick stone, (AIA 43) listed in the valuation as 'Free Stone' at a cost of £12, plus the 17s. 6d that was charged for the seven days it took John Yates to put it up. Pritchard's 'Staircase Brackets in Oak' (AIA 42) followed a pattern in Abraham Swan's *The British Architect;* carving each bracket cost 3s.[18] These are the only designs by Pritchard for this type of interior fitting.

Siena marble for the 'Best Chamber chimney piece' with the slips, soffits, 'noseings' and other parts of the surround came to £10. 15s. 2¾d, while the carving was £6. 9s. 1½d. and included 'Gadroon moulding, Ropeing, Cove with Palmira Foliage, Band and Flower, Bead and Space ... a Neat Freeze with Palms and wreaths of Flowers.' The accounts contain entries for packing and moving the chimney pieces from Shrewsbury. The cases were made of rough board for prices ranging from 12s. 17d. and £2. 3s. 2d. and 18s. was paid for 'freight of Chimney pieces' at one stage. The Westmorland slates were transported to Chepstow for only 13s. 3d., then by the River Severn to Bridgnorth for a further £1. 2s. 6d; carriage of chimney pieces was an expensive business.[19]

The drawing and valuation for the dining room chimney piece survive and provide a good picture of prices and the ornament used. The design for the chimney piece (AIA 62) was drawn in detail, apart from the centre tablet which is blank. It was later filled in with a carving of a 'Shepherd and flock in *Bas Relievo*' at a cost of £3. 10s. which took Nelson and van der Hagen 18 days to execute while the two side pilasters were a further £2. This type of pastoral scene was a favourite in the mid-eighteenth century and popularised by such sculptors as Henry Cheere. The total price was £19. 10s. 9d. for the carving and £10. 4s. 1¼d. for the veined grey Dove marble.[20]

20-6: 'Center Chamber'. (AIA 30)

Although there are valuations for the stuccoed cornices in the various rooms, there is no mention of the fine plasterwork in the dining room. The reason for this could be that the work, probably designed by Pritchard, was sub-contracted to a plasterer, such as Joseph Bromfield, who then submitted his own account. The plasterwork at Hatton has been compared to the dining room at Hagley Hall, especially the agricultural motifs, but this work is attributed to Francesco Vassalli because of the signed overmantel in the hall and he is known to have been there between 1759 and 1763. At Hagley the stylistic differences between the Classical plasterwork in the hall and lobby and the Rococo of the dining room adjoining the hall are so marked that it seems hard to believe they are by the same person, but no references to Pritchard or to Joseph Bromfield have been found in the archives. The dates for the building of Hagley, 1756-60, are outside the major documented jobs for Pritchard but he could have worked on the house as part of the team or been to see it as he had connections with the Lyttelton family of Hagley through Thomas

Johnes and the Knights of Wolverley. Similar motifs were found in pattern books available to all, such as the 'design for a side of a room' illustrated by Thomas Johnson in 1758.[21]

From these pattern and other architectural books, there was plenty of information about how work should be done. In *A Complete Body of Architecture*, Isaac Ware advised architects

> to raise an ornament like that of the other parts of the room from the chimney piece to the ceiling; and in such manner to adapt this to the chimney-piece itself, that it shall seem naturally to rise from it, and to be connected with it, that it shall be a regular and proportioned part of the chimney-work, at the same time that it is also a regular part of the ornament of the room.

This was good advice as the dining room at Hatton is the most successful overall scheme of decoration by Pritchard; here the plasterwork on the walls complements the chimney piece and the pastoral scene reflects the farming motifs around the walls. The niche for the service of food, shallower than the one at Gaines, has splendid plasterwork decoration within Pritchard's typical type of depressed arch. He was also following current fashion in the decoration of the dining room as Robert Adam recommended that dining rooms be 'fitted up with elegance and splendour, but in a style different from that of other apartments. Instead of being hung with damask, tapestry, they are always finished with stucco, ... that they may not retain the smell of the victuals,' – a very practical suggestion.[22]

The drawing room, next to the dining room, has another elegant chimney piece with black and yellow marble and a design which included raffle leaf, 'Antique Thermes richley ornamented, a Neat Tablet with Convalvolas and Roman Dish.' (AIA 29) In the centre of the tablet is a ram's head, one of the Slaney's prize sheep perhaps. The carving of this elaborate chimney piece cost a total of £9. 8s. 6½d. and took several weeks to complete. The marble for all these chimney pieces was accounted separately; Jasper marble was £13. 7s. 1d., while the slightly cheaper Dove marble for the dining room was £10. 4s. 1d.

The chimney piece for the 'Dressing Room at Hatton' (AIA 58) is an attractive mix of 'Cove with Gothic Arches of Water Leaf' and 'Two Gothic columns with Neat Capitals and Wreaths of flowers'; £8. 8s. 6d was paid for the carving. The chimney pieces in the upstairs chambers have various styles, with Rococo in the 'center' chamber, 'gadroon' and 'ropeing' for the 'best chamber' while the common parlour chamber has a 'Purple marble chimney piece' with 'bead and space' and flowers. The accounts for Hatton also include the work carried out on the butler's pantry, water closets, 'and three Bath Stove Grates with Pollish'd Barrs'.

John Cornforth commented on the 'idiosyncratic' choice of Rococo and Gothic for 'the otherwise Classical Hatton' but this is entirely in keeping with Pritchard's work.[23] The rooms in the medieval Croft Castle have Classical and Rococo motifs while in some rooms at Hatton the Rococo chimney pieces do not conform with the Classical cornices. The Classical elements in the dining room could be considered at odds with the Gothick cornice. Is this ignorance or deliberate design? More likely it was the latter as throughout his mature work Pritchard showed a non-conformity by combining a Rococo interior design within an earlier or Classical shell.

Hatton Grange remains Pritchard's most complete existing work. Externally the main block is innovative, with the backward stretching arcades designed to conceal an existing building, while the interior decoration goes further to reinforce Pritchard's skill as a designer, arising from his training as a joiner and his thorough knowledge his trade. Hatton Grange is a comfortable house suitable for a country estate and an influential family.

21:6. High Hatton Hall.

HIGH HATTON HALL.

22-6: *Chimney piece at High Hatton Hall. (AIA 30)*

High Hatton Hall is a smaller house for a smaller estate, but nevertheless stands up impressively in the flat landscape around. As a generalisation, all the existing houses by Pritchard have the same qualities – logical form leading to a practical space for living, spacious, light rooms and sufficient design detail to make the building interesting but not eccentric. Most of them are designed for living in, not for showing how grand or rich the owner was.

High Hatton Hall fulfils all these criteria with its fairly conventional mid-Georgian square block design. Externally, interest is provided by the pyramidal roof and bay window. The entrance on the east side leads up stone steps into the hall. The stairs rise up on the right and directly ahead from the front door is the present dining room; to the left is the drawing room. The house is positioned to catch the eye on approach and take advantage of the views from the windows.

Inside, the form of the rooms is functional as they have ample space without being awkwardly large and the size and number of them point to the occupants being part of a fairly small unit. The house was intended for Richard Corbet as *The Drawing Book* has a design for a chimney piece for 'Ric^{d} Corbet Esqr Highhatton'. (AIA 80) If the designs are in chronological order, it can be dated to about March 1769 but this is seven years later than a datestone on the external wall of the house. Seven years seems a long time from the beginning of the house to the designing of the chimney piece so building might have started and then stopped and commenced again at a later date for some reason. Research into the Corbet family tree has shown a connection between the Prynce family of Whitehall and the Corbets, so the RPC on the datestone is Richard Prynce Corbet, born 1735 and died 1779.

23-6: *Screen at High Hatton Hall.*

The Corbets of Hatton were also of Moreton Corbet through the male line and Shawbury through the female. The theory might be that High Hatton was developed when Richard, as a younger son, married Mary, daughter and heiress of John Wickstead of Wem. As Richard's brother Andrew did not marry, High Hatton Hall could have been planned as a house for an 'heir-in-waiting' but unfortunately Richard did not outlive his elder brother and Pritchard probably designed the monument for him in St. Bartholomew's Church, Moreton Corbet.

Pritchard's chimney piece (AIA 80) with a frieze of oak leaves, is in the dining room.[24] Careful restoration has been carried out and the carving has not been repainted so the bare wood shows the high quality of the work. The chimney piece in the 'main' upstairs bedroom, above the dining room, has a very interesting Rococo design with raffle leaf or scrolling foliage used extensively and interwoven with it are Chinoiserie motifs. A small hut with a thatched roof is in the centre of the frieze and a ho-ho bird on the right; the one on the left is missing.[25] Other designs by Pritchard that include Chinoiserie are a chimney piece at Sherford House, Bromyard and the 'Glassframes' for Croft Castle. (See Chapter 2, 4-2) Another bedroom at High Hatton also has a chimney piece with a slightly Rococo form that could safely be attributed to Pritchard.

Generally in the house, lugged architraves to the chimney pieces and doorcases and the stairs of fine quality with three balusters, two twisted to one plain, to the tread are all typical of Pritchard's carefully crafted work.[26] he house still has its original cast iron grates, door furniture and ironwork to the front steps.

A puzzling detail on the ground floor is the three-bay screen with its idiosyncratic capitals. This screen does not appear to serve a purpose as the room is not big enough to need dividing up and in a new building it would not be necessary to provide support for an existing upper storey as at Bitterley Court. In style it looks back to baroque examples as large abaci were a feature of the work of James Gibbs and the Hiorn brothers. To break the classical rules so much by adding the bay leaf frieze is further than they go and does not seem typical of the known work by Pritchard so perhaps these columns are later additions.

In terms of comfort and appearance, High Hatton Hall represents many people's ideal of a Georgian house with its well-proportioned light rooms and decorative detailing.

DOWNTON HALL.

Looking towards the Corvedale from Bitterley Court it might be possible to catch a glimpse of Downton Hall, spectacularly perched up on a ridge. The red-brick house that is there today dates back to 1738 when the owner, Wredenhall Pearce, inherited enough money to be able to erect a substantial house, probably built around an existing one, in this splendid position.

CHAPTER 6

A folio of architectural drawings has recently been rediscovered which show positive proof of Pritchard's involvement with Downton. The folio contains plans and elevations as well as drawings for nearby Hopton Cangeford Church. The sequence of 18th century building at Downton is not clear owing to the work which was done on the house in about 1830. Although Avray Tipping had access to the architectural drawings when he wrote his 1917 *Country Life* article on Downton,[27] other documentary evidence was scant and he skimmed over parts of the building process; it is this lack of documentation that handicaps us today. The house has recently undergone restoration and some of the 19th century work has been demolished which will leave a more compact, but still large house which could well appear more coherent in 18th century terms.

The estate had been in the Wredenhall family for many years and through lack of male heirs all the property, plus other inheritance, came to Wredenhall Pearce. The drawings show Pritchard was involved with the extensions for Pearce's son, known as W. Pearce

24-6: Pritchard's plan of Downton.

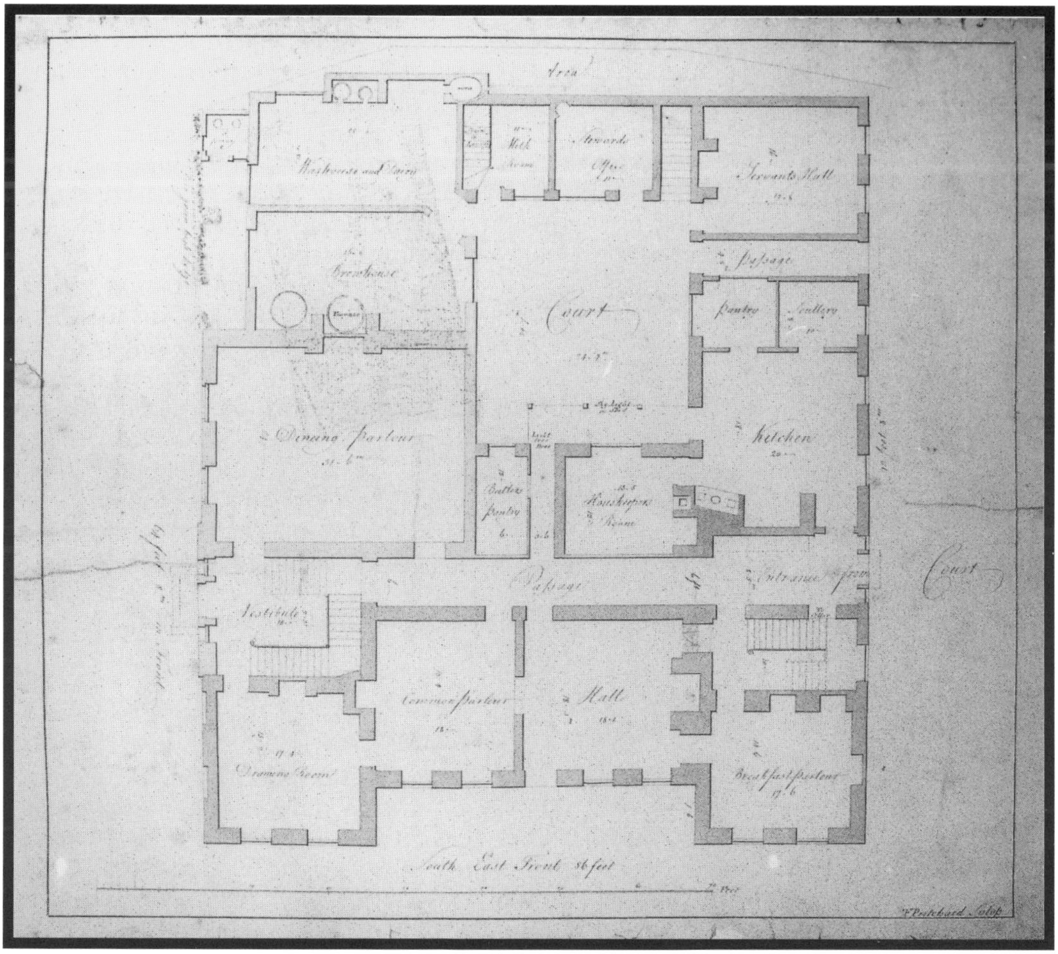

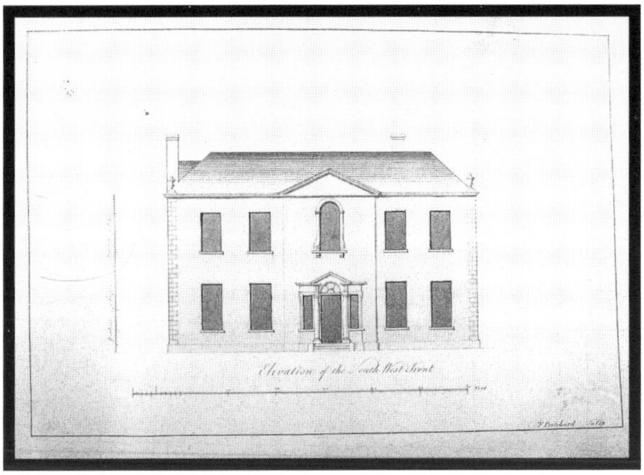

25-6: Elevation of Downton by Pritchard.

26-6: Plan of South front of Downton attributed to Pritchard.

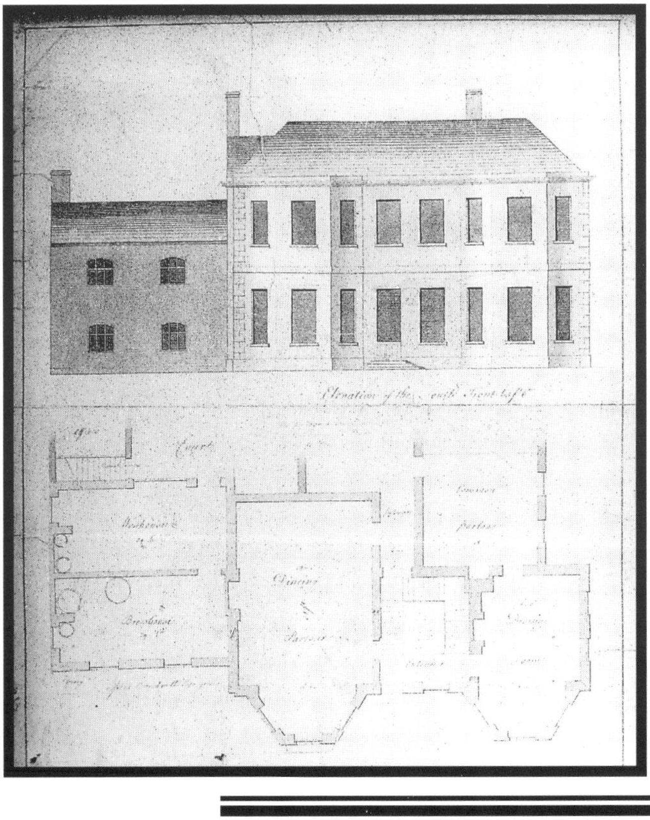

Hall. The possible date for this work is either the late 1750s or the early 1760s, just before the start of *The Drawing Book.* Pearce's son, soon after the death of his father in 1748, enlarged the house and this may have prompted the survey drawing to be made.

The survey shows that the south front consisted of five central bays with two projecting wings of two bays each. The central block contained the hall and dining parlour, the drawing room was on the west side and a breakfast parlour on the east with staircase and kitchens behind. In the centre of the building there was a 'best staircase', hall and an open court surrounded by the household offices. On the west side was a garden with a privy. In a drawing which could be a first proposal, Pritchard showed that he intended to create a new vestibule, staircase and 'dineing parlour' on the west side. The old dining room was to become the common parlour. The privy is moved away from the main rooms and 'covered with ever greens' but the brewhouse remains alongside the new 'dineing parlour'. This plan and the accompanying drawing of the 'south west front' both have Pritchard's name on them. This drawing shows a house of five bays with a wide central bay stepped forward. The central bay has a Venetian door, with fanlight over it and above a round-headed window with supporting brackets. The brewhouse is not shown.

Two other drawings show an elevation and plan of the 'south front' and this time the brewhouse is included. The elevation shows the stone quoins which are such a prominent feature of Downton Hall today. Canted bays have now been added to the dining parlour and the drawing room. Were these bays to take advantage of the superb view from the position of the house? These drawings are undated, so had time passed and fashion changed, as it did at Tern Hall? Pritchard's name is not on them but the style is so similar to the other drawings that they must be his work; further evidence is that the word dining contains an 'e', a form he often used.[28]

The early 19th century print of Downton Hall shows that this last plan is the most likely one to have been used. There is a similar sequence of bays: the front door, to which a small pediment has been added, is placed asymmetrically. At the side is the two-storey building which we know from the other plans to be the brewhouse.

The rich interior of Downton proves even harder to ascribe to anyone. Avray Tipping had recently visited Kyre and thought that the carver Benjamin King and the plasterer Vassalli might have been involved at Downton. The scheme is very elaborate and much more Baroque than most of Pritchard's plasterwork. His earliest datable interior design, 1765 for the chimney frame at Shipton (AIA 3) of 1765, shows a Baroque influence which is not apparent later as the designs become lighter and more Rococo in form.

The house was altered in 1824 by Edward Haycock so what is there today reflects these alteratioons and somewhere under them is Pritchard's work.

27-6: 19th century print of Dowton Hall.

The drawings for Downton Hall are important as they show that Pritchard was involved with one of the major country houses of south Shropshire.

This survey of the documented work carried out in Shropshire demonstrates that Pritchard worked all over the country for many of the families that had power and influence. They were members of Parliament and local corporations and involved with charitable institutions such as the Infirmary in Shrewsbury. Their wealth came from different sources, new and old, and while their incomes may not have been comparable with landowners and gentry in other richer areas, they nevertheless possessed a sufficient income to be able to refurbish their old houses or build new ones.

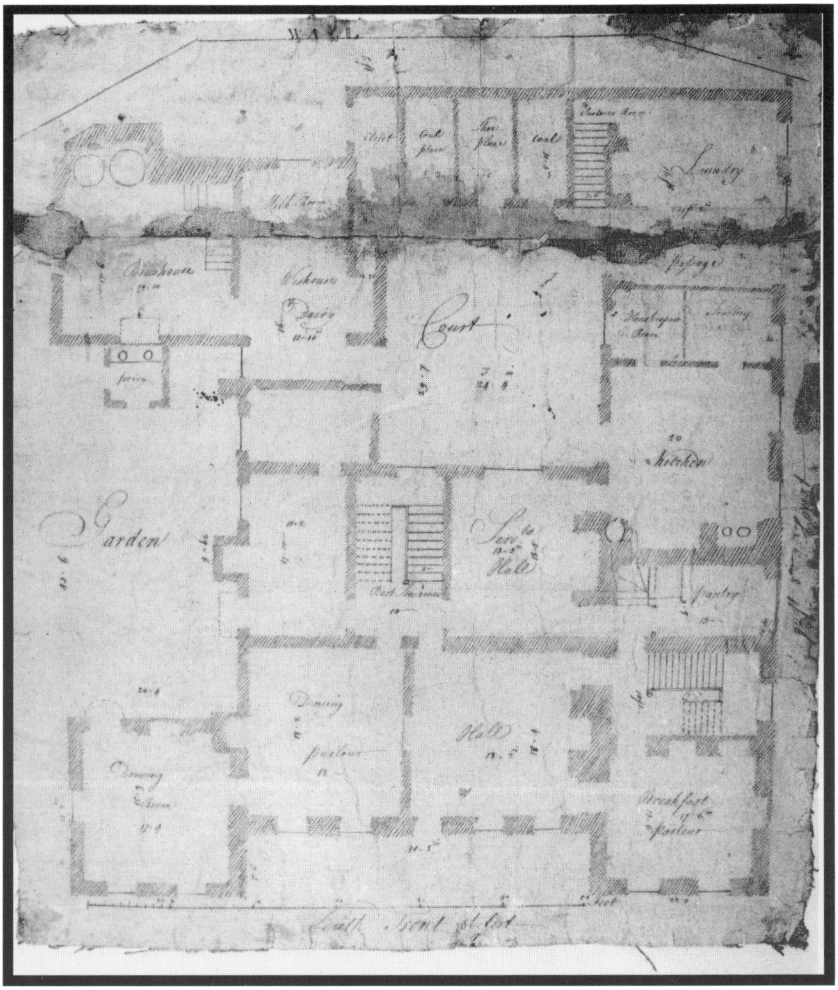

28-6: Survey of Downton Hall.

1 Clive was not the only person to bring in East Indian money to the county; see Namier, *The Structure of Politics at the Accession of George III.*

2 H. E. Forrest, *The Old Houses of Wenlock*, Shrewsbury, 1922, pp. 63-4. See also H. Avray Tipping, 'Shipton Hall', *Country Life*, 19 March 1910, pp. 414-421.

3 An older staircase remains at the other end from the extended section.

4 These are similar to those in the library at Houghton Hall in Norfolk.

5 James Gibbs, *Rules for Drawing the Several Parts of Architecture*, London, 3rd Edition, 1753, plates L and LI.

6 For further information on stoves in general and Buzaglo in particular, see Christopher Gilbert and Anthony Wells-Cole, *The Fashionable Fireplace*, Temple Newsam Country House Studies, No. 2, 1985. I am grateful for the information about Buzaglo given to me by Claude Blair and George Freeman. Thanks also to Liza and Wallace Gusler and John Davies of Historic Williamsburg for their help and hospitality.

7 Julia Ionides, 'Bitterley Court', *Country Life*, 11 September 1997, pp. 107-110.

8 This ornamental design, based on the curving leg of an animal, moved from Roman tripods to European furniture over the centuries. Earlier in the 18th century Kent had used a heavier form of the cabriole leg for the furniture he designed, particularly at Houghton, but by the 1750s a lighter, more Rococo style was illustrated in many publications of furniture designs, including those by Ince and Mayhew and Thomas Johnson.

9 Gadrooning is considered as a Renaissance motif and much used in the 18th century, particularly as an ornament for silverware.

10 Gunnis, p. 98.

11 All information about Hatton Grange from SRRC Chaplin Papers Ref: 5336/5/11/20 and 21, a leaflet about the house written by the present owners and privately owned documentation.

12 Letter in *Country Life* from John Cornforth in response to a letter from James Lees-Milne, 4 April 1968, p. 815.

13 Pritchard was not alone in rebuilding on top of an earlier house or incorporating it into the newer one. At Kenwood in north London and Saltram in Devon, Adam built on the foundations of earlier houses while he fashionably encased others such as Newby Hall in Yorkshire.

14 For further information on Hatton, see John Cornforth, *Hatton Grange*, Shropshire, Country Life, 29 February 1968, pp. 466-470.

15 Cornforth, pp. 466-470.

16 SRRC, Chaplin Papers, 5336/5/11/20-21.

17 Cornforth, p. 468.

18 Abraham Swan, *The British Architect*, London, 1745, plate xxxix.

19 The Hiorns paid 19s. for transporting chimney pieces (number unspecified) from Warwick to Stratford for work at Kyre Park while 'sundry' packing cases cost 18s.

20 A similar account by the Hiorns for Kyre itemised the materials used and prepared for the chimney pieces rather than the whole article, with the carving done separately by Benjamin King, so that comparisons are difficult to make. King's account itemises 'two Bracketts by the side of Marble Jambe with Festoones of flowers & foliage and Moseak [mosaic] work ...' WRO, Kyre Park, Baldwyn Childe Papers, 4707/4; Ref: b899:396, Parcel No. 4.

21 Thomas Johnson, 1758. Illustrated in *Rococo,* V & A Exhibition Catalogue, London, 1984, p. 205.

22 Quoted in Mark Girouard, *A Country House Companion*, Leicester, 1992, p. 72.

23 Cornforth, p. 469.

24 This popular design, illustrated by Gibbs and copied from him by Batty Langley, often has laurel or bay leaves and originated as a garland with binding around it. Gibbs, Plate L. Langley, *The Builder's and Workmen's Treasury of Designs*, London, 1741, Plate LXI. Pritchard used laurel leaves in a similar design for Mr Good, but he also used oak leaves and acorns in various other designs, such AIA 9 for Mr. Powis, Gravel Hill and AIA 12 for Mr. Bather, Mardol, both of Shrewsbury. Pritchard also used this design for AIA 41b for Mr. Davies. Oak leaves and acorns were used for a door frieze at Croft Castle, AIA 10d. The laurel or bay leaves were a symbol of glory and honour as well as eternity as they were evergreens. Oak leaves are classical motifs sacred to Jupiter and also to the Druids and acorns symbolised life and immortality.

25 The ho-ho bird is the oriental equivalent of the phoenix and although the birds are somewhat similar, according to their legend, phoenixes are usually shown rising from the ashes, often with only their head, while the ho-ho is perched on rocks or branches. The phoenix heads are included in some friezes for chimney pieces, notably AIA 7 for 27 Broad Street, Ludlow and AIA 8, a door case for Croft Castle.

26 The valuation for the Guildhall in Ludlow mentions both round and turned balusters being made.

27 H. Avray Tipping, 'Downton Hall', *Country Life*, 21 July 1917, pp. 60-66. These drawings are privately owned.

28 The survey and the two plans both have this spelling which is also used for the design for Bitterley Court. However, the designs for Hatton Grange and Tern Hall do not have an 'e' so this form of identification is far from conclusive but could help towards attribution.

CHAPTER 7

'... to assist you in your Designs'. Houses in Cheshire.

Although much of Pritchard's work was in Shropshire, as we have seen he also worked in Herefordshire and Worcestershire. To the north of Shrewsbury, he worked in Cheshire and westwards over the Welsh Border in what is now Powys. These jobs were for important clients such as the Egerton family at Tatton Park and Lord Powis at Powis Castle.

There are other houses in Cheshire, for instance Rode Hall near Congleton and nearby Betchton Hall and Ramsdell Hall, that might be connected with Pritchard, but lack documentation. There is also no evidence for his work at Peover Hall but the demolished Georgian wing shows a strong resemblance to his other work and this link is reinforced by the presence of a carved chimney piece in his style. Tatton Park is about forty miles from Shrewsbury so is the northernmost building that Pritchard is known to have worked on and. All these buildings extend the geographical area he covered.

WYNNSTAY.

1-7: 19th century print of Wynnstay.

Wynnstay is north of Shrewsbury near Wrexham and the estate had belonged to the Williams Wynn family from the 17th century. The family were prominent in the area and Wynnstay was their principal country seat. Originally a Jacobean house, it was rebuilt in the 1730s by Francis Smith of Warwick.[1] The stone stable block he built still survives but the 18th century house, after a series of alterations and some remodelling, was destroyed by fire in 1858 and rebuilt in the style of a French château.

Among the Wynnstay papers is 'A catalogue of Plans and elevations in the lower bookcase in the stucco parlour Wynnstay.'[2] This catalogue, destroyed in the 19th century fire, included plans and elevations for Wynnstay by Adam, Brown, presumably 'Capability' and Smith's plans and elevations. Item 7 is 'Prichard's plan of Llanvorda' and item 8 is 'Prichard's work for Wynnstay.'

In November 1768 Sir Watkin wrote ' ... the sooner Pritchard begins to repair & Beautify the Chancel of Ruabon Church the better. I hope to God that scheme will take place for I think that I had much better be there than in any house near London.'[3] It may be that the 'scheme' refers to the building of the 'Great Room' as well as work on Ruabon Church which was going on at the same time. Pritchard also worked on 'Great Rooms' at Powis Castle and Tatton Park, usually added for a celebration in a way that Isaac Ware would have disapproved of, but even he had to admit that sometimes it was required as the 'present custom is to see them [company] all at once and entertain none of them; this brings in the necessity of a *great room.*'[4]

At Wynnstay the work was carried out for the coming of age of the fourth Baronet, Sir Watkin Williams Wynn, in 1770 and was probably 'only intended as a temporary erection but so well-proportioned and convenient was it found to be, that it was allowed to remain and bedrooms built over it.'[5] Lord Torrington, who saw this room when he visited Wynnstay in July, 1788, disagreed. 'The house which is awkwardly approach'd, has been built at different periods, and is a bad uncomfortable mansion; the dining room is well wainscotted, the chapel tolerably well, but the drawing room is out of all size, and was built as a feast room, on Sr W.'s coming of age.' He added as a footnote: 'There stands Wynn Stay House: as ugly, as inconvenient ... The improvement of this place must be the work of some future Wynn.'[6]

An undated print shows this 'Great Room' projecting out from the main block. It is two storeys high and made up of four bays terminating in what appears to be a canted or semi-circular bay; it is indeed 'out of all size' in comparison with the rest of the house. This view is confirmed by an 18th century water-colour showing the 'Great Room' jutting out prominently from the main building.[7]

The estate accounts for 1770-72[8] show that work was being done at Wynnstay in the early 1770s as there are entries for bricklaying and the delivery of Bath stoves. In June 1770 Pritchard's plasterer, Joseph Bromfield, was 'paid in part his bill for work done at Wynnstay.' A further amount in September settled the remainder of his bill and he was also paid for work at Ruabon Church. Richard Lee, the carpenter who worked with Pritchard at the Foundling Hospital, also worked at Wynnstay and Ruabon Church. We know from a letter sent by Thomas Leggett, the landscape gardener, to Noel Hill at Tern Hall, that Pritchard was at Wynnstay in July that year.

When Torrington visited Chirk Castle, not far from Wynnstay, he regretted that the 'fine old wainscotting' had been 'lately removed' and praised the 'old, well varnish'd wainscotting' in the dining room at Wynnstay which, in his eyes, had become 'the ornament of the house.'[9] This retention of old material indicates that Pritchard might have had a hand in some of the interior decoration of the house, but not all; a bill dated 1772 for £53. 13s. in the Wynnstay accounts records that a marble chimney piece was put in the saloon by Charles Bromfield of Liverpool, who also worked at Chirk Castle.

Llanvorda, another Wynn house referred to above, was rebuilt in the 19th century, demolished in 1949 and now only remains of the stables survive. They are of an earlier design than the house which is dated to 1780 and described as a 'plain and low' building.[10] Is it another Pritchard 'fall-out' house, designed by him but constructed after his death? He was not an old man when he died and could have had work in hand when he was taken ill in 1776. This work may have been carried out after 1777 by his capable assistants.

ST. MARY'S CHURCH, RUABON.

2-7: Ruabon Church, 1794.

3-7: Postcard of Ruabon Church before the 19th century restoration.

While Pritchard was at Wynnstay he was also doing work on St. Mary's Church. Sir Watkin had written in 1768 about the urgency for Pritchard to begin 'to repair and Beautify the Chancel' in time for the baronet's coming of age. A petition to build a north east 'aisle' or chapel was put forward in 1769 at the same time as permission was sought to 'raise the Roof and Pillars of the Parish Church ... to a proper height – to place and fix an Organ – to ornament the same, to take down the present Reading Desk and pulpit etc. ...'[11] This work is thought to have been done by Pritchard who 'retained the piers of the perpendicular arcade and added his own semi-circular arches and circular clerestory windows.' The work was carried out remarkably speedily considering that first there was the death of Lady Henrietta, Sir Watkin's first wife, in 1769, just three months after her marriage and then the death of the vicar in 1770.

The Wynnstay accounts for 1770 record that Joseph Bromfield was paid for 'plaisterers' work on the church, and Richard Lee, the carpenter, who received £19. 14s. 6d. In 1771, both Bromfield and Lee were paid further sums, Bromfield for further plastering, Lee for laths and for work on the organ loft at the west end of the church which housed the organ given in 1770 by Sir Watkin.[12]

A Buzaglo stove was installed in the organ loft in February 1771.[13] In 1774 Thomas Steary was paid £11. 7s. 6d 'for lettering the commandments board in Ruabon Church'. A delightful font was designed by Robert Adam; a postcard of the interior shows the church before the 19th century alterations with this font at the back.

Little survives of Pritchard's work except for a blocked window with a heavy surround and central stepped voussoir at the east end.

TATTON PARK.

Pritchard's involvement with Tatton Park in Cheshire is also unclear. Lord Torrington rode through the park in 1790 and remarked that it is 'a house, a patchwork thing, standing ill, with no plantation on the lawn.' If Torrington had paused for a little longer and at an

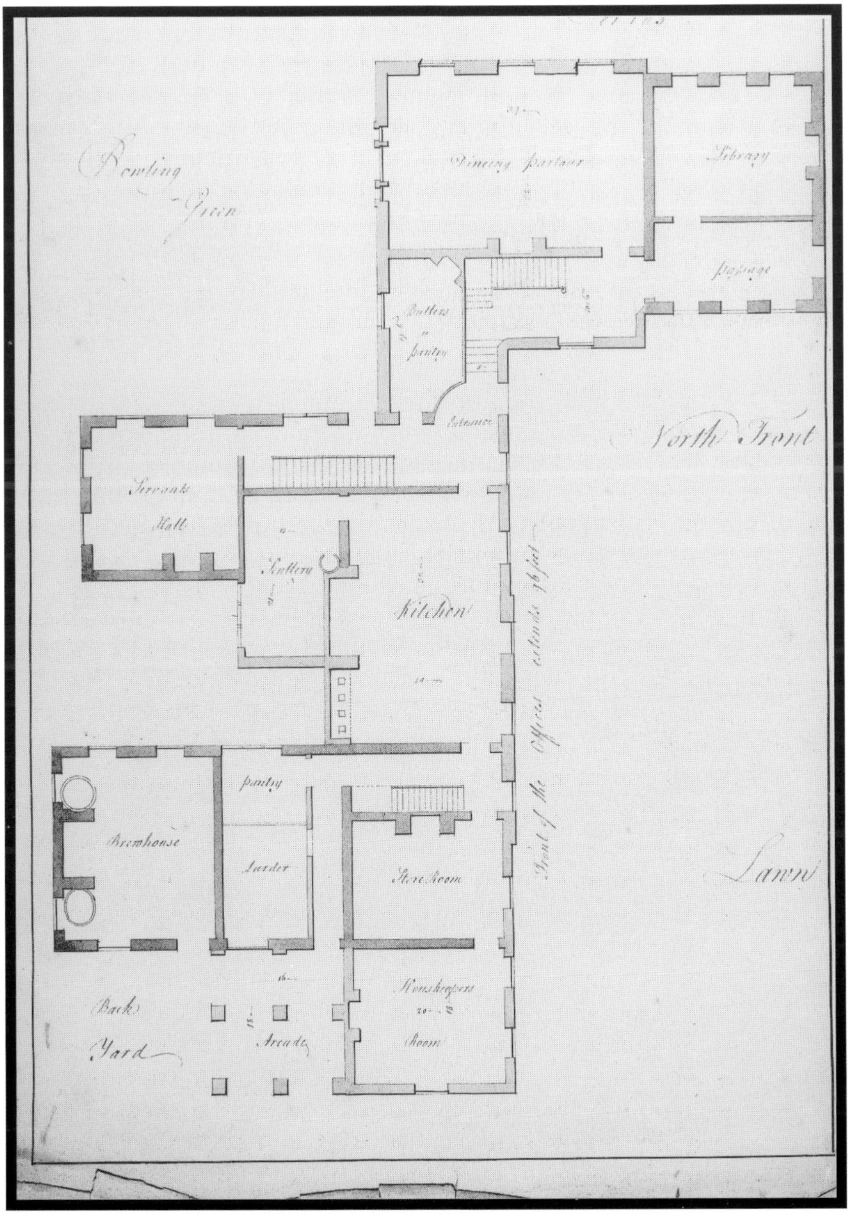

4-7: Plan for Tatton attributed to Pritchard.

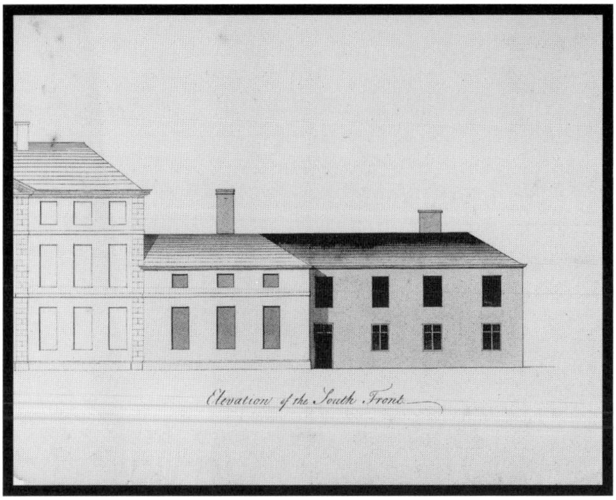

earlier time of day at Knutsford, he might have had time to make a sketch of Tatton but he was usually more interested in old churches or ruined castles.

At Tatton Pritchard may have added on another 'Great Room.' The Egertons of Tatton were related to the Hills of Hawkstone and Tern Hall so it is not surprising to find a letter from Rowland Hill of Hawkstone, dated 1 January 1760, to his relative Samuel Egerton, recommending Pritchard. 'The bearer is Mr Pritchard, who Mr. Kynaston desired me to send over to assist you in your Designs of building a large room.'[14] Isaac Ware would not have approved of this and took another opportunity in his book 'to rally that practice as the common race of builders now execute it.'[15]

5-7: Elevation of Tatton attributed to Pritchard.

From this letter we know that Samuel Egerton was planning an extension to the house but there is no firm evidence that Pritchard worked on it. Just as Noel Hill, another wealthy relative of Samuel Egerton, subsumed Tern Hall inside Attingham Park not long after it was built, so Tatton went through many stages of architectural metamorphosis before emerging as it is today. Despite the fine collection of architectural drawings still in the house, it is not clear

6-7: View of Tatton from the Green Frog Service.

precisely what building processes took place in the mid-eighteenth century and what Pritchard's rôle might have been.

Several drawings and plans in the collection at Tatton have been attributed to Pritchard and these include two plans showing alternative designs for 'a new Dineing Parlour.' Tatton [3] 1-2, and an 'Elevation of the South Front' Tatton [3] 3 have all been dated to around 1760. The kitchens at that time were on the eastern side of the house and so the proposed 'Dineing Parlour', shown as a large three-bay room on the plan Tatton [3] 2 and elevation Tatton [3] 3, would have been near them. This plan was executed as later survey drawings of the house by Samuel Wyatt show. The presence of this 'large room' is confirmed in the only known view of Tatton Park before extensive alterations were carried out later in the 18th century. This view appears on the 'Green Frog Service' made for Catherine the Great of Russia by Josiah Wedgwood, which also illustrates other Cheshire properties and scenes such as Tabley Hall and Rostherne Mere with Rostherne Church in the background. In the drawing, originally by Samuel Stringer, the south front of the house has a three-bay wing on the east side which is probably 'the large room' rising the height of two storeys.[16]

A detailed account for painting, covering the years 1767-8, from William Hunt indicates that work was going on in the 'Great Dining Room' in August and September of 1768.[17] The account for this room includes 'Painting the Ornaments on the Walls 3 times over Dead White after the stone colour was finished.' This job took William Hunt and a man nearly a month to complete at a cost of £7. 7s. as an extensive area had to be covered. The Egertons were not happy with the colour of this room and the stucco was painted again 'on account of its being prefered to be done Green as first designed.' The problem is, designed by whom?

On the two alternative schemes for the new room, the word dining is spelt with an 'e', a form often used by Pritchard, at Downton Hall for instance; a small clue but it may be significant and could help to verify Pritchard's involvement. As he had been given an introduction to Egerton and designed at least four chimney pieces for him there is a strong probability that he was also responsible for the architectural work there. From the evidence of the architectural plans and apparent similarity of this room at Tatton and the 'great room' at Wynnstay, it is possible that Pritchard carried out this work for Samuel Egerton.

One of Pritchard's designs for a chimney piece for Mr. Egerton is elaborate. (AIA 18) It is drawn from two different perspectives, front and side, with therms which have vines trailing below them; the vines could indicate that it was for the new dining room. The carved frieze has an animated griffin, or wyvern, on it and, according to Hunt's account, the whole chimney piece was given five coats of paint or limewash.

On the western end of the south front is the drawing room, now the dining room. This can be seen in the 'Green Frog' view as a canted bay which was later removed and replaced with a tripartite window. Some of the elaborate plasterwork of this room could be Pritchard's as it is considered to date from the middle of the 18th century.

Hunt's account also shows that work was done for a ' new bedchamber' and this links with the fact that about 1766 Pritchard designed some chimney pieces for Miss Egerton's rooms. Although no name for a property is given on his drawings, it is assumed that these are for Tatton but only two (AIA 41 and AIA 56) are designated for specific rooms; one, with 'gothick arches and leaves', was for Miss Egerton's 'bed chamber.' Was this the 'new bedchamber'? The other chimney piece, similar to one at Kinsham Court, was for 'Miss Egertons rooms.' Another item on Hunt's account was for painting the carving on the chimney pieces in the bed chamber and dressing room, perhaps because they were newly installed. None of these chimney pieces survives in the house.

The Tatton papers reveal little more information for work done at this time except for an estimate for 'compleating the Chancel in the Best and most Elegant Manner' at a cost of £380. This estimate, dated 20 July 1763, is signed by Pritchard and assumed to be for the Egerton Chapel in Rostherne Church.[18] As Pritchard had worked on Ruabon Church at the same time as he was engaged at Wynnstay, it is quite likely he did the same at Rostherne while involved at Tatton. As house and church are closely linked, I have included the latter in this section rather than Chapter 11 which covers church projects.

In May 1765, permission was sought

> to take down part of the East End wall of the Parish Church of Rosthern ... and to take in part of the church yard thereof to enlarge the Chapel of Samuel Egerton of Tatton ... called Egerton's Chapel situate at the south east end of the said church adjoining eastward to the East Wall, Westward to a seat or pew of Peter Brooke of Mere esquire Northward to the chancel arch and southward to the south wall in Length nineteen feet and a half and in breadth twelve feet or thereabouts and to enlarge the tomb vault or burial place underneath the said chapel, ... to assign and confirm the said new chapel with the seat or seats therein when erected to the said Samuel Egerton and his family to and for the use of standing sitting kneeling and hearing divine service and sermons therein and the said tomb vault or burial place underneath the same for the use of interring his and their dead therein ...[19]

Drawings, entitled 'Plans intended for rebuild[g] and enlarge[g] the Chancel belonging to Sam[l] Egerton Esq at Rosthern' exist at Tatton Park that are thought to be by Pritchard.[20]

These drawings, undated and unsigned, show the area as 'at present' and the scheme to be carried out, together with details of the arches and wooden screen on the west and south sides of the chancel and an 'Elevation of the South side of the Chancel'.

This work would appear to have been executed as *Bagshaw's Gazetteer* of 1850 mentioned the side chapels attached to the manors of Agden, Tatton and Mere. The author noted that 'there is a sumptuous monument in the Tatton chancel which occupies nearly the whole of the east end.'[21] The church today is mainly the work of Arthur Blomfield who restored it in 1888, but the measurements of the Egerton Chapel correspond to the dimensions given on Pritchard's drawings.

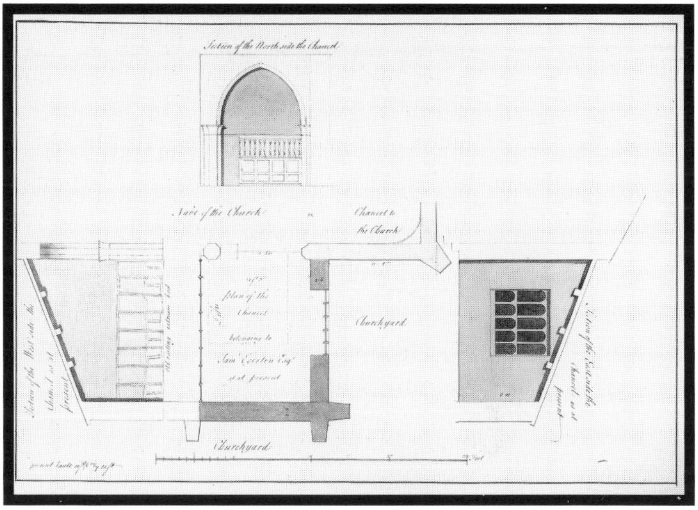

7-7: Chancel of Rostherne Church 'as at present', c. 1763.

In the Tatton accounts and correspondence other links with Pritchard appear; John Wilkinson, the iron master, supplied ironmongery in 1768 and Colonel Congreve, one of the governors of the Foundling Hospital, is mentioned in an undated letter.

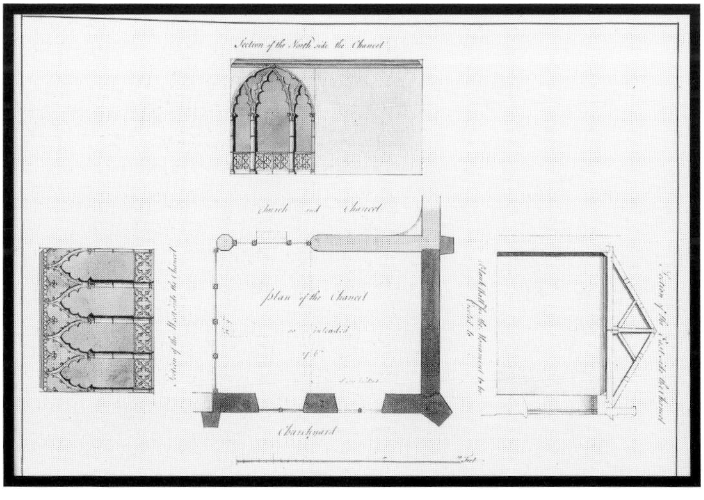

8-7: Chancel of Rostherne Church, 'as intended', c. 1763.

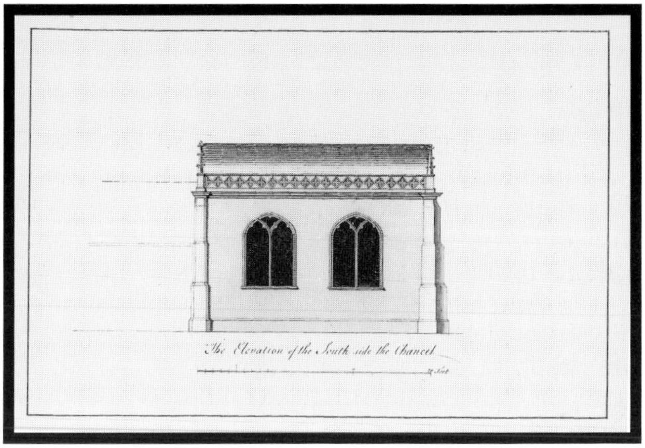

9-7: 'Elevation of the South side of the Chancel' of Rostherne Church.

10-7: Rostherne Church today.

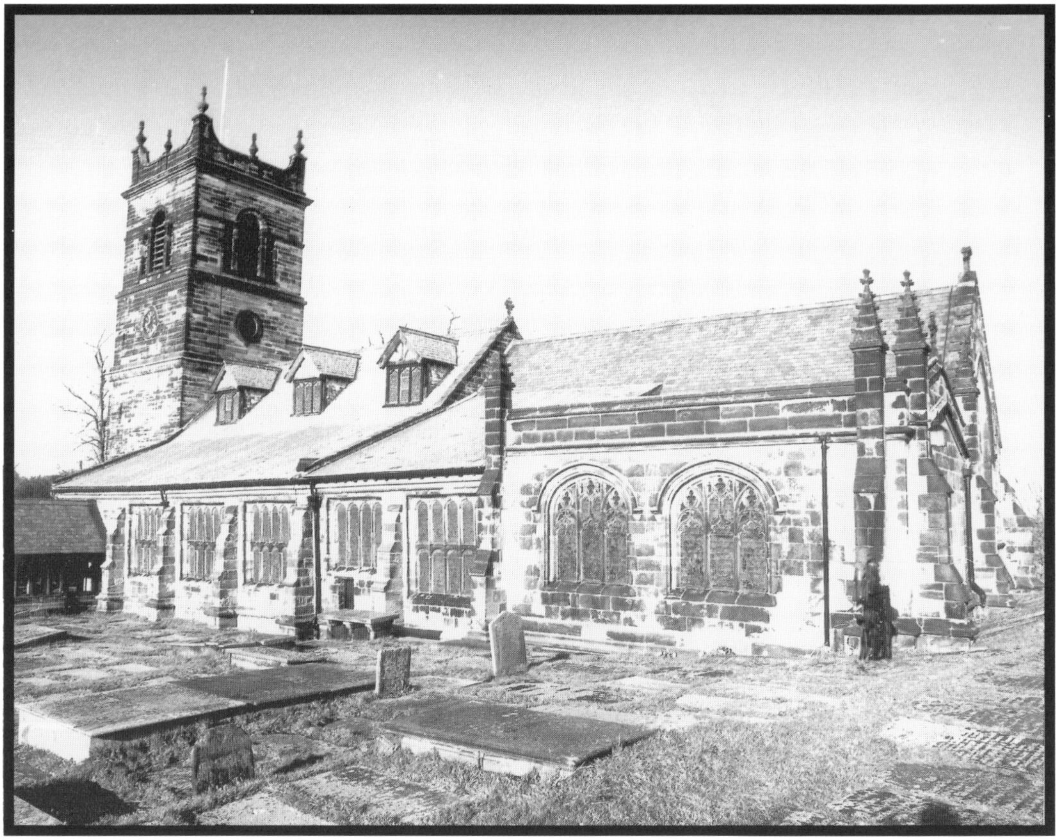

CHAPTER 7

In summary, Chapters 5, 6 and 7 contain a survey of work by Pritchard around the Welsh Border Marches and include some of his major commissions for important clients. He demonstrated that he could work in a variety of styles, efficiently producing what his clients required. His Gothick work at Croft Castle is probably the best example of this style, but Gaines could eventually prove that he was also at the forefront of technology by his use of cast iron in a domestic building. Pritchard also showed that he could work with some of the richest landowners in the area such as Sir Watkin Williams Wynn as well as designing for 'middling people' both in the town and the country.

1 'Wynnstay, Denbighshire - 1', Peter Howell and T. W. Pritchard, *Country Life*, 23 March 1972, pp. 686-689.

2 NLW, Wynnstay Box 115/28/1.

3 NLW, Wynnstay MSS122, P 5ff. I am grateful to The Venerable T. W. Pritchard for sharing this information with me and for his assistance generally.

4 Ware, p. 295.

5 Quoted in Howell and Pritchard, p. 689.

6 *The Torrington Diaries*, Volume 1, 'A Tour to North Wales', 1784, p. 175.

7 Illustrated in Howell and Pritchard, *Country Life*.

8 National Library of Wales (NLW), Wynnstay Estate Rentals, R40; other information is from R39, 1768-9 Estate Rentals; R41, Rent Roll; Catalogue of plans, Wynnstay Box 115/28/1.

9 *The Torrington Diaries*, Volume 1, p. 180.

10 Dated in *The Buildings of England,* Shropshire, p. 170 and described by Peter Reid, *Burke's and Savills Guide to Country Houses*, London, 1980, p. 96.

11 NLW, Wynnstay , 122, P5F and Wynnstay Rentals, R39.

12 There was a grand opening with an oratorio and several solos performed by 'Mr Paxton, the first violincello, and Signior Giardagni, the first singer in the Kingdom.' Details of Ruabon Church from the Guide Book by The Venerable T. W. Pritchard. I am grateful to him for supplying me with information on both Ruabon Church and Wynnstay.

13 It is interesting that another was put into Halston Chapel, near Oswestry and not far from Ruabon which remained in situ until early this century, according to Dean Cranage.

14 Egerton Tatton Muniments, Rylands Library, Manchester, ref. 5/3/13.

15 Ware, p. 433.

16 My thanks to Michael Raeburn of the Cacklegoose Press for his help and for supplying the photographs of both the views of Tatton and Tern Hall. His Press has published a book containing views from the entire 'Green Frog Service', a marvellous pictorial record of country houses and landscapes in the 1770s. *The Green Frog Service*, Ed: Michael Raeburn, Ludmila Voronikhina and Andrew Nurnberg, London, 1997.

17 Egerton Tatton Muniments, 2/3/411. Hunt's very detailed account includes the use of 'mohogony colour' on a staircase, and 'Dead White after the Stone' in some places. Miss Egerton's apartments were painted 'Dead White, Mohogony & Straw colour' at a cost of £10. 16s. 2½d., an amount that indicates that it covered an extensive area.

18 Egerton Tatton Muniments, 2/3/353.

19 Cheshire Record Office, Bishop's Register EDA2/6, folio 497.

20 Ref: Tatton [62].

21 *Bagshaw's Gazetteer*, 1850, Rostherne Parish, p. 563.

CHAPTER 8

'A substantial and workmanlike manner'. Town Houses.

1-8: Gothick doorway in Shrewsbury.

In the 18th century there was a rapid development of urban streets and terraces as we can see today from many of our towns and Shrewsbury was no exception. Originally it was a town with many timber-framed buildings, but as its prosperity grew many of these were replaced by brick or stone buildings. The area of St. John's Hill and Swan Hill Court would look very different now if the mid-eighteenth century development had not taken place.

Two of the town houses, in this chapter, 27 Broad Street, Ludlow and Swan Hill Court House, have a Palladian form with their symmetrical and unadorned front elevations. This form follows the country houses such as Hatton Grange and Brockhampton House. In this respect Swan Hill Court House and 27 Broad Street might not be considered as town houses apart from the fact that they are both in an urban situation. As both houses had a considerable amount of space around them they could afford to spread unlike the houses on St. John's Hill which, for commercial reasons, needed to be strictly specified and fitted into the space.

It is difficult to find documentation about much of the work that Pritchard carried out in Shrewsbury, although there is little doubt that he was involved in buildings that have now disappeared or cannot be identified. Indeed it would have been strange if, as Shrewsbury's leading architect of the time, he had not worked on a number of properties there. The doorway in the Square, Shrewsbury, with its elaborate ogee arch and finial at the top and cluster columns at the side is very characteristic of his style.

Much of the work was likely to have been on updating older properties rather than on building new ones. *The Drawing Book* shows that he designed chimney pieces and other interior details for Mr. Powis in Gravel Hill (AIA 9) and Mr. Lloyd in Raven Street (AIA 16a and 32) and Mr Scot Draper in Grope Lane (AIA 16b). There are two chimney pieces for Henry Powis at The Abbey (AIA 66 and AIA 67) and three for Mr Bather (AIA 12a-c) together as well as two candle stick brackets (AIA 15a) and a shield for a book case (AIA 15b). In 1765 the Bathers probably lived in the town; they did not own Meole Brace Hall until 1779 although they may have tenanted it before that date.

The front room of Hardwick House on St. John's Hill, owned by Roger Kynaston, has revealed that it was modernised in the middle of the 18th century. Essentially the older and heavier features have been altered to make the room lighter and larger. The size of the chimney breast was reduced so that a smart new fire place could be installed and in other rooms there are carved chimney pieces either by Pritchard or reflecting his style. The windows of the front room were changed to let more light into the room by cutting back the rebates and using lighter frames and the panelling was covered with hessian to take wallpaper. Older houses, often dating from earlier in the century, such as No. 5/6 Belmont were given similar treatment. In particular, 15 Belmont with its handsome front bay windows has a chimney piece that could have come from Pritchard's workshop which was nearby.

These comparatively small jobs may have required little in the way of documentation, perhaps a visit by Pritchard to the house and a trip by the client to Pritchard's yard to select a design for a chimney piece that would best suit the building. The whole project would have been carried out on a more informal basis than the work for the big houses. Pritchard and many of his local Salopian clients moved in the same circles and, as today, business would have been discussed in the inns or coffee houses of Shrewsbury, much as it was in London. It had been observed in 1722 that 'Shrewsbury had the most coffee-houses ... that ever I saw in any town, but when you come into them they are but ale-houses, only they think the name of coffee-house gives a better air.'[1]

There are houses in many Shropshire towns that have 18th century work of the kind that Pritchard and fellow builders and architects carried out. An example is 17 Green End in Whitchurch, Shropshire, a handsome town house containing many provincial details which appears to date from the first decade of the18th century.[2] It has a large cornice with dentil course on the front elevation and a sizeable, but plain hood over the front entrance. Interior details reveal that the house was updated later in the century, probably about 1740-50. The older stairs have been retained but carved tread ends may have been added; pediments, broken in one case, have been added to doorways and a carved Rococo chimney piece is in a downstairs room. These features, and the fact that the house was in the ownership of the Morhall family, for whom Pritchard designed a monument, are the only indications of his involvement, but equally the work could also have been carried out by another experienced builder.

Pritchard's work on public buildings has survived in the offices of lawyers and owing to the complex legal situation the papers for Swan Hill Court House, a property of the Newport estate, have also survived and are able to give us a good idea of Pritchard's work on a major town house for an important client. There are also records for the troublesome houses on Wyle Cop.

2-8: *Wyle Cop today.*

WYLE COP, SHREWSBURY.

Pritchard carried out work between 1752 and 1754 on two houses in Wyle Cop. They are originally on the lower side of the present Lion Hotel and now incorporated into it. The owner was Charles Gibbons and his account book records payments to Pritchard.[3] The work involved refronting one of the properties while the other was rebuilt completely.

Gibbons recorded that he had 'Paid Mr. Pritchard, Builder, for rebuilding this whole house (and front of part of the next) £350.00.' Pritchard also supplied plans but was only paid for these in February 1754. There is a begrudging entry of £3. 3s. for the plans 'of this and other houses (too much far).' Gibbons was not satisfied with the work to the house next to the Lion.

> N.B. Mr Pritchard shd have finished this house (accordg to Agreemt) by Laday 1753; but did not til after Laday 1754, by wch I lost a year's Rent. Mr Rogr Kinaston et all were abt it. Pritchard complaind yt he had lost by this contract, but if he did, he own'd he was cheated by his Bricklayer; & besides my losing sd year's rent, I was imposed on in the 3 guin[s] pd pro [for] his Plans; & I have bn forc'd to be at the charge of altering sevl Chimney Places and turning the water-courses under ground.[4]

Did the recourse to Mr 'Kinaston' lead to a litigation? A later entry refers to 'suing Prichard', written without a 't'. A Thomas Prichard, cart whip maker, is recorded as one of Gibbons' tenants with rent arrears, so it may have been him. In any case, the situation did not seem to affect Thomas Farnolls Pritchard's relationship with Roger Kynaston which was apparently cordial when he was closely involved with him as surveyor for the Foundling Hospital. Without Pritchard's own account it is hard to tell what went wrong, but as today, the relationships in a building project are often uneasy. Gibbons had a long memory; in 1757 he wrote that 'I've laid out here in Improvements £29. 14s. 2d since the house rebuilt per Mr. Pritchard & left as compleat.'[5]

Another job in Wyle Cop was on the upper side of the Lion, probably for John Ashby, who is thought to have owned a red brick three-storey building with keystones over the windows.[6] Ashby was attorney and agent to many of the prominent families around Shrewsbury such as the Clives, the Earls of Powis and the Foresters at Willey Hall near Broseley. At various times he was town clerk and mayor as well as a member of the Shrewsbury Hunt, an exclusive club which gave balls and dinners. Pritchard designed two chimney pieces for Ashby, one for the parlour. (AIA 36 and 37) They are surprisingly plain for a man who was becoming prosperous as the very efficient and trusted agent to the rich country landowners; rentals from Clive's Shropshire estates amounted to £18,000 in 1774.

There is no evidence that Ashby actually owned the Lion, but he could have had a financial interest in it as it was becoming the most popular venue in the town and a centre for the increasing coaching trade.

3-8: St. John's Hill, Shrewsbury.

ST. JOHN'S HILL, SHREWSBURY.

It is quite possible that Pritchard worked on some of the houses built on St John's Hill in Shrewsbury and even if he did not, they provide an interesting picture of speculative building in the middle of the 18th century and today the street is one of the most handsome in the town.[7] Behind the tall houses are walled gardens.

In 1761, the area of St John's Hill on the south-west side of the town was occupied by 'several old ruinous tenements.'[8] The land was leased for ninety-nine years by Hugh Owen of Woodhouse, West Felton, to Thomas Gittins, a shoemaker and William Harrold, a wool merchant

4-8: Doorways of St. John's Hill.

and draper of Birmingham at a yearly rent of £6. Two houses, later numbers 26 and 27, replaced three tenements, and five houses, numbers 19-23, were to be built on the site of further tenements.

A strict specification was laid down for numbers 26 and 27 for the 'two good substantial dwelling houses of brick.' They were to be 'forty feet front to the street and forty one feet long backwards of two stories above the ground besides garrets.'[9] The lower floor was just over six foot high and the house included cellars and two pantries, and on the first floor, a hall, two rooms, staircase and two closets and 'a closet to the front and two rooms backwards and hall' on the second floor.

The front wall was two bricks thick to the first floor and a brick and a half thickness to the top of the second floor. Five sash windows of 'good carpenters or joiners work' for the front of each house; two in the lower storey of six feet high and three foot broad and 'also to make three such sash windows to each house backwards.'[10] These were glazed with the 'best common glass' and locks, hinges and keys provided. The ground floor and brewhouse were paved with bricks. 'Inch Oak and deal Boards' were specified for the first floor and 'Ash Oak or deal boards' for the second.[11] 'Two vaults of Brick' for privies and a brick wall around the garden completed the specification for these two houses which had to be completed in eight months. This was a tight timetable considering much of that time was during the winter.

The specification for the St. John's Hill houses includes the direction that in the 'cellar story the lower floor thereof shall be six feet two inches to the bottom of the wiretree the ground floor nine feet and a half to the bottom of the wiretree the story over to be nine feet and a half high to the bottom of the wiretree ...'[12]

These houses are typical of the town house that Pritchard might have been working on as a speculative venture and of the type which made an area a more fashionable one. In the case of St. John's Hill, the name was changed from Swine Market to reflect its new status.

5-8: Garden elevation of Swan Hill Court House.

SWAN HILL COURT HOUSE, SHREWSBURY.

Not far away from St. John's Hill is Swan Hill Court and at the end of this street is Swan Hill Court House standing imposingly within the old town walls. It is built of red brick with cream stone detailing with a pediment over the central bays and pavilions on either side.

Carriages would have approached from the road alongside the town walls through the imposing gates. Fitting into its comparatively cramped situation, or 'spot of land' as Pritchard called it, with the town crowding on one side and the town walls blocking the other, the house needed to provide adequate access from both sides. No plans or drawings survive, but Pritchard's accounts for the house exist and amount to a total of £750. 4s. 7d. The measurements included in the accounts correspond to the size of the present main block of the house. Like much of his work the project was constrained by an existing structure or was an addition or extension.

In 1668, Swan Hill had been an area of textile workers, but it changed in character over the century. In 1731 only three clothworkers and a weaver were left and by the middle of the century the area boasted a watchmaker, three gentlemen and four esquires,[13] so it is not surprising that this sizeable site was used for a house of some importance. In 1761 Pritchard and John Corfield made an oath:

> that they have carefully viewed a piece of Garden...situate near the Walls of the said Town of Shrewsbury...and these deponants say that the Same is a very pleasant and Commodious situation for building upon.....Pritchard for himself saith he hath made an Estimate of the Expence which will attend the Building of an house upon this piece of Ground in a substantial and workmanlike Manner according to a plan .....and that the same will....amount to seven hundred and fifty pounds or thereabouts.[14]

Was this the same John Corfield who was Pritchard's cousin and who, as a relative, was left five pounds in the will of Anne Farnolls, Pritchard's grandmother? In the Swan Hill documentation he is described as 'a gentleman' of Bestlow in Shropshire. He signed the 1761 affadavit and was not mentioned again.

The documents for building were drawn up in Chancery 'between the Right Honourable William, Earl of Bath and others ... and The Right Honourable Thomas Earl of Bradford, a Lunatick by his Guardians and Committers, John Newport, Esquire a Lunatick by his Guardians and others ...Defendants.'

A complex situation had arisen with the death in 1734 of Henry, Viscount Newport, later Earl of Bradford. The heir to the estate was John Harrison, his illegitimate son, who took the name of Newport. His mother, Anne Harrison, was a friend of William, Earl of Bath and when she died in 1742 she made him a trustee of her 'bastard' child John, the 'lunatick'. Thomas Newport, the other lunatick named above, was the boy's uncle and he also left him property. Whether a streak of insanity ran in that branch of the family or whether there had been a ploy to get John declared insane so that his money could be used, is not clear. What does seem clear is that Bath was using trust money to build Swan Hill Court House for political purposes as it was considered that he 'acquired the vast estates of the Bradford family by devise under the will of the mistress of Lord Bradford.'[15] As William Pulteney, Lord Bath had a career of political manipulation and although 'a fine classic scholar, a brilliant political writer and an eloquent public speaker' he 'wanted power without responsibility.' He accepted the Earldom of Bath but found he had no power in the House of Lords, so planned to put up his son, William Pulteney, as MP for Shrewsbury using the influence of the Bradford Estates. Robert Clive was adopted instead and Bath formulated alternative plans by offering to raise and pay for a regiment with Shrewsbury as the headquarters and Pulteney as the lieutenant-colonel. Pulteney was sent to Shrewsbury to 'canvas for the borough.' Eventually he had to withdraw his candidature owing to the opposition of the Shropshire Whigs,[16] although the political connection of the Pulteneys continued after the death of Lord Bath and his son. The heir to the Bath estates through marriage, William Pulteney formerly Johnstone, contested the Shrewsbury seat first in

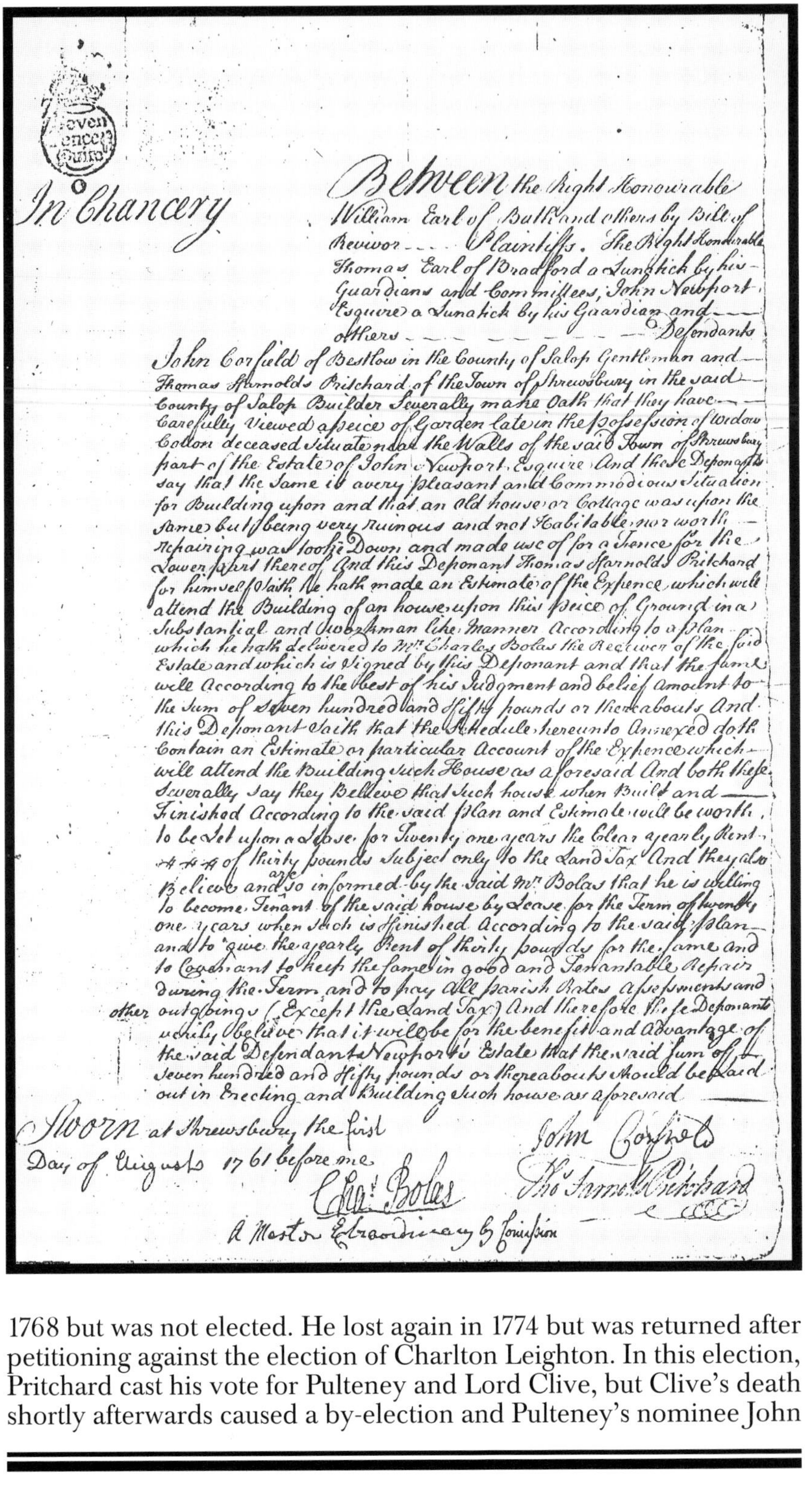

In Chancery

Between the Right Honourable William Earl of Bath and others by Bill of Revivor — Plaintiffs. The Right Honourable Thomas Earl of Bradford a Lunatick by his Guardians and Committees; John Newport Esquire a Lunatick by his Guardian and others — Defendants

John Corfield of Bestlow in the County of Salop Gentleman and Thomas Farnolds Pritchard of the Town of Shrewsbury in the said County of Salop Builder Severally make Oath that they have Carefully Viewed a peice of Garden late in the possession of Widow Cotton deceased situate near the Walls of the said Town of Shrewsbury part of the Estate of John Newport Esquire And these Deponents say that the same is a very pleasant and Commodious Situation for Building upon and that an old house or Cottage was upon the same but being very ruinous and not Habitable nor worth repairing was took Down and made use of for a Fence for the Lower part thereof And this Deponant Thomas Farnolds Pritchard for himself saith he hath made an Estimate of the Expence which will attend the Building of an house upon this peice of Ground in a Substantial and Workman like Manner According to a plan which he hath delivered to Mr Charles Bolas the Receiver of the said Estate and which is Signed by this Deponant and that the same will According to the best of his Judgment and belief amount to the Sum of Seven hundred and fifty pounds or thereabouts And this Deponant saith that the Schedule hereunto Annexed doth Contain an Estimate or particular Account of the Expence which will attend the Building such House as aforesaid And both these Severally say they Believe that such house when Built and Finished According to the said plan and Estimate will be worth to be Let upon a Lease for Twenty one years the Clear yearly Rent of thirty pounds subject only to the Land Tax And they also Believe and are so informed by the said Mr Bolas that he is willing to become Tenant of the said house by Lease for the Term of twenty one years when such is finished According to the said plan and to give the yearly Rent of thirty pounds for the same and to Covenant to keep the same in good and Tenantable Repair during the Term and to pay all parish Rates assessments and other outgoings (Except the Land Tax) And therefore these Deponants verily believe that it will be for the benefit and Advantage of the said Defendant Newport's Estate that the said sum of Seven hundred and fifty pounds or thereabouts should be laid out in Erecting and Building such house as aforesaid

Sworn at Shrewsbury the first Day of August 1761 before me
Chas Bolas
A Master Extraordinary by Commission

John Corfield
Thos Farnolds Pritchard

6-8: Extract from Pritchard's estimate for St John's Hill Court House, 1761.

1768 but was not elected. He lost again in 1774 but was returned after petitioning against the election of Charlton Leighton. In this election, Pritchard cast his vote for Pulteney and Lord Clive, but Clive's death shortly afterwards caused a by-election and Pulteney's nominee John

Corbet of Sundorne was elected.

During his lifetime, Lord Bath maintained these political interests and needed a base in the town, so Swan Hill Court House was known as 'Bath House' and Lord Bath himself probably lived there when he was in Shrewsbury carrying out his duties as Lord Lieutenant of the county. The plans to build Swan Hill Court House were delivered to his agent, Charles Bolas, who was to be the tenant of the house at an annual rent of £30 on a 21 year lease.[17]

In a town like Shrewsbury, Pritchard would have been aware of the political complexities of the day, but unlike some other architects does not seem to have been attached to patrons of one side or another. James Gibbs, as a Catholic, tended to work for Tories, while Robert Adam is more associated with Whig patrons. The situation in Shrewsbury was by no means clear cut and 'the party leaders agreed to leave Shrewsbury to the Whigs and the county to the Tories.'[18] In general terms, after the death of the Earl of Bradford in 1734, which left a gap at the top, the county was divided between the Tory country gentlemen, who represented the rural area. The Shropshire Whigs, who tended to represent the town and urban seats, were led by the Earl of Powis in the 1750s, but this situation was challenged by the Bath faction. Pritchard's clients were supporters of both parties and included John Ashby, a Whig lawyer and town property owner and Sir Richard Lyster, a Tory landowner.

Although Pritchard called it 'a spot of land', the site of Swan Hill Court House is large for a town house, but the attempt to build a country-style house on it produced problems. A three-bay projecting section with pediment would look cramped since there would be only one bay on each side so the immediate effect on the main elevation is that the centre block is restricted to five bays. The result is that the impressive pediment somewhat dominates the building. For reasons of space, there are no connecting arcades to the pavilions and they are pressed hard against the sides of the main elevation.

In spite of the grand garden elevation, the house was intended to be only one room deep in most places, but this has been rather obscured by the later additions on the Swan Hill Court side. A small hall or vestibule was added after Pritchard's time so that his original Venetian door, similar in style to 27 Broad Street, Ludlow, is now inside the house as an interior doorway. The principal living rooms overlook the garden and are separated by an octagonal ante-room or hall. The ante-room at Swan Hill is octagonal, then a fashionable shape being used by Kent in the 1730s at Holkham Hall for the statue gallery or at Belcombe Court in Wiltshire by John Wood the elder in 1734 and very grandly for Basildon Park in 1776 by John Carr. There is an oval drawing room, leading into the garden, at 14 St. John's Hill, Shrewsbury, a house, thought to be by Edward Haycock, where the design may have been influenced by Pritchard's work at Swan Hill.

The kitchen block incorporates the older timber-framed building, although another old house or cottage 'being very ruinous and not Habitable' had already been removed and 'made use of for a

7-8: Plasterwork at Swan Hill Court House.

Fence.' This service area now occupies the pavilion wing on one side while the pavilion on the other side contains a large room running the width of the house. This could have been used as a ballroom, perhaps for entertaining prospective political supporters. With the rising popularity of private entertainment and routs in the mid-18th century Isaac Ware wrote that 'the common practice is to build ... an out of proportion room: this always hangs from one end, or sticks on one side, of the house and shows to the most careless eye, that, though fastened to the walls, it does not belong to the building.'[19] This criticism cannot be applied directly to the ballroom at Swan Hill as architecturally the wings of the pavilions are important to the balance of the central block with its large pediment, but it could be applicable to other 'Great Rooms' as we have seen. The ballroom at Swan Hill can be reached without going through other rooms in the house. Was this because people, who were not equal in status to the owner, might be entertained for political or other reasons?

Stylistically Swan Hill Court House bears a resemblance to other work by Pritchard with external features such as Venetian windows, carved pediment and internally carved Rococo chimney pieces and low relief plasterwork.

There is no reference in the accounts of the attractive ornamental plasterwork for the 'ballroom', which was probably carried out by Joseph Bromfield as it resembles the Powis Castle ceiling. The 'plaisterer' stuccoed '222 yards of wall in Hall and Parlour' for £12.19s. and other walls were prepared 'to hang paper on'. Wallpaper was becoming fashionable; Isaac Ware commented that 'Paper has, in a great measure, taken the place of sculpture; [plasterwork and stucco] and the hand of art is banished from a part of the house in which it used to display itself very happily.'[20]

8-8: Chimney piece at Swan Hill Court House.

Four years later though Pritchard designed the splendid plasterwork for the dining room at Hatton Grange. Was paper considered more suited at this time to a town house? It was cheaper than decorative plasterwork, in spite of the taxes imposed on it. In London, by 1773, 'unpapered plaster walls were acceptable only in the entrance hall.'[21]

Although Lord Bath amassed a huge fortune, as he and his wife were renowned for their 'acquisitive and thrifty habits', economy could have been an important issue with them. 'Four marble chimney pieces with ornaments' are listed in the 'Estimate' at a cost of £25. As Swan Hill Court House was built in 1761-2, it comes outside the range of *The Drawing Book* so there are no designs for these chimney pieces, but it does show that Pritchard was supplying them in the years before the book starts. It hardly seems possible that four chimney pieces could have been made of marble for £25 and it is more likely to refer to the inner marble surrounds and the 'ornaments' are the wooden carved parts; the chimney pieces which survive in the house today are all made of wood. They are not elaborately carved but as they have been stripped of paint the fine carving associated with the work of Nelson, Swift and van der Hagen shows up well. It is assumed that they are in their original positions, although some were removed a few years ago, taken to be sold and only recovered by chance.

Swan Hill Court House is an imposing house and in the 18th century it would have been even more impressive. It demonstrates that Pritchard could design a house suited to a restricted urban site and yet be imposing enough to play a rôle in the town's social and political life.

above 9-8: Chimney piece at Swan Hill Court House.

left 10-8: 27 Broad Street, Ludlow.

11-8: Chimney piece at 27 Broad Street. (AIA 7).

27 BROAD STREET, LUDLOW.

Like John Ashby in Shrewsbury, Somerset Davies, the lawyer, is omnipresent in Ludlow. As collector of the Land Tax and Bailiff of Ludlow his name appears on documents in both Shrewsbury and Ludlow.

In a painting of Broad Street by Samuel Scott, Davies stands proudly outside his front door surveying the scene. His neighbours are busying themselves in the street and many of the people in the picture have been identified.[22]

Davies was described by Mrs Lybbe Powys as 'a gentleman of very large fortune, and having been formerly an eminent attorney, of course acquainted with the surrounding families. She is a very clever, agreeable woman.'[23] Davies had previously lived in nearby Old Street and 27 Broad Street was a much grander house, in fact the grandest house in the street and the only one built of stone. Again, it has the appearance of a country house, or at least one standing in its own grounds, rather than being attached to the smaller brick houses on either side. Its grandeur, though, adds to the interest of Broad Street, considered one of the finest streets in the country.[24]

Pritchard had come into contact with Somerset Davies in 1759 when he worked on the rebuilding of Hosier's Almshouses and for the Corporation of Ludlow. When Davies bought the house in Broad Street, formerly owned by the Charlton family, in 1764 Pritchard was the natural choice to modernise it, although the only actual evidence of his involvement is the vigorous Rococo chimney piece still in the house. (AIA 7)

In the early 17th century, the building had been divided internally to form two dwellings and in the 18th century was returned to one house and given a cohesive front stone façade and a new Venetian front door with windows on either side and a new window above. These features immediately created the desired effect of a new, modern street elevation and 'only at the rear is it evident that there were once two houses.'[25]

The two parts of the building had used the same solid Jacobean staircase which was moved to the back of the house. Isaac Ware had advised that a 'good house should always have two stair-cases, one for show and the use of the company, the other for domesticks. This latter should be thrown behind, but the other is to be shewn ... In considering the place for his stair-case, the architect must have two things in his eye; the giving it a *good light,* and allowing a spacious *landing place.*'[26] Pritchard put this advice into practice and created a new staircase in the hall, a fashionable position at that time as well as adding a tall round-headed window on the garden side to let light into the new stairwell. Pritchard later built a similar handsome new staircase and window at nearby Ludford House, a building owned by the Charlton family.

To the right of the entrance hall at 27 Broad Street is the dining room with the kitchen behind it. On

above 12-8: Chimney piece at 27 Broad Street. (AIA 7). Detail.

left 13-8: Staircase at 27 Broad Street.

far left 14-8: Hall of 27 Broad Street.

the left is the present study and library, probably once a common parlour, and behind that is the drawing room with a large Venetian window looking out on to the garden. The hall leads past the stairs into the extensive gardens behind.

The dining room is elegantly fitted with panelling which may date from earlier in the century or have been re-used from another part of the house. It is hard to tell whether it is by Pritchard as his joinery work does not reflect any particular 'signature', but we have come to expect from him a neat and 'workmanlike' job and many 18th century craftsmen would have turned out similar work.

There is no doubt about the chimney piece for Somerset Davies and although it does not include the name of the room it has probably always been in the drawing

15-8: The Gazebo at 27 Broad Street.

16-8: The interior of the Gazebo.

room. It is a splendid Rococo design, dated November 1765, with cornucopia, raffle leaf and the phoenix heads. The design differs slightly from the actual chimney piece as the sides of the fire surround are lugged, a feature not on the drawing.

The Gazebo in the garden behind, a building which reflects the spirit of Batty Langley, helps to make this house very special. It cannot positively be attributed to Pritchard as no documentation for it survives, but it seems almost certain that he carried out the work. The word is thought to come from 'gazeabout' and implies a building on a high point with a view all around. This delightful Gazebo, situated above the large garden of 27 Broad Street, lives up to its name with windows on three sides that overlook the town walls and the south side of the town.

The Gazebo has all the Gothick attributes synonymous with the style: traceried windows, crow-stepped battlements on the front, ogee arches over the windows and inside a hint of vaulting ribs. A flight of steps, with iron handrails on either side, leads to the upper room through a curved entrance. The unusual tracery of the curved doors and all the windows could be contemporary as no alterations seem to have been made to the Gazebo since it was built. The upper room has a plaster rose in the middle where the lightly indicated vaulting ribs meet. A most pleasant feature is the fireplace, with its original cast iron grate, so that the building can be warm all through the year.

The two-storey structure of the Gazebo is very evident when it is viewed from the garden on the south side.This view also reveals the two lower windows with ogee arches over them, matching the two on the other side which have a wooden door, also ogee topped, between them. The north side is also decorated with ogee-arched windows and two blank circles.

27 Broad Street is a very distinguished town house in a street of major architectural interest. It reflects the status of the owner but conceals the size of the series of gardens behind so that visitors cannot fail to be surprised and impressed when they first catch sight of them from the house.

BROAD GATE HOUSE, LUDLOW.

Further down Broad Street in Ludlow, situated over the one remaining gateway into the town, is the Broad Gate House. This extraordinary and unusual house straddles both the Gate and the town walls. Its Gothick battlements terminate this end of Broad Street and look directly up towards the classical Buttercross.

In the mid-eighteenth century the Broad Gate House was leased by Samuel Sprott, a doctor practising in Ludlow, whose family came from the Marsh, Much Wenlock. Samuel Sprott's wife was Mary Child (or Childe) of Kinlet, near neighbours of the Blounts of Mawley Hall.

There is no documentary evidence that Pritchard worked at the Broad Gate House, but as he was responsible for Dr. Sprott's monument in Ludford Church, which is very similar to the Blount monuments at Mamble Church, it is very likely that he also carried out work on the house. Although Dr. Sprott died in 1759, the lease ran until 1760;[27] Pritchard might have carried out the work when he was employed on Hosier's Almshouses.

17-8: The Broad Gate House, Ludlow.

Stylistically, there are indications of Pritchard's hand; the mock battlements, made of wood, have been discussed elsewhere but the interesting Broad Street entrance, with its curved entablature, fretted frieze and cluster columns at the side, is indicative of the sort of work that he carried out.

The Broad Gate doorway leads into the hall where the slightly depressed arches resemble those at the White House at Suckley and also on the first floor at Croft Castle, both buildings connected with Pritchard. The elegant drawing room, decorated in the neat, understated way that could be considered as one of Pritchard's characteristics is adjacent to the garden which is on top of the walls.

Mark Girouard, in *The English Town*, wrote that 'on stylistic grounds ... most of Ludlow's Georgian houses are likely to have been the work of Ludlow craftsmen working from contemporary pattern books and producing safe, sensible façades like hundreds of others all over England.'[28] This could be true for many of the Ludlow houses, but it does seem very possible that Pritchard did work at the Broad Gate House bearing in mind the connection between him and the Sprott family.

18-8: The entrance hall of the Broad Gate House, Ludlow.

BROSELEY HALL AND BENTHALL HALL.

19-8: Rear elevation, Broseley Hall.

Broseley Hall, and The Lawns nearby, stand in their own large gardens close to the centre of the town of Broseley. Broseley Hall is a red-brick mid-Georgian house of medium size, five bays wide. The spacious entrance hall, with living rooms on either side, leads to the curved staircase. This is lit by a tall round-headed window similar to the staircase window at Ludford House and 27 Broad Street, Ludlow, so the house could have been designed by Pritchard.

The owner, originally called Francis Turner, had inherited Broseley Hall from his sister, Anne Brown, in 1766. He had been High Sherriff of Shropshire in 1755 and was on the committee of the Foundling Hospital so would have known Pritchard from that time. As heir to his uncle in Warwickshire, Turner took the additional name of Blythe and became Francis Turner Blythe. His second marriage brought him around £10,000 so he was in a position to spend money on a house.[29]

The change of names creates some confusion. Two of Pritchard's designs, a chimney piece and the garden temple at Broseley Hall, were made for 'Blithe Turner Esq. of Broseley'; the temple is dated April 1769. Two more, also still at Broseley Hall, were for 'Mr. Blythe' but with no property name. The inference is that the first two, which could be dated to 1766, were made for Mr. Blithe when he first came to the Hall, but after he inherited from his uncle, it was felt that he had risen in the world and had become 'esq' when the other two designs were done.

20-8: Chimney piece at Broseley Hall. (AIA 39)

Pritchard's Rococo-style chimney piece, with a hint of a cornucopia in the centre, is in the drawing room to the left of the front door. (AIA 38) In the room behind is the simple and elegant 'Darby marble chimney' made for 'Blithe Turner esq.' with 'Bead and Flower' and '7 Leafe grasse'. (AIA 70) The design for the 'Bed Chamber Chimney' which has

a Rococo cartouche in the centre and sprays of leaves on either side is still in one of the bedrooms. (AIA 39)

The garden temple also for 'Blithe Turner esq.' terminates the view from the house at the end of the garden. (AIA 71) The slender cluster columns, supporting the cusped ogee arches with finials, are made of wood, not cast iron as might have been expected, considering the proximity of Broseley to Coalbrookdale and the ready availability of cast iron.

Broseley Hall stands next to the church and opposite The Lawns, a house which could date back to the late 17th century. It was owned by John Wilkinson, the iron master. Pritchard had worked on a monument for Ann, Wilkinson's first wife, when she died in 1759 and designed a chimney piece for him in 1769, so he may have done work on the house as well. (AIA 79)

21-8: Garden Temple at Broseley Hall. (AIA 71)

22-8: The Lawns, Broseley.

The situation over names is also complicated by a design for a chimney piece for 'Mr Francis Turner', dateable to the year 1766. (AIA 24) This is now in the present drawing room at Benthall Hall, near Broseley, where there is also a Rococo chimney piece in the dining room which is likely to be by Pritchard. In 1746 the Benthall estate was owned by the Brown, or Browne family of Caughley Hall near Broseley and then passed to the Harries family. Also on the Browns' Caughley estate was a small pottery run by Thomas Turner. The juxtaposition of all these names at Benthall and the name of the owner of Broseley Hall would indicate that the same families owned these properties and therefore involved Pritchard at Benthall. Family connections in the 18th century were very important. Edward Blythe Harries, who owned the estate in the mid-19th century, was the son of the Rev. Edward Harries of Cructon, one of the original investors in the Iron Bridge company. Pritchard's brother, Samuel, married Mary Harries, daughter of William Harries, also of Cructon and Benthall. Mary was considered to be a direct descendant of Anne Plantagenet, Duchess of Exeter and sister of Edward IV and Richard II. Her son, John Pritchard, referred to himself as 'A Humble Sprig of Nobility.'

However, these genealogical complications do not explain if Francis Turner Blithe of Broseley was the same person as Francis Turner for whom the chimney piece at Benthall was made. The design for the drawing room chimney piece, with therms, swags of flowers and a pinecone, contains a table set out in a different way from the designs apparently done at the same time. It is interesting to note that Pritchard often changed the way he set out the pieces to be carved and the time taken. For this piece, he had filled in the time for the therms and this showed that all three carvers worked on them – Nelson, Swift and van der Hagen. The time for the other elements of work was not recorded, apart from a brief amount for some mouldings. It is a matter of speculation why Pritchard did not always complete the information and how he calculated what he had to pay the craftsmen if a complete record was not kept.

The photograph shows the chimney piece in the dining room and, like the one in the drawing room, it deliberately blends in with the Jacobean overmantel and does not intrude on it; a very typical approach by Pritchard. He does not seem to have been involved with other work at Benthall Hall where most of the work had been done at an earlier date.

23-8: Chimney piece at Benthall Hall.

WOLVERHAMPTON: WORK FOR THE NEWPORT ESTATE.

Other documented work on town buildings was for the Newport estate and because all the specifications and accounts had to go through Chancery they have survived almost intact.[30]

One of these jobs, in 1763, called for repairs to the 'House called the Red Lyon Inn', then occupied by Mary Badger, a widow, and her son. Pritchard 'carefully viewed and inspected' the buildings and found them in 'very bad repair' and some parts of them 'ruinous.'[31] He considered that it would be costly to put the property into good condition, even before enlarging it as required for Mrs Badger and her son as they frequently had to send guests elsewhere. Pritchard suggested taking down the ruinous malthouse and 'making and Erecting the new buildings Additions Alterations and Conveniences.' Pritchard made a plan of the new buildings which has not survived, and an estimate of the expenses which came to £1560. 17s. 6d 'or upwards to compleat them' after an allowance for the old materials; the amount of this allowance led to a dispute.[32] The Badgers paid an annual rent of £260. l0s. and were willing to pay an extra £50. l0s. after the work was done; this considerable sum indicates the good trade that they were doing at the Inn. Pritchard ended the document by saying that it would be 'a great conveniency to the town of Wolverhampton, which is a large trading town' to have these alterations made.

The extensive and detailed accounts include three marble and two stone chimney pieces. In the original estimate these come under work done by the 'Carpenters & Joiners': '2 Stone Chimney pieces in Parlours' for £5 and '3 Marble Chimney pieces with plain Mouldings to Dineing & Drawing Room' at a cost of £27. Perhaps the latter was the design in *The Drawing Book* (AlA 8) which is for 'Two Chimneys for the great Room' carved by van der Hagen. In the valuation following the dispute, the work on the chimney pieces is assigned to the Mason, which included carving bubble and husk as well as making packing cases and carriage. A variety of marbles, such as 'Vein'd Italian' and 'Dove', was used for the surrounds; the Painter's account included £1 for painting '4 chimney pieces Marbled'. He also charged 9s. for '3 windows in passage & 2 Chinese.'[33] The estimated sum included such items as 'London Crown Glass' for the windows, cast iron stoves and grates for the kitchen and stucco and 'plaistering'. The building also had Venetian windows as well as nine blank windows 'painted on Stucco'.

A frame, with gadrooning, is also included for the Great Room (AIA 6) for a picture measuring 2ft. 6in. by 2ft. 1in. Nelson and van der Hagen both worked on it, using five books of gold. All these details indicate a building of considerable size and prosperity. If the chronology of *The Drawing Book* is correct then the designs for the

Red Lion were being done at the time the dispute was being settled over the account for the rest of the work. The itemised estimate came to just over £1821 and the old materials to £260 and this led to problems which arose from the valuation in the original estimate of the old materials of the malt house and outhouses; it was not resolved until two years later. At the time of making the estimate Pritchard had valued the old materials at £260, but when they were taken down they were found to be much worse than expected, especially the timber which was 'very much decayed and a great part of it not fit for use' and consequently he valued the materials at £116. 8s. 4d. The final account was disputed and William Baker and Robert Bromfield, a builder from Stourbridge, were called in to examine and measure the work and make a valuation. They were considered as 'persons well skilled in the Nature of Buildings.' They valued the work at £1,906. 13s. 3d. and the old materials at Pritchard's estimate of £116. 8s. 4d. and therefore recommended payment of £1,790. 4s. 11d. This document concludes with Pritchard asserting that he 'justly honestly and fairly deserves the said sum' and 'that he never contracted or agreed to do and perform the said work according to the said estimate mentioned in the said report and if he had done so he should have been a very great loser thereby.'[34] As both Bromfield and Baker recommended that Pritchard should be paid what he was owed, it has to be hoped that he was, as this job had dragged on for over two years.

The Red Lion Inn was in Snow Hill in Wolverhampton and today there is no trace of it and there is no indication of what it looked like, apart from a photograph taken before the alterations were made in the area. This shows, rather indistinctly, a small part of the front elevation and the name Red Lion Inn on a board on the front.

Before this dispute arose, Pritchard was involved in another with the Newport estate and their agent, Thomas Badger, presumably of the Red Lion, over the Deanery House, Wolverhampton. Again the building has not survived and 19th century prints and drawings of it do not show the alterations that Pritchard made to the property.

The work this time was an inspection of the property, which was divided into two tenements and in a very bad state of repair and to build a new 'compting house' for £30 for one of the tenants, Benjamin Corson; the total cost, with other repairs, came to £234. 12s. For another tenant, James Perry, Pritchard was to build a new kitchen with a room over it for £60, with additional repairs making a total of £198. Pritchard also seemed to have been carrying out negotiations for the tenants and arranging how much extra rent they would pay in exchange for the work. Corson was to pay an extra 'one pound ten shillings' a year and Perry an extra £3. Pritchard concluded by saying that the work would 'tend to the benefit and advantage of the said Lunatick's Estate.' Below he gave short schedules of the costs involved and the whole job seemed to be a simple one.[35]

Whether Pritchard miscalculated or the parsimony of Lord Bath prevailed, Pritchard presented a bill which was more than

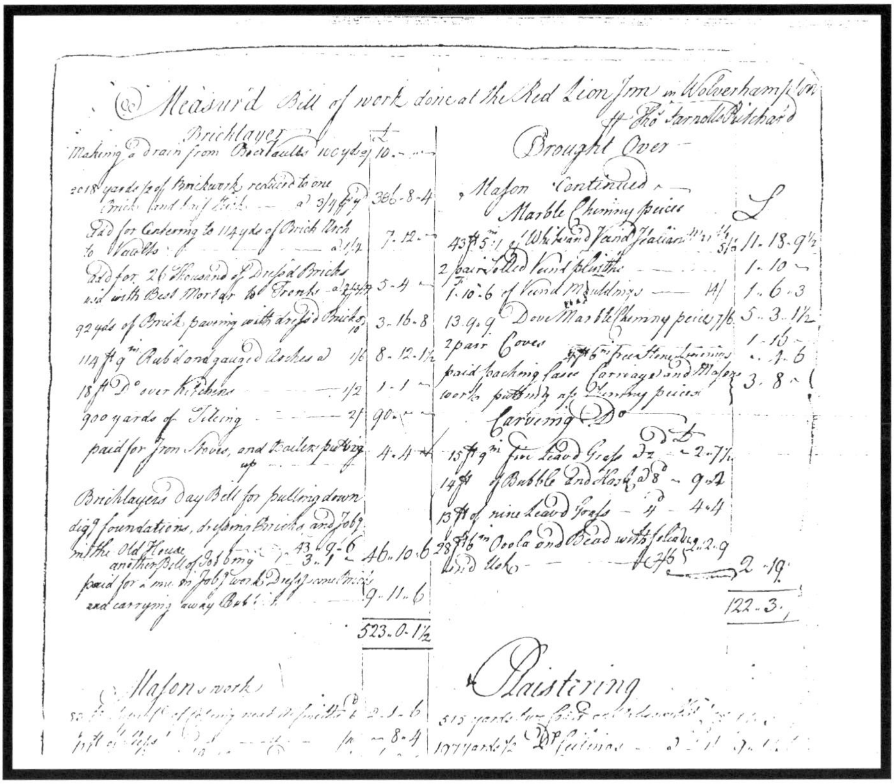
Measur'd Bill of work done at the Red Lion Inn in Wolverhampton
by Thos Farnolls Pritchard

Bricklayer

Brought Over

Mason Continued

Marble Chimney pieces

Carving

Plaistering

523.0.1½

122.3.

24-8: Extract from Pritchard's valuation for the Red Lion Inn, Wolverhampton, 1763.

the estimate. Again Bromfield acted for the Newport estate and Baker for Pritchard. The arbitrators 'carefully examined and measured the said work' and 'particularly enquired into the value of the materials made use of' and following this 'they made several Deductions.' Pritchard claimed that he would be the loser by the work as much of the existing building was in a worse state than expected and that it had been necessary to 'introduce new Timber Joists and Girders.' In the end, and it took some time to settle finally, Bromfield and Baker decided that Pritchard 'justly honestly and fairly deserve' £480. 1s. 9¼d., which was £47. 9s. 9¼d. more than the estimate.[36] Baker and Bromfield appeared to be tired of these disputes; Bromfield wrote on the Deanery House account 'What is wrote at the Back of the Red Lyon Bill is Applicable to this Bill' and underneath Baker put 'what I had said upon the back of the Red Lyon Bill is also relative to this.'[37]

With the frugal Lord Bath in charge of the Newport estate, these disputes probably occurred regularly and do not necessarily indicate incompetence on Pritchard's part. The estimate that he gave for the work was a thorough one and for both jobs, much as happens today, the dispute was over the value of old materials and the amount of decay in the old buildings that could not be assessed until work started.

CHAPTER 8

The work at Deanery House was a small job in comparison with many that Pritchard had in hand at the same time and it shows that his practice was not very different from that of a small architectural practice today. It consisted of some time spent designing, time on the road and more administration that he would perhaps have liked. The Deanery House papers ran to three pages for the original estimate but the itemised accounts that he had to draw up to answer the queries in the dispute ran to several more pages in addition to an introduction which outlined the problem.

Even a small job like Deanery House would have required his presence at some time, but without a diary it is difficult to know exactly how he organised his time. The estimate for the Red Lion was given in November 1763 and work probably began shortly afterwards. The work on Gaolford Tower started in June 1763 when he presented the survey and continued until at least 1764 and probably into 1765. He gave the first estimate for Deanery House in February 1764 and presumably work commenced as soon as the weather improved. Building work at Hatton Grange dates from 1764 and continued for five years; the schedule for Hatton chimney pieces is dated 1765. Two of the early designs in *The Drawing Book* are dated November 1765 and include the Red Lion, 27 Broad Street, Ludlow, Croft Castle and Shipton Hall. Over a two-year period Pritchard was working in Wolverhampton, Ludlow, Croft near Leominster, Shipton in the Corvedale and possibly at Gaines in Worcestershire, although the exact date of this work is not certain. At least three monuments are dateable to this period, but that work could have continued in the workshop while other was progressing on site.

Compared with Robert Mylne this is not a heavy schedule, but for a one-person practice it was quite a considerable workload and that is only judging from the work which is documented. Wolverhampton was a day's ride from Shrewsbury therefore such a trip there would have involved three days and the same would have applied to Ludlow with another day to visit Croft Castle.

As there is so little mention of assistants or other people working for him, it is assumed that Pritchard did most of the supervision himself. We do know that he had a small, but very competent team of craftsmen to call on, headed by Nelson and van der Hagen, but he seems to have had sole responsibility for the architectural side of the jobs. Jonathan Reynolds is the only person referred to in this connection as the workman on site who carried out the day-to-day running of the contract. Pritchard would have been required to visit the site himself to measure and draw up the valuations. Disputes such as The Red Lion and Deanery House would have put extra pressure on his time.

1 T. Auden, *A Historical and Topographical Account of the Town of Shrewsbury*, London, 1923, p. 228.

2 Madge Moran has recently surveyed the older houses of Whitchurch and gave me this useful information.

3 SRRC, I am grateful to Bill Champion for this information.

4 SRRC, 6001/2737, f.267-68.

5 SRRC, 6001/2737, f.267-68.

6 J. D. Nichol, 'Social and Political Stability in 18th century Provincial Life. A Study of the Career of John Ashby (1722-1779) of Shrewsbury', *Transactions of the Shropshire Archaeological Society*, lix, 1969-74, p. 61.

7 Michael Sayer, who lives at 23, St. John's Hill, has carried out some research into the houses and I am grateful to him for sharing this with me.

8 SRRC, Salt collection, Box 57, Salt 802.

9 SRRC, Salt collection, Box 57, Salt 802.

10 SRRC, Salt collection, Box 57, Salt 802.

11 SRRC, Salt collection, Box 57, Salt 802.

12 SRRC, Salt collection, Box 57, Salt 802.

13 See Angus McInnes, 'The Emergence of a Leisure Town: Shrewsbury 1660-1760', *Past and Present*, No. 120, 1988; Peter Borsay, 'The English Urban Renaissance: The Development of Provincial Urban Culture', in *The Eighteenth Century Town*, London, 1990.

14 All details of Swan Hill Court House: PRO Ref: C110/6 287.

15 Quoted in H. Avray Tipping, *Country Life*, 13 March 1920, p. 339.

16 SeeBarrie Trinder, *A History of Shropshire*, Chichester, 1983, p. 67 and *The Structure of Politics at the Accession of George Third*, London, 1957, pp. 235-298.

17 In 1771, as agent for the Newport estates, Bolas repaid the money that Pritchard had expended upon the Eyton house at Eyton.

18 Victoria County History , *A History of Shropshire*, Volume III, p. 268.

19 Isaac Ware, *A Complete Body of Architecture*, London, 1767, p. 468.

20 Ware, p. 295.

21 Dan Cruickshank and Neil Burton, *Life in the Georgian City*, London, 1990, p. 165.

22 David Lloyd and Peter Klein, *Ludlow: A Historic Town,* Chichester, 1984, p. 68-9.

23 P*assages from the Diaries of Mrs. Philip Lybbe Powys*, ed. E. J. Cleminson, London, 1899, p. 135.

24 By writers such as Alec Clifton Taylor and Christopher Hussey.

25 '27 Broad Street, Ludlow, Shropshire', Michael Hall, *Country Life*, 25 July 1996, pp. 57-62.

26 Ware, p. 325 and p. 327.

27 *Broad Street its houses and residents through eight centuries*, Ludlow Historical Research Paper No. 3. Birmingham, 1979, p. 27.

28 Mark Girouard, *The English Town*, 1990 edition, p. 107.

29 Rachel Labouchere, *Abiah Darby*, York, 1988, p. 74.

30 Wolverhampton information from PRO C110/6.

31 PRO, Estimate dated 1763, C110/6, 287.

32 PRO, Estimate dated 1763, C110/6, 287. The plan has not survived.

33 PRO, Red Lyon Account 1765, C110/6, 23647.

34 PRO 'Red Lyon Account' 1765, C110/6, 23647.

35 PRO The Deanery House Account 1764, C110/6, 23647.

36 PRO, The Deanery House Account November 1765, C110/6, 23647.

37 PRO The Deanery House Account November 1765, C110/6, 23647.

CHAPTER 9

'This Ancient Structure'. Work on older buildings.

1-9: A general view of Broad Street, Ludlow.

As I have said, Broad Street, Ludlow is considered one of the finest streets in a provincial urban town in the country but what makes it even more interesting is that most of the houses hide their earlier origins under the fashionable updating that took place in the middle of the 18th century. I heard a visiting teacher telling his school party about Ludlow's architecture; he described the buildings in the top half of Broad Street which include some timber-framed ones as older and the Georgian-fronted ones in the lower part down to the Broad Gate as newer. Of course he was partly right, but that was only half the story and the whole explanation of the modernisation scheme might have proved more interesting to the group of children standing freezing on the street corner.

Today Broad Street is appreciated for its elegance as it slopes gracefully down towards the river, but the rather obvious point has to be remembered that once it was modern and new. As now, not everyone admired the new: Lord Torrington, who admittedly preferred the 'antique', visited Coombe Abbey in Warwickshire in 1789. 'The old part of the abbey is venerable; the newer tasteless and ugly', he remarked. He had hoped that 'modern taste, join'd to antiquity, ... wou'd produce great taste.'[1] When he saw Foremark, in Derbyshire, which was then thirty years old he found it 'of vile architecture'[2] and near Bakewell he walked around the outside of 'a very old house ... which having been lately repair'd and sash'd, wou'd afford no charms for my inspection.'[3]

Fortunately not everyone had the same opinions as Torrington, otherwise there would have been little refurbishment work for architects such as Pritchard. In this type of work, Pritchard showed he was an architect capable of combining originality with an unusual respect for the past. Houses evolve according to necessity, fashion, finance and change of status and at least one of these criteria can be applied to most of the older buildings on which Pritchard worked.

Was his apparently sympathetic approach unusual? There was an appreciation of older buildings, especially Gothic ones, among some of Pritchard's contemporaries. Batty Langley wrote in the *Grub Street Journal* in 1735, 'I cannot but stop and observe the shameful demolition of the tower of S. Margaret's Church.'[4] Langley thought that as 'the materials were as sound as the first day they were lay'd' the tower could have been restored instead of being rebuilt. Although Langley was not an innovative thinker in much of his work, his *Gothic Architecture, Improved By Rules and Proportions*, did follow a new line of ideas and showed sympathy with at least some parts of the ancient buildings. John Gwynn, Pritchard's near-contemporary 'carpenter turned architect' and fellow Salopian, wrote in 1766

> This custom of mixing Gothick and Modern architecture in the same pile of buildings, has also been practised in the university of Oxford, with great success, and serves to show that very little attention is paid to taste and elegance in places where one would expect to find hardly anything else. If these things are suggested to be done merely because they may produce variety, they should be told, that variety may be produced in Gothick architecture without changing the stile, and that at the same time, a harmony may be produced without destroying the connection of what is already built; in short, very great, noble and elegant things may be done in the Gothick taste, and with proper attention, nor prove so expensive as may be imagined.[5]

Perhaps the word 'expense' could be one of the keys to the amount of work that Pritchard carried out on older buildings. Shropshire landowners, living in a county out of the mainstream of fashion, were perhaps more concerned with cost than their wealthier counterparts and in Pritchard they found an architect who could bring their ancestral houses and castles up to date without too much expenditure.

THE OLD MANOR HOUSE, SUDBOROUGH.

Necessity was certainly the case according to the survey of the 17th century Old Manor House at Sudborough in Northamptonshire, mentioned in an earlier chapter when Pritchard went with Edward Smith, a carpenter, and Robert Braybrook, a mason, to look at the work and give an estimate of the cost. Northamptonshire is a good distance from Shropshire, a drive of three hours today, and in 1776 he was involved in the Iron Bridge designs, the surveys of Powis Castle and Kyre Park, Ludlow Guildhall and in looking after

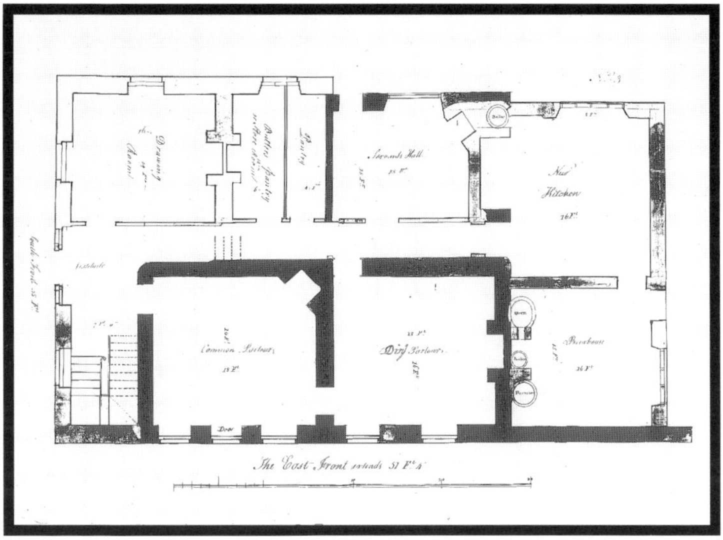

2-9: *Plan of The Old Manor House, Sudborough, 1776, probably by Pritchard.*

his own estate at Eyton. The fact that he died in 1777, after a long illness, also indicates that he would want to delegate to someone locally, such as Edward Smith and Robert Braybrook.

In a document dated June 1775, Pritchard said that he found 'that great part of the Roof is in so ruinous a State and Condition that it will soon fall in unless it be taken down.'[6] An addition in brackets noted that Pritchard had made this assessment 'according to the best Judgement and belief.' The gable end on the east front, 'being composed of bad small stones is much rent and shaken and the old kitchen and Brewhouse is in so bad a state that it cannot with safety be Inhabited, the Roof Stairs Floors and falling Ceilings being very rotten', so Pritchard considered that it would be better to take down most of the old house and rebuild it.

He drew up a plan and made an estimate which came to £566. 7s. 5d. for repairing and rebuilding the house according to the plan. This seems a small sum considering that the east front was 51ft. long and the depth 38ft. The plan shows the old house in black and the new parts as lighter lines. The entrance door and the drawing room are on the south side with the common parlour and dining room on the east. The plan shows that Pritchard had to rebuild most of the south front and the north side.

The thought of parting with even that amount of money may have been too much for the Newport estate, or change of ownership may have delayed the matter as it was nearly a year before Pritchard swore another affidavit regarding the repairs. It was now proposed that £450. 12s. 8d. 'may be laid out in repairing the Old Manor House.' The reason for this was that it would greatly benefit the 'lunatick's Estate' as there was no other house in the area suitable to accommodate the committee of the estate when they visited the area, which they did frequently. Additionally, as there was furniture 'bed and other things' in the house, it would be of no value if the house was not made water-tight.

Unfortunately the remainder of the document is missing, but it would appear from the house there today that the work was carried out according to Pritchard's original estimate, which drew up a schedule of work for foundations for the new walls, new floors, ceilings, plaistering and stuccoing and plumbing. The materials to be used included Crown Glass and '50 Bushel of lime for pargetting.' The use of the word is interesting as it does not occur in any of Pritchard's other schedules. Terminology in the 18th century was not precise and the three words, pargetting, plaistering and stuccoing, mean almost the same thing but today pargetting is a word used almost exclusively on the eastern side of the country to refer to a type of decorative exterior plasterwork.[7] Does this reinforce the idea that Edward Smith and Robert Braybrook were local men and drew up the estimate with the aid of Pritchard's plans?

The estimate also refers to the installation of a sky-light over the back stairs. The drawing room and dining parlour were papered at a cost of £9. 5s. while the common parlour was stuccoed. The timbers in the roof were renewed and old materials from the house used where possible, but oak was brought in for the 'Sash frames' and 'Yellow deal' for 'the styles of the runners.'

The house, built of coursed local limestone with a hipped slate roof, has been extended since Pritchard's time and its original three bays increased by another two bays on the south front. This addition can be seen in the photograph. The Venetian style 'New Front Door case cramped and leaded to a stone frame' is still there and to the right of the front door, just visible through the window, is 'the neat Oak Staircase with Ramps, Rail and Balusters' which cost £15 including 'Landings'.

3-9: The Old Manor House, Sudborough, in 1947.

The Old Manor House at Sudborough is the furthest point from Shrewsbury that Pritchard is known to have worked. The estimate is dated 19 June and the journey there in summer to carry out the survey would not have been too difficult. However, the actual proposal to spend the money on the building was not put forward until March 1776 and it would be interesting to know if Pritchard went there again but no records for this survive. None of the Newport estate estimates include a fee for him which would indicate that he was acting as the contractor and getting a percentage from the materials used.

It is just possible that the later extension may have been carried out by Thomas Telford. William Pulteney, who had come into the estate of Lord Bath through marriage, commissioned Telford to work on Sudborough rectory and perhaps he did the extension to the Old Manor House at the same time.

CHAPTER 9

LUDFORD HOUSE, LUDFORD.

4-9: Garden elevation of Ludford House.

The work at Ludford House in Ludlow in 1769 was also essential as the medieval timber framing of the ground floor was rotting. The way in which the work was carried out illustrates how fashionable updating could be combined with the retention of older fabric and demonstrates Pritchard's skill at blending in old and new and how well his sense of design was developing by creating a Gothick interior in keeping with the history of the building. At the same time it shows him conforming with the conventions of the period with the fittings advised by Isaac Ware. The work at Ludford is always interesting but never intrusive and it is unfortunate that no correspondence exists from the owner, Sir Francis Charlton, to give us an idea of what he required from the work and if he was satisfied with it when it was completed.

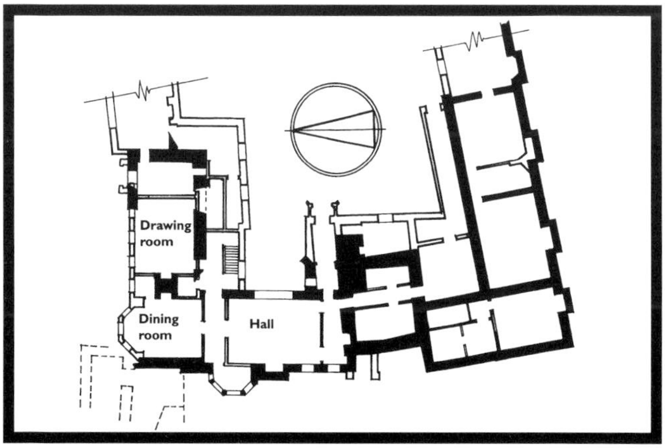

5-9: Plan of Ludford House.

6-9: *The hall at Ludford House.*

Originally the leper hospital of St. Giles, Ludford House was sold at the time of the Dissolution of the Monasteries in the sixteenth century. In 1769 Pritchard drew up the schedule of work for Sir Francis.[8] The Charltons were a family who acquired land and wealth at the time of the Dissolution. The plan was to modernise the ground floor to provide more comfortable living accommodation and 'to shoar up carefully the Old Timber framing of the Chamber story next to the Terras' so that rotten timber could be replaced.

Today the East, or garden, front of Ludford House is a mixture of this 'Old Timber framing' over a stone wall. Pritchard also planned to take down

> the present staircase and partition adjacent to the chimney in the intended drawing room. To take down the stone wall and place in large sash frames and sashes made of fine oak and glazed with London Crown Glass. To shoar up carefully the timber wall about the present staircase, take down the stonework and erect the intended wall as laid down in the plan.

7-9: *The entrance passage at Ludford House.*

Unfortunately Pritchard's plan does not survive, but later work on the house has revealed that brick piers were built to underpin the older work above when the staircase was removed. The plan shows the new 18th century work in light outlines. To get from the courtyard into the medieval hall a new entrance passage was created, with a round vaulted ceiling with shallow ribs, to give an impression that it has always been there; the medieval screens passage was retained. The hall was divided and a depressed arch leads into another newly formed passage which was put across one end of it. The other half of the hall, or it may have been the parlour, was transformed into a dining parlour with a bow window on the garden side. The medieval oriel window on the north wall of the old hall was left intact, but on the other side of the hall a larger Gothick-style sash window was inserted 'to light the staircase and passage.'

The work for the new dining parlour included plans to 'alter and new set the chimney piece and fit up the room with the present old wainscot in the best manner with new door and architraves.'[9] Pritchard's inclusion of the wainscot is another example of the use of the old materials, as he had already done at Bitterley Court. By this date panelling had gone out of fashion although ten years earlier Ware had recommended it for a parlour as being 'the neatest.' Pritchard did not usually include wooden panelling in any of the best rooms of the houses that he built; they were all plastered and stuccoed. However, at Ludford the panelling was also retained in the drawing room where there is a carved chimney piece, probably by Pritchard. The Rococo style of the scrolling foliage echoes the sinuous design of the earlier plasterwork on the beams above it, another sign of Pritchard's skill at interpreting the character of a building.

8-9: The stairs at Ludford House.

The new staircase was 'intended to be wrot. with fine oak with neat moulded hand rail and baluster.' At this period the staircase had become a prominent feature of a house;[10] Pritchard either replaced it or made a fine new additional staircase in a more conspicuous place, as he did at 27 Broad Street, Ludlow, and Gaines, among others. All the staircases are of high-quality workmanship and with the introduction of smaller and slimmer newel posts the balusters had become lighter as the century progressed.[11]

9-9: Windows at Ludford House.

In the main first floor bedroom, leading out onto a balcony created above the bow window of the dining parlour, are Gothick windows and a door made up of pointed arches containing cusped arches and supported by cast iron cluster columns with stiff leaf capitals. Did Pritchard design this wonderful range of windows? If so, they are an early example of Gothick cast iron and it would be a real tribute to him if he had the flair and imagination to create them. Regrettably, the specification says nothing about them.

The cost of all the work at Ludford, including instructions to 'finish and make good the whole intended alterations and repairs according to the plan so that the parlours, staircase and the whole of the Old Building, occasion'd by the alteration be made substantial and compleat' came 'to the sum of two hundred and eighty pounds'. The finished house contains many typical Pritchardian details such as the shallow ribbed 'vaulting' in the entrance hall, Gothick windows, depressed arches along the passages and a carved chimney piece in the drawing room.

In his *Country Life* article, Avray Tipping did not approve of the restoration work and considered that 'The garden gains nothing from the front of the house which looks on to it, for the Victorian treatment of windows and the modern slating of its roof make it disappointing after enjoying the picturesqueness of the north and west sides that retain so much of the ancient character.'[12] The roof was reslated in the 19th century and Tipping knew about the imminent collapse of 'the superstructure ... so that a local mason was called in to set up rough stone walling that sadly mars the original design, but might easily be removed and the old arrangement replaced.' Eighty years after he wrote that, the 'rough stone walling' is still in place.

POWIS CASTLE.

The work at Ludford House illustrates Pritchard's practical and sympathetic approach to work on older houses and another example is the survey of 1772 of Powis Castle, an even older building. This project demonstrates his skill at redesigning an interior to suit both the client and the situation, but unlike Ludford House, this work was not carried out or if it was, it no longer survives in the same form.

Powis Castle, near Welshpool, is basically a medieval Border Marches castle, which had been 'the fortress of a dynasty of Welsh princes.'[13] It stands in an elevated position above the 'old-fashioned' gardens, which have been renowned for over two hundred years.[14] Today the red sandstone castle retains its fortified appearance with round towers, turrets and battlements that have been added over the centuries to give it a very asymmetrical appearance. By the 18th century, the castle was much in need of repair. 'About £3,000 laid out upon Powis Castle would make it the most august place in the Kingdom,' Lord Lyttleton wrote in 1756.[15] Bishop Pococke, visiting at about the same time, agreed: 'on the whole, for a situation of this kind, it is the finest place I ever saw.'[16]

The castle had been owned by the Herbert family since the 16th century, but their Catholic affiliations with the Stuarts caused them to be stripped of their titles and estates in 1688. These were restored to the family in 1722 but their financial fortunes were not

revived until later in the century when a daughter married the second son of Lord Clive of India. Shortage of money could explain the hesitation about carrying out the work as proposed by Pritchard.

Some of the varied sources of income for carrying out work have already been mentioned; others include the Charltons of Ludford House who were lawyers working for the Council of the Marches and a 17th century member of the family was Lord Chief Justice of Chester. The money for the improvements to Croft came from industry, as the Knights of Downton were wealthy iron masters, but major work on the Castle only became feasible when Elizabeth Johnes inherited money on the death of her father.

Pritchard was involved with work at Powis

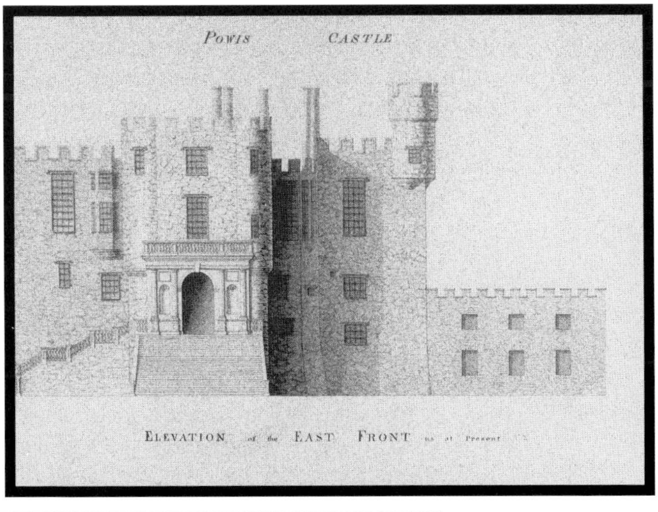

10-9 & 11-9: East elevation of Powis Castle.

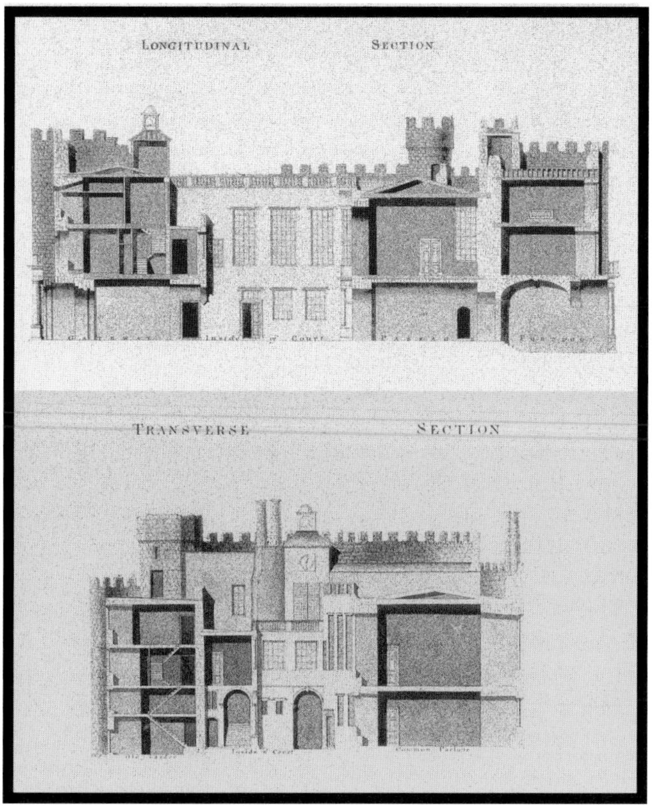

12-9 & 13-9: Longitudinal and transverse sections of Powis Castle by Pritchard, 1772.

Castle over at least six years. The Powis Castle papers contain an account for two guineas dated 3 and 4 September, 1770 for 'My journey to Powis Castle attending Mr. Pryce surveying the castle and makeing a report in writing of the same.'[17] Pritchard continued to work there during 1771 when he 'attended' the agent, Mr. Probert and made a 'survey of the kitchen and rooms adjacent' and put forward a proposal for the servants' quarters to be completed in the 'plainest and least expensive manner.'[18] In October he travelled to the castle to direct the plumber's work and survey the building for another two guineas. In November he went again to supervise the workmen and included surveys of the chancels of Montgomery and Welshpool churches on the way. Richard Lee, the carpenter from Shrewsbury, was working at the Castle in 1771 and was paid £23. 18s. 3d. in an account signed by Pritchard.

Also in October 1771 Pritchard was instructed to make minor alterations to the offices of Powis Castle based on his earlier survey of 1770. Mr. Probert, together with Mr. Hodges, had to organise materials for the work. Over the winter 'sufficient timber, boards and bricks' were to be prepared 'for making the alterations on the south side.' It was instructed that the bricks must be made in some of the meadow ground in case clay cannot be found elsewhere but let a thorough search be first made above the Castle particularly in the Vale on North side.' As 'the timber at Kingswood will not then be proper for all uses except boards ... Let enquiry be made as to that matter with the price and quality thereof. Will not Dale [deal?] be much cheaper had at Bristol and brought up the Severn than any other way.'[19]

The notes of journeys made are the only ones existing for Pritchard, unlike Mylne whose diary records almost every mile. Powis Castle is about twenty miles from Shrewsbury and as Pritchard went there regularly to survey the work it has to be assumed that he did the same on other jobs and therefore would have often been on the road during his busy periods. Torrington's diaries describe in detail the pleasures and miseries of travelling by horseback and Pritchard's experiences, although not so far afield and on more familiar territory, would have been similar.

Pritchard had begun work at Powis Castle for the first Earl of Powis and the survey was drawn up before his death in 1772. He was succeeded by his seventeen-year-old son as second Earl of Powis, described rather vividly by Torrington some years later as 'a mean silly man, the bubble of his mistress (and of his steward consequently) who rarely comes here, to sneak about for a day or two.'[20]

As Lord Lyttleton had noted, by the middle of the 18th century Powis Castle needed modernising; it was run down and out of date as well as being inconvenient to run as a domestic dwelling. Pritchard was therefore 'order'd' by the Earl and Countess of Powis to make 'a Plan of the Present Castle and Buildings with a Plan and Section of the ground 60 yards round them ... so as to enable His Lordship to have the whole further considered in London.'[21] Lord Powis was a friend of Thomas Hill, and John Ashby, the Shrewsbury lawyer, was agent for the Powis Estates, so Pritchard was a natural choice as architect. The survey was found tucked into a folio together with 'A copy of Mr. Pritchard's Letter to the Earl of Powis Which shews a description and reference to the Improved Plans according to his design,' dated 'Salop 14th Feby. 1772.' The package, for which Pritchard received a fee of thirty guineas, consisted of sixteen plans, only some of which have survived, together with a survey of the whole site including the gardens.

In his survey, Pritchard showed a definite sympathy with the 'antique.'

> The Dining and Anti Room ceilings are ornamented with historical paintings and the Drawing Room Ceiling enriched with very old stuco'd ornamental figures representing the Celestial Sphere, the windows are large, modern sashes, the flooring tho' old and out of level in places, is in a tolerable good condition. The whole of this apartment makes a noble appearance and ought to be preserved nearly in the present state.

The appreciation of the 'very old stuco'd ornamental figures' is interesting; at Ludford House no attempt had been made to update the earlier plasterwork. Although this work is not comparable with the quality of the work at Powis, it was nevertheless allowed to remain. Similarly at Bitterley Court, when a new Rococo chimney piece was installed the earlier unsophisticated plasterwork frieze in the room was not changed.

Pritchard's survey of Powis involved all the rooms as well as listing the contents of some areas. In the Long Gallery there are 'the curious Busts of the Caesars wrought in the purest statuary marble with vestments of fine Jasper and other choice marbles.' As he used a variety of marbles for both monuments and fireplaces, Pritchard showed a particular interest in the busts.[22]

He considered that 'the Bed Chamber on the South side, known as the King's Chamber, has a most elegant appearance and should be preserved to keep up the stile and dignity of the Old Castle', but he also wished to improve the facilities and make the most of the magnificent views. Bearing in mind the problems at Tern Hall with the high windows, he commented that from the Terrace 'you command one of the most pleasing views in Britain' and for this reason he criticised the rooms on the South side as being 'low and of small dimensions, the windows of a disagreeable figure and proportion, and not at all suitable to the dignity of this ancient structure and the uncommon fine prospect it commands ...'

He pointed out several places where the building was in need of repair, especially the grand painted staircase where 'the back wall has set from the sides ... This wall with care may be supported so as to remain in its present state, then the crack in the plastering may be made good and an artist found to finish the paintings.' The roof was also in need of attention. It was covered with 'lead of about eight or nine pounds to a foot' and 'wanted recasting and relaying.' Pritchard cautioned that some of the roof timbers that lay 'on the stone walls' might 'be found old and decayed at the ends, as is commonly the case with old buildings.'

The arrangement for the servants was also criticised as 'the communication from the kitchen offices to the Castle, is at present extraordinary bad and inconvenient, the Servants are oblig'd to go under the landing of the best stairs to the parlours; at this place there is a doorway cut through in order to go down stairs to the offices which is liable to damage the building and a better way ought by all means to be contrived for this communication.' Here Pritchard is showing concern about the fabric of the building as well as the practical aspects of running the castle and 'the inconveniences and ineligant parts.'

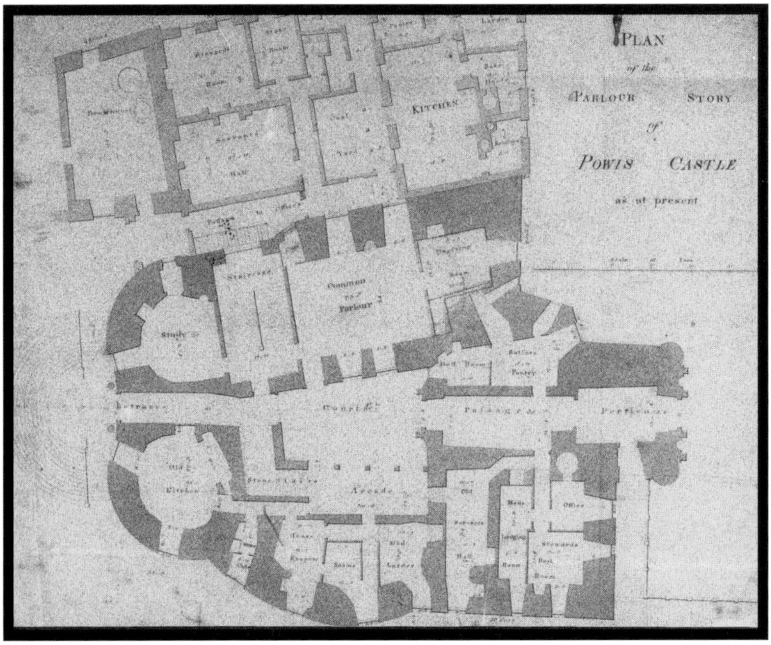

14-9: Plan of the 'Parlour Story' by Pritchard, 1772.

One of the biggest problems in the Castle was 'the want of Good bedchambers' on 'the Parlour Story.' 'The Old Dining Room and the Ante Room to the Drawing Room, now being handsomely finished and very elegant in themselves, I fear will be thought too good to be converted into two Bedchambers and a Dressing Room much wanted on this story', although he did intend making Bedchambers in the attic storey. In order to light a 'long narrow arched passage, without which it will be dismal indeed' at the top of the staircase to the upper story, he 'intended a circular skylight.' Is this an early use of the word here? By 1783 it had travelled over to America and was in use there.[23] Pritchard was much concerned with lightness as he wanted the Courtyard 'kept white washed which will add great chearfullness' to it. Pritchard recommended that the 'rough stone work [walls] be pointed with a proper cement for on this high situation, no stucco will endure or be proper,' a reference to the position of the castle which is exposed to the elements. On the practical side again, 'The drawing room when the alterations are made will be used as a Breakfast Room.' Was this another early example of a word being used?[24]

15-9: Plan of the "Chamber Story' by Pritchard, 1772.

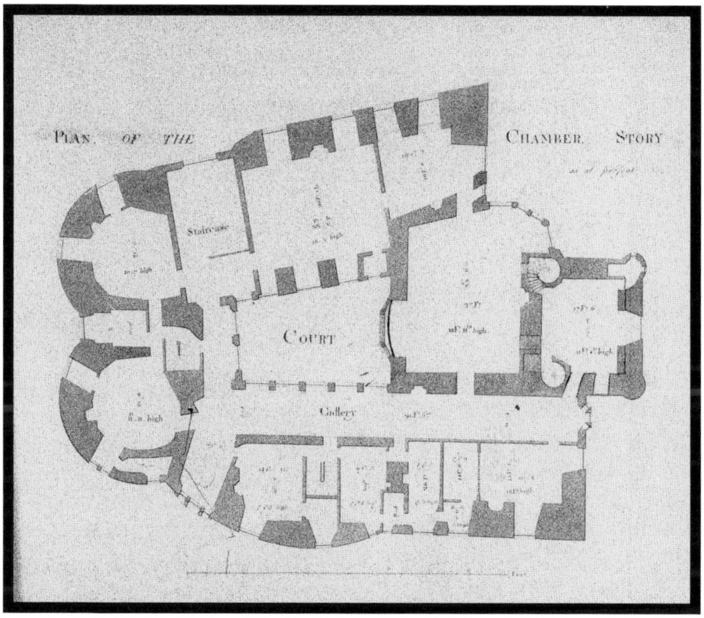

The Plans also included a water closet, 'advantageously placed under the Landing of the Best Staircase.' Although this does not seem to be the most advantageous place, other houses show that this was not unusual as Robert Mylne placed it there in his 1775 plans which he drew up for The Wick in Surrey.

Pritchard tactfully ends the account of the 'Improved Plans': 'In regard to finishing the inside of the rooms proposed by these alterations, Lady Powis will best judge what elegance and expense she chuseth to ornament them.' Lord Powis died in 1772: the work was postponed but some activity must have taken place as Pritchard travelled there in June 1772 to survey 'the Peir that was sunk in the kitchen.' He also gave directions about supporting it and measured the work done by the joiners and 'plaisterers' and charged three guineas instead of the usual two guineas for just surveying. In July he was there again, 'attending Mr. Probert and makeing a plan in order to convert part of the Long Gallery into a Repository for records and other writings.'[25]

The Old Long Gallery, above the stable block, was required for the second Earl of Powis's 21st birthday. 'The only money that has of late years been (mi)spent here was to fit up, over the old offices, a long narrow Ballroom, 108 feet long, and 20 feet broad, in which was given an entertainment, when his l'ship came of age,' commented Lord Torrington in typical caustic style when he visited Powis Castle in 1784.[26]

In his survey Pritchard wrote:

> ... that the Old Long Gallery is not finished having only the naked flooring framed, a coved ceiling and very old semicircular sash windows, glazed with common green glass which is by no means suitable to the room. The walls ... are of the same rough stones as the Castle are very thick stand upright and well. The roof is in tolerable good condition and when repair'd may last a great number of years.

16-9: Balcony in the ballroom at Powis Castle.

In his recommendations he suggested that the walls 'be dashed with fine rough cast in the manner of Stucco.' Work eventually began on the Old Long Gallery in March 1774 and one of the workmen was William Haycock, a carpenter and grandfather of Edward Haycock. Ornamental plasterwork was done by Joseph Bromfield who was paid directly for the work.[27] The gallery at one end of the Ballroom retains its decorative plasterwork by Bromfield, similar to the work at ures or remains in ghostly form oromfield, similar to the work at ures or remains in ghostly form on the walls in the style that Pritchard and Bromfield used, for example, at Gaines.

The Powis Castle accounts for the period March 1774-April 1777 show work carried out on the Ballroom and domestic offices came to almost £2000.[28] This sum included payments to Pritchard: '200 dozen of flooring Quarries for the use of the Ballroom' for £5. 5s., seven tons of brick quarries transported 'from new quay' to the Castle for £2. 9s. and 'the carriage of 200 dozen quarries from Broseley to New Quay' for £3. In March 1777, Pritchard also purchased ironmonger's goods 'for use of the Ballroom, offices etc. as particular account £105. 7s.' and he was paid £3. 19s. as the balance of his surveying bill. In February 1776 he had been paid £80 for 'work done at the new offices at Powis Castle' and in April a further £50 'on account' so altogether he earned a considerable sum from this job.

In 1775 the Earl asked for estimates for the work outlined in the 1772 proposals for the Castle which included 'stuccoing the walls with neat Ornamental plaister cornices, putting up Marble Chimney pieces with suitable Ornaments, papering the Chambers, with Handsome New Doors, Locks and Hinges.' A new brewhouse, wash-house and laundry were also proposed, together with repairs to the kitchens and a housekeeper's room.[29] The total sum for 'thoroughly repairing and finishing the castle in a very handsome and substantial manner' was £10,000. The Earl, through Mr. Probert, asked for a breakdown of the figures. The exterior work came to £2,115 and the alterations to the chamber storey £2,880, large sums then.[30]

By the time of Pritchard's death the proposed work, with the exception of the Ballroom, had not been carried out. When Torrington visited the castle in 1784 he found it 'sadly neglected, and hourly falling to decay. The staircase is painted in the pompous stile of King William's time, the dining room dark, and gloomy; but the upper floor which consists of large, shutter'd apartments commands a most extensive, and glorious prospect ... There is a long gallery fill'd with family pictures; and some pompous bed chamber, but all in dampness, & uninhabited.'[31]

The situation was not much better in 1793 when he visited Powis again. 'It is one of the most neglected, sorrowful places I ever saw. How grievous is the sight of such deserted houses; and to have them possess'd by such owners as Ld. P: who has indeed, trick'd up a frenchify'd drawing room. – The dining room is a gloomy dungeon.'[32]

Pritchard had noted that the drawing room has 'a noble antique appearance' and should be left in its present state. There was nothing in his plans to indicate he would do anything except renew some of the windows as they needed replacing by 'large modern sashes.' What the 'frenchify'd' decoration was is not known; work was carried out to the Castle in the early 19th century by Robert Smirke and again early in the twentieth century by G. F. Bodley. Bodley also shortened the Ballroom and replaced the sash windows.

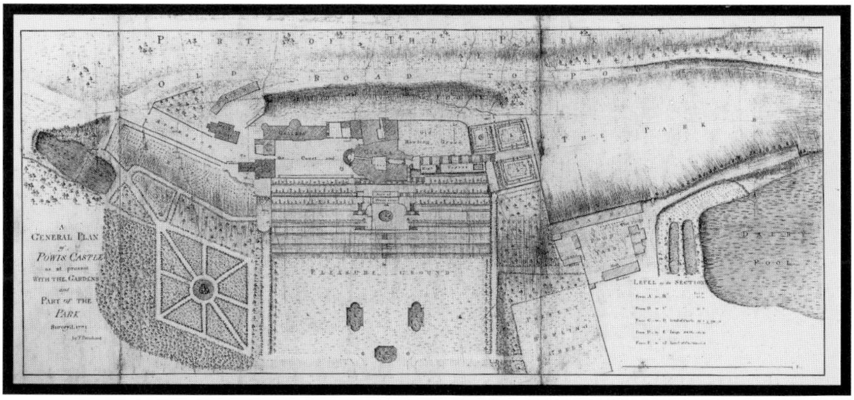

17-9: 'A General Plan of Powis Castle' by Pritchard.

The 1771 'General Plan of Powis Castle as at present with the grounds and Part of the Park' by Pritchard is interesting as it is the only existing drawing of a landscape and garden by Pritchard. It was probably drawn for William Emes 'layer out of Lands and pleasure grounds' who was consulted about 'the Park and Lawns around it.'[33] Pritchard is thought to have worked with Emes at Brockhampton House and Tatton Park.[34]

Pritchard's descriptions of the Castle, the survey and the intended plans, show a sensitivity to the older fabric combined with a practical approach to the restoration of the building from a sound and professional architect. The work represented a major commission for Pritchard spanning many years and involving detailed surveys and drawings. The documentation gives important information about his work generally and shows him as an architect and surveyor making detailed reports and drawings of the castle as well as supervisor of the work and procurer of materials. This sort of long-term supervisory work is the basis of the income of many architects' offices today and was probably just as welcome to Pritchard in the 18th century as it is now.

18-9: The Norman Chapel at Ludlow Castle, by Francis Towne, 1777.

CHAPTER 9

LUDLOW CASTLE.

Another survey of a historic building was the one that Pritchard made of Ludlow Castle in 1771. The castle had been the headquarters of the Council of the Marches until 1689 and then ownership passed to the Crown. It had a romantic past as the home of the young Plantagenet princes in the 15th century and the venue for the first performance of Milton's masque Comus in 1634. Today, although roofless, it still dominates the hill on which Ludlow is built.

In 1868 Thomas Wright, whose father had lived in Ludlow in the late 18th century, wrote about this survey:

> It is certainly not generally known that before the property was alienated from the crown, the government contemplated the demolition of the whole building, and the sale of materials, for which purpose a surveyor from Shrewsbury, named Pritchard, was employed to value it, and to him we owe the following report. It is evident that Mr. Pritchard sought to save the building by wonderfully undervaluing the materials, so as to shew that they would not pay for the work of destruction; and we have to thank him partly, without doubt, for the prevention of so extraordinary an act of Vandalism.[35]

Pritchard's survey of the general decay of the castle concludes:

> Great difficulty will arise in attempting to put a value on so prodigious a quantity of rough stones ... Many of the stones are rotten and perishable. And were the whole premises ordered to be converted into one mount of land or gardens, the stone walling would be of little more value than the expense of taking down, clearing, and carrying away rubbish, levelling and making good the land.

The Ludlow Castle survey was done on the instructions of Somerset Davies, the Ludlow lawyer, and sent to the Surveyor General. Davies's attached letter arouses suspicion that protection of the ancient fabric was not uppermost in his mind, whatever Pritchard's opinion. Davies rather too vehemently emphasised the worthlessness of the castle and the materials and the waste of money paying a Governor £30 a year, especially as there were no arms or ammunition to protect. He considered that it would be 'some advantage to the Crown to be relieved from such unprofitable charge.'

There is no way of knowing what was in Pritchard's mind but it is interesting that someone, not all that long after his death, should have considered that preservation of the old castle was his aim. What then had Davies in mind for the castle? Was he planning a profitable deal to let it to the Earl of Powis who took the lease in 1771, but he died a year later? His widow laid out the walks around the

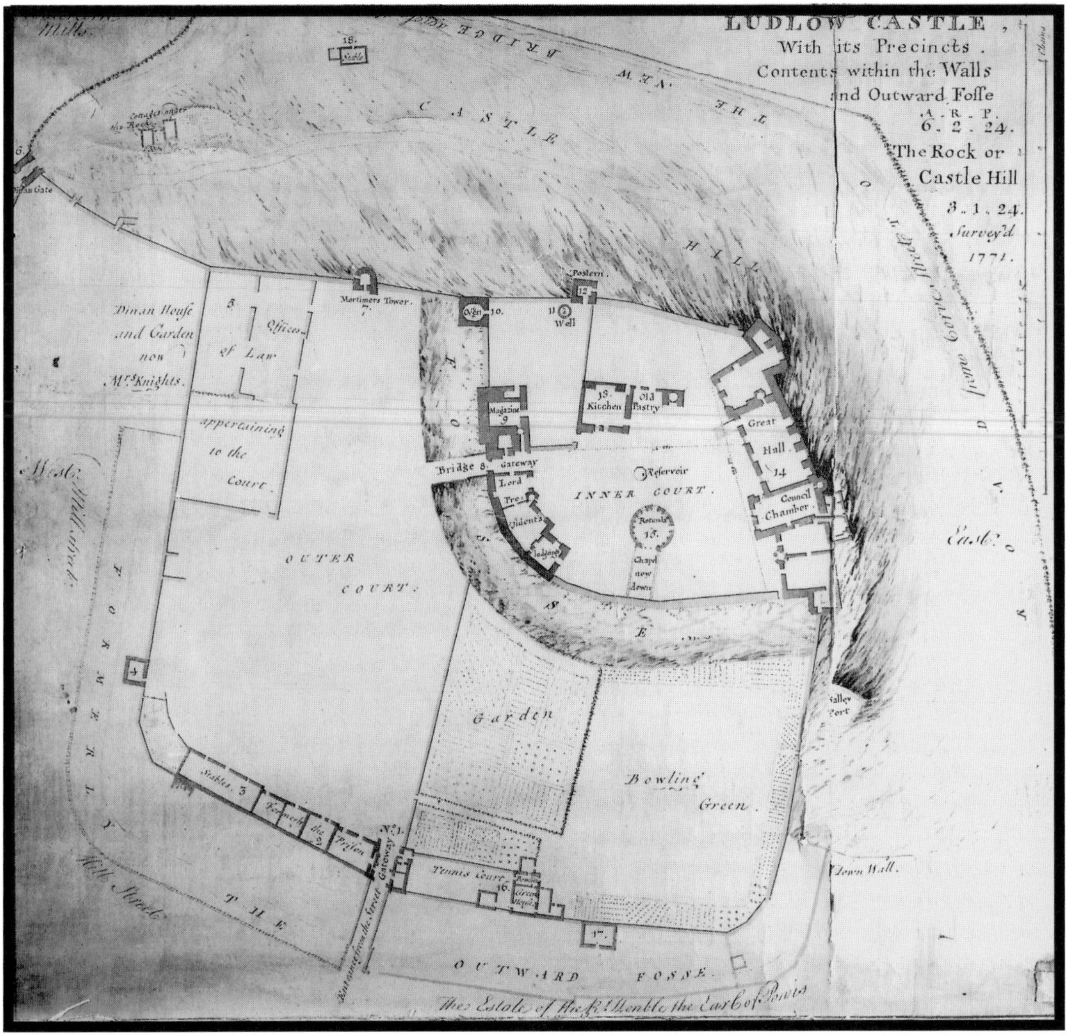

19-9: Plan of Ludlow Castle by Pritchard, 1771.

castle walls. The couple knew Ludlow well as the Earl had been a member of the Corporation for many years.

Pritchard's survey, while emphasising the ruined nature of the fabric, gave a good description of the various areas as well as information about Hill, the tenant of Bowling Green House, who occupied the castle's stables. He paid £18 annual rent with responsibility for repairs but had let the roof get in a bad condition. Pritchard allowed his admiration of the chapel to creep into the survey: 'the doorway and a few small pillars with arches over them being rather perfect, are the only ornament left about the castle.'

Torrington when he visited Ludlow in 1784 remarked, with relief, that 'the late Prince of Wales sent a surveyor to inspect ... the castle, who reported its great decay, and the large sum that wou'd be required to render it habitable and princely, all thoughts of its restitution were dropt; so now Ludlow Castle is devoted to devastation.'[36]

EYTON TURRET, SHROPSHIRE.

What sort of houses did Pritchard live in? In Shrewsbury his house at the top of Pride Hill no longer exists, so the information about the house at Eyton on Severn is all the more valuable. Eleanor Pritchard died the year after her husband took the lease of 'a Farm and Lands at Eyton' at 'Ladyday at several yearly rents amounting together to the sum of Forty seven pounds a year.'[37] The farm was leased from the estate of 'John Newport Esquire, the Lunatick'.

The history of the Newport house on this site is unclear; there had been a 'vast mansion' which may have been built in 1607 by Francis Newport, but evidence suggests that there was a much earlier building on the site as pieces of carved stone now lie on the ground and are incorporated in walls and architraves. There is also some carved stone around the gate in the garden wall and springing for vaulting nearby. With its proximity to the river and high ground vantage point it does seem likely that a building was there from a relatively early date.

By the time that Pritchard took over the lease in 1767, there was only a ruin. Some of the work that he carried out to get the farm and land into order included 'raising up the Foundation, levelling the Old Mount and carrying away the Stones and Rubbish whereby about three Acres of good arable Land has been made where the Old Hall and Offices with their Appurtenances stood and which was of no Service when he first became Tenant ... nor for sometime afterwards and until [he] begun to level and improve the same.'[38] Pritchard remarked in his evidence that 'there also being two old Turrets in the Wall in the Garden which did belong to Eyton Hall before the same was demolished and taken away.'[39] From all accounts it would appear that there were the remnants of the mansion left; now nothing remains except some humps and bumps in the field between the two turrets.

20-9: Eyton Turrett in 1814.

21-9: Pritchard's house at Eyton on Severn, probably in the 19th century.

Pritchard took over one of the ogee-capped turrets which he 'repaired' and 'made such an additional Building thereto as made the same a compleat and convenient Dwelling House' for himself and his family. Unfortunately the turret that Pritchard repaired and incorporated into his 'Dwelling House' no longer survives and the only evidence of its original hexagonal shape is an angled wall in the present farmhouse. The ogee cap was still there in 1814 as a view by David Parkes reveals, but it had gone by the time the photograph was taken.

It appears, from examination of the timbers in the attic storey, that there was an older building on the site of Pritchard's house. In some of the first floor rooms there are heavy beams which have been left exposed, or papered over, indicating that essential structural beams were left in place. One of the roof timbers was re-used from an older building as there is evidence that it once joined onto a wind brace.

In the document listing the work carried out Pritchard stated that as 'a Builder' he 'constantly employs several workman.' He made the point that the work he had done at Eyton 'would have cost any other person, not in the same Business, a much larger Sum,' as he had not charged for his own 'trouble attendances and loss of time.'[40] He made this point again when he listed the workmen involved in the schedule of expenditure he drew up. Although Pritchard must have had a workshop to keep up with all the work he was involved in at that time, this is the only reference found to his employment of labour.

He also referred to 'my team carrying lime, stones and other materials 40 days at 5s. per day.' To justify keeping a team he would have been regularly supplying materials and if he kept this team in Shrewsbury, his yard near St. Mary's Church must have been large to house them as well as a quantity of materials. An extra team was hired for a week in March 1767 for carrying soil from the foundations at a cost of £1. 16s. In total for 1767, over seventy days were spent by a team and five horses carrying materials at a total cost of £18. 15s.

When work started in earnest payments were made for brick and stone work to J. Birch and W. Croft the Brickmaker; to Joseph Dale the Carpenter and to John Chilton for sinking the well. Peck of Wenlock was paid for lime. Peck was also the supplier of lime for the Foundling Hospital, an example of the same names occurring over the different projects. Mr. Higgins of Wellington was paid for nails, while sprigs (small nails) came from George Goodby. Pritchard supplied 1000 feet of better quality flooring boards from his own yard at a cost of £12. 10s.

Pritchard listed the wages to the workmen in 1767 and the weekly amount paid out during June, July, August and September averaged around £8. In October 1767 as Pritchard was working away from the area 'Edward Loyd' was instructed to pay the workmen £11. 0s. 2d.[41] Is this the same 'Edward Lloyd', the lawyer in Shrewsbury who had witnessed the will of Sir Richard Lyster two years previously?[42]

Some of the slates for the work came from Llangwynog, near Bala and Pritchard brought along 1000 feet of 'better quality from my yard',[43] an indication of the quantity of materials stored there. An expensive item was glass with a total of £16. 1s. spent in one year.[44] In December a further payment was made for sinking a well and supplying pump.

A large amount of hair was used in the construction for the plaster – nine stone on 8 August came from Mr. Hesketh while six days later twenty eight bushels came from Mr. Corbet in Wenlock. In December more hair was bought and paid for in advance up to March 1768 to the value of £9. 6s. White deals, yellow deals of varying sizes and 7000 nails were supplied for the work in early August 1767. Other materials included linseed oil, whitening and red lead and 'Bristol Lime'. After the glass, one of the most expensive items was locks; £8. 10s. 6d. was paid to Mr Lane of Wolverhampton for 'locks and carriage' confirming that property in the 18th century was no more secure than today, a fact borne out by the number of crimes reported in the *Shrewsbury Chronicle.*

Lodgings were obtained for the workmen and regular payments made for this; Percks the shoemaker was one of the people who provided lodgings. Four dozen candles were supplied for them in December. It was more practical for them all to lodge on the spot than walk or be transported from Shrewsbury daily as the five or so miles travelling could take time, especially in the winter months. It is impossible to know if the men – John Dale, Steenton and Beddows – were from Pritchard's own yard or had been hired for this job, but we do know that Yates, the stonemason at Eyton, worked regularly with Pritchard.

The items for the interior give clues to Pritchard's own choices for his home. The parlour floors had oak boards; a 'set of ogees' and 'two entablatures' were carved at a cost of £5 and three of the chambers were papered. There is an entry for 'hanging bells.'[45] Were these bells for the servants? Mr. Prosser supplied 'colour for the chamber,'[46] but there is no indication of what colour it was. Hinges, latches, catches and 'front plates' were all bought.

One of the largest amounts, £13. 16s. 3d., paid in 1768, was to 'Edw.[d] Wilcox in full for Smiths work done, as Iron Barrs to windows casements Chimney Barrs &c.'[47] In addition £6. 18s. was paid for 'ironmongery goods used in the building' with a further £3. 4s. for some more of the same in 1769. A chimney piece was made by Swift who was paid £1. 11s. 6d. for nine days' work carving the ornaments for it.[48] Expense was not spared and the last item in the account is 'to five marble and one Bidford stone chimney piece £33. 6s.'[49]

Unfortunately these chimney pieces have not survived and there is only a small piece of carving around an internal arch to tell us of the quality of the work that Pritchard put into his own house. Some of the original cast iron grates, no doubt from Coalbrookdale, remain in the upper rooms and attic storey.

22-9: Pritchard's house today.

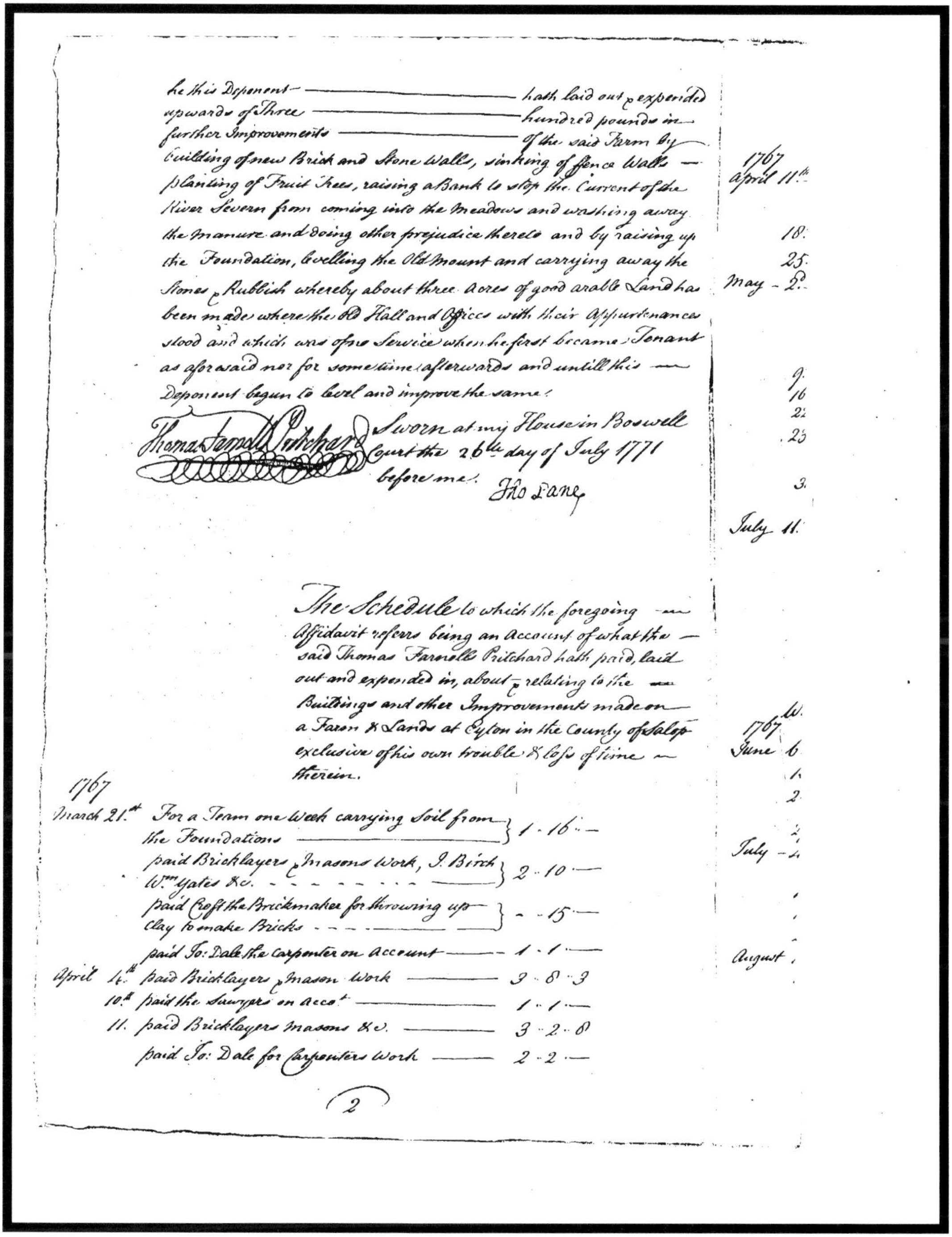

he this Deponent — hath laid out & expended upwards of Three hundred pounds in further Improvements of the said Farm by building of new Brick and Stone Walls, sinking of Fence Walls — planting of Fruit Trees, raising a Bank to stop the Current of the River Severn from coming into the Meadows and washing away the Manure and doing other prejudice thereto and by raising up the Foundation, levelling the Old Mount and carrying away the Stones & Rubbish whereby about three Acres of good arable Land has been made where the Old Hall and Offices with their Appurtenances stood and which was of no Service when he first became Tenant as aforesaid nor for sometime afterwards and untill this Deponent begun to level and improve the same.

Thomas Farnolls Pritchard

Sworn at my House in Boswell Court the 26th day of July 1771 before me.
Tho Lane

The Schedule to which the foregoing Affidavit refers being an Account of what the said Thomas Farnolls Pritchard hath paid, laid out and expended in, about & relating to the Buildings and other Improvements made on a Farm & Lands at Eyton in the County of Salop exclusive of his own trouble & loss of time therein.

1767			
March	21st	For a Team one Week carrying Soil from the Foundations	1 · 16 · –
		paid Bricklayers & Masons Work, J. Birch Wm Yates &c.	2 · 10 · –
		paid Croft the Brickmaker for throwing up Clay to make Bricks	– · 15 · –
		paid Jo: Dale the Carpenter on Account	1 · 1 · –
April	4th	paid Bricklayers & Mason Work	3 · 8 · 3
	10th	paid the Sawyers on Acct	1 · 1 · –
	11.	paid Bricklayers Masons &c.	3 · 2 · 8
		paid Jo: Dale for Carpenters Work	2 · 2 · –

(2)

23-9: Extract from Pritchard's valuation for the work done at his house at Eyton, 1771.

Pritchard looked upon the work with pride as he wrote 'paid ... for painting my house &c £6. 16. 6.'[50] He remained at Eyton for the rest of his life as he had 'a Lease for 21 years' but unfortunately he only enjoyed six of them. He had put a great deal of effort into the house and its proximity to Iron Bridge was a positive factor due to his increasing involvement with the use of iron for architectural purposes. His only surviving child, Anne, was married at nearby Wroxeter Church.

1 *The Torrington Diaries*, Volume II, p. 113.

2 *The Torrington Diaries*, p. 163.

3 *The Torrington Diaries*, p. 191.

4 Quoted in Alastair Rowan, 'Batty Langley's Gothic', in *Studies in Memory of David Talbot Rice*, Edinburgh, 1975, p. 204. It was written by Batty Langley in the *Grub Street Journal*, LV, 6 February 1735.

5 John Gwynn, *London and Westminster Improved*, London, 1766, p. 46.

6 PRO, Newport Papers, C110/6, 23647, The Manor House, Sudborough.

7 Richard Neve, *The City and Country Purchaser and Builder's Dictionary*, London, 1726, defined pargetting as 'the plastering of walls', p. 215.

8 Plan and Schedule for Ludford House are at the SRRO, Morgan Collection Box 25.2, Ludford Park 783.

9 Ware, pp. 327-8. Cupboards were made in the spaces either side of the fireplace as advised by Ware, who had a word to say on almost every aspect of Georgian house building. 'In planning out the several rooms, the architect must not forget, on any occasion, to make the best of all natural recesses for closets ... There is a multitude of things that must be always at hand and never in sight ... nothing can be more needful than a place of reception for them.' We would all agree with that!

10 Ware, p. 487. He advised, 'there is no part of a house where the eye is more naturally directed upwards than the stair-case ... in passing upstairs the eye is naturally directed to the sides and top and this justifies the finishings usually bestowed upon these parts of an edifice.'

11 According to Langley, the 'twisted rail at the lowermost Stair' was only considered appropriate to small buildings; 'magnificent Buildings' required 'a grand Staircase with a Pedestal' following the 'Custom of the Ancients.' Batty Langley, *The Builders Compleat Assistant*, 2nd Edition, c.1750, p. 166.

12 H. Avray Tipping, 'Ludford House', *Country Life*, 3 March 1917, pp. 208-209 and Arthur Oswald, 'Ludford House', *Country Life*, 2 September 1949.

13 Further information from *Powis Castle*, a National Trust publication, 1989.

14 George, Lord Lyttleton, *A Journey into Wales*, 1757, p. 40. Quoted in *Powis Castle*, p. 40.

15 *Powis Castle*, p. 4.

16 Richard Pococke, Bishop of Ossory and Meath, *The Travels Through England of Dr. R. Pococke*, 2 Volumes, London, 1888, Volume ii, p. 17.

17 National Library of Wales, (NLW) Powis Castle Deeds and Documents (Powis Castle), 20590.

18 NLW, Powis Castle; for further information see James Lawson and Merlin Waterson, 'Pritchard as Architect and Antiquary at Powis', *The National Trust Yearbook, 1975-76*, London, pp. 8-11.

19 Lawson and Waterson, pp. 8-11.

20 *The Torrington Diaries*, Volume III, pp. 295-6.

21 The information is taken from a typescript of the 'Survey and Description of the Improved Plans' which was at Powis Castle at the time we saw and photographed them.

22 Over twenty years later, Torrington remarked on their 'great size and weight' and he would exchange them 'for some comforts' in the Castle as there was 'not one carpet, not one bed fit to sleep in, nor, probably one hogshead of wine!!' *The Torrington Diaries*, Volume III, p. 296.

23 Carl R. Lounsbury, *An Illustrated Glossary of Early Southern Architecture and Landscape*, Oxford, 1994, p. 333. There is also the reference to the skylight at Sudborough in 1775.

24 The term was used on the plans at Downton Hall. Mark Girouard, (*Life in the English Country House*, London, Penguin edition 1978, p. 234) referring to the middle of the 18th century, wrote that 'many houses had a breakfast room or breakfast parlour, used not only for breakfast but also as a morning sitting room.' John Carr included two Breakfast Rooms at Basildon Park in Berkshire in 1776; an octagonal one on the ground floor and a rectangular one on the floor above.

25 NLW, Powis Castle, 20590, 20 July 1772.

26 *The Torrington Diaries*, Volume I, p. 137.

27 This could explain why accounts for ornamental plasterwork are not included at Hatton Grange and other buildings. If Bromfield was the plasterer for these buildings, he would have submitted his own accounts which do not appear to exist now.

28 Payments and information from NLW, Powis Castle, 21209.

29 NLW, Powis Castle, 12390.

30 NLW, Powis Castle, 12390.

31 *The Torrington Diaries*, Volume I, p. 137.

32 *The Torrington Diaries*, Volume III, p. 296.

33 For further information see Gervase Jackson-Stops, *An English Arcadia, 1600-1990.* London, 1991.

34 Keith Goodwey, an authority on Emes, has found no direct connection between the two men. As discussed in Chapter 10, another case of mistaken identity could have arisen at Powis Castle from the casual reading of a forthright letter written by Lord Powis August 1767:

'I am told by Lady Powis that there is a deep rutt made by a cart from one end of the garden at Powis Castle to the other which makes the garden appear as if there were an high road through it. I beg to have the matter explained by you. I mean that by your application to Mr Pritchard about it, I may learn how it came about. I cannot conceive what business a loaded cart could have in the garden! But be that as it will, I desire the rutt aforementioned may be laid smooth and level directly and an account of the expense of doing it kept and delivered to me when I come there ... Having been at no small charge to make the house commodious for my residence I am not a little displeased that Mr Pritchard and the gardener showed the garden to be abused in the manner I hear it is and they must be accountable for it.' (NLW, Powis Castle, 1295.) In this case Pritchard was an estate tenant and Thomas Farnolls is not recorded as working at Powis Castle until 1770.

35 PRO, LRRO 1/19.

36 *The Torrington Diaries*, Volume I, p. 132. Torrington added a note that the amount for repairing the castle was '£30,000 only.' The Prince of Wales was Frederick, father of George III.

37 Public Record Office, Newport Estate papers, (PRO, NE) C110/6 287, f.1.

38 PRO, NE, f.2.

39 PRO, NE, f.1. In 1868 Mrs Stackhouse Acton remarked that a 'small portion remains of the house' and she thought that as it resembled Aston Hall near Birmingham, it could be dated to the early part of the reign of James I. The rather fanciful illustration shows the two surviving turrets, both with their ogee caps, linked by the garden wall with a door in it. This drawing also shows part of an ancient wall with two pointed, or ogee, headed doorways. Mrs. Stackhouse Acton, *The Castles and Old Mansions of Shropshire*, Shrewsbury, 1868, pp. 44-5.

40 PRO, NE, f.1.

41 PRO, NE, f.4.

42 See Chapter 11 for Pritchard's work on the monument for Sir Richard Lyster.

43 PRO, NE, f.3.

44 On 14 August £10. 16s. was paid to Mr. Dewberry for glass (5s. to Mr Bather for carrying it) and on 30 October a further £4. 5s was paid to Mr. Lewis for a case of Bristol Glass.

45 PRO, NE, f.5.

46 PRO, NE, f.6.

47 PRO, NE, f.6.

48 PRO, NE, f.6.

49 PRO, NE, f.7.

'The blunder of an Architect ...' or was it? Some problems at work.

The relationship between client and architect has often been, and still is, an uneasy one. The architect's rôle is a complex one involving designs for the building, providing working drawings, supervising the construction and valuing it to make sure that it conforms to the standard set. The client needs to have confidence in the architect so that the building will fulfil his expectations and be ready on time to the agreed specification and budget. This relationship is not always straightforward and the standard of the workmen involved in the project can sometimes be a deciding factor.

In the 18th century the amateur gentleman architect could make the life of the architect or surveyor carrying out the day-to-day work more difficult. While most clients appear to have been satisfied with Pritchard's work, some accusations of bad workmanship and incompetence have been sometimes wrongly ascribed to him.

SHOBDON COURT, HEREFORDSHIRE.

1-10: The pulpit at Shobdon Church, Herefordshire.

One of these accusations concerned work at Shobdon Court in Herefordshire for Richard 'Dicky' Bateman. This would be less important if it did not lead to Pritchard being ruled out of consideration as the architect for the Strawberry Hill-style Church of St. John the Evangelist, Shobdon and his involvement there is still a matter for debate.[1] The Bateman family had owned the Shobdon estate since the beginning of the 18th century and Sir James Bateman built a large house for himself there.[2] John, 2nd Viscount Bateman, had the estate managed by his uncle, 'Dicky' Bateman and extensive correspondence exists between him and Fallowes, the steward. This correspondence contains many references to Pritchard and concerns 'shoddy work', 'bad materials', absence from duties and many other faults.[3] Other letters reveal that this Pritchard is one of the tenants on the estate who is in charge of the children from the workhouse. Bateman instructed Fallowes to pay Pritchard monthly for the children and keep the account separate from others. A year later Pritchard complained that as Fallowes had let 'the brick ground' and taken it from him, he had 'no ground to keep his cows and consequently he does not know how to support the poor.'[4]

So clearly Thomas Farnolls Pritchard was not involved in the unsatisfactory work and it was a case of mistaken identity which recent writers on the subject have not put right. Pritchard, or Ap Richard, son of Richard, is spelt in a variety of different ways and is a common name along the Welsh Borders.

DOWNTON CASTLE.

Downton Castle on the Shropshire-Herefordshire border is another place where Pritchard's competence has been considered as questionable. In a much-quoted letter of 1772, Richard Payne Knight, wealthy young owner of the Downton Estate, wrote to his uncle, Samuel Nash: 'Let Pritchard's bill be paid in full, but do not tell him I have no intention of imploying him again.'[5] Two months later when Pritchard submitted his bill, Nash wrote to Payne Knight: 'Mr. Prich[d] has this day sent his bill viz. atending 3 times at Downton to fix on a spot for the new byllding, consulting about muterriells and making plans as delivered in, £10.10s.0d.'[6]

2-10: Downton Castle, Herefordshire.

Payne Knight was apparently following the advice of Lord Chesterfield and using a practical person to pick the site and the materials and organise mundane items such as drains. At the time, Payne Knight was on the Grand Tour, learning about Classical architecture on the spot as well as the latest fashions for building and intended to carry out the design of the new house himself.

By 1772 Pritchard was a well-established and respected architect in Shropshire and neighbouring counties and Payne Knight probably did not want to 'dismiss' him completely in case he needed help again on any of the practicalities of the work. The fee of ten guineas paid to Pritchard for the plans compares with other fees for similar work, such as the extensive survey and drawings of Powis Castle for which he was paid thirty guineas. The case against him at Shobdon Court is clearly one of mistaken identity and the dismissal at Downton Castle occurred as a result of a shift of emphasis in the building programme. The problems that arose at Tern Hall are more complex to unravel.

TERN HALL, SHROPSHIRE.

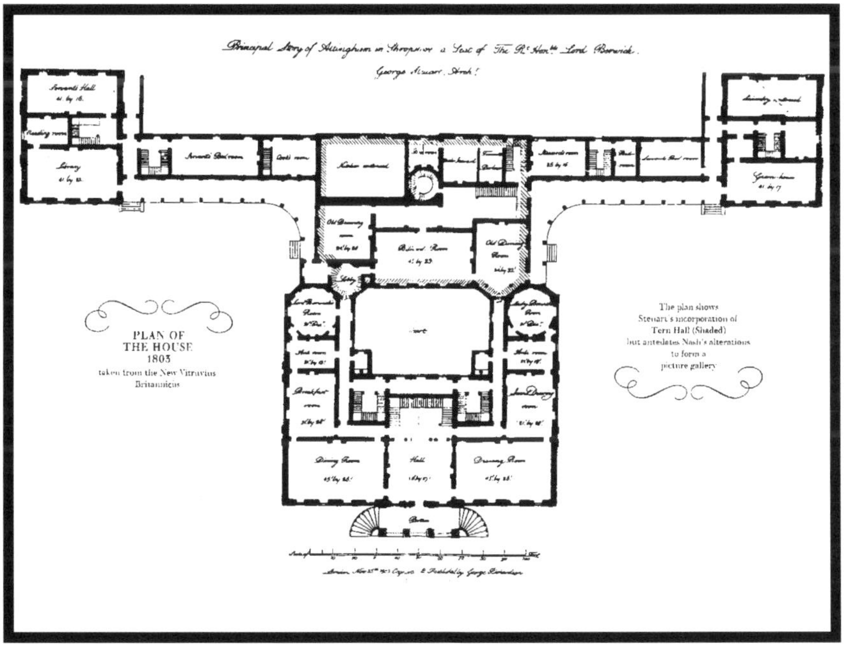

3-10: 'The Principal Story' of Attingham, 1803.

A plan Attingham Park of 1803, taken from *New Vitruvius Britannicus*, shows that Tern Hall survived until alterations by John Nash in 1805 swept most of it away. The old house is indicated by hatched lines and acted as a link between the new building and the two wings. It housed a billiard room, kitchen and servants' rooms and at the front the 'Old Drawing Room' and 'Old Dining Room' which has a canted bay. Drawings by George Steuart show how he incorporated Tern Hall into the new building of Attingham Park and that both canted bays survived his work in the basement area. The shape of one of the canted bays is now reflected in the curved door at the end of the internal passage running down the west side of the building.

The information that we have about the building sequence of Tern, and Pritchard's rôle there, comes from contemporary letters and accounts.[7] One of the only two known illustrations of Tern Hall was made by James Craig in 1775, not long before work started on its replacement. This shows a large house with canted bays at each corner of the front elevation and a stepped bay in the centre of the five-bay central section. Behind the main block is the two-storey 17th century house linked to the new one, but not shown clearly in the Craig picture.

Another view has been identified on The Green Frog Service, a dinner set made for Catherine the Great of Russia;[8] here the house, under the title *Vue de la riviere Severn*, is drawn from a different perspective. One elevation is shown with seven bays and on the other the canted bays have gables over them, a feature confirmed by the Craig drawing.

4-10: View of Tern Hall by James Craig, 1775.

The senior branch of the Hill family had their seat at Hawkstone Hall in the north of Shropshire. Richard Hill, who inherited the Hawkstone estate in 1700, was Deputy Paymaster to the Army in Flanders for William III and royal envoy for the king and later for

5-10: *View of Tern Hall from the Green Frog Service, 1770.*

Queen Anne. He became a wealthy man and used this wealth to improve his Hawkstone properties and to buy the Tern estate for Thomas, son of his sister Margaret; she was married to Thomas Harwood, a member of the Drapers' Company in Shrewsbury. As Richard Hill was not married, he wanted his name to continue and so young Thomas took the name of Hill.[9] He trained as a banker and is thought to have spent some time abroad during this period. His first wife was Anne Powys, a member of a prominent Shropshire family.

Anne Powys died in 1739 and Hill's second wife was Susanna Maria Noel.[10] For much of the year they divided their time between London and Tern Hall, then a modest house close to the Tern Works, an ironworks leased by Thomas Harvey of Stourbridge, one of the Quaker iron masters and a brother-in-law of Abraham Darby I. The lease ran until 1760, but it was given up early and the works were demolished.

The estate at Tern was administered from 1734 for forty years by Thomas Bell, a north country man, and the correspondence between Bell and his employers gives a revealing picture of mid-18th century life in Shropshire.

The 1700 house was '47ft long, 30ft broad and 34ft high with a roof of slate.'[11] Sarah Hill, aunt of Thomas Hill, tenanted the house from 1733 and the rooms listed in an inventory include a little parlour, drawing room, best parlour, hall as well as several garret rooms. A drawing, dated about 1701, shows a two-storey house of six bays with dormer windows and an asymmetrically placed front entrance. After Sarah Hill gave up the tenancy, Thomas took over the lease and ordered that Richard Scoltock should carry out some repairs as rain was coming in. This was to be an emergency measure only as he did not want to spend 'any more money on the house' but he told his father that if he made enough money he would build a better one.

Shortly after her marriage in 1740, Susanna began to show an interest in the house and gardens; the removal of the ironworks, which were noisy and offensive, gave an added impetus to making improvements, but it is not known if Pritchard was first involved then. By 1742 work was progressing well; Bell reported that 'a new stone Chimney piece and Grate to fill up the fireplace in the flaged Hall ...'[12] had been installed and the labourers had been busy 'sinking foundations and cellars.' During refurbishment in 1745, Bell wrote that the painter was at work and thought that the staircase should be painted in a 'mohogany Couller' while the stucco in the parlour and the common parlour was also painted. In 1758 the garrets were prepared for the children and the staircase walls, which had become grimy, were repainted in a more fashionable lighter colour and Pritchard was certainly involved by 1759 which was a busy year at Tern.

Regarding the 'intended alterations' Bell was asked by Thomas Hill to consult Sir Richard Corbett, a neighbouring landowner, and show him the plan,[13] but there is no indication in the correspondence of whose plan it was and this is important as far as later events are concerned.

Apart from surveying, Pritchard arranged for the supply of Grinshill stone for which he was paid ten guineas.[14] This sandstone, which comes in a broad range of colours, is quarried in an area north of Shrewsbury and for centuries was used extensively in Shropshire and all over the country. The Grinshill stone travelled down the River Severn to Atcham and Bell, on Mr. Hill's behalf; 'Pd. the Bargemen to drink that bought the stone down the River.'[15] A month later drink was supplied to the quarrymen at Oakengates and there is an entry recording the carriage of the stone that they had quarried at Oakengates; this cost £4. 10s.[16]

Carriage was a heavy item throughout the accounts; the slate cost £16. 4s but moving it was £32. 8s; Pritchard was repaid this amount in September. The movement of materials usually took place in the summer and autumn months, as the roads were difficult during the winter and wetter periods, so it was a responsible job to make sure that everything necessary was on site. Later entries confirm that Pritchard was acting as contractor as well as surveyor as he was paid for 5371 foot of boards at 3d. per foot and later on for more 'Board and Wainscot' to the sum of £27. 6s.

Around the same time John Yates, the stone mason,[17] Richard Scoltock and Richard White, a carpenter,[18] were involved in a variety of projects on the Atcham estate; they pulled down the forge and the ironworks and rebuilt the corn mills. As Scoltock had worked on the estate over several years, it was natural that he should continue his connection with the house when the rebuilding took place.

Progress was being made as Pritchard was paid £50 'on Acc't for Surveying' on 11 January 1760 and nine months later he was paid another £20 for a further survey. [19] These are quite large sums which suggest that Pritchard also drew up some plans, or at least made working drawings based on a main plan.[20] There are no entries in the accounts for plans drawn by Pritchard, but there is one, dated 24 February 1761, for three guineas to 'Mr. Baker for Drawing a Plan.'[21] This could be William Baker although there must have been some earlier plans which were shown to Sir Richard and subsequently left in London as a letter from Bell to Hill of 14 January 1760 reveals:

> I presume if theres any Plans of the Building here they are in Mr. Prichards possession and as things are wrong he'l not care to produce them but I remember the plan of the front of the House (Elevation as the Builders call it) was left in London by mistake after the Building was begun and Prichard was obliged to draw another, which made him curse and swear a Great Deale and Very Probably that may be found in London still for I dar say it never came here and if you can find it Mr Prowse may find what Hight the Windows were designed to be however I will enquire if Scoltock or White has anything that will shoo it.[22]

Barbara Coulton in her work on Tern Hall implies that these plans were drawn by Pritchard, but there is nothing in the above letter or the accounts to indicate this and Bell does not say what was 'wrong'. If the plans were Pritchard's, Bell would almost certainly have made it clear and it would not have been such a problem to draw another set. The question of 'what Hight the Windows' should be festered for eleven years and came to a head in 1771.

The tone of Bell's references to Pritchard indicated that he regarded him as one of the workmen rather than an architect. Bell appeared to want someone to lay the blame on and Pritchard, as surveyor, was a convenient target. The type of angry behaviour described does not accord with the character that Pritchard projects through his work, although we have no contemporary descriptions of him and no letters from him survive. Another architect who worked at Tern was Robert Mylne and he was known for his 'violent temper' which was as 'hot as pepper' and he had 'a contempt for every art but his own, and for every person but himself.'[23]

Mylne, however, did not arrive in London, after a two-year Grand Tour, until 1759 and there is no record of him in Shropshire until 1766, when he was consulted over the English Bridge. We know that he visited Condover Hall in May that year and 'surveyed Miss Leighton's house.' He produced designs for Tern Hall from 1769 as he recorded in his diary, 'Gave Mr Hill a Drawing of a Cornice for Drawing Room at Tern' and ordered a chimney piece 'of Mr Deval for Mr Hill', but, as far as we know, he was not actively involved with

Tern Hall until 1773.[24]

Pritchard was paid £33. 9s. in September 1760 'for Marble Chimney Piece ... ac. Asp.,' which confirms that he was supplying chimney pieces for the house before those included in *The Drawing Book* which probably date from around 1769. They all contain a record of the work carried out by his own craftsmen, so the chimney piece ordered by Mylne must have been an additional one. In addition Pritchard was paid £20 in April 1764 for another 'marble chimney piece &c. £7. 6s' so this must have been another extra one .[25] None of the designs for Noel Hill in *The Drawing Book* (AIA 69, 72, 73, 74, 75, 76 and 77) can be dated before about 1768 or 1769. They are elaborate designs with a variety of colour marbles – 'New Dove, Sienna French Black and Yellow Vein'd and Jasper' – for the surrounds.

Mrs. Hill died in early February 1760, but this did not prevent the work continuing. Bell reported that

> the Dineing Parlour will be finished in six weeks the Plasterers have Rough Scrated (as they call it) best part of the Rooms the Hall excepted and they propose to prick up the Cornish [cornice] in the two middle bedchambers and to finish them as soon as they conveniently can be done which Mr Prichard says is agreeable to the orders he Received as to what Cornish or ornaments is to be done in other rooms. it will not be begun until there be proper orders given for doing thereof.[26]

Bell said he had seen his Mistress's letter to Mr Prichard:

> and don't find anything contrary to her orders, the Cieling and Cornish is finished in the Dineing Parlour the Wainscot is put up and the Plasterers are now stuckoing the Walls and the Joiners propose haveing the room finished in about a month's time the other Cielings are all lathed and plastered over ... The glass came safe and in good time and the Dineing Parlour and the Room over it are Glassed.[27]

Mr. Kynaston came to Tern and 'look'd at the Building both above and below and liked everything very well.'[28] In the same letter 'the Old House' is mentioned, and the link with 'the new Building' which was not going to be completed for another month or so. Linking the old with the new house probably also happened at Hatton Grange and at Swan Hill Court House. In November Richard White made 'alterations in the Old House' and provided some 'Chinese Gates' and in December Scoltock had built 'the Haha wall and part of the Paddock wall' at a cost of £24. 8s. 8d.[29]

After this flurry of activity, work slowed down over the next few years. Running alongside the work at Tern was work on the Talbot Inn at nearby Atcham. Bell reported that an 'octagon' window was being put in and he asked Hill to give him instructions about what was to be done there.[30] If Pritchard was supervising the work Bell does not mention him in this context.

A change of ownership altered the emphasis at Tern. The estate had been in the hands of Samuel, Thomas Hill's elder son and heir from 1762. Samuel died in 1766 and the estate was taken over by Noel when he married in 1768 so the chimney pieces must date from around this time as they were all made for him.

Bell wrote to Noel Hill in October 1768 about the floor boards for the drawing room, which were to be finished quickly. Mrs Mainwaring, the housekeeper, had spoken to Pritchard about this and Bell said that the work could be carried out as there were boards in the house for it. After that the plasterers could come in and do the walls.[31]

In January 1769, Bell wrote to Hill

> As to the Building affair there is nothing going forward at present nor anything said about it I presume Mr Prichard has drawn out some plans and that Mr Hill intends consulting some London Builders about the same and to take advice of his friends upon what he will have done.'[32]

Bell was writing as if little was happening at Tern, but this was the period when Pritchard was designing the chimney pieces. Bell's terminology is not always precise, so 'the London Builders' could refer to Mylne as he was carrying out designs for Tern by this date.

In August, 1769, Thomas Hill wrote to Noel that things 'now begin to go on expeditiously at Tern' and he thought that the alterations 'will be pleasing to those who are to live there.'[33] The other area of activity was in the garden, where Thomas Leggett, the landscape gardener, was drawing up plans and sending in planting schemes. In a letter of 27 July 1770, he wrote to Noel Hill from Wrexham and added that when he 'went to Wynnstay (he) was inform'd Mr Pritchard was return'd to Tern' so Pritchard was still working at Tern after eleven years.[34]

Opinions differed as to whether anything had been done to the house; in December 1770, Noel's wife, Anne Vernon, asked for an increased allowance for work on Tern Hall 'as nothing had been done here this fifty years.'[35] In any case, Noel was not satisfied with the house and the window problem arose again. As he told his father in 1771:

> The only Room finished in the new Building at Tern was oblig'd to be pulled to pieces again owing to the Blunder of an Architect who built the Windows so high from the Ground that no one sitting could look out of them. I was advised & I think you approved it to alter the Windows round the House before I finished the other Rooms.[36]

It is by no means certain that the 'Architect' was Pritchard and it might have been William Baker. 'The blunder' was probably due to a change in fashion as lower windows would be more consistent with the current desire to feel part of the landscape around the house. Pritchard appreciated this when he surveyed Powis Castle in 1772 and wrote, 'the windows (which command a delightful prospect) should be kept low ... The east window in the Drawing Room is introduced on account of the beautiful prospect there is from it.'[37]

What appear to have gone unnoticed in the Attingham accounts are payments of interest due on a bond of £1000 by Noel Hill to Pritchard. These occur between 1771-1776 and Pritchard's signature, on the receipts, illustrated on documents in other chapters, is unmistakable. The first payment was for '£9. 4s. 9d. paid by John Oliver, jun. on behalf of Noel Hill to Thomas Farnolls Pritchard interest due at Michaelmas Dec. 11 1771'.[38] This is followed by further payments on 14 January each year of 'a years interest of £1000 due upon bonds at Christmas last.' The sums paid in interest vary between £40 and £50. Noel Hill had also borrowed money from other people such as Thomas Amler of the Mansion House, Ford, and Robert Burton of Longner Hall, another of Pritchard's clients.

Apart from the fact that £1000 was a considerable amount and gives an indication of Pritchard's financial situation, these receipts raise interesting questions about his relationship with both Thomas and Noel Hill. If Pritchard was the architect who made the mistake ten years before, as Bell intimated in the letters, his involvement there would have ceased by 1771 if not earlier, and Noel Hill would not have borrowed money from him. If Noel had financial dealings with Pritchard, then it is even more unlikely that the 'blunder of an architect' does refer to him.

However, it does seem strange that Noel Hill did not ask Pritchard to carry out the list of 'alterations and amendments recommended to be made to his house at Tern, in its present state.' This item, as 'sent to Mr. Hill', is entered in Mylne's diary for 16 February 1773. A month later Mylne gave Mr. Hill 'a plan, elevation and section of a large set of stables' and so the entries continue with work at Tern over the next year, combined with visits to other sites in the area such as Loton Park and Sundorne Castle. It can only be conjectured that Pritchard had become interested in other projects; his farming activities at Eyton were taking up his time; an entry in the Tern Hall accounts records £40 paid to Pritchard 'on account of hay sold this winter to Mr. Rowlat.'[39] In addition, his involvement with bridges and the use of cast iron in their construction was a new and exciting area of work. Several major jobs are recorded for these years such as renovations to the Guildhall in Ludlow and a survey of Powis Castle. It is easy to speculate that he may have become tired of dealing with difficult clients such as Noel Hill.

The letters and papers relating to Tern Hall illustrate the elite, almost claustrophobic, nature of society in Shropshire where an able and economical craftsman-turned-architect such as Pritchard would be well received and recommended to the close-knit and often related circle. Rowland Hill of Hawkstone's introduction of Pritchard to Samuel Egerton of Tatton Park is an example and this kind of 'network' would have been essential for obtaining architectural work. In the Attingham Collection there are letters to and from people such as Francis Turner Blythe, Mr Fowler of Atcham, Mr. Bather and Somerset Davies. Rather than just being names on Pritchard's designs, these people take on a personality and character. Sir John Astley, Mr. Kynaston and John Ashby all feature in the documents and in one letter John Newport, the 'lunatic' is referred to. In the 1770s Noel Hill bought hats, bands and buckles from Samuel Pritchard. The letters read like a panorama of mid-eighteenth century Shropshire life and reveal much about the period.

Recorded payments for Tern Hall total just under £2,400 and Pritchard's fee was £70. In addition he bought, and was repaid for, materials to the value of about £200; these included stone, timber, slate and the marble chimney piece.

Within twenty years Noel Hill had begun to build Attingham Park. Richard Lee, carpenter from the Foundling Hospital and Wynnstay, was involved in the preliminary work to prepare the old house for its altered status. Tern Hall was incorporated into Attingham Park when a new house was designed for the site by George Steuart. Work began there in 1783 and finished in 1785. At that time, Tern was reduced in size, although in the Moses Griffiths painting of 1792 it is still clearly visible behind the new mansion.

It was reduced further during the work by John Nash in 1805 and now only fragments remain. There is no indication of what happened to the six chimney pieces that Pritchard designed for Noel Hill or evidence to show what the problem was with the height of the windows.

6-10: Attingham Park by Moses Griffiths, 1792.

1 See Julia Ionides, 'Shobdon Church - Who Done it?', *The Picturesque Society Journal*, No. 4, Autumn 1993, pp. 1-4. John Harris wrote ' ... Shobdon provided Pritchard with the inspiration to create a fashion for gothic in Shropshire and Herefordshire,' and this may be the situation as discussed in the section on Croft Castle. (Harris, p. 18)

2 The house has now been demolished. See Peter Reid, Burke's and Savills, p. 56 and *Country Life*, 10 November 1906.

3 Bateman Papers, Hereford Record Office (HRO). Ref: G39/III/E/1-360, in particular 131, 132, 136, 141, 148 and 149.

4 HRO, Bateman to Fallowes, 28 February 1748/9, G39/iii/E/211.

5 Downton Castle Papers, HRO. Ref: T74 . Bundles 199-416. T74/414, Letter from Richard Payne Knight to Samuel Nash, 25 September 1772.

6 HRO, T74/414, Nash to Payne Knight, November 1772.

7 Such as the Attingham Collection and Pritchard's designs in *The Drawing Book* for Tern Hall for the then owner Noel Hill. For more information on Tern Hall, see Barbara Coulton, *A Shropshire Squire*, Shrewsbury, 1989, p.104 and 'Tern Hall and the Hill Family: 1700-75', *Transactions of the Shropshire Archaeological and Historical Society*, Volume LXVI, 1989, pp. 97-105.

8 For details of the Green Frog Service see Tatton Park Chapter 7.

9 Thomas Hill was Member of Parliament for Shrewsbury and Treasurer of the Infirmary. He lent £300 to the churchwardens of St. Julian's Church to get the project started and here he would certainly have met Pritchard during work in progress.

10 Eventually the family assumed the name Noel-Hill.

11 Coulton, p. 97.

12 Coulton, p. 101.

13 This would seem to be Sir Richard Corbett of Longnor, a not too distant neighbour. There are other letters to Sir Richard Corbett of Longnor in the Attingham Collection. The extensive Corbet, or Corbett family in Shropshire are confusing and as a generalisation the southern Corbetts from Longnor, near Church Stretton, spell their name with 'tt' while those from north Shropshire use one 't'. In any case Bell's spelling cannot be relied on as he usually spells Pritchard without a 't'.

14 Information from the SRRC, Chaplin Papers, 5336/5/5/19. 23 June 1759.

15 Information from the SRRC, Chaplin Papers, 5336/5/5/19. 20 June 1759.

16 Information from the SRRC, Chaplin Papers, 5336/5/5/19. 21 July and 28 August 1759.

17 John Yates was involved with Pritchard on many projects such as Hosier's Almshouses, Pritchard's house at Eyton and Hatton Grange.

18 Probably from the same family as William White who worked with Pritchard on St. Julian's Church.

19 Information from the SRRC, Chaplin Papers, 5336/5/5/19. 11 January and 6 September, 1760.

20 Robert Mylne was paid £35. 15s. in settlement of his account in 1778, so the sums are comparable.

21 Information from the SRRC, Chaplin Papers, 5336/5/5/19, 24 February 1761.

22 SRRC, Attingham Collection 112/23/175, Bell to Thomas Hill, 14 January 1760.

23 Colvin, 1995 edition, p. 681.

24 For information on Robert Mylne, see *Robert Mylne*, A.E. Richardson, Batsford, London 1995 and the Robert Mylne Diaries, Series 5, in the RIBA library, London.

25 SRRC, Chaplin Papers, 5336/5/5/19. 21 April 1764.

26 SRRC, Attingham Collection, Ref: 112/6/23.178. Bell to Thomas Hill, 7 April 1760.

27 Coulton, p. 103. Bell to Thomas Hill, 21 April 1760.

28 SRRC, Attingham Collection, Ref: 112/12/23/181. Bell to Hill, 19 May 1760.

29 SRRC, Chaplin Papers, 5336/5/5/19. 28 November 1760.

30 SRRC, Attingham Collection, Ref: 112/12/23.186. Bell to Thomas Hill, 21 January 1761.

31 SRRC, Attingham Collection, Ref: 112/12/23.245.

32 SRRC, Attingham Collection, Ref: 112/12/23.247

33 SRRC, Attingham Collection, 112/6/Box 26, 26.92, Thomas Hill to Noel Hill, 17 August 1769.

34 SRRC, Attingham Collection, 112/6/Box 41. 41.526

35 Quoted in Dorothy Woolley, 'Thomas Hill of Tern, 1693-1782', *Archives*, XXI, no. 92, October 1994, p. 170.

36 SRRC, Attingham Collection, 112/6/Box 41/526. Noel Hill to Thomas Hill, 15 February 1771.

37 Improved plans for Powis Castle by Pritchard, dated 1772. Plans document p. 3.

38 SRRC, Attingham Collection, 112/6/Box 41. Document Nos. 41.70, 41.86, 41.143.

39 SRRC, Attingham Collection, 42.39, entry dated 3.8.72.

CHAPTER 11

'The State of the Church'. Work on Churches.

An extraordinary amount of building and restoration of churches took place in Shropshire in the 18th century.[1] Much of this work is demonstrated by the valuable water-colours executed by the Reverend Edward Williams in the 1780s and 1790s and John Homes Smith between 1823 and 1850.[2] These paintings illustrate the extent of the work and reveal that during this period church after church added a new tower, replaced its windows with Gothick tracery and rebuilt naves and chancels. The buildings they both painted range from small and modest chapels, such as Moreton Chapel at Llanyblodwell, to major buildings like St. Alkmund's at Whitchurch. Additional information is given by Archdeacon Plymley in his visitation reports on Shropshire churches at the end of the century.[3]

Pritchard's documented church work is small considering the amount that was being done in the area of the Border Marches, especially Shropshire, but it is possible that he was involved in rebuilding and restoration schemes for which evidence does not survive. St. Andrew's Church, Quatt, has been attributed to Richard Colley, but it is possible that he was the contractor and Pritchard the architect. Other churches, such as St. Edith's Church, Worthen and All Saints Church, Pulverbatch, have similar rebuilt or restored towers, while a late 19th century sketch of St. Mary Magdalen's Church, Battlefield shows that the interior resembled Pritchard's work at St. Julian's, Shrewsbury. Outside Shropshire, he surveyed the parish churches in Welshpool and Montgomery and carried out alterations and additions to St. Mary's Church, Rostherne in Cheshire and St. Mary's Church, Ruabon in Denbighshire, now part of Clwyd.

There are many examples in Shropshire of standard early to mid-Georgian square towers, often retaining the older fabric of the base, as Pritchard did at St. Julian's, the first Classical church to be built in Shrewsbury. It followed the 'preaching box' pattern recommended by Sir Christopher Wren as both 'beautiful and convenient.'[4]

ST. JULIAN'S CHURCH, SHREWSBURY.

1-11: South elevation of St. Julian's Church by Pritchard, 1748.

If the John Pritchard, churchwarden of St. Julian's Church in 1743 and 1747, was Thomas's father, then it is not surprising to find that Pritchard worked on the rebuilding project. This was his first architectural work for a church and was a co-operative business. Pritchard drew up the plans and worked with experienced craftsmen; William White, a carpenter, and Samuel Smith and Richard Scoltock, both bricklayers. On 12 September 1748, he swore that 'the roofs walls & pillars were much decayd & incapable of being put in a durable repair' and it was agreed at a public parish meeting that 'the church shou'd be taken down & rebuilt According to a plan designed by Mr Pritchard.'[5]

Two drawings of the medieval, pre-1749 church show that on the south side the nave had four bays with sturdy buttresses between them. The chancel was also of four bays but with no such apparent buttressing. On the north side, at the east end, there was a battlemented chapel, probably St. Mary's or the Shearman's Chapel, and three gabled buildings built onto the nave. In the drawings, the windows have late Perpendicular tracery with square hood moulds. The small porch at the west end of the chancel and another small addition built against the tower appear to be constructed of wood. In these drawings the church has not been made to appear as ruinous as the Reverend Hugh Owen reported, when he wrote in 1808 that 'part of the chancel had fallen away'.[6]

The first stone was laid in February 1749 and the church was opened on 26 August 1750. The 'comparatively small sum of £1700,' for the work was raised in various ways;[7] Thomas Hill of Tern Hall lent the Church Wardens £300 to get it started, £100 came from the patron, Sir John Astley, an M.P. for the town, and £50 from the Drapers' Company, while £800 came from contributions throughout the area. The balance of the sum required was borrowed on the parish rates, with a small part being raised by annuity.

2-11: St. Julian's in the 18th century.

Pritchard's drawing for the new south elevation shows that a more simple building was intended. There is no pediment over the south doorway and apparently no dentil course. The height and placing of the windows would have been dictated by the requirements of the galleries inside.

3-11: Interior of St. Julian's in the 19th century.

The fabric of the old church was used in the new foundations which were 7ft. 6in. deep at the chancel. Pritchard retained the square tower but rebuilt the top, adding a balustrade, and the urns considered 'hideous' by the Reverend Owen;[8] but then he thought that the church 'has no pretensions to beauty or architectural taste, externally. It is a plain Grecian fabrick of red brick.'[9] A contemporary engraving shows a tidy 'preaching box' with a long, wide nave, flanking aisles and a shallow chancel, very much in keeping

4-11: North elevation of St. Julian's today.

with the conservative form and style of the time. It also shows that a pediment, supported by columns, was added to a south porch. Along the sides are five tall round-headed windows with keystones and four small square ones underneath, all with the luggs so typical of Pritchard's work. The influence of James Gibbs can be seen here, and windows such as these were put on many churches around the county at this time, as the views painted by the Reverend Edward Williams demonstrate. The prominent quoins on each corner of St. Julian's were made from Grinshill stone, and roof slates came from Chester, while sale of the old lead from the roof amounted to £56. 11s. 3d.[10]

In the interior, Pritchard also put in 'a high and remarkably acute arch' between the old tower and the new nave, [11] and a contemporary wrote that 'the galleries are supported by pillars of the Tuscan order, and upon these stand another row of pillars, of the Doric order, with a full entablature supporting the roof and the whole of the inside of the church is neatly finished.'[12] This entablature, without its galleries, now seems rather eccentrically oversized, somewhat in the manner of Daventry parish church, Northamptonshire, built by the Hiorn brothers.

Pritchard's Venetian window at the east end remains, but is now filled with 19th century painted glass. In 1808, it contained a painted figure of St. James which came from Rouen during the French Revolution and was bought in London for £30. In 1861, St. James was moved to the south window of the chancel and was replaced by a copy of Raphael's Transfiguration, the work of David Evans who lived in the parish. In 1754 Pritchard was paid just over £25 for an 'Altar Piece' a sum which may have included making and carving it; Mr. Bowen received £11. 7s. for painting it and 'Writing the Commandments.'[13] These sums suggest that it was an elaborate piece of work.

Since Pritchard's time, the church has been altered; first in 1819 and again in 1846, when the Reverend Richard Scott 'embellished the [external] south wall with pilasters, cornice, balustrade &c., which are now so prominent a feature.'[14] These additions have changed the clean lines of Pritchard's building thereby altering its character. The Greek key-patterned apron beneath the windows, an enlarged dentil course as well as the balustrade and pilasters, make this elevation fussy and out-of-step with the older unadorned fabric of the tower. The north side of the church was left plain and reveals the original clarity of the building.

Further work took place in 1883-4 under the direction of S. Pountney Smith, another Shrewsbury architect. New vestries were added and the church now seated 500 people. At the same time, as the change of brick shows, the south entrance was moved from the west end of the nave to the base of the tower. Dean Cranage thought that 'both vicar and architect are to be congratulated on the vast improvement which was effected.' He was usually sympathetic to the ancient fabric of a building, so one can only assume that St. Julian's had been in need of some 'restoration'.[15]

The interior was also altered. A 1906 photograph shows it after the 1883 work, which cost £3000. The wooden ceiling, decorated with 'Gothick' roses from the ancient beams, remained. The Reverend Owen thought it was 'an incongruous decoration for a Grecian church' but that it 'had no bad effect.' The galleries, over the side aisles and at the west end, seemed to have been taken away during the 1883 repairs as there is no sign of them in the 1906 photograph. The church is now a busy craft centre with the interior divided into sections; the cherubs from the 'Altar Piece' decorate other parts of the interior. Pritchard's simple brass memorial tablet, recording his name, his wife's and their three children who died young, is on the south side of the tower arch. They were buried in the churchyard but their graves are no longer there.

5-11: South elevation of St. Julian's today.

It is clear from the outset that Pritchard intended to use the Classical style throughout St. Julian's, instead of rebuilding the church in Gothic form as he might have been expected to do in a town of ancient houses, medieval abbey and churches. He showed a confidence and maturity for his twenty five years by building the first church of a new style in Shrewsbury.

ST. MARY'S CHURCH, KINNERLEY, SHROPSHIRE.

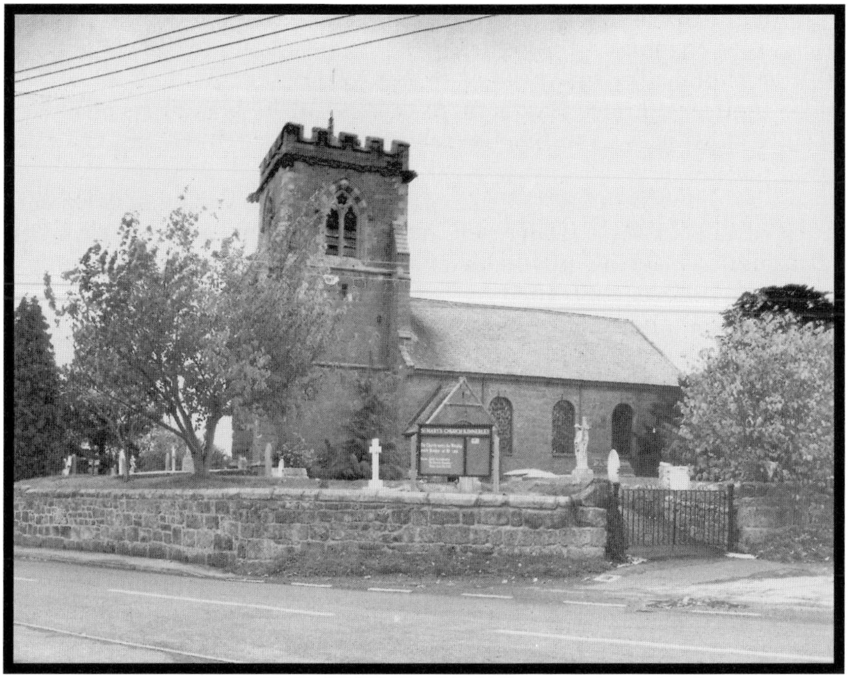

6-11: St. Mary's Church, Kinnerley.

Kinnerley Parish Church, north of Shrewsbury, was rebuilt in 1773-4 after much discussion, procrastination and indecision. Work had been urgently needed for some time as the parish accounts show that estimates were being obtained in 1767.[16] In the entries for 1768-9, 2s. 6d. was recorded for 'going to Salop to see for Mr Pritchard,' as well as going to 'Salop for ye Plan' and 'fetching ye Plan and Estimate' cost 5s. 1d. A further 1s. 6d. was spent 'going to Oswestry for to see Mr Pritchard,' and another 2s. 'Pd when Mr Pritchard was Looking [at] ye Church.' In January 1769, the Quarter Sessions granted a certificate to raise a brief to 'build a Parish Church for £1,232 11s. to be collected from House to House throughout the counties of Salop, Stafford, Hereford and Worcester.'[17]

In 1769, the church wardens paid Pritchard £2. 13s. 6d. for 'Coming over and drawing the Plan for ye Church.' The situation must have been getting rather worrying as timber was purchased 'to support the arch of ye Church.' At the same time, a sum was paid to John Pugh for repairing the churchyard wall. After he had drawn up the plans, Pritchard apparently played no further part in the work.

In 1771, 'Mr. Haycock' was paid for 'a Journey to View ye Repairs of ye Church.' Presumably the brief had not raised the expected money, as the Churchwardens waited until 1773 before drawing up a faculty for 'taking down the said old decayed Church and in the place and room thereof to build and Erect a handsome And more convenient Church and Chancel.'[18] The faculty stated that as the church was in such a ruinous condition the parishioners could no longer worship there safely. An 'experienced person' was appointed to oversee the job and make sure 'that the Builders execute the same in a workman like manner according to their contract.' The person appointed was James Baylis of Knockin and he was to receive £25 'as a recompense for his troubles as soon as the work shall be completed.'

The sum of £192. 12s. was paid 'To the Builders, according to Contract for Rebuilding ye Church' This may have been a first instalment as, according to Dean Cranage, writing in 1906, an 'article had been entered into to rebuild the church for £639.' The name of the builders was not recorded.

7-11: Kinnerley Church by the Rev. Edward Williams, 1786.

The 1786 water-colour by the Reverend Edward Williams shows the church from the south-west side. This reveals that the stone tower had a wooden bellcote with a pyramidal roof.[19] The base is supported by corner buttresses. The new body of the church was built of red sandstone. The entrance on the south side had a pedimented doorway with an off-set semi-circular window above it; this feature was removed, or concealed, when a porch was added. A similar door and off-set window survives on the north side; the door has now been blocked up. At the east end is an apse with a conical roof.

The church today does not reveal many clues about its architect. The strong projecting buttresses still support the tower but the wooden top has been replaced by stone with traceried windows. The three round-headed nave windows have plain surrounds with keystones and clear glass in them. The window details are very similar to those on several Shropshire churches which were built, rebuilt or restored during the 18th century.

The simple interior consists of a nave and chancel which retains its elegant altar piece, topped by urns; perhaps the parishioners of Kinnerley did not disapprove of urns as much as the Reverend Hugh Owen. Whether Pritchard designed the altar piece, or whether

8-11: The interior of Kinnerley Church today.

the church we see today conforms to his plan is no longer possible to determine, since further information does not exist. There is only a plan of 1774[20] which was drawn up to demonstrate how the pews would be 'all of one decent regular and uniform order ... according to a certain Scheme Chart or Plan exhibited [and] also to erect ... in the Area Body and Chancel ... handsome and convenient new Seats or Forms in a regular and uniform manner' as stated in the faculty.

The church has been attributed to Pritchard for many years on account of the entries in the churchwardens' accounts quoted above and Dean Cranage refers to them in his book. Pritchard's original scheme may have been more extensive, but as the brief seems to have raised only £100, it may have been necessary to modify it. In any case the tower was left in place and the body of the church rebuilt and this work could have been what he put forward in 1768.

CHAPTER 11

9-11: Hopton Cangeford Church by the Rev. Edward Williams, 1791.

HOPTON CANGEFORD, SHROPSHIRE.

At the end of the 18th century Hopton Cangeford Church, or as it was called, Hopton Chapel, near Ludlow, was described by Archdeacon Plymley as

> modern AD 1766, uniform & of the Grecian order. It has been very neatly finished ... In the belfry Pidgeons make their habitation & the smell is offensive ... & must be injurious to the part of the building so occupied. The west window wants mending and the windows in general are not quite whole. There is a bad crack over the window on the south side this is nearest the west end and some slates are off the same side. I have ordered the Pidgeons removed and these repairs attended. I wish also the Ch: to be re whitewashed; it is nearly as it should be and a little attention will keep it so.[21]

10-11: Elevation and plan of Hopton Cangeford by Pritchard, undated.

There is an undated drawing, with Pritchard's name on it, for the 'South Front of Hopton Chapel' among the collection of architectural drawings at Downton Hall. This shows it much as built and as it is today.

The church, both in the drawing and as built, has a sturdy square tower topped with a pyramidal roof and three windows along the nave while the shallow chancel is lit by a single window. The order of the windows on the tower has been reversed with the circular window at the top now. The plan of the interior shows the arrangements of the pews. The comment about the re-whitewashing, which is also in a report by Plymley on Worthen church, supports the fact that the stone or brick carcass was not meant to be exposed, as it is today.

11-11: Hopton Cangeford Church today.

ST. ANDREW'S CHURCH, WROXETER, SHROPSHIRE.

When Pritchard moved to Eyton in 1767 Wroxeter became his local church and his daughter Anne was married there. The ancient fabric incorporates masonry from the nearby extensive Roman town. The churchwardens' accounts reveal that Pritchard was already connected with the church, as in 1763 he received £4. 4s. for unspecified work. This probably corresponds to an entry dated 17 March reading 'An account of Money paid by Mr Claytin [Richard Clayton] for the use of the Church by Mr. Pritchard.'[22] At the same time several payments, amounting to £232, were made to Richard White and Richard Scoltock; the latter had worked with Pritchard on St. Julian's in Shrewsbury. The church today still retains the vestry that was part of the rebuilding of the south side of the church that had been demolished.

ST. MARY'S CHURCH, WELSHPOOL AND ST. NICHOLAS' CHURCH, MONTGOMERY.

In November 1771 when Pritchard was working at Powis Castle he also made surveys of the chancels of Welshpool and Montgomery parish churches, much as he did in conjunction with work at Tatton and Wynnstay. He charged three guineas for 'attending Mr. Probert to survey the chancel at Welshpool.'[23] This sum included his travel and surveying the workmen at Powis over two days. The work was badly needed as the church was described in 1742 as 'dirty & nasty as all ye rest of the Welsh churches are.'[24] Although work was carried out at Welshpool in the middle of the 18th century there does not appear to be any mention of Pritchard in the documentation. However, in 1772 a vault for the Powis family was built under the chancel and Pritchard could have been looking at the building for this purpose.[25]

As far as Montgomery is concerned, perhaps he was satisfied with the fabric and decided that no work was needed as there is no mention of any further involvement.

Monument of Sir Richard Lyster, AIA82

CHAPTER 11

'The Monument Lately Put up'. Work on Monuments.

13-11: Sketch for a monument by Henry Cheere.

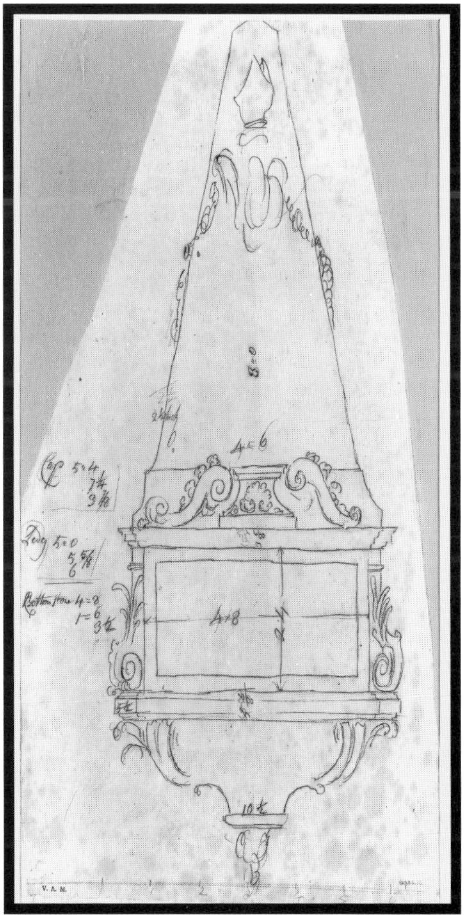

In the Preface to *An Essay on Design*, John Gwynn criticised the untidy assortment of monuments in Westminster Abbey. He considered that ' ... in Architecture, as well as Sculpture, nothing should be crowded in, that was not Part of, or analogous to, the Builder's original Design.'[26]

The design and production of monuments and wall tablets was an important part of the income of stonemasons and carvers over many centuries, especially during the winter months when outside building work was not possible. Pritchard's contemporary, John Platt of Rotherham, recorded 'A frost broke which lasted 5 weeks and not a man I had could work.'[27] The Platts charged between sixty and eighty pounds for a monument and over the years they recorded the monuments they had put up around the area, as well as the supply of materials, including black marble for a sarcophagus at Lowestoft. This transaction proved unprofitable since Platt noted in 1793 that he 'received £30 for the Bl^{k} marble Coll^{m} sent to near Lowestoft in Suffolk & was paid £16 short. lost.'[28] He was paid £60 for a monument in Tankersley church, Yorkshire, supplied in the same year.[29]

Pritchard was no exception to other architects of the period in designing and producing church monuments. *The Drawing Book* contains designs for only three, but it is known that he was responsible for others as his name is on them and there are more that can be considered as his work on stylistic grounds. For instance, the monument to John Dod in St. Peter's Church, Cound parish church, appears to have been executed by John Nelson whose name it bears, but the similarities to other monuments by Pritchard would indicate that he designed it before he died.

Nelson was working for Pritchard as well as on his own account in the 1760s; he signed a monument to Beatrice Peck in Market Drayton Church.[30] After Pritchard's death in 1777, Nelson continued to work independently and his later monuments are plainer than those he made with Pritchard, but then the fashion had changed and elaborate Baroque monuments were no longer required. Nelson's monument to Thomas Hanmer (1794), in St. Mary's Church, Overton, Flintshire, is an elegant but simple oval tablet with two columns at the sides. In the same church there are two monuments by van der Hagen whose work was also less elaborate later on; his monument to Mrs. Hanmer of 1770, also at Overton, is in a similar style, while a later one of 1780 has a draped and ornamented urn backed by an obelisk.

Contemporary comments on new church monuments are rare. Lord Torrington is no assistance as he only noted interesting inscriptions in his diary or included 'ancient' works; 'rich in monuments of antiquity' is a typical entry.[31] In 1772, Parson James Woodforde wrote in his diary that his father's monument cost £14. 14s. He sent the lengthy Latin inscription to Mr. Ford, the Bath statuary, to be added to the monument which was a neat one of white marble. In 1796, he reported that he went to see 'the Monument put up lately by Mr. Townshend for his Friend and Relation Mr. Du Quesne. It was the plainnest I ever saw, it is marble but nothing more than a mere Slab, only wrote on. The Character given of him is very great.'[32] This sounds like a criticism by Woodforde, but as the century progressed the monuments became simpler and he was probably more accustomed to the elaborate ones of his younger days. The choice of monument would have been dictated by the price; some monuments, especially the Baroque ones by famous sculptors, were very costly.

Pritchard's documented work in this field ranges from the very detailed imagery on the monument of Sir Richard Lyster in Alberbury church, and the decorative work at Acton Round, both in Shropshire, to his earliest known work, a straightforward wall tablet to Ann Wilkinson in St. Giles' Church, Wrexham, Denbighshire, now part of Clywd. In addition, there are some fine monuments in churches in the Shrewsbury area that could with some justification be attributed to Pritchard. The monument at Cound to Edward Cressett, Bishop of Llandaff, who died in 1755, for example, has a cartouche which resembles the one on the Offley monument at Pontesbury. In the same church, the palm fronds bound with ribbons on the monument to John Dod, who died in 1774, are comparable to those carved on the Lyster monument in Alberbury church. The similarities between the heads of the cherubs and other details on several monuments are striking, particularly on the monuments of Edward Cressett, Richard Corbet at Moreton Corbet and Edward Cludde at St. Peter's Church, Wrockwardine. Some of the monuments attributable to Pritchard are included in Appendix 1.

14-11: *Monument of Ann Wilkinson.*

MONUMENT OF ANN WILKINSON, ST. GILES' CHURCH, WREXHAM.

Ann Wilkinson, who died in 1756 aged twenty three, was the first wife of John Wilkinson, the iron master from Bersham. Her monument, bearing Pritchard's name, is on the south wall of Wrexham church. The contact between Pritchard and Wilkinson is significant as Wilkinson was to become one of the partners in the project to build the Iron Bridge.

At the top of the monument is a pediment and at the bottom crossed palm leaves, a motif which Pritchard often used elsewhere. The inscription in the centre is surrounded with an edge of black marble, with a black marble tablet under it. The monument, made of veined marble, is plain compared with later ones designed by Pritchard. It is thought that he began to use a wider variety of coloured marbles after Nelson and van der Hagen had joined him.

15-11: *Monument of John Lloyd.*

MONUMENTS OF JOHN LLOYD AND OF MARY MORHALL, ST. MARY'S CHURCH, SHREWSBURY.

The Reverend John Lloyd, who died in 1758 aged 40, is commemorated by a monument on the north nave wall of Shrewsbury's St. Mary's Church. Pritchard's name is on the soffit. The inscription in Latin, like that of Doctor Sprott at Ludford, perhaps indicates academic achievements. This idea is reinforced by the books, two open and two closed, perched on the sides of the monument while below them Rococo scrolls swirl down to the supporting brackets.

The monument of Mary Morhall, who died in 1765, is on the north side of the chancel in St. Mary's and is also signed under the soffit. This monument, of different coloured marbles, has a draped urn at the top and three cherubs' heads at the bottom, while bell-flower and twined leaves decorate the sides.

16-11: Monument of Mary Morhall.

The monument, and its position in the chancel, reflects the importance of the Morhall family, who owned Onslow Hall, a house north of Shrewsbury where Robert Mylne worked in 1774. A Rococo chimney piece was in the Hall before it was demolished in 1955.[33] Perhaps this was another one designed by Pritchard for Mylne but as it has disappeared there is no way of knowing.

MONUMENT OF RICHARD HOLLINGS, OLD ST. CHAD'S, SHREWSBURY.

In 1788 the tower and much of the fabric of Old St. Chad's Church, Shrewsbury collapsed, as Thomas Telford had warned. The Hollings monument, with Pritchard's name on it, is in the remaining part of the church. Richard Hollings, who died in 1741, is commemorated by an elegant wall monument with a draped urn at the top and foliage and bell-flower down the sides and on the apron.

17-11: Monument of Richard Hollings.

MONUMENT OF SAMUEL SPROTT, ST. GILES' CHURCH, LUDFORD, SHROPSHIRE.

The simple and dignified monument to Samuel Sprott is on the west wall of St. Giles' Church, Ludford. The Latin inscription gives little information about him. Doctor Sprott, who died in 1760, was the tenant of the Broad Gate House in Ludlow where Pritchard is believed to have worked.

The monument is topped with a draped urn and at the bottom is a Rococo cartouche containing his coat of arms, with flanking upturned palm fronds. The arms are skilfully painted, but as so little documentation exists for Pritchard's monuments, there is no indication who undertook this work. On one side Pritchard's name is shown prominently at the front, with his characteristic T and F forming one letter and on the other is 'Salop. Arc^{t}.' An almost identical monument to Henry Sprott, also of The Marsh, with no maker's name on it, is in St. Giles' Church, Barrow, near Much Wenlock.

18-11: Monument of Samuel Sprott in Ludford Church. 19-11: Monument of Henry Sprott in Barrow Church.

20-11: Pritchard's name on the monument of Samuel Sprott in Ludford Church with the characteristic T and F joined together.

MONUMENT OF RICHARD WARD OFFLEY, ST. GEORGE'S CHURCH, PONTESBURY, SHROPSHIRE.

21-11: Monument of Richard Ward Offley.

The dating of monuments in a chronological context is sometimes difficult. For example, the design for the monument to Richard Ward Offley on the north wall of the chancel of Pontesbury church, near Shrewsbury, is dated 'January the 28th, 1769'. (AIA 64) Offley died in May, 1762, so it was nearly seven years before this work was carried out. This was not an uncommon practice, just as monuments were sometimes made before the death of a person, but dating the work is made more difficult when there is no other evidence.[34]

This monument took three craftsmen, Nelson, van der Hagen and Swift, nearly eleven weeks between them to complete, indicating the time-consuming nature of detailed carving in marble and stone. In the margin of the preparatory drawing, a line appears to point to the amount of time taken by Nelson and £11. 18s. 9d. alongside it which if correct means that Nelson was paid 10s. a day.

The monument, made of white veined marble, has a broken scrolled pediment at the top enclosing a coat of arms surrounded by a Rococo cartouche. From this bell-flower swags are draped along the sides and on the apron at the base are crossed palm fronds. The inscription is filled in with red pigment, not the customary black. The surround for the inscription is a coloured marble of the alabaster type.

Offley's house, Hinton Hall, is located about a mile north of Pontesbury, so he was very much a local man and, as the inscription reads, 'attended the true interest of this Parish and Neighbourhood.'

CHAPTER 11

MONUMENT OF SIR EDWARD BLOUNT, ST. JOHN'S CHURCH, MAMBLE, WORCESTERSHIRE.

A design for the monument of Sir Edward Blount is in *The Drawing Book* and could be dated to 1768-9. (AIA 48) The monument was erected in the 16th-century Blount Chapel on the north side of Mamble church. As the Blounts were a Catholic family, their Chapel, which has now fallen down, was built outside the main body of the church. According to the inscription, Blount died on 15 February, 1758, at Mawley Hall, about ten miles away.

Left.
22-11: Monument of Sir Edward Blount by Pritchard, in 1949. (AIA 48)

Right.
23-11: the same monument today.

Left.
24-11: Another Blount monument, probably by Pritchard, in 1949.

Right.
25-11: the same monument today.

Only the neglected remains of the monument, made of 'Sienna' marble and jasper, now survive on the north wall. This is unfortunate as the design has a lighter Rococo form than any other work by Pritchard on a monument. In the design, the edge of the apron is made up of 'C' scrolls, with more of the same at the top surrounding the cartouche and supporting the Greek cross. Foliage swags flow down the sides.

A monument to another Sir Edward, who died in 1756, was on the south wall of the Blount Chapel until recently when a blocked window expanded, pushing much of it off the wall. Photographs show that the style of this monument, although lacking the Rococo character, appears so similar to its counterpart opposite that it is almost certainly by Pritchard. An old photograph shows two lamps at the top, with a floriated Greek cross between them.[35] Both of these monuments might once have had Pritchard's name on them.

MONUMENT OF SIR WHITMORE ACTON, ACTON ROUND CHURCH, SHROPSHIRE.

26-11: Monument of Sir Whitmore Acton.

Pritchard was not the only architect in the Welsh Border counties designing monuments. In his payment book William Baker recorded work on three monuments with payments varying between £8. 10s. for 'my trouble & plan of a Monument' and £27 paid 'in full for a monument put up at Leighton Church.'[36] The most interesting of the entries concerns the monument of Edward Acton 'at Acton on the Hill' now Acton Scott, as Pritchard could have worked with Baker on this project. When Sir Richard Acton, uncle of Edward Acton, commissioned a monument for his father, Sir Whitmore Acton, more than ten years later it was to Pritchard that he turned. Sir Whitmore Acton had died in 1731 and his wife in 1759, so there was a long gap between their deaths and the creation of the monument.

Acton Round is a small stone church in eastern Shropshire where Pritchard designed one of his most important monuments for the newly-built chapel on the north side. The monument, with Pritchard's name on it, has been called 'a remarkably early piece of Gothic Revival in a Rococo vein'[37] but its pioneer status is no

27-11: Acton Round Church with the Acton Chapel on the left.

longer sustainable on the present knowledge of the use of these styles in the 18th century. Yet this does not detract from its splendour and the employment of a wide variety of styles and motifs; this is Pritchard at his most eclectic. In the centre of the monument is the white marble commemorative tablet to Sir Whitmore Acton with swags of flowers around it. Under it, the black marble sarcophagus, with winged talons for feet, contrasts with the dark grey veined marble behind. Similar designs to the Classical sarcophagus are in James Gibbs' *A Book of Architecture* (1728). Other Classical motifs on the monument include the four lamps at the top, two of them with flames, while at the very top are Rococo scrolls and a 'finial' enclosing a 'sun-burst'.

The cornice of the chapel is decorated with Gothick pendants which stand out against the black painted wall behind and around the monument. This use of black paint to set off a monument was probably quite usual during the Stuart and Georgian period, but few examples survive.[38]

It is the mixture of motifs and styles that makes the monument striking as well as particularly interesting. The influence of Batty Langley's *Gothic Architecture* can be seen in the frieze and capitals, the columns and the form of the cusped arch.[39] The soffit of this arch is in different veined marbles and the spandrels at the sides contain diaper work.

It is the only monument by Pritchard for which a record of payment exists. On 6 January, 1763 Sir Richard Acton paid 'sixty pounds on account of erecting a monument by his order.'[40] The receipt is signed by Pritchard, but unfortunately no other documentation survives so there is no way of knowing if this sum was for the whole monument, or for part of it and if so which part.[41]

The workmanship is of the high standard that reflects the quality that Pritchard and his craftsmen were then attaining. The two pointed windows contain clear glass with 'y' tracery cames at the top[42] so it is very possible that he was also responsible for the new chapel. Did he also put in the ogee-headed priest's door on the south side of the chancel?

MONUMENT OF SIR RICHARD LYSTER, ST. MICHAEL'S CHURCH, ALBERBURY.

While the Acton Round monument is Pritchard's most important in the Gothick style, his most intriguing is the one to Sir Richard Lyster on the north wall of Alberbury Church on the Shropshire-Welsh border. The design for the monument is in *The Drawing Book* (AIA 82) and Pritchard's name is on the front of the finished work. Nearby, to the north west of the church, is Loton Park, seat of the Leighton family for many generations; Pritchard designed two chimney pieces for Sir Charlton Leighton.

The influence of Sir Henry Cheere on Pritchard's work has already been discussed and is evident on this monument which demonstrates Pritchard and his craftsmen at their best. There are weeping putti on either side of the urn in the centre; one is holding a scroll in his hand and at the feet of the other are the scales of justice, tossed to the ground. This area is so sketchily indicated in the original drawing that it is hard to tell if the object was intended at the time or added afterwards. In the design the foot of the putti is much closer to the base of the urn so the object could have been added afterwards. Behind the other putti is a stick with a floppy garden-type hat on it. The symbolism of some of the other items carved on the monument denotes death; the closed urn for mortality and the crossed palm fronds for victory over death.

28-11: The monument of Sir Richard Lyster. (AIA 82)

Pritchard made out a table of the time taken on the monument and this shows that Nelson worked for twenty-nine days on the three cherubs' heads. Unfortunately the rest of the table is not filled in. On separate pages of *The Drawing Book* are sketches of cherubs' heads, some with wings. (AIA 86 and 87) After Nelson's hard work, it is unfortunate that the heads, designed for the bottom of the monument, have been removed to make room for a tablet to Lyster's wife Anne, who died in 1781. This was put up by van der Hagen, whose name appears on the side.

Sir Richard died on 13 April, 1766 at the age of 74 and the inscription on the tablet eulogises his many virtues. During his life he served his county in five successive Parliaments with 'unshaken integrity, unwearied attention and steady attachment to the true Interests of his Country.' This paragon of an 18th century gentleman was also a Magistrate and a 'Friend to the Church and to Religion'. Perhaps the most apt comments in this typically 18th century catalogue of praise are that 'His House like his Heart was open to his Friends and more a Model of ancient than modern Hospitality.'

Apt because Sir Richard was described as 'a typical old Tory knight of the shire':[43]

> The establishment of Mr. Lyster was administered upon the most ample scale of ancient English hospitality: one day in the week his table was open to every class of his constituents, from the very highest to the lowest ... His progress to London to attend the duties of parliament in which he is ... very assiduous, had (a) feudal cast ... He travelled in his coach and six, and was a week upon the road: his principal tenants and tradesmen accompanying him as far as Watling Street, where they were entertained as his expense. At Highgate he was met by a select body of his London tradesmen, and thus ushered to his town house, in Bow Street, Covent Garden: and the same ceremonies were repeated on his return into Shropshire. All this cost was maintained by a rental of £1800 a-year.[44]

This account portrays the old-style Shropshire gentry as much as it also reflected on the county's politics. Lyster was well known and popular and was also 'considered a Jacobite'.[45] The old Shropshire families, such as the Myttons, Kynastons and Leightons, dominated the Parliamentary seats and formed a network of connections; these are also the families that Pritchard worked for and contact with them was important for him, so the Lyster monument was a most prestigious work.

Lyster's parliamentary career was somewhat chequered in its early days; he was first returned for Shrewsbury in 1722, but lost the seat in the next year when the 18th century equivalent of boundary changes took place in an arbitrary fashion. The change affected the Abbey Foregate area of Shrewsbury where Lyster gained much support. Lyster appealed to his fellow Parliamentarians, but they decided against him whereupon he put on his hat and turned his back on the Speaker ' ... and when Members called him to order, he looking round, with a firm and indignant tone said, "When you learn justice, I will learn manners ..."'[46] This explains the significance of the hat. Lyster felt that the firm stand he had taken against the decision of Parliament, by breaking the rules of the House and keeping his hat on, had made his point and he wished all the world to remember it after his death.

29-11: Detail of the Lyster monument - the 'hat on the stick.' (AIA 82)

References to hats appeared to be in fashion; Thomas Hill wrote to Robert Moore saying that Mr Lyster thought that he might as well 'kick his hat against the moon' regarding the opposition in Shrewsbury.[47] In the frontispiece of John Gwynn's *London and Westminster Improved*, Britannia is shown in the company of Mercury and a bas relief of George II. Above is a sword with a similar hat on its point.

The hat can be considered as Lyster's reply to the ruling of the House of Commons, but does it have a deeper significance? John Wilkes, described as 'radical demagogue and pamphleteer' began publishing his radical anti-Government paper, *The North Briton*, in 1762. He was imprisoned in the tower for criticising the King's speech but was released after demonstrations and riots. The slogan of the demonstrators was 'Wilkes and Liberty.' In cartoons by William Hogarth, Wilkes is depicted with the Cap of Liberty. Could the hat on Lyster's monument also be a cap of liberty?[48] The tradition of the 'cap on the stick' is a very old one and a significant one to Lyster as a supporter of 'Liberty and Justice'.

The radical views of John Wilkes were approved by many people at the time. Thomas Turner recorded in his diary on 13 July 1763 ' ... in the even read several political papers called *The North Briton*, which are wrote by John Wilkes esq., member for Aylesbury, in Bucks, for the writing of which he has been committed to the Tower, and procured his release by a writ of *habeas corpus.* I really think they breathe forth such a spirit of liberty that it is an extreme good paper.'[49]

Lyster was returned again for Shrewsbury in 1727, together with Sir John Astley, his colleague for many years, but lost his seat again in 1734 when the returning officer showed a 'partiality' towards the Whigs. He gained a seat for the county at a by-election in 1740 and held this until his death in 1766.

This review of the work on churches and monuments carried out by Pritchard helps to establish him in a leading position as architect and designer, especially in Shropshire. The church projects ranged from rebuilding St. Julian's in Shrewsbury in the modern Classical style to surveys of the large parish churches in Montgomery and Welshpool. Hopton Chapel was the only completely newly built church for which drawings exist, and although mention is made of his plan for Kinnerley, this has not survived. Hopton Chapel is in effect the estate church for Downton Hall, just as the Coton Chapel was used by the Lee family for several generations. The clients for the church work include a wide range from parish meetings to owners of large estates. The work on the monuments has a similar range extending from the industrialist iron master, John Wilkinson to the wealthy Tory squire, Sir Richard Lyster. As I have indicated there are more monuments that are attributed to Pritchard but these cannot be verified. The hope is that in the future more evidence will come to light.

Cherubs over the chancel arch in St. Julian's Church, Shrewsbury.

1 Terry Friedman, 'The Golden Age of Church Architecture in Shropshire', *Shropshire History and Archaeology, Transactions of the Shropshire Archaeological and Historical Society*, Volume LXXI, Shrewsbury, 1996, pp. 83-134. I would like to acknowledge the work done by Dr. Friedman on the 18th century churches of Shropshire and for generously sharing this information with me.

2 SRRC 6001/372 and 6009/114.

3 The Reverend Joseph Plymley's Visitation Reports, SRRC 6001/6860-6865.

4 Friedman, p. 85.

5 Presumably this oath was a measure of safeguard against unscrupulous surveyors who made out that the buildings were in a worse state than they actually were. The plan is SRRC, 6001/MS 299, f.264. These are all names familiar in Shrewsbury building records. Richard Scoltock, with Edward Massey, a carpenter, designed and built Millington's Hospital in Shrewsbury in 1747-8. Massey affirmed, in the estimate for the Hospital, that he and Scoltock had 'for several years been very much employed making plans of publick and other great Buildings and making calculations of the expenses of the building thereof.' (James Lawson, 'The Architect of Millington's Hospital, Shrewsbury,' *Shropshire News Letter* 42, May 1972, p. 10). In the Salop Fire Office Policy Books, Jonathan Scoltock, also of Sutton, is described as an 'architect'. Sutton to the south of the centre of Shrewsbury, then a small village, is now a large housing area and one of the roads is called Pritchard Way; but there does not seem to be a Scoltock Way there.

6 The Reverend Hugh Owen, *The History of Shrewsbury*, Volume II, Shrewsbury, 1808, p. 427.

7 Owen, p. 427.

8 These were later replaced by 'eight handsome pinnacles'. Owen, p. 426.

9 Owen, p. 427.

10 SRRC, 6001/MS 299, f.266.

11 Owen, p. 426.

12 T. Philips, *The History and Antiquities of Shrewsbury*, Shrewsbury, 1779, p. 107.

13 SRRC, MS 299, f.264.

14 The Reverend D.H.S. Cranage, *An Architectural Account of the Churches of Shropshire*, Part 10, Wellington, Shropshire, 1906, pp. 919-922. His account of St. Julian's and many of the churches of Shropshire are still regarded as standard works.

15 Happily the small statue in a niche under a canopy on the south side of the tower survived. It is thought to represent St. Juliana, martyred in the fourth century to whom the church was dedicated.

16 All information in this section, unless otherwise indicated, from SRRC P151/B/2/2. Churchwardens' Accounts 1757-97. Unpaginated.

17 SRRC, Shrewsbury Quarter Sessions, 1779.

18 SRRC, P151/B/3/1.

19 There are several churches along the Welsh Borders with wooden bell-cotes such as Kerry Parish Church. It would have been a cheaper option for what was not a prosperous area.

20 SRRC, P151/B/3/3.

21 The Reverend Joseph Plymley's Visitation Report, SRRC 6001/6862, f.79.

22 SRRC, 2656/21, Churchwardens' Accounts 1763-1827.

23 NLW, Powis Castle Collection, 20593.

24 British Library, Add.MS15,776, f.151, a 1742 tour.

25 The Reverend Roger Brown, Vicar of Welshpool, kindly supplied information on research he is carrying out on the church.

26 John Gwynn, *An Essay on Design*, London, 1749, Preface, v.

27 For further information on the Platts see J. D. Potts, '*Platt of Rotherham Mason-Architects 1770-1810*', Sheffield, 1959.

28 Potts, p. 17.

29 Potts, p. 18.

30 Gunnis, p. 270.

31 *The Torrington Diaries*, Volume II, p. 138.

32 James Woodforde, *The Diary of a Country Parson*, ed. James Beresford, Oxford 1978, p. 529.

33 Information from John Harris.

34 The life-size monument to Thomas Spackman by John Deval, the younger, in Cliffe Pypard church, Wiltshire is thought to have been ordered before his death and details of it are given in his will of 1782. Nicholas Penny, *Church Monuments in Romantic England*, Yale and London, 1977, p. 18.

35 This cross resembles one on the monument of another Catholic, Dame Mary Smythe, who died in 1764, in Acton Burnell Church which is thought to be by Pritchard.

36 Oswald, p. 134.

37 Pevsner, p. 52.

38 Clodock Church on the Welsh-Herefordshire border has a good example.

39 Langley, in particular plates IX and L.

40 SRRC, 1093 Acton Collection, Box 32.

41 'On account' could mean a part payment or 'because' the job had been done.

42 Richard Neve, *The City and Country Purchaser and Builder's Dictionary*, London, 1726, defined 'cames' as 'the slender Rods of Cast-lead, of which the Glazier make their turn'd Lead.' The glass, clear diamond-shaped or stained glass is then inserted and held in place by the cames.

43 Lewis Namier, *The Structure of Politics at the Accession of George III*, London, 1956, p. 240.

44 Quoted in Namier, p. 240, taken from J. B. Blakeway, *The Sherrifs of Shropshire*, Shrewsbury, 1831, p. 145.

45 Namier, p. 239.

46 Namier, p. 240.

47 SRRC, Attingham Collection, letter Book ref. 112/12/22/71, to Robert Moore, 6 February 1754.

48 The origins of the cap of Liberty date back to Roman times. When a slave was freed, a small Phrygian cap was placed on his head and he was termed *liberttinus* or freeman. Similar caps were hoisted onto spears and carried in triumph after acts of liberation in Rome, the murder of Julius Caesar being one of these occasions.

49 ed. David Vaisey, *The Diary of Thomas Turner 1754-1765*, Oxford, 1985, p. 275.

CHAPTER 12

'Inventor of Cast Iron Bridges'. Work on Bridges.

The Iron Bridge, and the surrounding area, is so important in the history of industrial development that it was declared a World Heritage Site by Unesco in 1986, the first such site to have received this recognition. The significance of the Iron Bridge itself, and the iron masters who created it, has been the subject of many books over the years, but until recently Pritchard's contribution had been somewhat overlooked. It could be said that it is a designer's bridge, and in this respect Shropshire gained a symbol that is instantly recognisable and can be utilised to fit many circumstances. The daring use of cast iron and the ostentatious size of the ribs indicate that this was a spectacular self-promotion exercise by the iron masters and as Pritchard played a major part in this innovative project he can be considered as one of the early architect-engineers together with Robert Mylne and Thomas Telford.

THE ENGLISH BRIDGE.

Pritchard's interest in the construction of bridges dated back to at least 1765 when he carried out a survey of the old bridge in Shrewsbury, known then as the Stone Bridge, and drew a design to widen and improve it.[1] Trustees, appointed to gather subscriptions and oversee the project, included Sir Edward Smythe, Sir Richard Corbett, Robert Burton of Longner, John Ashby, Charles Bolas, Mr. Fowler and Roger Kynaston, all familiar names on Pritchard's client list.

At the general meeting of the Subscribers held at the Infirmary in Shrewsbury on 20 November 1765, Pritchard showed his plan of the 'bridge in its present state' and his 'design for the improvement of it.' Somehow this did not seem to satisfy the meeting as 'Mr Baker', presumably William Baker, was then 'desired to make a plan ... with an estimate of expenses thereto.' Baker was also directed to take note of the houses on the north side of the bridgework which may have needed to be purchased and taken down 'for the executing of his schemes.'

It was decided that both plans should be laid before Robert Mylne, John Smeaton 'or any other architect as the committee ... shall direct for his opinion ... if such an architect cannot frame a good plan out of these two without taking a view of the place he be desired to come down for that purpose and prepare a design of his own.'

John Smeaton was a bridge engineer who had collaborated with John Gywnn in 1759 on the proposals for Blackfriars Bridge where they recommended the use of semi-circular as opposed to elliptical arches. In the end Smeaton could not accept the invitation to come for three months as he was very busy, so Mylne was asked to travel to Shrewsbury as soon as possible. Mylne, not well known in Shropshire at this stage, was described by Farington as 'a sociable man, much addicted to conversation', as well as being 'extremely exact in all his affairs'[2] and his diaries bear this out with their meticulous entries. The Trustees of the English Bridge asked for his advice after he had won the competition to build a bridge over the Thames at Blackfriars.

When Mylne visited Shrewsbury in May 1766, he took into account the 'ruinous condition' of the nearby Abbey Bridge at Coleham Head and said that it should be rebuilt. He also gave recommendations for improving the Stone Bridge which included taking away the island and erecting piers and arches in its place. The Trustees were impressed and asked him to prepare a design which would include these recommendations within the budget.

In June, it was agreed that Pritchard should be the surveyor of the works on the following terms which I have quoted in full as they differ very little from the work that an architect and a clerk of works have to carry out today:

> To make estimates of every sort of work relating to the edifices to be pulled down and to treat and contract with the proprietors if required
>
> To prepare all drawings necessary for the work and particularly such as the trustees shall require
>
> To make all enquiries relating to materials and workmanship to prepare particulars of the different species of work so that the workmen by understanding what is required to be done may give in the proper proposals
>
> To examine and give his opinion of the contracts to be made
>
> To superintend the execution of all the works under the direction of the Trustees in which he is not to give direction for anything beyond the order of the trustees nor alter anything they have ordered unless in cases of exigency and even then he is to consult one or more of them whose presence can be procured
>
> To measure all materials delivered by contract and enter account of them in books
>
> To measure the work when executed
>
> To take charge of the materials and stores
>
> To sell or dispose of to the best advantage for the use of the trustees all materials which they shall direct to

> be sold or otherwise disposed of
>
> To examine and sign all bills and enter them in books of the respective works
>
> To engage workmen when required and take care of the time of such as are to be employed by the day that they be well applied and work their full time
>
> To keep a clerk at his own expence to be constantly attending on the spot while work is going foreward at such times as he cannot attend himself who is to act as his deputy must be of good character, skilful in the works an accountant and a person agreeable to the trustees
>
> Mr Pritchard in consideration of the services he has already performed and of his executing the office of surveyor as aforesaid is to be paid by the trustees after the rate of three and a half per cent for all the money hereafter to be expended by them in widening and repairing the said bridge and the avenues thereto under his inspection except as underwritten (for example, the salaries of officers) and if he discharge the trust to the satisfaction of the trustees he is to receive from us a half per cent more.

These terms also demonstrate the amount of work that Pritchard was expected to carry out during a very busy period when he was involved also in other large projects such as Hatton Grange and Croft Castle. Other than the craftsmen we know about, he must have had additional people working with him, but for most jobs there is no direct mention of an assistant such as Jonathan Reynolds.

Work was to start almost immediately to take down the tower of the bridge, which had already collapsed. Pritchard was to sell the lead and safely lodge the timber, stone, iron and glass to be re-used and to make an estimate of the price of those houses which needed to be bought up before demolition started. In the end the purchase of the houses dragged on for a long time as the owners cannily refused to sell at the estimated prices.

Mylne's designs 'for widening and repairing the bridge' were approved and Mylne was paid fifty guineas for his work which included attending parliamentary committees and travel. It was agreed to advertise in Birmingham, Chester and one of the London papers for master builders and masons to 'send in proposals for undertaking the work.' Sir John Astley recommended that his bricklayer, Samuel Scoltock, should 'take down the houses during the winter season.'

It was intended that stone for the bridge would come from 'Miss Leighton's Rock in Condover Park' and Pritchard was ordered to contract for one hundred and fifty tons, but in October Mr Kynaston reported that Miss Leighton 'will not permit the stone to be carryed between Michaelmas and Lady Day.' In the end most of the stone came from the Grinshill Quarry and, surprisingly, it came by horse-drawn carts, not down the river. A team of twelve horses hauled the keystone for the centre arch.

In October, Mylne was asked if a new bridge, similar to one he had sketched already, could be built for the same money or whether an entirely new design could be made for the same price. Mylne replied that it could not.

In January 1767, Pritchard submitted a plan for a new bridge. The Trustees consulted several workmen about this and then decided to ask Mr. Mylne's opinion. In the meantime, the Trustees advertised for proposals for a temporary bridge, but in the event, floods delayed this; Shrewsbury is still flooded today when the River Severn rises quickly.

1-12: The English Bridge during rebuilding, 1770.

In August, Lord Clive donated the considerable sum of £500 to the fund. Complaints were made that the scantlings for the temporary bridge were not of the specified size and when this was discovered, Pritchard was ordered to 'strictly examine and survey what has been done' and report back. In September yet more designs were produced, this time by John Gwynn. These were for 'an entire new bridge consisting of seven semi-circular arches and another of seven elliptical arches.' Pritchard's design also had seven arches. After examination by Mr Buddle, a London mason, regarding the execution of the designs, it was 'resolved unanimously that Mr Gwynn's semi circular Design' should be adopted.

Why was Pritchard's design not accepted? He was working for many of the Trustees at that time and was well known to them. On the other hand, Gwynn had been short-listed for Blackfriars Bridge, although he had not won the contract and was subsequently embroiled in a controversy over the advantages of the differing shape of arches. In 1767, Gywnn's work on bridges was yet to come; Atcham Bridge in 1769, Worcester Bridge in 1771 and Magdalen Bridge, Oxford in 1772. However, he was a London architect and had published *An Essay on Design* and his important *London and Westminster Improved* had just come out, so the Trustees may have felt that he was the older and more experienced man for the job.

Architects such as Pritchard and Gwynn had enough experience with the techniques of building and the management of materials to undertake the design and construction of a bridge. The fact that Pritchard put forward plans indicates that he was interested in the design of bridges but it was not until 1773 that he was able to work on one at Stourport. It is ironic that Shrewsbury's best-known 18th century architect, whose plans were rejected for the English Bridge, then went on to produce the first design for the Iron Bridge, one of the most famous bridges in the world.

In October 1768, perhaps with some relief, Pritchard presented his bill for £72. 7s. 6d. 'for business done as surveyor' on the English Bridge, but as he had purchased 'sundry old materials' for £43. 15s. only £28. 12s. 6d. was due to him. The Trustees also queried him on 'the reasonableness of some articles charged in his bills' and he assured them that he had charged everything 'at a fair and customary price' and many of them much lower than he frequently

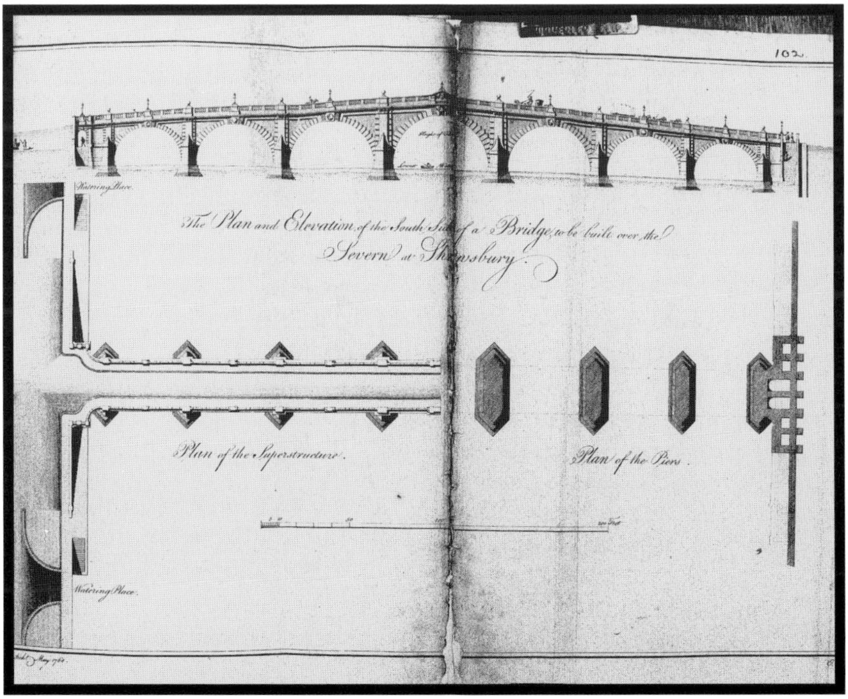

2-12: Design by John Gwynn for the English Bridge, 1768.

made on similar occasions which he would submit to the judgement of any workman but nevertheless would 'contribute 5gns more to the design of the trustees which was accepted.' Does this suggest that they had a point or that he felt it was not worth disputing? He was treading a careful path between retaining their patronage and making a living for himself.

Gwynn then took over as surveyor and although Pritchard was no longer directly involved he no doubt watched the progress of the bridge with interest and would have used this route when travelling between Shrewsbury and his new home at Eyton. The process of building which followed Pritchard's departure reveals interesting details on the construction of a bridge in a provincial town and the minutes show the typical problems faced by architects and surveyors, whether in the 18th century or today, so for this reason I have continued the English Bridge story.

One of Gwynn's first actions was to prepare a model of the 'intended new bridge' and to send it down 'with all convenient expedition together with a stand for the same to lie thereon' as he had been ordered by the Committee. He was also to send down an engraving on copper plate of his design; these items were for fund-raising purposes. When the model arrived Benjamin Reynolds, a carpenter, was paid 8s. 2d. for unpacking it and putting up a fence to guard it. He was given half a guinea for 'his trouble in attendance' and a later minute reveals that the model, made by a Mr. Thacker, cost £98. 7s. 6d. This amount had been sent but no acknowledgement had been received.[3]

The workmen on this job seemed to justify Taylor White's opinions of the team at the Foundling Hospital. Messrs. Thompson and Lowden were not carrying out their tasks properly, although this was 'repeatedly pointed out and insisted on by the surveyor.' Mr Buddle, the London mason, was absent so much that the 'subscribers and public in general' became 'very impatient to see the undertaking set on foot.' Mr Buddle said he was absent through illness, and was questioned by the Committee, who had every right to be suspicious as in July 1768 he had entered into a contract to build the Atcham Bridge for £5,000.[4] Buddle was dismissed and Gwynn took over, together with his agent, William Hayward of Shrewsbury; eventually Buddle's account was settled by arbitration.

Suppliers of materials also caused difficulties. Before Buddle was dismissed he clashed with Martha Walford, who ran the quarry at Grinshill and had supplied stone to the Foundling Hospital. She broke her agreement with Buddle and 'refused to furnish him with any more stone, without he would comply with a very exorbitant and unreasonable demand in respect to a sum of money to be advanced.' Mr. Hill of Hawkstone, who owned the Quarry, offered the Trustees the free use of another quarry adjoining provided

> they or Mr Buddle would be at the expense of opening it or otherwise a continuance of the present quarry from

Lady Day next (when the present occupier's tenure therein will expire) at the customary rate of three pence per ton royalty. The said Martha Walford attending and being called in and examined expressed great penitence for her misbehaviour and promised Mr Buddle should, agreeable to his contract, have whatever stone he had further occasion for unmolested.

3-12: The English Bridge after rebuilding.

The foundation stone for the bridge was laid, 'amidst acclamations of a great number of spectators' on 29 June 1769 by Sir John Astley as 'his great munificence gave birth to the design.' The 'great munificence' amounted to a very generous £1000 and the 'acclamations' were for the lack of tolls on the new bridge. A general meeting of the contributors and friends to the bridge was held on 24 October 1770 when Samuel Pritchard was present, but not Thomas; he had retired out to Eyton by then. In 1921 the English Bridge was carefully dismantled and using the same stones was rebuilt with a lower crown and wider carriageway. In 1769 the total was eventually £16,000: the 1921 work cost £86,000.

In January 1769, Pritchard had been paid three guineas by the Quarter Sessions for unspecified work; this could have been connected with a survey of Atcham Bridge over the River Severn as its condition was causing concern,[5] but Gwynn and Buddle went on to build the bridge there. Berrow's *Worcester Journal* of 14 April 1774 advertised for 'several masons and labourers to work at the New

Bridges. Any such applying to Mr. Gwynn's office near the Bridge may meet with employment. N.B. None need apply but such as are sober and good Masons.'

Gwynn's Atcham Bridge still stands today as an elegant monument to him.[6]

4-12: Stourport Bridge, 1776.

STOURPORT BRIDGE.

By 1773 Pritchard was well prepared to act as surveyor for a new bridge over the River Severn at what is now Stourport. In the Prefatory Notice in *On Cemetitious Architecture*, Pritchard's grandson, John White, wrote proudly about his grandfather's achievements:

> In the year 1773 Mr. Pritchard was engaged in making a design for Stourport bridge, where the Severn requires water-way sufficient to permit a rise, in flood-times, of 18 feet, and an aperture of at least 136 feet. He originally meditated on the construction of a Timber bridge, similar to that which then crossed the Thames at Walton: but not being satisfied with the material, and at the same time being unwilling to employ brick or stone in the buttresses of the bridge in such a manner as would impede the current, he made his first design for a brick bridge on an iron centre, lightened in the buttresses and in part over the arch, by circular perforations ...[7]

John White's article showed Pritchard's drawing of the 'Design of a New Bridge at Stourport' dated 1773. Was this the timber one that Pritchard first contemplated putting across the river?

The bridge was required at Stourport to cross the Severn, near Redstone in Worcestershire. The basin for the Staffordshire and Worcester Canal at Stourport had just been built and therefore there was an important commercial motive. The first notice of the scheme was put into Berrow's *Worcestershire Journal* on 2 September 1773.[8] Trustees had already been appointed to 'put into execution the Act of Parliament for building a Bridge across the River Severn ... and for making proper Avenues and Road to and from the same ...'[9] and a meeting was called for 14 September. The main business was to ask for:

> any Person or Persons willing to contract with the said Trustees, ... for building a Stone Bridge across the said River, to consist of three Arches, the center Arch thereof to be 18 feet wide at the Wall, and 17 Feet wide in the Clear for passing over, and 132 Feet clear for the Water to flow through the said Arches, from and out of the Meadow of Mrs. Pougher, above and near Stour-port ... to the Meadow of Daniel Zachary, Esq. in the Parish of Lower Areley ... on the opposite side of the river, together with the Arches of Communication across the Meadows

on each Side ..., are desired to deliver in, the same day, to the Trustees, Plans and Estimates thereof sealed up.[10]

At the same meeting the Trustees intended to borrow and 'take up, on Mortgage of the Tolls granted by the said Act (of Parliament) the sum of Seven Thousand Pounds.' This was to be advanced in instalments as the Trustees directed and as required. At the next meeting in December the sum of £2500 was to be laid out in 'building a substantial commodious and permanent wooden bridge ... and it being intended to contract for building the said bridge agreeable to a plan fixed upon for the purpose.'[11] The work was to begin in the spring.

5-12: Two designs for bridges by Pritchard, 1773-4.

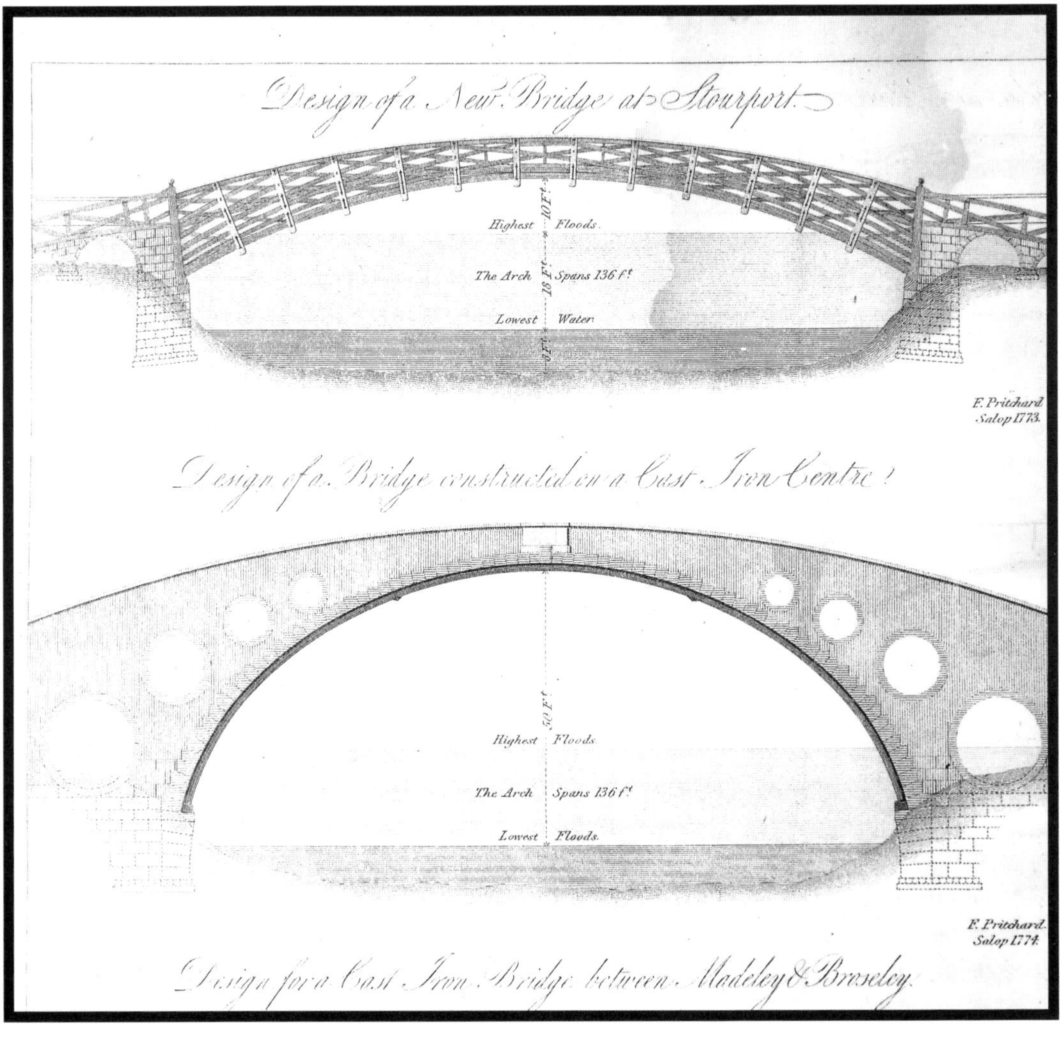

The notice for the first meeting of 1774 showed that the Trustees were now appointed 'by Act of Parliament'and the sum of £3000 was to be borrowed for purchasing 'necessary land ... making Satisfaction for Damage.' The wooden bridge was to have 'stone abutments at each end and brick arches to support a Road of Communication.' The Trustees were also ready to contract with someone to build the bridge, 'or any different part thereof ... agreeably to a plan designed by Mr. T. F. Pritchard, appointed surveyor of the intended work.'[12]

This was the first mention of Pritchard, although he must have been appointed in the autumn of 1773 in order to draw up the plans. There is no indication of why the bridge was changed from stone to wood, but the mention of the wooden bridge bears out what his grandson wrote.

White had said that Pritchard was 'not satisfied with this material' and by the summer of 1774 seemed to have reconsidered the design. The Trustees were called for a meeting to discuss 'Business of some Consequence' and it was hoped that as many as possible could attend. Pritchard's 'Design of a Bridge constructed on a Cast Iron Centre' is dated 1774 but no month is given.[13]

There is no report or further information about this important business but meetings were called frequently over the summer and autumn of 1774, suggesting a more urgent timetable and perhaps another change of plan as in August contractors were sought for building a stone bridge. The meeting of 15 September was called to agree to borrow £1000 'to be laid out in compleating the said Bridge.'[14] In November the Trustees decided that 'in order for proper and speedy completion of the Bridge it being not only expedient to examine the state of the accounts but also necessary to provide some particular materials in the winter ... so as to start again in the spring as early ... as the season will permit.'[15]

None of the Notices for meetings mentions cast iron, so we are left to work out what exactly was used in the way of materials. There is no dispute that Pritchard's first design was for a wooden bridge, although the original specification was stone, but the design changed back to stone sometime in 1774. Pritchard's design of 1774 shows a stone bridge with what seems to be iron around the arch and which could have been the iron centre referred to by John White.

No interim details of the bridge were reported before its completion by October 1775 and a notice was published that it was 'now commodious & convenient for Herses and Carriages to pass and repass over the same.'[16] It was announced that a drawing by James Sherriff of Stourport, 'dedicated to the Proprietors of the Staffordshire and Worcestershire Canal ... will soon be ready for publication.'

The range and area of the news covered in Berrow's *Worcester Journal* at that period was extensive. For instance, in January 1774, when Pritchard's plans for the Stourport Bridge were put out for tender, the same edition carried a notice about the Adelphi Lottery.[17] The *Journal* also surprisingly mentioned Shrewsbury and Shropshire news such as the notice for Noel Hill standing for election, Ludlow races with Richard Morhall as Steward, a man being tried for stealing Nathaniel Scoltock's black mare and the generous contribution of £794 towards the 'relief of the poor' made homeless by a fire in Abbey Foregate, Shrewsbury. Familiar names appear such as Pritchard's client, Jonathan Pytts of Kyre, who is Steward of the Worcester Races and the publication of the *Life of Clive of India* is advertised; it was also in the *Shrewsbury Chronicle* at the same date.[18]

As the Stourport Bridge was damaged in a flood of 1795 and had to be replaced it is not possible to know what use was eventually made of cast iron. In contemporary illustrations, there is nothing to indicate the use of iron in the centre and the bridge appears to have been made of stone with lighter-coloured stone keystones, edges to arches and circular perforations.

The River Severn was important as a means of transport with a 'timetabled service from Shrewsbury to Gloucester and Bristol.'[20] The number of cargo-carrying boats in 1756 on the Shropshire stretches of the Severn was about 250 so the river itself and its bridges were of considerable economic importance to the area.

6-12: Pritchard's Stourport Bridge.

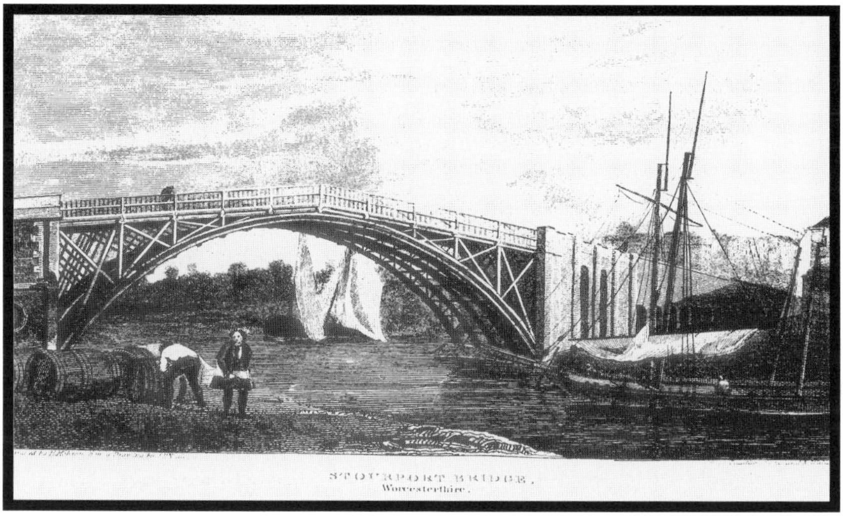

7-12: Stourport Bridge, probably a replacement of the one built by Pritchard.

John White was in no doubt about his grandfather's achievements:

> The interest which I feel in recording the advancement of Science, and the respect which I entertain for the memory of my maternal grandfather ... have induced me to draw out (as far as recollection and the materials in my possession enable me) a brief account of part of the consecutive designs which led to the first application of cast iron for arches in the construction of bridges; an application which ... originated with him ...[19]

Looking at the site of the bridge today, it seems likely that the bases of the land arches were those laid down by Pritchard in 1774 or 1775. There is no sign of any other land arches in the immediate vicinity and this might have persuaded the builders of the new bridge to use them on practical and economic grounds.

There is a resemblance between the replacement bridge and the design that Pritchard drew for 'a New Bridge at Stourport' in 1773. The Trustees, in possession of Pritchard's earlier design, could have decided to use it. There is little information about the second bridge. *The Cambrian Travellers' Guide* wrote that 'this bridge was built by ironfounders in the district, possibly by Messrs. Baldwin, Son and Co. at their works in Foundry Street.' It would be interesting indeed if this replacement bridge used Pritchard's original design and was built of iron, but it has also been replaced.

The Use Of Cast Iron.

John White wrote that Pritchard was not satisfied with the 'arrangement' at Stourport and

> planned various bridges of these materials; till at length, encouraged by the patronage of the spirited Iron-masters of Colebrook Dale, he made a design for the bridge now existing near that place ...[21]

We have already seen that Pritchard was acquainted with John Wilkinson, the fanatical iron master, that he had designed a cast iron grate for Shipton Hall and columns made in cast iron for Gaines, so it seemed natural that he would want to take the process further and when the chance arose progress towards 'THE FIRST INTRODUCTION OF IRON AS THE CONSTITUENT MATERIAL FOR ARCHES OF A LARGE SPAN.'[22]

The third drawing illustrated by White is for a 'Design for a Cast Iron Bridge between Madeley & Broseley,' dated 1775. Assuming that what he wrote is correct regarding the 'first application of cast iron for arches in the construction of bridges,'[23] then this design is of great importance in the history of the use of cast iron. Darby's great grandfather had smelted iron with coke in the early 18th century, but this method was slow to be adopted and in 1759 when the Carron works were founded much of their pig-iron was smelted with charcoal.

If Darby's methods were slow to have been taken up in Britain, the same would apply to the other iron-producing countries such as Sweden and Russia. They both had plentiful wood as a source for charcoal and therefore little incentive to change their methods. It would follow, therefore, that no other country was advanced enough at that time to be able to use cast iron for bridge building. We know for certain that the Iron Bridge was the world's first cast iron structure of any size, and it could almost certainly be said that the Stourport Bridge was the first to be constructed using cast iron as one of the materials.

Wrought iron had been used for construction for many centuries; the use of it in the Gothic spire of Salisbury Cathedral is a famous example. As far as bridges are concerned, there are records that it had been used for iron chains on suspension bridges; some chain bridges are recorded in China and Kashmir in 65AD.[24] In Britain, the *Leeds Intelligencer* reported on 2 January 1770 that:

> A few days ago was finished by Mr Tobin of this town a most curious bridge of one arch, six feet wide, and 72 feet in span; made entirely of iron ... It has also iron balustrades, which are ornamented with roses of the same metal ... [25]

Accounts from Kirklees Estate show the payment, in 1769, of £157.10s. to Maurice Tobin from Sir George Armytage for '1 Ormanented Iron Bridge'.[26] An illustration from the estate map of 1788 shows this bridge in situ and it is not dissimilar in style to the timber bridge designed by Pritchard. Unfortunately the Kirklees bridge no longer exists so it is not possible to know if it was made of cast or wrought iron. The latter seems most likely as Maurice Tobin was a well-known whitesmith and ironmonger in Leeds and his obituary described him as 'the most eminent in his profession of any in the North of England'.[27] Tobin worked for John Carr and Robert Adam supplying fenders and grates among a range of items. He also made 'railings, gates, staircase balustrades and other ornamental cast-iron work',[28] so it is just possible that the Kirklees Bridge was made from cast iron in which case it predates the Iron Bridge by ten years, but with only these brief facts it is hard to be certain.

The first use of cast iron for structural purposes seems controversial. It is believed that the Greeks of the classical age used cast iron sections to strengthen the undersides of marble beams.[29] I have already referred to the 1752 example in Portugal and the columns in the House of Commons.[30] Over twenty years later cast iron was used for a staircase in the Louvre in Paris around the same time as the Iron Bridge was first opened.[31] The earliest dateable cast iron columns in this country are thought, by Raymond Lister, to have been in Old St. Ann's Church, Liverpool, built in 1770-2 but as the church was demolished in the middle of the 19th century no evidence remains.[32]

It is indisputable that the Iron Bridge was the biggest and most daring use of cast iron at that date, so impractically daring that it is now considered that Darby and Wilkinson looked on it as an advertisement for their businesses.[33]

THE IRON BRIDGE.

It is often thought that Thomas Telford or Isambard Kingdom Brunel were involved in the scheme to construct the Iron Bridge, but Telford did not arrive in Shropshire until after it was built and Brunel was born twenty-seven years after its completion.

The 'proposal to build an iron bridge between Madeley and the south shore of the Severn' originated in a letter written in 1773 by Thomas Farnolls Pritchard ... to John Wilkinson.'[34] Pritchard was, as we have seen, encouraged by the 'Iron-masters of Colebrook Dale', to make the design. In February 1774 the Worcester and Shrewsbury newspapers reported on the proposal for a petition to Parliament to build a bridge over the Severn near Coalbrookdale.

A meeting of interested parties took place on 15 September 1775 at Abraham Cannadine's house at Broseley. At this meeting it was agreed 'that Mr. Thomas Farnolls Pritchard and Mr. Samuel Thomas be desired to prepare estimates of the said bridge against the next meeting.'[35] The identity of Samuel Thomas is not known and he is never mentioned again. At the next meeting a month later it was agreed that the noblemen and gentlemen of the area should be named as commissioners who would put their names to the petition for the bridge to be presented to Parliament. Pritchard had worked for many of the influential people named – Sir Richard Acton, Plowden Slaney and Roger Kynaston. Pritchard himself was also included on the list. In February 1776 the petition, which put forward sound commercial reasons for building the bridge, was presented to the House of Commons. Lord North, the Prime Minister, saw the plans by Pritchard and they 'gave great satisfaction.'[36]

8-12: Prtichard's design for 'A Cast Iron Bridge', 1775.

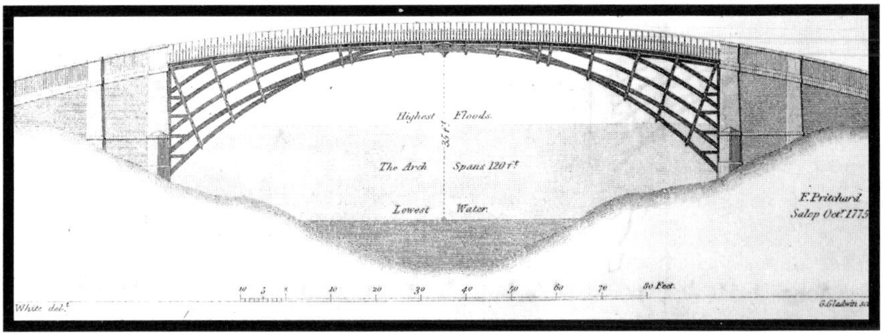

Also at this meeting it was agreed to 'defray all expenses in erecting the intended Bridge in a substantial manner, according to a plan this day produced by Mr. Thomas Farnolls Pritchard or as near it as may be for the best and safest manner.' Pritchard himself was present at this meeting and presumably discussed the plan with them; this must be the plan that is dated October 1775 and definitely states 'for a Cast Iron Bridge.'

The span for the arch is 120 feet, a size that was adhered to throughout the planning stages. An estimate for the bridge, which came to £3,200. 11s., was drawn up by Darby and Pritchard, together with a subscription list, which brought in a total of £3,150, Darby and Wilkinson being the largest subscribers. Pritchard subscribed £105, a respectable sum for that time. The eventual cost of the bridge was in the region of £5000.

The next meeting was held on 15 May 1776 at the Swan Inn, Coalbrookdale, owned by Nicholson, one of the subscribers. At this meeting is was agreed to advertise, in Birmingham and other papers, for someone to build a single arch bridge of 'stone brick and timber.' The sizes are given as 'one arch of 120 feet span, the superstructure 18 feet in the clear and the centre 35 feet above low water.'[37] These are the sizes on Pritchard's drawing of 1775. Why was this advertisement necessary? Pritchard was present at this meeting and must have put forward his case for iron. Perhaps he felt that any doubters on the committee could be swayed if no one suitable came forward and this proved to be the case because at another meeting on

June 28, at which Pritchard was also present, they 'agreed to advertise' for someone 'to undertake the stone and brick work of a bridge ... according to a plan produced this day by Mr. Thomas Farnolls Pritchard.'[38] This would appear to indicate that work was for the abutments and other structural parts necessary for the bridge as ' ... a far greater and more wonderful piece of Architecture is now in agitation, a Fabric which England or the whole Globe cannot equal. This is an Iron Bridge ... the whole will be of Cast Iron without an ounce of any other sort of material about it ...'[39]

Now that they had managed to generate publicity, the committee settled down to serious business as the abutments were a critical part of the structure. They have been strengthened and altered over the years and are vital in keeping the unstable ground of the embankments under control. A month later, on 24 July 1776, at another meeting at the Black Swan, 'it was agreed that Mr. Thomas Farnolls Pritchard should prepare a model of a Bridge according to a plan by him produced; that application be made to proper persons to find out proper stone and clay for making bricks for building the bridge.'[40] Pritchard was not present at this meeting, but by this period he was a busy and successful architect and was working on or drawing up plans for buildings as far apart as Kyre Park in Worcestershire, at Sudborough in Northamptonshire and The Guildhall in Ludlow; in August, 1776 he was in Ludlow measuring and abstracting the work.

In October he attended the meeting where Mr. Jennings, one of the original subscribers who put up £525, and Mr. Wilkinson, who subscribed £630, 'agreed to let Mr. Darby have their shares in consideration of him giving the security that an Iron Bridge shall be erected ... in 2 years from Christmas next and Mr. Darby agrees to take the said shares on the condition ...'[41] Later that month, there was a reassignment of shares and Darby's 'supporters' paid £5 per share. The final assignment of these shares did not take place until 20 October 1777 and Pritchard took two shares. Work eventually started in November 1777. Pritchard died a month later, after being ill for a year.

In 1781, not long after the bridge was completed, the committee agreed to print 10,000 tickets for the tolls with the name 'Iron Bridge' on them and so it became official and has been used almost since then; until then it had been called the 'intended Bridge'. In the next year the iron masters capitalised on the publicity generated by the bridge and issued a drawing by William Ellis and so the bridge became famous both here and abroad. In September 1779 £40 was paid to Samuel Pritchard for his brother's drawings and model.

The Iron Bridge, as Wilkinson and Darby had intended, soon became 'One of the Wonders of the World'[42] and visitors flocked to see it. Even before the bridge was opened Darby had paid 'for advertising the views' and engravings of the bridge were sold in a package which included the engineering drawing by Ellis.[43]

Visitors had been coming to the Gorge for some time to see the ironworks and other industrial activity and the motives of the visitors varied from a scientific interest in the minerals of the area and how they were used, to industrial espionage by a French spy. Whatever the reason, nearly all visitors were impressed by the activity in the Gorge and after the construction of the bridge they were even more impressed. One of the first references to the bridge was made by Arthur Young the agriculturist in 1776 when, crossing on the ferry, he noted where 'Mr. Darby has undertaken to build a bridge of one arch of 120 feet, of cast iron.'[44] Once the bridge was in place, admiration for it soon followed. Samuel Butler in 1782 commented that 'The Bridge itself makes a light and elegant appearance tho' apparently no ways deficient in Strength.' He had heard that the 'expence of this undertaking is said to have been 5000 Guineas.'[45]

Torrington came to the Gorge in 1784. He was impressed by the bridges of Shrewsbury, Atcham and Berwick, now called Tern Bridge, and called them 'new and magnificent.' He went on to eulogise about the Iron Bridge 'which we cross'd, and where we stop'd for half an hour, what shall I say? That it must be the admiration, as it is one of the wonders, of the world ... the county agreed with the founder to finish it for 6000£ and have, meanly, made him suffer for his noble undertaking.'[46] This entry illustrates the high cost of the bridge, but the results must have been worth every penny to the builders. Berrow's *Worcester Journal* advertised premises to let close to 'the cast Iron Bridge, so universally admired in the centre of a most romantic Country, and within ten Minutes of the Coalbrookdale Iron-Works.'[47]

In later years, Pritchard's rôle became eclipsed. Writing in 1863 Samuel Smiles attributed the design of the bridge to Thomas Gregory, Darby's foreman pattern maker:[48]

> Mr Pritchard, a Shrewsbury architect, prepared a design of a stone bridge of one arch, in which he proposed to introduce a key-stone of cast iron, occupying only a few feet at the crown of the arch. This plan was, however, given up as unsuitable; and another, with the entire arch of cast iron was designed under the superintendence of Mr. Darby.[49]

After he had dismissed Pritchard, Smiles quoted admiringly:: 'If we consider that the manipulation of cast iron was then completely in its infancy, a bridge of such dimensions was doubtless a bold as well as an original undertaking, and the efficiency of the details is worthy of the boldness of the conception.'

9-12: *The Iron Bridge by C. Varley, 1802.*

More significantly, Thomas Telford wrote about the influence of the Iron Bridge and considered its original design formed 'an Era in bridge building.' He continued to say that Pritchard's grandson, 'Mr John White, a London architect, has favoured me with the perusal of the original documents, dated 17 October 1775 and I consider it only justice to the ingenious artist to record his merit on this occasion.'[50] Praise indeed from one of the greatest bridge builders.

There are many accounts of the Iron Bridge over the two centuries of its life, so I will end by quoting from an article in a leaflet on the British Construction Awards for 1995. The small project winner was the Jackfield Bridge across the River Severn. The judges called it 'A worthy near neighbour to its world famous forebear.' David Hayward, who wrote the article, said that the Jackfield Bridge was 'less than 1km. downstream from arguably the most architecturally challenging bridge to complement. The presence of the world's first iron bridge just around the corner has dominated virtually every aspect of the new crossing's location, design and construction.' The architects themselves, Percy Thomas Partnership, were very conscious of this and in the end they believed they had 'complemented rather than conflicted with the Iron Bridge ... one of our major headaches was designing the apex of the tower ... we went for a stiffening ring to complement the circles featured on the Iron Bridge.' Visitors to the area will probably agree that the new bridge is a very striking structure and fits well in the Gorge.

It is interesting, however, to compare the costs. Torrington said that the Iron Bridge cost '6000£'; the new Jackfield bridge cost £2 million.

Today the Iron Bridge is a symbol of Shropshire, of industrial archaeology and is recognised around the world. It is used for advertising the whole area and Pritchard has now been assigned to his rightful place as the original designer.

10-12: The Iron Bridge today.

11-12: The Forge Bridge.

FORGE BRIDGE AND CASTLE BRIDGE, DOWNTON.

By the time that Payne Knight was building Downton Castle, Pritchard was turning his attention to bridges generally and the use of cast iron for them in particular. For a long time, it has been considered that Pritchard could have been the architect of the Forge Bridge at Downton. Recently, doubts have been cast on this theory, notably by John Van Laun in an article for the Woolhope Club. He based his evidence on an estate terrier of about 1780 which 'shows only the old bridge ['a very venerable old bridge'] lying slightly upstream from Forge Bridge.' Van Laun continues: '... it is most unlikely that he [Pritchard] was involved in the construction of the Forge Bridge.'[51] Without further evidence the matter is inconclusive.

12-12: The Castle Bridge at Downton today.

Comparisons have been made between the Forge Bridge and the Iron Bridge, but these are not convincing enough to be evidence of Pritchard's authorship of the former. Both bridges have a semicircular form, which make a full circle when reflected in the water, but Pritchard's first design for the Iron Bridge had a lower arch and we have no surviving knowledge what his next stage was. The arched abutments at the side of both bridges are for practical purposes; for the Forge Bridge it was to allow water in the leet to pass through to run the power for the forges and for the Iron Bridge to allow horses and men to tow the boats upstream.

The Castle Bridge at Downton has also been attributed to Pritchard and the design for this could have formed part of the plans that he drew up for Payne Knight in 1772. References to the Castle Bridge appear in documentation by 1780, but it may have been built earlier to convey building materials to the site. The bridge has three elegant arches with stone facings over a rubble core. Recently it has been restored after deteriorating into a rather poor state; the stone facings were being pushed away from the rubble core by frost and damp and now the bridge has been returned to its former elegance. Again, there is no firm evidence for Pritchard's involvement in this work, but it was certainly within his capabilities.

As I have said, there is a logic in the construction of a bridge, and these masons and joiners, such as Pritchard, could transfer their skills from buildings to bridges, which if the principles are known and recognised, most skilled craftsmen are able to do. These men were very much what we today would call 'design and build'; that is they carried out both tasks and in their minds there was no difference between them. Although so little work on bridges is positively attributed to Pritchard, there is no doubt that he made a definite contribution to the construction of bridges and the use of new materials for them. He is credited with giving the impetus to the plan for building the Iron Bridge in cast iron and this alone brings him to the forefront of early industrial architects and perhaps justifies the claim on a now-vanished portrait that he was an 'Inventor of Cast Iron Bridges.'

13-12: Downton Castle and the Bridge in the early 19th century.

1 Minutes of the Trustees of the English Bridge, Box LXXV, No: 2677. This is the source for all information on the building of the English Bridge. Unpaginated.

2 Colvin, p. 681.

3 This cost is comparable with today's prices for a high-quality model.

4 Anthony Blackwall, *Historic Bridges of Shropshire*, Shrewsbury, 1985, p. 12.

5 SRRC, Shrewsbury Quarter Sessions, 1769.

6 William Hayward, another Shrewsbury architect, built the bridge over the River Tern at Atcham. He was a member of one of several Shropshire families of craftsmen-architects. He himself was the third generation of this line of work and his sister Ann married John Carline I, a mason from Lincoln and thereby established another two generations of mason-architects. Hayward's grandfather came from Whitchurch and had probably worked as a foreman for William Smith of Warwick. His grandson came to Shrewsbury and involved himself with the building of the English Bridge, acting as deputy to John Gwynn. He supervised Gwynn's work on the Magdalen Bridge in Oxford from 1772 and built the Tern Bridge in 1773. Sadly Hayward died at the age of 42, having caught a cold and fever from 'giving up his place inside a coach to a woman on a stormy night', which illustrates one of the hazards of 18th century travel. In 1932 Hayward's masonry formed the basis for the widening of the Tern Bridge on the busy A5 London to Holyhead road. (Colvin, pp. 482-5.)

7 John White, 'On Cementitious Architecture', from *The Philosophical Magazine and Annals*, London, 1832, p. 1.

8 Information about meetings of the Trustees for Stourport Bridge from Berrow's *Worcestershire Journal* from 1773-1775 held at Worcester Records Office, (WRO) County Hall, Worcester.

9 Berrow's *Worcestershire Journal*, 2 September 1773.

10 Berrow's *Worcestershire Journal*, 14 September 1773.

11 Berrow's *Worcestershire Journal*, 2 December 1773.

12 Berrow's *Worcestershire Journal*, 3 February 1774.

13 The meetings of the Trustees took place in the 'dwelling house' of Mary Roden at Stourport and the meetings were called by Richard Colley, who is discussed in connection with Quatt Church.

14 Berrow's *Worcestershire Journal*, 1 September 1774.

15 Berrow's *Worcestershire Journal*, 17 November 1774.

16 Berrow's *Worcestershire Journal*, 9 October 1775.

17 The Adelphi was the speculative London building project by the Adam brothers.

18 Not everyone was happy with the new arrangements. A petition was presented to Daniel Zachary, esq., owner of the meadows in Lower Areley from the Bailiff, Burgesses and the inhabitants of Bewdley. They said they had already spent money on repairs to the bridge and that unemployment would be caused on the river. In addition, the owners of boats also intended to petition against the bridge as they felt that it would obstruct navigation and make it much more dangerous and expensive 'which will be a heavy clog upon trade in general.' Their petition did not carry much weight as the Act was passed.

19 White, p. 1.

20 Information from 'Bridgnorth Port' by Alan Webb in *The Shropshire Review* Sept./Oct. 1997, p. 8.

21 White, pp. 1-2.

22 White, in the title of his short article about his grandfather.
23 White, p. 1.
24 See Nikolaus Pevsner, *Pioneers of Modern Design*, London.
25 York Archaeological Society, Industrial History Section, *A Preliminary Report on the Kirklees Iron Bridge of 1769 and its builder,* David Nortcliffe. Unpaginated.
26 Nortcliffe, unpaginated.
27 Christopher Gilbert and Anthony Wells-Cole, *The Fashionable Fireplace 1660-1840*, Temple Newsam Country House Studies Number 2, 1985, p. 61.
28 Gilbert and Wells-Cole, p. 61.
29 Letter in *Building Design*, May 1997 from Miles Scott. Reference: W. B. Dinsmoor 'Structural Iron in Greek Architecture', *American Journal of Archaeology*, Volume 26, 1922.
30 See Chapter 5, note 31.
31 Pevsner, *Pioneers of Modern Design*, 1986 edition, p. 118.
32 Raymond Lister, *Decorative Cast Iron Work*, London, 1960, p. 155
33 Shropshire was proud of its connection with iron. In Wrockwardine churchyard, in Shropshire, there is a cast iron stand for a sundial. The sundial itself, in brass, is inscribed with the date 1750 and the names of the churchwardens, who were the donors. One is Thomas Onions. The Onions family were involved in the Benthall ironworks near the Iron Bridge and John White said that Mr Onions, together with Wilkinson and Darby, promoted 'the completion of the Colebrook Dale bridge.'
34 Neil Cossons and Barrie Trinder, *The Iron Bridge*, Bradford, 1979, p. 17.
35 SRRC 6001/3698. MSS Iron Bridge Committee Minute book, 15 September 1775, unpaginated.
36 SRRC, February 1776.
37 SRRC, 15 May 1776.
38 SRRC, 28 June 1776.
39 Quoted in *Iron Bridge*, an Ironbridge Gorge Museum Trust publication.
40 For many years this model was at Acton Burnell Hall, but has since disappeared.
41 SRRC, 1 October 1776.
42 *The Torrington Diaries*, Volume 1, p. 184.
43 *The Iron Bridge and Town*, Ironbridge, 1995, p. 15.
44 Quoted in Barrie Trinder, *The Most Extraordinary District in the World*, Chichester, Second Edition, 1988, p. 34.
45 Trinder, p. 37
46 *The Torrington Diaries*, p. 184-5.
47 Berrow's *Worcester Journal*, 6 April 1786. I am grateful to Dr. Terry Friedman for giving me this reference; he remarked that it was very interesting that proximity to the Iron Works should be considered an asset then. Presumably it was their novelty that drew people, just as they were attracted to the Iron Bridge itself.
48 Samuel Smiles, *Industrial Revolution: Ironworkers and Toolmakers*, (1863) pp. 89-90
49 *Life of Thomas Telford*, Samuel Smiles, London 1867, pp. 170-171.
50 *Life of Thomas Telford*, ed. J. Rickman, London 1838, p. 29.
51 John Van Laun, 'Bringewood Furnace and Forge Site - a Reassessment,' *The Transactions of the Woolhope Club*, 1987, p. 787.

APPENDIX 1

Attributed Work.

In this appendix are houses, churches and monuments that Pritchard may have worked on but for which there is no supporting documentation. All have either a stylistic resemblance to his other work, or family, business or geographical connections. William Baker is the link for such places as Mawley Hall and the proximity of Peover to Tatton Hall presents a geographical connection. The similarity of the cherubs on the Cludde monument, which does not have Pritchard's name on it, to cherubs on monuments which bear his name, almost certainly point to the same designer.

As in the other chapters the work is grouped by county.

WORCESTERSHIRE.

THE WHITE HOUSE, SUCKLEY.

1-A1: The staircase at the White House at Suckley.

The White House at Suckley, close to Gaines, had come into the possession of Thomas Freeman in 1742 and his family lived there for a further six generations. When Freeman's father died in 1764 he started to spend money on the building. Thomas's older sister, Betty, was married to Bartholomew Barnaby of Brockhampton so Pritchard, who worked at both Gaines and Brockhampton, would have been the obvious choice as architect for the work.

The White House is a tall, three-storey house dating from the time of Queen Anne. The first thing that catches the eye is a particularly fine hood over the front door with a plasterwork Rococo cartouche and sprays of flowers; another, less ornate one, is over the garden entrance at the back of the house.

The house contains several stylistic indications of Pritchard's involvement: the plasterwork over the fireplace in the dining room is so similar to plasterwork at Gaines that it would appear to be by Joseph Bromfield. The rather shallow arches beside the staircase are echoed at the Broad Gate House, Ludlow. There the modernisation seemed to have stopped and many interesting features from an earlier era were fortunately allowed to remain.[1]

Above
2-A1: Peover Hall with the Georgian additions.

Below
3-A1: Chimney piece at Peover Hall.

CHESHIRE.

PEOVER HALL.

The 18th century work at Peover Hall, near Knutsford in Cheshire, disappeared when the Georgian wing was demolished in the 1950s. Photographs of this demolished wing show a brick six-bay Georgian block somewhat awkwardly attached to the 16th century house built by Sir Ralph Mainwaring. Three of these bays on two of the elevations are slightly stepped forward and pedimented. On one elevation there is a central Venetian doorway with a wide pediment over it and above that a tall arched window, probably inserted to light a staircase. The other windows have lugged architraves. On another elevation the pedimented bays have similar windows but no Venetian doorway or rusticated surround. This block shows similarities to other known work by Pritchard and the sympathetic welding of the new wing with the existing Tudor building is in keeping with his style.

One of the Georgian chimney pieces from the demolished house is now in a first floor bedroom on the west side and as the style resembles Pritchard's designs in *The Drawing Book* it is very likely to be his work. The plain pedimented overmantel can be compared with one at Swan Hill Court House and there is high quality carving on the wooden chimney piece which is decorated with grapes and other fruits, indicating that it may have been originally in the dining room.[2]

Pritchard was involved at nearby Tatton Park and could have worked at Peover when he was in the area. William Emes is known to have carried out designs for the garden at Peover and the two men have been connected.

3-A1: The stables, Peover Hall.

The coach house is dated 1764 and its form resembles the stables at Shipton Hall, Shropshire. Both are long buildings with the entrance for coaches in the centre three bays. Two round windows in the centre at Shipton echo the circular windows at Peover along the whole façade. Both buildings are crowned with a cupola.

SOMERFORD PARK.

This house, demolished in 1926, has been firmly attributed to Pritchard by John Harris.[3] No evidence exists for this attribution apart from the exterior appearance of the house. The front elevation is nine bays wide with the centre three bays stepped forward and topped with a pediment. The wings were added later and before these additions, the house would have looked much more like Pritchard's customary style.

SHROPSHIRE.

LUTWYCHE HALL.

Lutwyche Hall near Much Wenlock is basically an E-plan brick building of 1587 but little is known about the history of this very interesting house except that the central area between the wings was filled in during the 18th century.

The riot of plasterwork in the large hall veers between Rococo and Baroque and Rococo-Baroque revival in such a way that it is hard to know how to date it. Some of this plasterwork could be said to resemble the work at nearby Shipton, but it has the general appearance of being later. A fine 18th century staircase has three balusters to the tread and carved tread ends which could indicate Pritchard's hand. Also more in keeping with Pritchard's work is the stable block with a cupola on it.

HENLEY HALL.

In 1771 Mrs. Lybbe Powys described the house as 'a fine old place badly situated. The house and furniture are quite antique, but one receives pleasure in these reviews of former times.'[4] Just after her visit, the house was sold by Sir Littleton Powys to Thomas Knight of the family of Shropshire ironmasters, so it would be entirely possible that the modernisation of the Jacobean house in 1772, a date confirmed on the rainwater heads, was undertaken by Pritchard who had connections with other members of the Knight family at Downton Castle and Croft Castle.

Henley Hall is a house of varied styles and building dates. The main block consists of three structural bays with pointed gables and, like Shipton, has a high towerlike entrance porch with a pitched roof. Mullion and transom windows have been retained along with casement windows with small panes. The Venetian doorway, seen in a *Country Life* article,[5] could easily be Pritchard's work. As the date of the renovations is outside the range of *The Drawing Book*, there is no information about interior work at Henley Hall.

Apart from the family connections, the other clue to Pritchard's involvement is the updated entrance hall. Its appearance is very similar to the other updated halls at Ludford House and Broad Gate House, both in Ludlow and nearby Bitterley Court. There are such features as depressed arches over the doorways and the plaster-covered, but not concealed beams.

The 1772 staircase elegantly rises with three balusters to the tread and a turned newel post at the bottom. There is carving on the tread ends and although this could be considered as a standard mid-eighteenth century job, it is all done in the 'neat and workmanlike' manner that is expected of Pritchard.

Although there is no proof, there is very strong circumstantial evidence, such as family connection, style and close proximity of other houses with similar work, that Pritchard was involved at Henley Hall in 1772.

ELTON HALL.

Elton Hall, south of Ludlow, is connected with the Knight family later in the 18th century, but in the earlier part it belonged to the Salwey family, who had bought Elton from the Littleton family. They also owned the Moor and the Lodge, both near Ludlow, in addition to three houses in Broad Street, one of them, No. 52, designed by William Baker.

A first glance at Elton Hall immediately says 'Pritchard'. Surely those ogee arched windows set into the red brick front elevation must be his? Here we need to pause and say 'Where else did he do windows like that?' and the answer is nowhere else that we know of except the

Broad Street Gazebo in Ludlow. Other clues might be the circular window under the pediment and the typically 18th century doorway which is almost identical to one at Henley Hall and to town houses in Ludlow.

The original house at Elton dated back to at least 1661 and was enlarged by Richard Salwey. Henry Salwey probably carried out the next building phase in 1737 when he sent his nephew Thomas 'a rude sketch of my house at Elton as it is designed to be built.' Existing drawings of Elton Hall may date from 1760 when alterations are thought to have been carried out for the widow of Thomas. These drawings show a larger house than is there today with wings added to the existing block. This work was never done, but it is likely that the windows were given their ogee tops at this time. There is speculation that these unexecuted drawings could be by Pritchard, but the style is not similar to his known drawings. There is a slight possibility that they might be by William Baker, as he already worked for the Salweys, but his plan for 52 Broad Street, Ludlow does not show much resemblance in drawing style to the plan for Elton by the unknown hand.[6] The creator of the front elevation at Elton with the ogee windows must therefore remain anonymous for the present.

5-A1: Elton Hall.

MAWLEY HALL.

Mawley Hall, near Cleobury Mortimer in Shropshire, is one of the county's grandest houses which cannot fail to be noticed on its elevated position overlooking the Teme Valley. The house that is there today was built in 1730 for Sir Edward Blount by Francis Smith of Warwick, who also built nearby Kinlet Hall and Davenport House, Bridgnorth. About 1768 Pritchard designed a memorial tablet for Sir Edward Blount for the Blount Chapel at Mamble Church in Worcestershire.

Mawley Hall's early 18th century origins show in the windows with large keystones over them and aprons under them and the sturdy pilasters, topped by urns, attached to the walls. Looking at these details, it comes as no surprise to find that William Baker's payment books recorded work at Mawley for Sir Edward Blount in 1748. Much of it is in his style, although the work is unspecified and some of the money might have been for the new stables.[7] For this work Baker received £289. 9s., the sort of sum that indicates that he was also acting in a contracting role and buying and supplying materials.

Mawley is sumptuous inside. When she visited Mawley in 1771 Mrs. Lybbe Powys described it as a 'very fine place ... every room is carved in the most expensive taste. The library, eating-room and larger drawing-room are all good.'[8] The 'eating-room' is of interest regarding Pritchard; Sir Walter Blount had redecorated it in about 1765-6 in the more fashionable Adam style, cool and classical compared with the exuberant Baroque of much of the house.[9] The grapes, acorns and crossed spears of the plasterwork in the recess are echoed on the centre panel of the marble chimney piece at Mawley. As far as we know none of Pritchard's chimney pieces of this date is marble. Marble slips were used for the fire surrounds, but the chimney pieces were not made entirely of marble. Where a material other than wood is used, he specified it, as for example, 'Painswick stone' for the Hall chimney pieces at Hatton Grange and Condover Hall. There was no reason for him not to use marble as both Nelson and van der Hagen were skilled carvers in this material as they showed with the Lyster monuments. The fact remains that he did not seem to use it or if he did the designs are not in *The Drawing Book.* As papers for Mawley have not survived one can only say 'probably' for the 'eating-room.'

6-A1: The chapel at Mawley Hall.

Much more likely is Pritchard's involvement with the chapel; was this the one which Mrs. Lybbe Powys 'much wanted to see' as she imagined 'it must be superb'? Why did she imagine it would be superb? Perhaps because she had seen, as she wrote, 'a thousand nick-nacks from abroad, as one generally sees in these Catholic families.'[10] Would she have been disappointed to find a chapel in a restrained style, rather like a country house drawing room or was she referring to a private chapel in the house?

The chapel has now been demolished but photographs show

that it had a shallow barrel-vaulted ceiling, round-headed windows and what appear to be Doric pilasters. In between the pilasters are panels with rococo plasterwork. From the photograph the plasterwork on the east wall seems to resemble that at Powis Castle, Gaines and the White House, Suckley. It is therefore quite conceivable that Pritchard carried out the work at the chapel at Mawley and if he did then this gives more credence to his involvement with the 'eating-room.'

TONG CASTLE.

7-A1: Tong Castle, the day before it was demolished in 1954.

8-A1: Tong Castle, the day before it was demolished in 1954.

Although Pritchard's name has been mentioned in connection with Tong Castle, there is no documentary evidence for his connection there. The Tudor Castle of Sir Henry Vernon was altered and given a Moorish-Gothic look by the owner George Durant. This work was carried out by 'Capability' Brown in 1765 and it has been suggested, from an existing fragment of plasterwork, that Pritchard was responsible for the interior decoration.[11]

This fragment does show similarities to plasterwork in the ballrooms at the Lion Hotel and Powis Castle and Pritchard could have carried out the work under the direction of Mr. Durant, who seemed to have fancied himself as an architect and was supplied with plans by Brown. Dorothy Stroud suggested that Durant could have 'made use of Brown's plans and passed them off as his own.'[12] If he did this, then he would have needed some expert advice on the practical side and this is where Pritchard might have come in. Tong Castle, reduced to a shell, was finally dismantled in 1954.

MONUMENTS.

Among the other splendid Shropshire monuments of the 1760s and 1770s is that of Dame Mary Smythe in the north transept of St. Mary's Church, Acton Burnell. Dame Mary died in 1764, aged forty. There is no name of the maker on the monument but the floriated cross at the top resembles the cross at Mamble Church on the Blount monument, not surprising perhaps as the Smythes and Blounts were both Roman Catholic families.

Also at Acton Burnell, on the north wall of the chancel, is a monument to Samuel Smith of Ruckley who died in 1733. This also commemorates his wife who died in 1768, a likely date for the making of the monument. This monument can be compared to that of the Sprotts, at Ludford and Barrow.

Another monument in Pritchard's style is that of Sir Richard Corbett of Longnor Hall in St. Mary's Church, Leebotwood. He was probably the Corbett who was involved with the plans for Tern Hall.

Just as every Gothick window and ogee-arched doorway in Shropshire is not by Pritchard, so every high quality carved monument is not by him. Without a list of his work or his workshop records it is hard to find out how many he was involved with. Again we come back to the problem that if Pritchard did not carry out the work on some of the more elaborate monuments in the area, then who did?

THE MONUMENT OF EDWARD CRESSETT.

There is a strong possibility that two of the splendid monuments in Cound Church are by Pritchard. When the late David George gathered the material for the guide book of Cound Church in 1979 he wrote that the monument of Edward Cressett, Bishop of Llandaff, who died in 1755, was 'designed by Thomas Pritchard.' He went on to say that the monument of 'Sir William Fowler and others, 1759' was 'another fine work of Thomas Pritchard.' David George's certainty about these attributions could be that he actually saw Pritchard's name on these monuments during work on the church, although nothing is visible today. He wrote that the Fowler monument was moved in 1968 from above the chancel arch to the west wall of the north aisle and this move could have revealed the name.[13]

On the north side of the chancel is the Cressett monument, with the many attributes of the Bishop finely carved out of white marble. It is in the style of Pritchard's Lyster monument and has a Rococo cartouche at the top which resembles the one on the Ward Offley monument at Pontesbury Church.

Also at Cound, on the west wall, is the monument of William Fowler and here Pritchard's involvement is more doubtful as it appears to be of a later date than the death of Fowler would suggest. Its clear cut, less adorned lines show the influence of the Neo-Classical revival more than the Rococo era. However, some of the ornamentation on both monuments is so similar that they do seem to be by the same person; there is a frieze of quatrefoils on one and flowers on the other, and both are enclosed within a fret. Pomegranates at the bottom act as supporters.

I have already referred in Chapter 11 to the 'fine Rococo marble monument' to John Dod who died in 1774. This is signed by 'J. Nelson, Salop,' but it could have been designed by Pritchard and executed after his death.

9-A1: Monument of Edward Cressett.

THE MONUMENT OF EDWARD CLUDDE.

There are a few monuments signed by Pritchard but more that could, stylistically, be linked with his work. The proximity of a house that he worked on can lead to the identification of a monument or it can be the other way round.

One instance is the monument to Edward Cludde in Wrockwardine Church, near Telford, which led to the Cludde family of Orleton Hall and the gatehouse which has Gothick features possibly connected with Pritchard.

The Cludde monument has so many similarities to that of Edward Cressett at Cound that they are almost certainly by the same person, in particular the carving of the cherubs' heads. Two of the cherubs on the Cludde monument are like those on Richard Corbet's at Moreton Corbet and the Cressett monument at Cound.

10-A1: Monument of Edward Cludde.

CHURCHES.

Taking into account Pritchard's prominent position as an architect in Shropshire in the middle of the 18th century and the amount of church restoration work being done, it would have been extraordinary if he had not been involved in a number of commissions. Two probable churches are Church Pulverbatch and Worthen, both in the Shropshire Hills near the Welsh border. The patronage of Worthen was in the hands of the Kynaston family who knew Pritchard's work well and the patron of Church Pulverbatch was Nicholas Smythe, of the Smythe family of Condover Hall. Pulverbatch was remodelled in 1773 and Worthen in 1761. Archdeacon Plymley comments on the latter that 'The chancel is of brick ... It is in bad taste but neat on the inside ... the N aisle wants new paving and the N. side to be whitewashed and if possible made drier for it is discoloured by damp.' He rather disapprovingly wrote that 'the altar piece is neat but unfortunately a mixture of Grecian and Gothic. The singing gallery is also of Grecian form.'[14]

11-A1: *St. John's Church, Wolverhampton.*

ST. JOHN'S CHURCH, WOLVERHAMPTON.

St. John's is a handsome 'preaching box' church with a tall tiered spire inspired by James Gibbs and it represents another connection with William Baker. From 1756 to 1759 Baker received payments as surveyor of St. John's, or Wolverhampton Chapel, as he called it. The church was rebuilt over this period, with the foundation stone laid in April, 1756. The Reverend Hugh Owen wrote a book about Shrewsbury's ecclesiastical buildings in 1808 and noted Pritchard's brass memorial plaque at the west end of St. Julian's: 'Mr. Pritchard was the architect of this church, and also of the handsome new church at Wolverhampton.'[15] As this was only thirty one years after Pritchard's death, Owen may have received this information from people who had known Pritchard.

Baker's account book lists payments for this job at Wolverhampton and as the more experienced architect, he would have been expected to actually carry out the work. By 1755, Pritchard had not been involved in many large projects, or any that are documented and St. Julian's Church is on a more modest scale than St. John's. What is more probable is that Pritchard worked with Baker at Wolverhampton and took over the supervision of the job, which was not completed until about 1758 when Baker began to play a less active part in architecture. Baker worked with the Wolverhampton builder, Roger Eykyn and over the time the church was being built received fees totalling about £190. This kind of sum indicates that Baker did much of the design of the church.[16]

Lord Torrington was not impressed with the handsome new church as he makes no mention of it when he visits Wolverhampton in 1792, preferring to stroll around the old church-yard of St. Peter's Church.

ST. ANDREW'S CHURCH, QUATT.

Sometimes knowing something about a church raises even more problems. St. Andrew's Church, Quatt for instance, was built or restored in 1763-66. It had been considered that the identity of the designer was revealed in the churchwardens' accounts: 'A true Estimate delivered in with plans by Richd. Colley for a New Church & Steeple.'[17] The estimate is dated 1766 and was for 'a new church and Steeple.' It included taking down the old church and clearing away the rubbish and making three stone doorcases, five semi-circular and two circular windows, wainscot pewing, glass, plaster and oak boards; a thorough job as the total of £1, 126. 1s. 6d. was a considerable sum then.

This would seem very straightforward and Sutton Maddock Church (1766-67), not very far from Quatt, is also attributed to Colley. Both Quatt and Sutton Maddock, which were altered rather than rebuilt, have similar surrounds to their doors and windows to those on St. Julian's Church in Shrewsbury and Hopton Cangeford Church. Quatt also has a circular window in the tower. On the face of it there is nothing unusual here as we have seen that many of the churches of the period had similar detailing. What does cause second thoughts is the fact that a mason called Thomas Colley worked at Pritchard's house at Eyton on Severn in 1767. A payment of one guinea to him is recorded.

12-A1: *Quatt Church by the Rev. Edward Williams.*

Regarding Quatt Church, one theory could be that Richard and Thomas Colley are of the same family and the entry 'delivered in with plans' should be taken literally and that is what he actually did – handed in plans which had been drawn up by someone else.

The similarities between Quatt and Sutton Maddock churches give rise to the thought that Pritchard may have been the designer and architect and the Colleys the contractors. Another complication is that Richard Colley, a mercer and draper of Kidderminster, was clerk to the Trustees for Stourport Bridge. Kidderminster is not far from Quatt, so either he was acting in the same capacity for Quatt Church and delivering the plans or it is another Richard Colley altogether.

There is no direct evidence for a connection with Pritchard; however, the form of the tower, the date for the refurbishment, the retention of much of the older fabric and the arch from the chancel into the chapel all seem typical of his work. Pevsner calls this arch 'puzzling' but 'without a doubt of the date of the chapel'[18] and it is the kind of detail that Pritchard would have retained. Quatt highlights the difficulties of sometimes unravelling the documentation and making a clear cut case for attribution.

ST. MARY MAGDELENE CHURCH, BATTLEFIELD.

Battlefield Church lies just outside Shrewsbury and was built as a chantry chapel to commemorate the dead at the Battle of Shrewsbury. in 1406. A water-colour by the Reverend Edward Williams shows that most of the nave was roofless in 1790. A sketch of the Church by the Shrewsbury architect S. Pountney Smith shows that the interior has Doric columns very similar to those at St. Julian's Church, Shrewsbury after the 1749 rebuilding. Restoration of Battlefield was undertaken at the same time but a few years later the nave roof fell in and some support was necessary for the chancel so four Doric columns were inserted and a brick wall built across the west end of the chancel. This was removed in 1861 when the church was restored by Pountney Smith, who sketched the church before carrying out the work.

There is no other evidence to link Pritchard with Battlefield apart from the similarity of the supporting Doric columns.

13-A1: Coton Chapel.

COTON HALL CHAPEL.

A footnote to the section on the churches, is the Gothick embellishment of an ancient chapel in the grounds of Coton Hall, near Bridgnorth. In the 18th century the house belonged to the Lee family and in *The Drawing Book* are 'Three frames in Burnished Gold for a Dessert table for Mr. Lee.' (AIA 55) If this work was for Mr. Lee of Coton Hall then it is very likely that Pritchard added the Venetian window with the ogee head and finial and the Rococo plasterwork of which traces remain around the east window. The chapel was in use until 1820 for family occasions. Henry Lancelot Lee also owned estates in Quatt and he could be a possible link with Pritchard's involvement at the church there.

14-A1: The Rococo plasterwork in the Coton Chapel, Coton Hall.

1 For further details, see John Cornforth, 'Love of Illusionism', *Country Life*, 4 February 1993, pp. 54-55.

2 Two downstairs chimney pieces are made of marble and probably came from the studio of Francis Haywood, made to designs by George Dance. 'Some time ago Sr. Henry Mainwaring wrote to me from Florence, & express'd great satisfaction for two designs of Chimneys I gave. He has got them executed in fine Marble there.' George Dance to his father, Rome, 2 November 1760. (RIBA Library Da Fam/1/2/1) I am grateful for this information from Hugh Belsey.

3 Save Britain's Heritage, *The Vanishing Houses of England*, 1982, p. 15. Peter Reid first gave me information about this house.

4 Mrs. Lybbe Powys, pp. 130-131.

5 Christopher Hussey, 'Henley Hall, Shropshire II', *Country Life*, 23 August 1946, p. 349.

6 See Richard Hewlings and Richard Garnier, 'The Salwey Saga', *Country Life*, 21 September 1989, pp. 208-212. Regarding the Lodge at Richard's Castle, the existence of a Rococo chimney piece is the only indication that he might have worked there.

7 Morrice, p. 244.

8 Mrs. Lybbe Powys, p. 139.

9 Jeffrey Haworth has drawn my attention to the similarities between the plasterwork in the dining room at Mawley and the present dining room at Brockhampton House near Bromyard, Worcestershire. The same circular paterae and bell-flower festoons can be found on the cornices of both rooms, the differences being that ribbons tie together the festoons at Brockhampton while at Mawley it is lyres.

10 Mrs. Lybbe Powys, p. 139.

11 John Harris, *Pritchard Redivivus,* p. 18-19. See also Christopher Hussey, 'Tong Castle', *Country Life*, 20 and 27 September 1946.

12 Dorothy Stroud, *Capability Brown*, London, 1975, p. 148.

13 *The Parish Church of Saint Peter, Cound*, Shropshire. The guide, written by David George, was first printed in October 1979, revised in 1986 and revised again in 1995 by Christopher Dalton. Copies can be obtained at the church.

14 Plymley, f. 198.

15 Rev. Hugh Owen, , M.A., *Some Account of the Ancient and Present State of Shrewsbury,* Shrewsbury, 1808, p. 300.

16 John S. Roper, *A History of St. John's Church*, Wolverhampton, 1958, pp. 6-7.

17 SRRC, 4237/Ch/29b-c.

18 Nikolaus Pevsner, *The Buildings of England, Shropshire*, London, 1958, pp. 233-4.

APPENDIX 2

Thomas Atkinson and William Buckland

THOMAS ATKINSON, YORK.

Information about Thomas Atkinson of York has been more difficult to find than information about Pritchard, but he seemed such an apt parallel provincial architect that he could not be ignored. Howard Colvin describes him as 'an able architect in both Gothic and classical styles' and this description could also be applied to Pritchard.

Atkinson's dates are very similar to Pritchard's as they were born within six years of each other and their most productive years were in the 1760s and 1770s. Like Pritchard, he also worked for

1-A2: Bishopthorpe Palace.

Catholic families in the area but Atkinson went further and converted to the Catholic faith. Most of Atkinson's known work was done within a fifty to sixty mile radius of York.

Their closest similar work is at Bishopthorpe Palace where Atkinson carried out 'elegant and effective essays in the Rococo Gothic of the 1760s.'[1] Externally the additions that Atkinson made to Bishopthorpe in 1763-5 are more elaborately Gothick than any work carried out by Pritchard with the profusion of ogee windows, string course with Gothic motif and the delightful porch. Internally the work, although more ornate, comes closer to Pritchard's work at Croft Castle and Shipton Hall. The plasterwork in the entrance hall can be compared with the staircase at Croft Castle. The drawing room is altogether more highly decorated with a ceiling similar to Arbury Hall at Nuneaton. All the work is of a very high standard of craftsmanship, particularly the woodwork of the doors in the entrance hall. Plasterwork in other parts of the Palace is very similar to work of Pritchard's craftsmen.

2-A2: The hall at Bishopthorpe Palace.

At the Bar Convent in York, Atkinson showed his skill with the classical orders 'to achieve interesting and original spatial effects.'[2] The street façade, dated 1786-7, is of seven bays, the centre three bays stepped forward and crowned with a pediment. The central window over the doorway is recessed in an arch and this provides architectural interest. This elevation can be compared with some by Pritchard and indicates the similarity of styles around the country at this time owing, in part, to the proliferation of pattern and architectural books and also to the sound training that was received by such craftsmen-architects.

The chapel for the Convent is hidden and there is no hint of it from the street. The circular space is elegantly decorated with gilded plasterwork but more suited to the Catholic nuns of York than the Anglican congregations of Shropshire.

Atkinson's monuments appear to be in northern cities such as Leeds, Durham and York and are 'of good provincial workmanship and carried out in coloured marbles';[3] again this statement could be applied to Pritchard. The range of Atkinson's work includes additions and alterations for private clients, such as William Constable at Burton Constable, Coxwold and Brandsby Churches, surveying new streets in Sheffield, a workhouse in York and a Mausoleum at Halsham. This last building, which is well documented, caused a great deal of trouble, far more than any endured by Pritchard, and was unfinished at the time of Atkinson's sudden death in 1798. The job was taken over by his son, John, but was not completed until 1802. Unlike Pritchard, Atkinson died 'insolvent', probably as a result of the mausoleum.

WILLIAM BUCKLAND, NEW ENGLAND.

Reference has already been made to William Buckland, arguably one of New England's most important architects of the mid-18th century. I have included this very brief account of his work to draw a parallel with Pritchard as Buckland was building houses in the states of Maryland and Virginia, which are often larger but very similar.

3-A2: Hammond-Harwood House, Annapolis, Maryland.

The similarity is not surprising as Buckland's early years were spent in England and he served his apprenticeship there. He was born in 1734 and died at a young age in 1774 but during his short life he designed some notable buildings. In 1755 Buckland went to America as an indentured joiner to George Mason of Fairfax County, Virginia. Here he worked on the completion of Mason's plantation house, Gunston Hall.

From the evidence of Buckland's surviving work, the sources for his work were similar to those that Pritchard used, such as James Gibbs, Batty Langley and Abraham Swan. This is especially evident in the chimney pieces, overmantels and doorcases which show an inventiveness based on the elements illustrated by these pattern books; a fine example is the main entrance door of the Hammond-Harwood House in Annapolis. In some interior details Buckland's own particular flair shows itself such as in the jib doors and the decorated panels and window lining around them. Like Pritchard, he took the basic design and adapted it to suit his purposes. Also like Pritchard he was an eclectic designer, including different styles within the same building.

4-A2: Hammond-Harwood House, Annapolis, Maryland.

The similarities to Pritchard's work reveal themselves in the elevations of the Hammond-Harwood House with its pedimented central bay, adjoining pavilions with canted bays as well as the hall of the Chase-Lloyd House which is comparable to the hall at Brockhampton House.

Both the James Brice House and the William Paca House show that externally at least Buckland had developed his own style suitable for his new country. Internally, his cornices, chimney pieces and other decorative details still refer to the old world and the pattern books common to all architects of the period.

1 Colvin, pp. 82-4, 1995 edition.
2 Colvin, pp. 82-4.
3 Gunnis, p. 22.

5-A2: Willam Pace House, Annapolis, Maryland.

6-A2: The Brice House, Annapolis, Maryland.

CHRONOLOGICAL LIST OF WORK BY THOMAS FARNOLLS PRITCHARD

Buildings which are documented or have dated designs in *The Drawing Book* have been included in this list, together with other important work that can be dated from this book. In some caseS, work on the houses may have started earlier than the date given on the design.

Date	**Place and Client**
1743-44	The Butter Cross, Ludlow
1747	Shrewsbury Infirmary
1748	St. Julian's Church, Shrewsbury
1749	Work for Shrewsbury Drapers' Company, thought to be 3 shops in Shoplatch, Shrewsbury
1752-4	Repairs to houses in Wyle Cop for Charles Gibbons
1757-68	General work at Shrewsbury School
1758-62	The Kan Office, Shrewsbury, for the Shrewsbury Drapers' Company
1758-9	Hosier's Almshouses Ludlow, for the Ludlow Corporation
1759-68?	Tern Hall, Attingham, Shrewsbury, for Thomas Hill
1759-63	The Foundling Hospital, Shrewsbury
1761	Swan Hill Court House, Shrewsbury, for the estate of John Newport
1764-5	The Red Lion Inn, Wolverhampton, for the estate of John Newport
1764-5	Gaolford Tower, for Ludlow Corporation
1764-5	The Deanery, Wolverhampton, for the estate of John Newport
1764-8	Hatton Grange, Shropshire, for Plowden Slaney
1765	Rostherne Church, Cheshire
1765	27 Broad Street, Ludlow, for Somerset Davies
1765	Croft Castle, Herefordshire, for Thomas Johnes senior
1765-6	Gaines, Worcestershire, for Mr. Freeman
1766	Mr. Bather, Mardol, Shrewsbury
1766	Shipton Hall for Mr. Mytton
1766	Condover Hall, Shropshire, for Miss Leighton and Mr Smythe
1766	10-11 High Street, Shrewsbury, for John Ashby
1766?	Downton Hall and Hopton Cangeford Church
1767	Tatton Park, Cheshire for Mr. Egerton
1768	Mr. Fowler, Atcham Vicarage, Shropshire

1768-9	Bitterley Court, Shropshire, for Charles Walcot
1769	Garden Temple for Broseley Hall, Shropshire, for Francis Turner Blythe
1768-9	House for Mr. Good, Shrewsbury
1769	The Lawns, Broseley, for Mr. Wilkinson
1769	Ludford House, for Sir Francis Charlton
1768-70	Restoration of Ruabon Church, Clwyd, for Sir Watkin Williams Wynn
1769	The Abbey, Shrewsbury, for Henry Powys
1772	Downton Castle, Herefordshire, for Richard Payne Knight
1773	Stourport Bridge, Worcestershire
1773-4	Kinnerley Church, Shropshire
1774	Plans to build the Iron Bridge
1774-6	The Guildhall, Ludlow, for Ludlow Corporation
1775-6	Sudborough Manor, Northants, for the estate of John Newport
1775-7	Powis Castle, for the 2nd Earl of Powis
1776	Kyre Park, Worcestershire, for Jonathan Pytts
1777-9	The Iron Bridge

Probable Work by Pritchard

Tong Castle, Shropshire
Henley Hall, Shropshire
Elton Hall, Ludlow, Shropshire
Hill Court, Ross on Wye, Herefordshire
Sherford House, Bromyard, Herefordshire
The White House, Suckley, Worcestershire
Peover Hall, Cheshire

Monuments with Pritchard's name on them or in *The Drawing Book*

Ann Wilkinson, St. Giles' Church, Wrexham
The Reverend John Lloyd, St. Mary's Church, Shrewsbury
Mary Morhall, St. Mary's Church, ShrewSbury
Dr. Samuel Sprott, St. Giles' Church, Ludford, Shropshire.
Sir Whitmore Acton, Acton Round Church, Shropshire, for Sir Richard Acton
Sir Richard Lyster, St. Michael's Church, Alberbury Shropshire
Sir Edward Blount, St. John's Church, Mamble Worcestershire
Richard Ward Offley, St. George's Church, Pontesbury Shropshire
Richard Hollings, Old St. Chad's Church, Shrewsbury

Select Bibliography

Primary sources - Manuscript.

Shrewsbury Records and Research Centre
Attingham Collection
Chaplin Papers
Kenyon-Slaney papers
Ludlow Borough papers
Morgan Collection

Worcester Record Office
Baldwyn Childe papers

Hereford Record Office
Bateman Papers
Downton Collection

National Library of Wales
Powis Castle Deeds and Documents

Public Record Office
Newport Estate Papers
Ludlow Castle Papers
Thomas Farnolls Pritchard's Will

Printed Primary Sources.

Pattern books and information for architects and builders.

Builders Dictionary, London, 1734.
Builders Price Book, London, 1776.
Robert Campbell, *The London Tradesman*, London, 1747.
William Chambers, *A Treatise on Civil Architecture*, London, 1759.
Thomas Chippendale, *The Gentleman and Cabinet Maker's Director*, London, 1754.
John Crunden, *The Chimney Piece Maker's Daily Assistant*, London, 1766.
Matthias Darly, *The Ornamental Architect*, London, 1771.
James Gibbs, *A Book of Architecture*, London, first published 1728.
James Gibbs, *Rules for Drawing the Several Parts of Architecture*, 1753 edition.
William and John Halfpenny, *The Country Gentleman's Pocket Companion*, London, 1753.
William and John Halfpenny, *The Modern Builder's Assistant*, London, 1757.

William Ince and John Mayhew, *Universal System of Household Furniture*, London, 1762, 1960 reprint by Tiranti.
Thomas Johnson, *Twelve Girandoles*, 1755.
Thomas Johnson, *A New Book of Ornaments*, 1760.
Thomas Johnson, *Genteel Household Furniture in the Present Taste*, 1762.
Thomas Johnson, *One Hundred and Fifty New Designs*, 1761.
N.B. Some of Thomas Johnson's publications do not survive in their original form and the published designs that do exist have been collected together in *Thomas Johnson and English Rococo* by Helena Hayward and published by Tiranti in 1964.
Batty Langley, *The City and Country Builder's and Workman's Treasury of Designs*, London, 1740. The 1745 edition includes designs for ironwork.
Batty Langley, *A Sure Guide to Builders*, London, 1729.
Batty Langley, *Gothic Architecture, Improved by Rules and Proportions*, London, 1747.
Richard Neve, *The City and Country Purchaser and Builder's Dictionary*, London, 1726.
Abraham Swan, *The British Architect*, London, 1745.
Abraham Swan, *Designs for Chimnies*, London, 1765.
Isaac Ware, *A Complete body of Architecture*, London, 1756.
Robert Wood, *The Ruins of Palmyra*, London, 1753.

Other Primary Sources.

E. J. Climenson (editor), *Passages from the Diary of Mrs. Lybbe Powys*, London, 1899.
D. H. S. Cranage, *An Architectural Account of the Churches of Shropshire*, Wellington, Shropshire, 10 Vols. 1903.
Daniel Defoe, *A Tour through the Whole Island of Great Britain*, first published 1724-6.
Celia Fiennes, *The Journal of Celia Fiennes*, Edited by C. Morris, London, 1947.
Francis Leach, *The County Seats of Shropshire*, 1891.
Rev. Hugh Owen, *Some Account of the Ancient and Present State of Shrewsbury*, Shrewsbury, 1808.
T. Philips, *The History and Antiquities of Shrewsbury*, Shrewsbury, 1779.
Rev. C. J. Robinson, *Mansions and Manors of Herefordshire*, 1872.
The Victoria County History of Worcestershire, London, 1908.
The Victoria County History of Shropshire, London, 1968.

General Bibliography.

T. S. Ashton, *Economic Fluctuations in the 18th century*, Oxford 1959.
T. S. Ashton, *An Economic History of England: The 18th Century*, Oxford, 1955.
Geoffrey Beard, *Decorative Plasterwork*, London, 1975.
Geoffrey Beard, *The Work of Robert Adam*, London, 1978.

Geoffrey Beard, *Craftsmen and Interior Decoration in England 1660-1820*, London, 1981.
Geoffrey Beard, *The Country House Interior*, London, 1990.
Peter Borsay (ed.), *The 18th Century Town*, London, 1990.
Burke's and Savills, *Guide to Country Houses: Herefordshire, Gloucestershire, Shropshire, Warwickshire, Worcestershire*, London, 1980.
Kenneth Clark, *The Gothic Revival*, London, 1928.
Howard Colvin, *Biographical Dictionary of British Architects 1600-1840*, London, 1995.
Howard Colvin, (ed.) Roger North, *Of Building*, Oxford, 1981.
John Cornforth and John Fowler, *English Decoration in the 18th Century*, London 1974.
Barbara Coulton, *A Shropshire Squire*, Shrewsbury, 1989.
J. Mordaunt Crook, *The Dilemma of Style*, London, 1989.
Dan Cruickshank and Neil Burton, *Life in the Georgian City*, London 1990.
Terence Davies, *The Gothic Taste*, London, 1972.
R. W. Douglas and S. Frank, *A History of Glassmaking*, London, 1972.
Kerry Downes (ed.), *Architectural Outsiders*, London, 1985.
Charles Eastlake, (J. Mordaunt Crook ed.), *A History of the Gothic Revival, London*, 1872, reprinted Leicester 1970.
H. E. Forrester, *The Old Houses of Wenlock*, Shrewsbury, 1923.
Christopher Gilbert and Anthony Wells-Cole, *The Fashionable Fireplace*, Leeds, 1985.
Mark Girouard, *The History of the English Country House*, Yale, 1978.
Mark Girouard, *The English Country Town*, Yale, 1990.
Rupert Gunnis, *Dictionary of British Sculptors 1661-1851*, London, 1951.
Eileen Harris and Nicholas Savage, *British Architectural Books and Writers 1556-1785*, London, 1990.
Nicholas Hills, *The English Fireplace*, London, 1983.
Christopher Hussey, *English Country Houses: Early Georgian*, London, 1955.
Elizabeth Inglis Jones, *Peacocks in Paradise*, London, 1950.
Barrington Kaye, *The Development of the Architectural Profession in Britain*, London, 1960.
Alison Kelly, *The Fireplace Book*, London, 1984.
Fiske Kimball, *The Creation of the Rococo Decorative Style*, New York, 1942.
David Lloyd and Peter Klein, *Ludlow: A Historic Town in Words and Pictures*, Chichester, 1984.
Nathaniel Lloyd, *A History of the English House*, London, 1931.
Michael McCarthy, *The Origins of the Gothic Revival*, Yale. 1990.
Pippa Mason and Michael Gregory, *Of Gilding*, London, 1989.
Morrice, Richard, 'The Payment Book of William Baker of Audlem', in *English Architecture Public and Private*, London 1993.
Lewis Namier, *The Structure of Politics At the Accession of George IIi*, London, 1957
Steven Parissien, *The Adam Style*, London, 1992.

Nikolaus Pevsner, Buildings of England Series - *Herefordshire, Shropshire, Worcestershire,* London, various dates.
A. E. Richardson, *Robert Mylne*, London, 1955.
Alastair Rowan, 'Batty Langley's Gothic', *Studies in Memory of David Talbot Rice*, Edinburgh, 1975.
John Rule, *Albion's People, English Society 1714-1815*, London, 1992.
John Rule, *The Vital Century, England's Developing Economy 1714-1815*, London, 1992.
Sacheverell Sitwell, *British Architects and Craftsman*, London, 1945.
John Summerson, *Architecture in Britain 1530-1830*, London 1953.
Torrington Diaries, (ed.) C. Bruyn Andrews, New York Edition, 1970.
Barry Trinder, *A History of Shropshire*, Chichester, 1983.
David Vaisey, (ed.), *The Diary of Thomas Turner*, Oxford, 1985.
Victoria & Albert Museum, *Rococo Art and Design in Hogarth's England*, Exhibition Catalogue, London, 1984.
David Watkins, *The Rise of Architectural History*, London, 1980.
Phyllis Williams, *Whitbourne, A Bishop's Manor*, Bromyard 1979.
Phyllis Williams, *Bromyard, Minster, Manor and Town*, Bromyard, 1987.
Michael Wilson, *William Kent*, London 1984.

Articles, Essays and Guide Books.

Ian Bristow, 'Ready Mixed Paints in the 18th Century', *Architectural Review*, April 1977.
Roger White, 'The Influence of Batty Langley', *A Gothic Symposium*, The Georgian Group, 1983.
Robin Chaplin, 'In Search of Thomas Farnolls Pritchard', *Shropshire Archaelogical Society News Letter*, No.34 - June 1968.
Howard Colvin, 'Georgian Architectural Practice', *Georgian Group Symposium Papers*, London, 1991.
Martha Blythe Gerson, 'A Glossary of Robert Adam's Neo-Classical Ornament', *Architectural History* 24: 1981.
John Harris, 'Pritchard Redividus', *Journal of the Society of Architectural Historians*, Volume 11: 1968.
John Harris, 'Cast Iron Columns', *Architectural Review*, CXXX, 1961.
J. L. Hobbs, 'Thomas Farnolls Pritchard', *Shropshire Magazine*, August/ September, 1959.
James Lawson and Merlin Waterson, 'Pritchard as Architect and Antiquary at Powis', *National Trust Year Book*, 1975.
A. McInnes, 'The Emergence of a Leisure Town: Shrewsbury 1660-1760', *Past and Present*, 120, 1988.
Robert Maguire and Peter Matthews, 'The Ironbridge at Coalbrookdale; a reassessment', *The Architectural Association Journal*, 1958.
The National Trust, Guide books for Croft Castle, Benthall Hall, Attingham Park, Powis Castle and The Vyne.
Arthur Oswald, 'William Baker of Audlem, Architect', *Collections for a History of Staffordshire*, London, 1954.

Veronica West, 'Broseley Hall and Thomas Farnolls Pritchard', Paper from a Seminar on Local History Research published in the Wilkinson Society Journal, 1974.
John White, 'On Cementitious Architecture', Extracted from *The Philosophical Magazine and Annals*, London, 1832.
Thomas Wright, 'A Survey of Ludlow Castle, May 1711', *Archaelogia Cambrensis*, 3rd Series XIV, 1868.

Articles from *Country Life*.

'Shipton Hall', 19 March, 1910.
'Benthall Hall', 30 June, 1917.
'Hill Court', 3 February, 1966.
'Hatton Grange', 29 February, 1968.
'Croft Castle', 5 May 1950 and 31 December, 1978.
'The Salwey Saga', 21 September, 1989.
'Brockhampton House', 4 January, 1990.
'Heaton Hall', 10 December, 1992.
'Love of Illusionism: The White House, Suckley', 4 February, 1993.

Please Note: As the whole book is about Thomas Farnolls Pritchard and his work, he has not been included in the index.

Ludford House 60, 105, 114, 125, 167, 171, 183-186, 187
Lutwyche Hall, Shropshire 119, 120, 273
Lyster, Sir Richard 34, 37, 44, 54, 73, 163, 196, 199, 232, 240-243, 276, 280

Pritchard's bills, valuations and specifications.

Historic written or drawn evidence in the world of architectural history can perhaps be divided into two categories. First, those letters and drawings that are for clients and are connected with the circumstances that generate the need for the buildings in the first place. Second, there are the documents that are connected with the actual design and construction. In this book there are facsimiles of Pritchard's drawings which were used to communicate between the architect and the craftsmen and there are also specifications and bills for the work. Generally, while research work continues on the first category of information little research seems to have been carried out on the second.

During the research for this book several examples of bills and specifications have been found. To illustrate the form of these, in addition to those in the text, some more are included on the following pages. In many respects these documents are not that far removed from the present form of a 'bill of quantities' as used in the construction industry at present. The procedure for making up such a 'bill of quantities' is set down in the *Standard Method of Measurement of Building Works* formulated by the Royal Institute of Chartered Surveyors and the Building Employers Federation. Although the first edition was not issued until 1922 this was essentially the clarification of practice. Clearly, changes are in hand to include the billing in Computer Aided Design programmes whereby the measurement and automatic billing becomes part of the normal design routine. Such programmes, when modified, could be come useful research tools for the architectural historian. However, in the 18th century there must have been some mutual understanding between architects and builders in the way that buildings were measured and there is a an unbroken line of development from the way the matter was dealt with in the 18th century and how it is dealt with now.

Some understanding of 18th century practice and its use a key to existing documents would add a considerable amount of information to what we already have on the buildings and their design. Spot measurements and calculations where both bills and drawings of Pritchard's work are available have so far proved unrewarding. It is sufficient to say that more work is needed. It is quite clear that these construction and billing documents contain a tremendous amount of information which needs to be understood and interpreted.

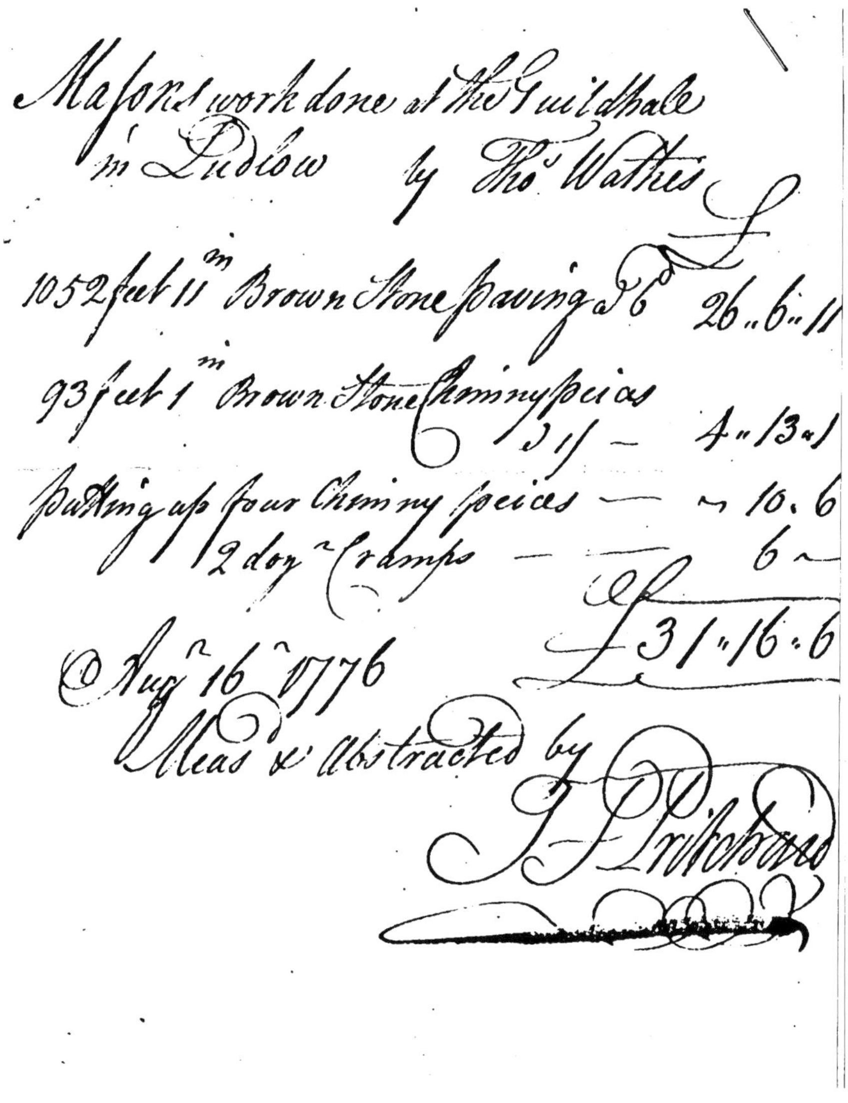

Masons work done at the Guildhall
in Ludlow by Thos Watkis £
1052 feet 11 in Brown Stone paving at 6d 26..6..11
93 feet 1 in Brown Stone Chimney peices at 1/- 4..13..1
putting up four Chimney peices — 10.6
2 dozn Cramps — 6
£31..16..6
Augt 16 1776
Meas & Abstracted by
T. F. Pritchard

1. Extract from the valuation for The Guildhall, Ludlow, 1776.

(Shropshire Records and Research Centre)

Bordering of free Stone round twelve Window recess'd into receive the Sash frames and Sash 12 foot Superficial Stone and Work as 2 1/4 foot to each Window	16.–.–
10 yds. Running of Weldon Stone Base – at 4/6	2. 5.–
Removing Stone Stairs in passage and carrying down Cellar Stairs	2.–.–
457 feet superficial Stone paving in the Vestibule & Staircase at 6	11. 8. 6
224 ft. Common Stone paving in Servants Hall at 3	2. 16.–
4 Ton of Weldon Stone for Quoins to the Building at 13/– Cube	4. 6. 8
354 Bushels of Lime for Walling delivered at 6d. p Bushell	8. 17.–
50 Bush. Do. for pargetting laying Floors and Extra Work	1. 5.–
digging 90 Cartloads of Gravel to make Mortar at 3	1. 2. 6
Altering and new setting three old Chimney pieces and Slabs	2. 4.–
One new Chimney Piece in Parlour	1. 5.–
altering and making good Stone Steps	–. 15.–
Cutting away and making good doorways to Parlour and Kitchen and contracting the fire Place	1. 10.–
	10,

...ter & Joiner's Work

Pulling down the Roof floors Partitions Stairs and all the Timber work of the decay'd part of the old Building	5.–.–
Taking up the Floor over the present Hall, raising it up to a level with the other Floors removing the Steps relaying the Floor and making good	2. 10.–
30 Squares of Common framed Roofing Sawing included at 12/6	18. 15.
2 Square 50 feet of Principal Rafters in Ditto 15/	1. 17. 6
210 feet superf. of Eaves Board and Guttering at 1 1/2	1. 6. 3
110 feet Running of Wood Cornice round the Building at 2/6	13. 15.–

Slater's Work	
387 Yds of Slating the Front, being to be new the remainder laid with the old Slates including lath Nails and rendering — at 2/	38. 14. –
Plaisterer	
388 yards of Plaistering on Walls including Materials — at /10	16. 3. 4
250 yds plain Ceilings to Rooms – Do. – at 1/4	14. 11. 8
add 289 yds of Stuccoing in Hall Staircase & Common Parlour 6	7. 4. 6
Wire Window and Shutter to the Larder	1. 10. 0
Glazier 210 feet Superfl. Crown Glass in 12 Sash Windows 1/6 and 4 Attic's	15. 15. –
20 Ditto in Sky Light	1. 10. –
50 ft. Glazing Brewhouse with old Glass at 4d	–. 16. 8
Plumber	
215 feet Superfl. of Lead in Flashing to Cornice Hips Valleys & Ridges — at 1/6	15. 7. 6
100 feet Ditto on Gutters Boarded – at 1/10	9. 3. 4
One Stack of Rain Water Pipes	5. –. –
Covering 4 Dormers with Lead	12. –. –
Sash Weights to Windows	2. 8. –
Painting all the Wood Work three Times in Oil	20. –. –
Removing & Repairing Servants Privy, with all Materials	6. 10. –
New Lead Pump with Pipe of Conduct to the Kitchen and Brewhouse	12. 12. –
Removing the Ground from both Fronts of the House paving the yard &c.	20. –. –
Ladders and Logs in Scaffolding allowed	2. 10. –
Papering two Chambers	9. 5. –
Carrying away Rubbish, Carrying Timbers to place and carrying of Deals to the building, Sand and Lead Pipes	26. 10. –
	237. 11. –
Amount £	566. 7. 5

5.

2 & 3. Extracts from Pritchard's valuations for The Old Manor House, Sudborough, Northamptonshire, 1775.

(Public Record Office)

In the Matter of John
Newport Esquire a Lunatick

Thomas Farnolls Pritchard of Eyton in the parish of Wroxeter in the County of Salop Builder maketh Oath that he this Deponent became Tenant of a Farm and Lands at Eyton aforesaid part of the Estate of John Newport Esquire the Lunatick at Lady day one thousand seven hundred & Sixty seven at several yearly Rents amounting together to the sum of Forty seven pounds a year and there being a want of a House upon the said Farm to live in and there also being two old Turretts in the Wall in the Garden which did belong to Eyton Hall before the same was demolished & taken away which Wall adjoined upon part of the said Farm and the said Turretts and this Deponent apprehending that he should have a Lease for Twenty one years granted to him of the said Farm and premises he this Deponent repaired one of the said Turretts and made such an additional Building thereto as made the same a compleat and convenient Dwelling House for this Deponent and his Family and also built a Stable Brewhouse Rickhouse or Barn and Cart house and new roofed the Dovehouses and made several other Improvements on the said Farm (which was, when he entered upon it, in a ruinous Condition, the Land having been greatly impoverished by the former Tenant and the Hedges being then in very bad Condition) by manuring the Land and laying thereon many Barge Loads of Dung brought from Shrewsbury to Eyton and by planting and rearing new Hedges, draining the meadow Lands and several other Improvements, all of which are lasting Improvements, and the Estate is of much greater yearly Value thereby. And this Deponent, who is a Builder and constantly employs several Workmen, hath laid out and expended in and about such Buildings Repairs & Improvements the several sums of money mentioned in the Schedule hereunto annexed amounting together to the sum of Seven hundred and seven pounds Nineteen shillings & three pence farthing and which would have cost any other person, not in the same Business, a much larger Sum, this Deponent not having charged any thing for his own trouble attendances and loss of time about the same, and this Deponent further saith that, over and besides the said Sum of Seven hundred and Seven pounds Nineteen shillings & three pence farthing and since the same was so laid out and expended by this Deponent,

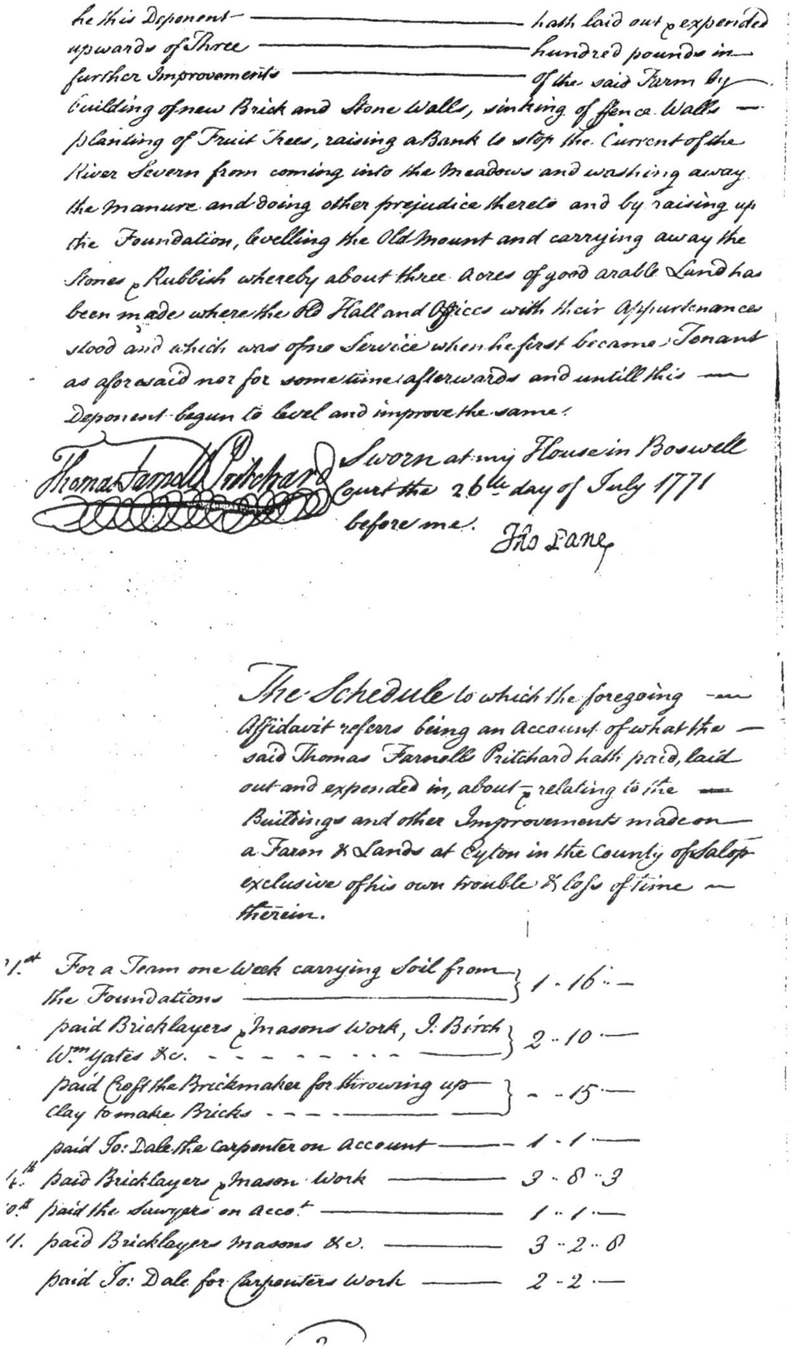

he this Deponent — hath laid out & expended upwards of Three — hundred pounds in further Improvements — of the said Farm by building of new Brick and Stone Walls, sinking of ffence Walls — planting of Fruit Trees, raising a Bank to stop the Current of the River Severn from coming into the Meadows and washing away the Manure and doing other prejudice thereto and by raising up the Foundation, levelling the Old Mount and carrying away the Stones & Rubbish whereby about three Acres of good arable Land has been made where the Old Hall and Offices with their Appurtenances stood and which was of no Service when he first became Tenant as aforesaid nor for sometime afterwards and untill this — Deponent begun to level and improve the same.

Thomas Farnolls Pritchard

Sworn at my House in Boswell Court the 26th day of July 1771 before me. Tho Lane

The Schedule to which the foregoing — Affidavit refers being an Account of what the — said Thomas Farnolls Pritchard hath paid, laid out and expended in, about & relating to the — Buildings and other Improvements made on — a Farm & Lands at Eyton in the County of Salop exclusive of his own trouble & loss of time — therein.

'1st	For a Team one Week carrying Soil from the Foundations	1 · 16 · —
	paid Bricklayers & Masons Work, J. Birch Wm Yates &c.	2 · 10 · —
	paid Croft the Brickmaker for throwing up Clay to make Bricks	— · 15 · —
	paid Jo: Dale the Carpenter on Account	1 · 1 · —
4th	paid Bricklayers & Mason Work	3 · 8 · 3
0th	paid the Sawyers on Acco.t	1 · 1 · —
11.	paid Bricklayers Masons &c.	3 · 2 · 8
	paid Jo: Dale for Carpenters Work	2 · 2 · —

2

4 & 5. Pritchard's contract with the Newport Estate for the rental of his house and land at Eyton on Severn, 1767.

(Public Record Office)

Black & Yellow Marble in Drawing Room

	ft		£	
Contents B & Yellow	12, 2, 3 @ 8		4, 17, 6	
Statuary Slips & Soffitts	4, 7, 9 @ 10		2 – 8 1½	
Statuary Mouldings	2, 2, 8 @ 10/6		1 – 7 – 9½	
Dove Nosings	2, 1, 5 @ 7/6		15 10½	
a piece of Dove plinths			18 –	
12 ft 2 in 3 Free Stone Linings to Slab			12, 2	
Cube Free Stone Linings Cramps & plaister				11 – 4 – 5½
Two Neat Cast Iron Bath Stoves				4, 15
Putting up the Grates & Cove Wm Yates 6 Days				17, 6

Carveing in Chimney peices

Dressing Room

8 ft	Ovola in Cornice with water Leaf @ 1/4		0, 10, 0	
4	Small Astragal with Bead & Husk @ 8		4, 0	
6, 3	Astragal at Foot of Cove with Beads and Fluted Space @ 8		4, 2	
	Cove with Gothic Arches & Water Leaf		2, 15, 0	
	Two Gothic Columns with Neat Capitals and Wreaths of Flowers		3, 0, 0	
			6, 4, 6	
	19 ft 5 in Mouldings in Do @ 1/4		1 6	6, 0, 6

Common Parlour

8 ft 4	Ovola in Cornice with water Leaf and Husk @ 1/4		11 1/4	
7	Cove to Cornice with Fluting and Raffled Leaf	@	17, 6	
7, 6	ft Astragal with Husks	@ 8	5	
6 8	Ovola to Cove with Egg & Tong	@ 8	4 5	
	a Neat Freeze with Foliage Laurel Leaves and Vase		2, 10, 0	
	Two Pilasters with sunk pannells and Drops of Laurels		2	
			6, 0, 1/4	
	19 ft 5 Deal Mouldings at 1/4		1, 6	
3	11 Cove Boards		1, 11	7, 15, 1¼
	Carried Over			32, 13, 4¼

85 ft ½ Cornice in Drawing Room Chamber 6 | 2-2-9
105 ft ¾ Cornice in Dressing Room enriched four Members — — — — — @ 2 | 17.7
136 ft ¾ Block Cornice in Gallery enriched four Members — — — — — at 8 | 4.10.8
60 ft Cornice enriched two Members in Study @ 4 | 1.2.8
110 ft ½ Block Cornice in Hall — @ 10 | 4.10.1
80 ft 6 Cornice in Common parlour enriched three Members — — — — — @ 4 | 1-9.6
113 ft 9 in Corinthian Cornice fully enriched in Drawing Room — — — @ 8 | 3.15.10
144 ft 10 Cove Cornice Dining Room enriched four Members — — — — @ 2 | 1.4.1½

Packing Cases for Chimney peices

16 June Common Parlour & Study Chamber Chimneys
25 ft ½ of Inch Rough board 47 ft of ½ Inch
2 C of 6 Nails 1 Days work by John Davies | 12.9½
6 Aug packing Cases for two Marble Chim Peices
80 ft of Inch Rough board 160 ft of ½ Inch Do
1 C ½ of 10d Na of C of 6 Nails 3 Days work | 2.3.2½
3 Oct the Hall Chimney Piece & Wand Sl..
124 ft of Inch Rough board 1 C of 2 Nails 3 C of
6 Nails 1 ¾ Days Work by John Davies — | 1.5.5½
To Cases for Dress J. Room Bed Chamber &
Common Parlour Chimney Pieces — — —
11 Oct 100 ft of Rough board Inch 2 C of 6 Nails
1 ½ Days Work — | 1-0 2
For the Carving of four Chimney pieces
64 ft Coarse inch 56 ft of half Inch 2 C of 6d
Nails ½ C of 2 Nails 1 Day ½ work — — | 17.2
26.2.3

5 & 6. Extracts from Pritchard's valuations for Hatton Grange, 1768.

(Shropshire Records and Research Centre)

The Drawing Book of Thomas Farnolls Pritchard

Introduction to *The Drawing Book* and the facsimile.

The identification of *The Drawing Book* was a significant factor in establishing Pritchard as a major provincial architect of the mid-eighteenth century. Previously he had been known for a handful of jobs which were recorded under public works for Ludlow, the churches of St. Julian's in Shrewsbury and Kinnerley in north Shropshire and for some monuments which carried his name. Little else was known about him.

The Drawing Book has been in the possession of the American Institute of Architects in their library in Washington DC since 1926. Prior to that the book belonged to John Tiranti, of the Tiranti firm who are now suppliers of artists' materials and at one time published art and facsimiles of pattern books. John Tiranti was a Gold Medallist woodcarver and it is thought that the book would have been of interest to him from this point of view.[1] There is no indication of where Tiranti obtained it from. The book then came to the attention of Lawrence Kocher of Pennsylvania State College and Institute Member of the New York Chapter of the American Institute of Architects. According to correspondence with Grahame B. Tubbs, an architect of John Street, London, this interest arose from the fact that similar chimney pieces had been imported into Pennsylvania from England. Tubbs said that he was 'originally going to edit the book' for Tiranti, but had given up the idea and thought that someone else might do it. The present John Tiranti has no information about this idea and why it was not carried out; perhaps an offer from Kocher to buy the book was too good to refuse.

In his letter dated 29 March, 1926, Tubbs remarks on the fact that the book contains 'a great variety of styles, some being Gothic, some in the French taste, and some typical English fireplaces in the middle of the 18th century.' He speculates on the owner of the book: 'there is no clue as to the name of the master carver, or as to where he worked, but I think he was probably a provincial craftsman working somewhere in the West of England.'[2] Tubbs was near the mark when he showed his appreciation of the variety of styles as this is one of Pritchard's characteristics. Tubbs pointed out that the 'sketches' contained 'the actual time taken by the craftsman employed on each, together with the total cost of the carving.'[3] It is these details, noted over seventy years ago, that make the book so important and it is for this reason that we decided that a publication about Pritchard could not be considered complete without including all of it.

It is not clear how *The Drawing Book* came to the attention of architectural historians in the 1960s, but when it was shown to interested people such as Mrs. Diana Uhlman of Croft Castle it aroused great speculation as to whose it was. Many of the clients and the properties could be identified as they were places well known along the Border Marches. At first it was thought the book might have belonged to William Baker until Edward Croft-Murray, who had a flat in Croft Castle, solved the mystery in a flash of inspiration. He linked the frieze on the chimney piece in his drawing room with the frieze on the monument of Sir Whitmore Acton in Acton Round Church which was signed by Pritchard. This started what one writer called a 'Pritchard industry' as more of his work came to light.

The book was conserved in 1984 before coming to London for the Rococo exhibition at the Victoria and Albert Museum. The conservator's report for this can be found at the end of the facsimile of the drawings. This is attached to the bound album in the Library. Unfortunately, the date of Pritchard's death is not corrrect and the date of birth has not been included.

Over the years some of the drawings have been included in articles on Pritchard's work but this is the first time that they have all been published together.

This facsimile shows several things, chiefly the quality of the drawings, and raises the question of where Pritchard learnt his drawing skills. While Shrewsbury would have had drawing masters for the increasing number of residents from the leisure classes coming to live there, there was, as far as we know, no studio or architectural office there for learning the sort of skill that these designs required. Secondly, the sequence of the drawings shows that the early ones are more Rococo and Gothick in style but towards the end the designs are becoming more strictly Gothick or Classical, or Neo-Classical, without so much of the Rococo.

Pritchard's designs comply well with Isaac Ware's advice on chimney pieces for small rooms: 'the workmanship in them is light and of little expense and with respect to materials those of the plainest colour are best for <u>both</u> because both depend in a great measure upon the sculpture which the lighter it is the more necessity there is that it should be seen distinctly.'[4] Matthias Darly recommended that 'the ornaments introduced on chimney pieces must be well carved and neatly finished.'[5] All good sound advice which Pritchard heeded.

It is not possible to tell from the book as it is bound today whether the drawings are in the right order. As far as possible they have been put in a chronological order and we have followed this arrangement in the facsimile. It is likely that the original drawings were not bound up as many of the pages have pencilled lines on them for setting up and this would have been difficult if the book was originally bound.

Perhaps once it was complete, and there are few blank pages, Pritchard himself had it bound as a record of the work he had carried out.

We are grateful for the help of Tony P. Wrenn, former Archivist at the American Institute of Architects Library and Archives for his assistance in photographing, listing and shipping the photographs of the book.

We would like as many people as possible to appreciate, enjoy and gain something from this facsimile and we are certain that Thomas Farnolls himself would have been, in his modest manner, pleased that it is being done. As a final thought, if one drawing book has survived unnoticed for two hundred years perhaps there are others around, so *Pritchard Part II* may appear one day.

It is important at this stage to make some technical comment on the drawings. The drawings were made on handmade paper with ink and pencil using traditional instruments as the front and back sheets show. The drawings were photographed by the American Institute of Architects. Those who have struggled with the photography of bound drawings will know the problems. The photographs were printed to be actual size but show certain discrepancies in the scaling and the size of sheet. It would appear that the scales are those used until recently in architectural drawings such as '½ ins represents 1 foot' and are to be found on an Armstrong scale, but this needs further examination. Some of the figures given appear to be related to measurement for pricing as opposed to measurement for building. For the purpose of this book the drawings are reduced to 90% of the prints to fit on the page. The writing on the drawings is very difficult to read because of its treatment in the past and for this reason the scans are calibrated to give the most readable result. The increase in contrast often shows the lay of the paper much more than is apparent in reality but on the other hand without the increase in contrast much of text is not readable with the naked eye.

1 I am very grateful to John Tiranti, grandson of John Tiranti, for this information. As many of us know, the high quality books published by Tiranti have been invaluable in our 18th century work and research.

2 Letter from Tubbs to Kocher in the possession of the American Institute of Architects. Ref: 804 5 16A 4.

3 Letter from Tubbs to Kocher. Ref: 804 5 16A 4.

4 Isaac Ware, *A Complete Body of Architecture*, London, 1756, p. 568.

5 Matthias Darly, Professor of Ornament, *The Ornamental Architect*, London, 1770, especially pl. lxxxix.

Detail of the chimney piece in the Croft Murray flat in Croft Castle.

The Drawing Book of Thomas Farnolls Pritchard: an annotated list of designs.

Dating the designs in *The Drawing Book* is not an easy task as there are few dates given on them and in some instances there is only the day and month with no year. The earliest date is 15 November 1765 for Somerset Davies at 27 Broad Street, Ludlow, AIA 7 and the last date 1 April 1769 for the Garden Temple at Broseley Hall, AIA 71. In between are about six other positive dates.

It is possible that all the designs for specific houses were originally grouped together and not separated as they are now. For instance, Mr. Good's two chimney pieces, AIA 63 and AIA 77 are both dated February but only one had 1769 written on it. It would be logical that they were both done at the same time although twelve pages now divide them. The designs for Tatton Park would tie in with William Hunt's painting account of 1767-8 and the designs for Condover Hall, if grouped in a block, could be linked with Robert Mylne's entries in his diary.

We know that work was completed on Hatton Grange in 1768 when Pritchard drew up the valuation for the job, so it therefore follows that the designs were carried out between the start of the building work in 1764 and the valuation four years later. The design for the pediment would have been required at a fairly early stage, as its position in the book could indicate, so the first quarter of 1766 is an appropriate date for this.

In some of the tables Pritchard has been very specific about days and hours worked by the craftsmen. On Mr. Fowler's frames, AIA 28, Nelson worked for fourteen and a half days while Hatton Grange's pediment, AIA 31a, took him seven weeks and five days. Where this information is not specified, then it is assumed that the figures refer to days and hours.

I have given each page and each design a unique number with the prefix AIA, as the drawings are in the ownership of the American Institute of Architects Library and Archives in Washington, D.C. This prefix is used when the designs are referred to in the main text, but to simplify the annotated list only the number has been given. There are other numbers on some sheets and some of these were given in more recent times. Pritchard's spelling has been used for the titles. References are given to the relevant chapters in the main book. An asterisk* denotes that the actual piece still exists.

John Harris's admirable article in 1968 identified and drew attention to *The Drawing Book*, thereby giving some prominence to Pritchard's work. We hope that the publication of all his drawings will carry this further forward.

1. Lettering and sketches of designs.

2. Cut sheet with figures for a 'frame' and a small piece of gadrooning.

3. *Mr Mittons Chimney frame.** Shipton Hall, Shropshire.

This chimney frame is still at Shipton Hall in the library on the first floor. It is more baroque than later designs by Pritchard and may reflect work that he had done at an earlier date. This can probably be dated to 1765. Halley was involved in this work but never appears again. Chapter 6.

4. *Time on the Liberary Chimney frame for Croft.** Croft Castle, Herefordshire.

5. *Chimney frame for the Liberary at Croft Castle.** Croft Castle, Herefordshire.

Not many of these designs are dated, but this can probably be ascribed to September 1765. This wonderful Rococo Gothick chimney frame is still at Croft Castle, but not in its original position. For some unexplained reason, it was moved from the library on the north east side to the ante-room on the east side. Throughout the book, Pritchard varies the way that he calculated the time Nelson, van der Hagen and others took to complete the work. The calculations on AIA 4 would appear to be the amount that was paid to the craftsmen, as the time taken is given on the actual drawing. Pritchard carried out a great deal of work at Croft, but few designs have survived. Chapter 5.

6. *This frame for Ld Baths Picture in the Great Room at the Red Lyon W:verhampton.* Snow Hill, Wolverhampton.

This and AIA 8 were for the Red Lion, a busy Wolverhamton inn which was part of the Newport Estate under the control Lord Bath. The Red Lion was demolished when the area of Snow Hill was redeveloped in the 1950/60s. For the involved situation of the Newport Estate, see Chapter 8.

7. *This Chimney Peice for Mr Somerset Davis of Ludlow.** 27 Broad Street, Ludlow

This design is dated November 1765 which helps with other dating. The lively design with a phoenix is the only drawing existing for 27 Broad Street where Pritchard carried out a modernisation scheme and built The Gazebo in the garden. Chapter 8.

8. *Two Chimneys for the great Room at the Red Lyon in Woolverhampton.* Snow Hill, Wolverhampton. Chapter 8.

9. *Chimney for Mr Powis Gravel Hill.*

This is presumed to be in Shrewsbury and like most of the clients there, neither Mr. Powis nor his house on Gravel Hill has been identified.

10. Four Designs for Thomas Johnes, Croft Castle, Herefordshire.

10a. *2 Door freezes to Saloon Room Croft.**

10b. *2 Door freezes to Mr Johnes Dressing Room Croft.**

10c. *Chimney freeze for the Bishop^s Room Croft.**

10d. *a Chimney Freeze to Bed Chamber South front Croft.*

Two of the door 'freezes' and the chimney 'freeze' are still at Croft; the one for the dressing room is now in the Saloon Room. Chapter 5.

11. *Glass frame and Chimney for Mr Pritchard.*

11a. Glass Frame

11b. Chimney

Mr. Pritchard has not been identified, but his 'Glass Frame' with its Rococo style contrasts with the Classical mouldings of the Chimney.

12. *These 3 Chimneys for Mr Bather in Mardol.* Shrewsbury.

The Bathers were an extensive Shrewsbury family, but it has not been possible to identify where Mr. Bather lived in Mardol, one of the old streets of the town.

12a. *Dineing Room.* December 28th, 1765.

12b. *Parlour.* Derbyshire Marble, March 8th, 1766. Pritchard has added to this 'Nelson 5 Days at additional ornaments'.

12c. *Attick Storey.* This is the only instance in the book of a chimney piece for this floor.

13. Two designs for Miss Leighton, Condover Hall, Shropshire.

13a. *Bed Chamber Chimney for Miss Leighton.*

13b. *Dressing Room Chimney for Miss Leighton.*

Danders appears here alongside Nelson and van der Hagen. These Rococo designs, in the style of Thomas Johnson and Ince and Mayhew, show Pritchard's light touch in designing these chimney pieces thought suitable for a young lady's room. Anna Maria Leighton, eldest daughter of Sir Charlton Leighton of Loton Park, was the heiress of Condover through her Owen grandmother. She married Nicholas Smythe, or Smith, from Gloucestershire.

14. *Drawing Room Chimney for Esqr Barnaby.* Brockhampton House, Herefordshire.

Bartholomew Barnaby, owner of the Brockhampton Estate, is thought to have commissioned Pritchard to rebuild the house for him in the 1760s. This interesting chimney piece, probably with one of Mr. Barnaby's hunting dogs and Diana the huntress in the centre, does not survive in the house. Definite figures and animals are not usual in Pritchard's work so this must have been requested by the client. Chapter 5.

15. Four designs.

15a. *2 Candle Sticks Bracketts for Mrs Bather.* Shrewsbury.

15b. *a Mahogany Scheild for a Book Case for Mr Bather.* Shrewsbury.

The Bathers seemed to like Rococo designs which is interesting as members of the family were in business in Shrewsbury as carriers of goods. There is a light pencil note of ' ½ day altering 2 girandoles for Mr Bather Nelson.'

15c. *Modele for a Machine grate for Colbrook Dale.* Shipton Hall, Shropshire.

This important piece is still at the Hall but perhaps not in the original position. It is discussed in Chapter 6.

15d. *Chimney Peice for Esqr Corbet ... Park.* The name of the venue is not clear but it was thought to be Shawbury Park, one of the Corbet houses north of Shrewsbury. However, this does not appear to be the name that is written there.

16. Two designs.

16a. *Chimney Peice for M^r^. Lloyd Raven Street.* Shrewsbury.

16b. *Chimney Peice for Mr Scot Draper Grope Lane.* Shrewsbury. Mr Haycock has been crossed out and Mr Scot inserted. Grope Lane is one of the old streets in central Shrewsbury, but these houses have not been identified.

17. *Chimney Peice for Mr Haycock in Wales.*

The client and location are not known. On this design Pritchard has written out detailed information about the lengths of the different mouldings required. Was this because Swift had just joined the team? He makes his first appearance in this design. The design includes a bird, which appears to be a ho-ho, on the frieze. Ho-ho birds and other Chinese motifs are on chimney pieces at High Hatton Hall and Sherford House that are believed to be by Pritchard.

18. *Freeze and Therms of this Chimney peice for Mr Egerton.* This may be for Tatton Park, Cheshire. Perhaps this one was never executed as there is no time given for the carvers or details of their work. As it is rather grand, with a griffin, or wyvern, and a lion's head, it may have been for the 'Great Room' that Pritchard is thought to have worked on there. Chapter 7.

19. *Common Parlour for Mr Freeman.* Gaines, Worcestershire.

Pritchard starts to use the style of tablethat is found throughout most of the book. John Freeman was the owner of Gaines at this time and it is presumed that Pritchard also carried out the extensions to the house. None of the chimney pieces remain at Gaines. Chapter 5.

20. *Chimney Peice for Mr Burton.* Longner Hall, Shropshire.

Longner Hall was rebuilt in 1803 by John Nash. Here Pritchard has used a different kind of table for keeping the times which he does not use again.

21. *French Marble Mr Freeman's Chamber.* Gaines, Worcestershire. Chapter 5.

22. *Chimney for Bed Chamber Mr Freeman.* Gaines, Worcestershire. Chapter 5.

23. No details for the client or the house are given for this chimney piece with a wild boar hunting scene.

24. *This Chimney Peice for Mr Francis Turner.** Benthall Hall, Shropshire.

This is an important design as it was made to reflect and complement the Jacobean overmantel at Benthall Hall. Francis Turner, also the owner of Broseley Hall, is listed under various names as his complicated history and inheritances show. Chapter 8.

25. *Chimney Piece for Mr Fowler of Penford.*

The location for this pretty design is not certain, but it could be Pendeford Hall, Staffordshire, now demolished, which was owned by the Fowler family.

26. *Chimney Peice for Blew Room Cundover.* Condover Hall, Shropshire.

Some designs have few details on them and no information about carvers or time. This may have been one of the designs that Pritchard did for Robert Mylne. On 26 June 1766, Mylne sent Miss Leighton a drawing for a chimney piece and another for door cases, but does not specify which room the chimney piece was for. Chapter 2.

27. *Common Parlour Hon^le Mr Harley.** Kinsham Court, Herefordshire.

This carving from this chimney piece is still at Kinsham Court, but has been used for the overmantel and for the edge of the marble fire surround. Chapter 5.

28. *2 Frames for Shell pieces for Mr Fowler of Atcham.* Delivered 19 May 1768.

Atcham is near Shrewsbury and Atcham Rectory was occupied by The Rev. Mr. Fowler in the 18th century and these were probably for him. His name appears on various committees such as the Foundling Hospital. This would seem to be for a picture made of shells; shells were in fashion and Mrs. Delaney was making marvellous creations with them. (See *Mrs Delaney and her flower collages*, Ruth Hayden, London, 1986).

Richard Corbett wrote that as Mrs. Hill (of Tern Hall) had promised to buy him some shells in London so that he could finish his grotto, he had 'taken the liberty of enclosing a list' of those he wanted.

(SRRC, Attingham Collection/112/12/24/265: Corbett to Hill, 12 November 1758) This drawing could possibly be in the wrong order as the designs for Hatton Grange would have been carried before it

29. *Drawing Room Chimney Esqr Slaney.** Hatton Grange, Shropshire.

All the designs for Hatton Grange are still in the house which has been altered very little internally. It is Pritchard's largest documented new domestic building. Chapter 6.

30. *Center Chamber Chimney Esqr Slaney.** Hatton Grange, Shropshire. Chapter 6.

31. Two designs.

31a. *Pedement for Mr Slaney^s^ house at Hatton.** Hatton Grange, Shropshire.

Nelson worked on this for over seven weeks, while Yates, the stone mason, spent fourteen days working on the pediment.

31b. *Two flower pots over the Doors in Liberary at Croft.** Croft Castle, Herefordshire. These are now in the present dining room over and around picture frames. These designs show that Pritchard was working on two very important commissions at the same date, probably about 1766. Chapters 6 and 5.

32. *This Chimney Piece for Mr Lloyd Raven Street.* Shrewsbury.

33. *Chimney Piece in Freestone for Esqr Smith Cundover.* Shropshire.

This classical design with Ionic columns and an Apollo's head and sunburst in the centre was for Nicholas Smith, also called Smythe, who married Miss Leighton of Condover.

34. *Dineing Parlour Chimney for Mr Wallcot Bitterley.** Bitterley Court, Shropshire.

The dining room is now the drawing room. This design was also used for Hatton Grange and both are still in the house. The Slaneys and the Walcots, like the owners today, would have known each other. Chapter 6.

35. *Best parlour Chimney for the Honor^le^ Mr Harley.** Kinsham Court, Herefordshire.

This is still at the house, complete with the lion's head in the centre. Chapter 5.

36. *Chimney Peice for Mr Ashby in High Street.* Shrewsbury. Chapter 2.

37. *Chimney Peice for Mr Ashby in High Street Parlour.* Shrewsbury.

These two designs are for the lawyer, John Ashby, who was agent for the Clive estates in the county.

38. *Chimney Peice for Mr Blythe.** Broseley Hall, Shropshire

Perhaps for a bed chamber for Francis Turner Blythe, but this is not specific. The mouldings have been drawn in detail. Chapter 8.

39. *Bed Chamber Chimney Chimney Peice for Mr Blythe.** Broseley Hall, Shropshire.

This was for Francis Turner Blythe, later of Benthall Hall and is still at Broseley Hall. Here Pritchard has drawn the mouldings to be used in larger and more detailed form than usual. Chapter 8.

40. *Chimney Peice for Samuel Egerton Esqr.* Tatton Park, Cheshire. *The same for The Honable Mr Harley* and *Same for Sir Charlton Leighton* of Loton Park, Shropshire, has been added. Chapter 7.

41. *This Chimney Peice for Samuel Egerton Esqr, Miss Egerton's Room.* Tatton Park, Cheshire. Chapter 7.

This chimney piece design was also made for 'Mr Harley for the Hall' and is now at Kinsham Court.* Chapter 5.

42. *29 Stair Case Brackets in Oak - Esqr Slaney.** Hatton Grange, Shropshire. This is a very typical 18th century design that can be found in such publications as Abraham Swan's *The British Architect.* Chapter 6.

43. *Hall Chimney in Painswick Stone - Mr Slaney.** Hatton Grange, Shropshire.

One of the three examples of stone used for a chimney piece. Nelson worked alone on this piece for fourteen days. Chapter 6.

44. Two designs.

44a. *Door case for Miss Leighton Cundover.* Condover Hall, Shropshire. This design for Condover might have been for Robert Mylne. Chapter 2.

44b. *Chimney Piece for Mr Davis* ... Perhaps of Ellesmere but he has not been identified.

45. Two designs.

45a. *Plinth Base to Salone Room at Croft.* Croft Castle, Herefordshire.

45b. *Chimney Peice for Miss Leighton Cundover.* Condover Hall, Shropshire.

The reference to the marble ornaments is unusual in Pritchard's known designs. Nelson spent over ten days working on the marble and seven on the wood. Danders, who has not appeared for some time, comes in to work on both the marble and the wood. There is no mention of van der Hagen, who would have been expected to work on the marble, but may have been busy with a monument.

46. *Drawing Room Chimney Esq*^{r} *Barnaby.* Brockhampton House, Herefordshire.

It is unfortunate that this attractive chimney piece no longer exists as the therms carry interesting motifs such as a pineapple and lion's head. Chapter 5.

47. *Dressing Room Esq*^{r} *Walcot Bitterley.** Bitterley Court, Shropshire.

This is one of the most popular designs that Pritchard carried out, in the Ince and Mayhew and Thomas Johnson style of Rococo. Pritchard wrote down the side that it was also for the 'Center' chamber at Hatton Grange where it still is today. Chapter 6.

48. *S*^{r} *Edward Blount.** The remains of this monument are now in the Blount Chapel, a Roman Catholic Chapel attached to St. John the Baptist's Church, Mamble, Worcestershire.

Pritchard used Rococo at the sides, top and around the cartouche, so it is all the more unfortunate that it does not survive intact. Jasper and Sienna marble are specified. Someone has written 'Aged 104 years.' The cross at the top gives valuable clues to link Pritchard with other monuments such as Dame Mary Smythe, another Roman Catholic, in St. Mary's Church, Acton Burnell, Shropshire. Chapter 11.

49. Two designs.

49a. *Dressing room for Cundover.* Condover Hall, Shropshire.

49b. *Common Parlour for Cundover.* Condover Hall, Shropshire.

50. *Chimney Peice for purple Room at Cundover.*

A wonderful example of a frieze of cusped Gothick arches. The name 'purple room' suggests something rather exotic.

51. *Hall Chimney Peice at Cundover - Painswick stone.* Condover Hall, Shropshire.

Stone must have been considered more suitable for a hall as it was used for this at Condover and Hatton Grange. This design, and the preceding design are much larger than most of the others in the book. Unlike the other Condover designs, there is no client specified, only the house and there are no details of the carvers, so this may have been a design that went to Mr Duval from Mylne. Chapter 2.

52. *Chimney for S*^{r} *Charlton Leighton.**

Sir Charlton of Loton Park was father of Miss Leighton. This is still at Loton Park and is very similar to AIA 40.

53. *Chimney Peice for M*^{r} *Bather.* Shrewsbury.

Another Rococo design for Mr Bather.

54. *Eight Gothick Colloums for Mr Freeman.** Gaines, Worcestershire.

Perhaps the most important design in the book. These were the wooden formers for the cast iron columns now at Gaines. Chapter 5.

55. *Three frames in Burnished Gold for a Dessart Table Mr Lee.*

The client is thought to be Mr Lee of Coton Hall, Shropshire and Pritchard may have worked for him on the chapel next to the house. Details of Coton Hall and the Chapel are in the Appendix.

56. *For Miss Egertons Bed Chamber.* Tatton Park, Cheshire.

William Hunt's painting account, dated May and June 1767 and 1768 lists work done on Miss Egerton's apartments including painting chimney pieces. These designs could date from early 1767 and be part of a rebuilding scheme for Tatton. The use of the term 'Gothick arches', listed at the bottom as 'Gothick coave', is interesting as well as the mixture of motifs - waterleaf and fluting. The same design was also done for *Capt Evans Best Parlour.* He has not been identified. Chapter 7.

57. *Hall Chimney for Mr Freeman.** Gaines, Worcestershire.

This chimney piece, taken out of the house either in the late 19th or early 20th century, was found dismantled in an outhouse at Gaines and in the 1950s it was taken to a house in Sussex where it is today. If it had not been removed at that time, it would probably have not survived at all. 'Fluteing and Gothick' have again been mixed. Chapter 5.

58. *Dressing Room Chimney Esqr Slaney.** Hatton Grange, Shropshire.

Another example of this popular design, usually used for an upstairs room. Gothick in essence but enhanced by the flowers twisted around the cluster columns. Chapter 6.

59. *Common Parlour Chamber Purple marble Chimney Esqr Slaney.** Hatton Grange, Shropshire.

The 'purple marble' refers to the fire surround. Chapter 6.

60. *Best Chamber Chimney Esqr Slaney.** Hatton Grange, Shropshire.

A design similar to AIA 41 for both Samuel Egerton and Mr. Harley of Kinsham as well as the frieze for the Bishop's Room at Croft Castle, AIA 10. Chapter 6.

61. *Freeze to Esqr Barnaby,* Brockhampton House, Herefordshire.

It is not clear what this account applied to, but it could be AIA 14. Above is another faint account in pencil.

62. *Dining Parlour Chimney for Esqr Slaney.** Hatton Grange, Shropshire.

At the time the drawing was made, the design for the central tablet had perhaps not been decided. A pastoral scene was executed by

Pritchard's craftsmen as the valuation tells us that both van der Hagen and Nelson worked on it. Chapter 6.

63. *Drawing Room Chimney Esqr Walcot, Bitterley.** Bitterley Court, Shropshire.

One of the best Gothick designs by Pritchard, dated February 4th 1769 and now in the dining room at Bitterley. '£6. 7. 7.' has been written alongside it. Was this the cost of the carving? If so, it seems low for such an elaborate piece, but the sum is comparable with the carving for Noel Hill and other clients. Chapter 6.

64. *Richard Ward Offley of Hinton Esqr, Aged 46 Dyed May 29 1762.** St. George's Church, Pontesbury, Shropshire.

Dated 'January the 28th 1769', so seven years had elapsed between his death and the making of the wall monument. This is the only monument design that lists the time taken by all three craftsmen and shows that Swift joined the regular team. From the table, we can see definitely that weeks, days and hours are listed, but the question is, can this also be applied to other tables? For example, did it take van der Hagen twelve days or twelve weeks to carve the tablet for the dining room chimney piece at Hatton Grange? (AIA 60) Twelve days does not seem long enough and twelve weeks too long, especially as Nelson worked on it as well. For Hatton it must be concluded that the times refer to days. Chapter 11.

65. *Derby Marble Chimney to Mr Good feby the 11th.* Shrewsbury.

As this was being worked on in February and van der Hagen's name is not included, this could show that he was still working on the Ward Offley monument which occupied him for five weeks. Mr Good's house has not been identified. Chapter 2.

66. *Dining Parlour Chimney - Henrey Powys Esqr the Abby.* Shrewsbury.

The Abbey House belonged to the Newport Estate and was rented by Henry Powys, another person whose name can be found on committees of public works in Shrewsbury.

67. *Alcove Bed Chamber Chimney - Henrey Powys Esq. the Abby.* Shrewsbury.

This design was originally for the dressing room and is another example of Rococo being used for an upstairs room.

68. Glass frame.

It would be interesting to know who this neo-Classical glass frame was for but there is no information on it.

69. *Bed Chamber over Dining Parlour Noel Hill.* Tern Hall, Shropshire.

This is the first of the series of chimney pieces designed for Noel Hill after he took over Tern Hall. It is an elegant mixture of Gothick and Classical motifs in true Pritchard style, with a 'New Dove marble' fire surround. He notes at the bottom that the carving cost £3. 4. 10. The Tern Hall drawings have a number on them in the top left hand corner indicating that they were a series. Chapter 10.

70. *Darby marble chimney for Blithe Turner Esqr of Brousley.** Broseley Hall, Shropshire.

Although this sounds as if it was made of marble, it is in fact wood. The date 1769 is in the top right hand corner and alongside it, faintly in pencil, is 'Bed Chamber Capt Evans'; he has not been identified. Chapter 8.

71. *Garden Temple for Blithe Turner Esqr Brousley.** Broseley Hall, Shropshire.

This wooden garden temple design, dated April 1st 1769, is still at the Hall. Faint lines can be seen under the drawing of an earlier drawing with what appears to be a rounded roof. Chapter 8.

72. *Dressing room Over Drawing Room - Noel Hill Esqr.* Tern Hall, Shropshire.

No. 2 in the Tern Hall series. The decorative frieze contains a vase and a Baroque recorder. 'Sienna' marble is used for the surround and the carving cost is given as £6. 1. 5½. Chapter 10.

73. *Bed Chamber over Hall for Noel Hill Esqr.* Tern Hall, Shropshire.

No. 3. Another elegant and elaborate chimney piece for Tern. Chapter 10.

74. *Right hand Chamber over Hall Noel Hill Esqr.* Tern Hall, Shropshire. *Same as Mr Tomkins.*

This is an account only. Mr Tomkins has not been identified and the drawing for him is not in *The Drawing Book.*. Another carver, Abram, is brought in indicating that much work needed to be done to complete all the Tern Hall pieces. Chapter 10.

75. *Chamber Over Drawing Room - Noel Hill Esqr.* Tern Hall, Shropshire.

No. 4. Chapter 10.

76. This appears to have been designed as No. 5, *Right Hand Chamber over Hall for Noel Hill* and this is the drawing to go with the account in AIA 74. The original title was crossed out and then it became the chimney piece for Mr Tomkins. *The same for Noel Hill* has been written down the side. There are some slight variations in the time taken and the price of the carving written at the bottom. Chapter 10.

77. *Dressing room over Dining Parlour - Noel Hill Esqr.* Tern Hall, Shropshire.

No. 6 in the series presumably, although the figure is written in a different way. The carving of the pastoral scene for the tablet took nearly twice as long and cost almost twice as much as the tablet for AIA 76. Here the pastoral scene is sketched in, unlike Hatton Grange, AIA 62, where the tablet is left blank in the drawing. This is a very elaborate chimney piece for a dressing room with a haut boy and possibly a drum carved on it. Chapter 10.

78. *Veind Marble Chimney Peice for Mr Good Feby the 18th*, 1769. Shrewsbury.

79. *Chimney Peice for Mr Wilkinson Feby 25th, 1769.* The Lawns, Broseley.

This was for John Wilkinson, the iron master.

80. *Chimney for Ric^d^ Corbet, Esqr Highhatton.** High Hatton Hall, Shropshire.

A member of the extensive Corbet family, Richard Corbet is from the north Shropshire branch. Chapter 6.

81. *Glass frame Mr Walcot Bitterley in Burnished gold.*

Unfortunately this no longer survives at the house. It must have been an elaborate piece as van der Hagen worked on it for 37½ days and twelve books of gold were used. Chapter 6.

82. *To the Memory of Richard Lyster Es^r^.* *Alberbury Church, Shropshire.

This detailed drawing is one of the most important in the book, but regrettably Pritchard has given little information about the carving times set out in AIA 83 and 84. Only Nelson's time for carving the cherubs' heads and the side palms is listed and this took him a total of twenty nine and six days respectively. The palms remain on the monument, but the cherubs' heads, over which he spent so much time, have gone; ironically they have been replaced by a tablet carved by van der Hagen. Behind the monument, there is an arch faintly sketched in, indicating its position in the church perhaps. There is a full account of this monument in Chapter 11.

83 and 84. *Account of Time on the Within Monument.*

85. Sketches of two cherubs.

Written alongside is '*2 frames for Ld Bal ...*' and an item for Mr Harley, as well as for other clients, one being Mr Johnes of Croft Castle.

86. A sketch of a capital with possible acanthus leaves.

87. Figures, sums and pen strokes.

88. Another cherub and some flowers.

Credit:

The American Institute of Architects Library and Archives in Washington, D.C.

The designs from *The Drawing Book* in their physical context.

Until quite recently *The Drawing Book* was available in this country in the form of poor photocopies of a microfilm. This present book contains the facsimile of *The Drawing Book* which is being published for the first time.

Besides *The Drawing Book* there are also now more of Pritchard's drawings available for analysis. Not many similar documents are available and for this reason they are very important. Drawings were and still are, analogues of the final form that is intended. In short it is a simple but effective message. Not unreasonably very few messages are kept after their content has been communicated. It so happens that *The Drawing Book* has, by some accident, been preserved albeit in a previously neglected condition.

The Drawing Book, since it was to communicate designs to Pritchard's craftsmen, illustrates drawing techniques of the period and also the vernacular techniques employed with classical moulding. In addition, it provides us with information on the terminology of the workman. There can be little doubt that the spirit of the designs are carried forward into reality although in the detail there may be differences. For example the depth of relief of certain details will show work by different craftsmen.

As part of this new access to the drawings certain simple visual comparisons have been used to compare weights of detail and the degree of change between the design and the construction. It seems likely that these will be of interest to the reader and some of these are included in this book. These examples have been put together using fairly standard computer graphics programmes. This work is still very much in hand but it was felt worthwhile to show some examples. Clearly, these are raster files but we are making progress in the conversion of these to vector programmes which are much more accurate and extensive in their ability to manipulate the solid geometry. Vector analysis on sophisticated programmes such as AutoCAD R14 will begin to show interesting comparisons between present forms and Pritchard's designs. In certain cases 3D modelling could be used to compare present buildings with the original design to determine the various stages in development.

Peter Howell, RIBA.

Monument of Richard Ward Offley, AIA64

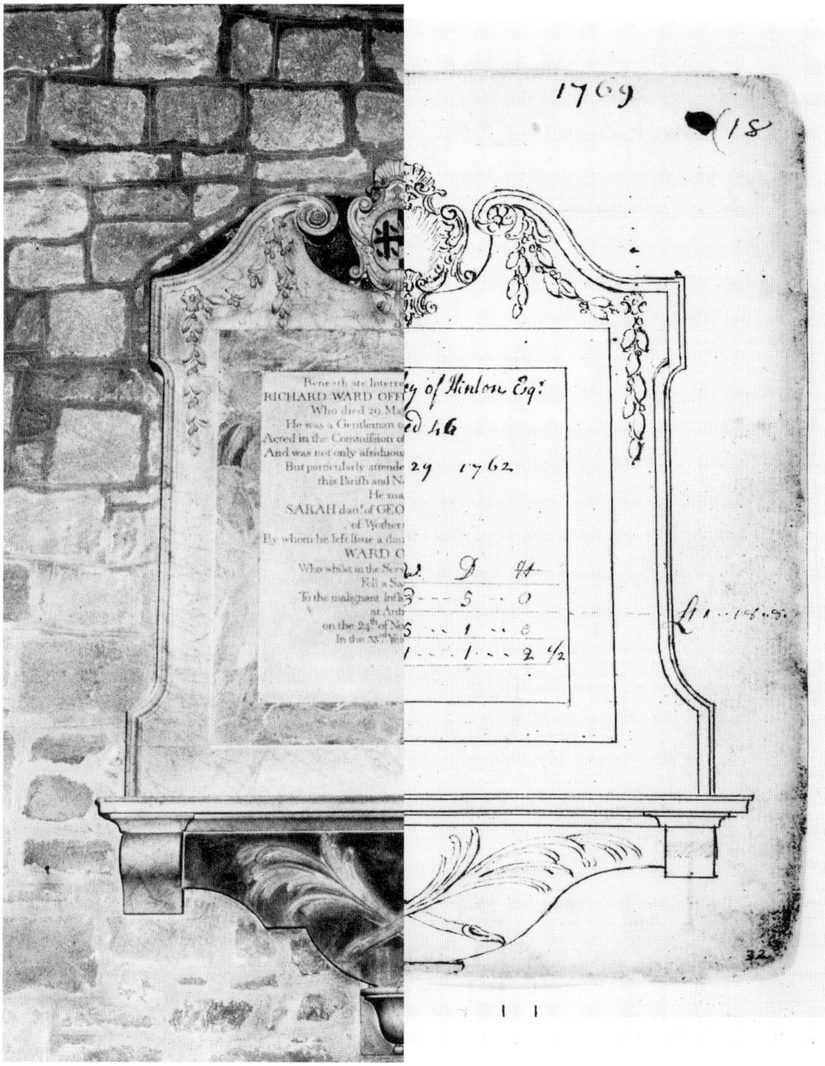

Nelson
Vanderhagen
Halley

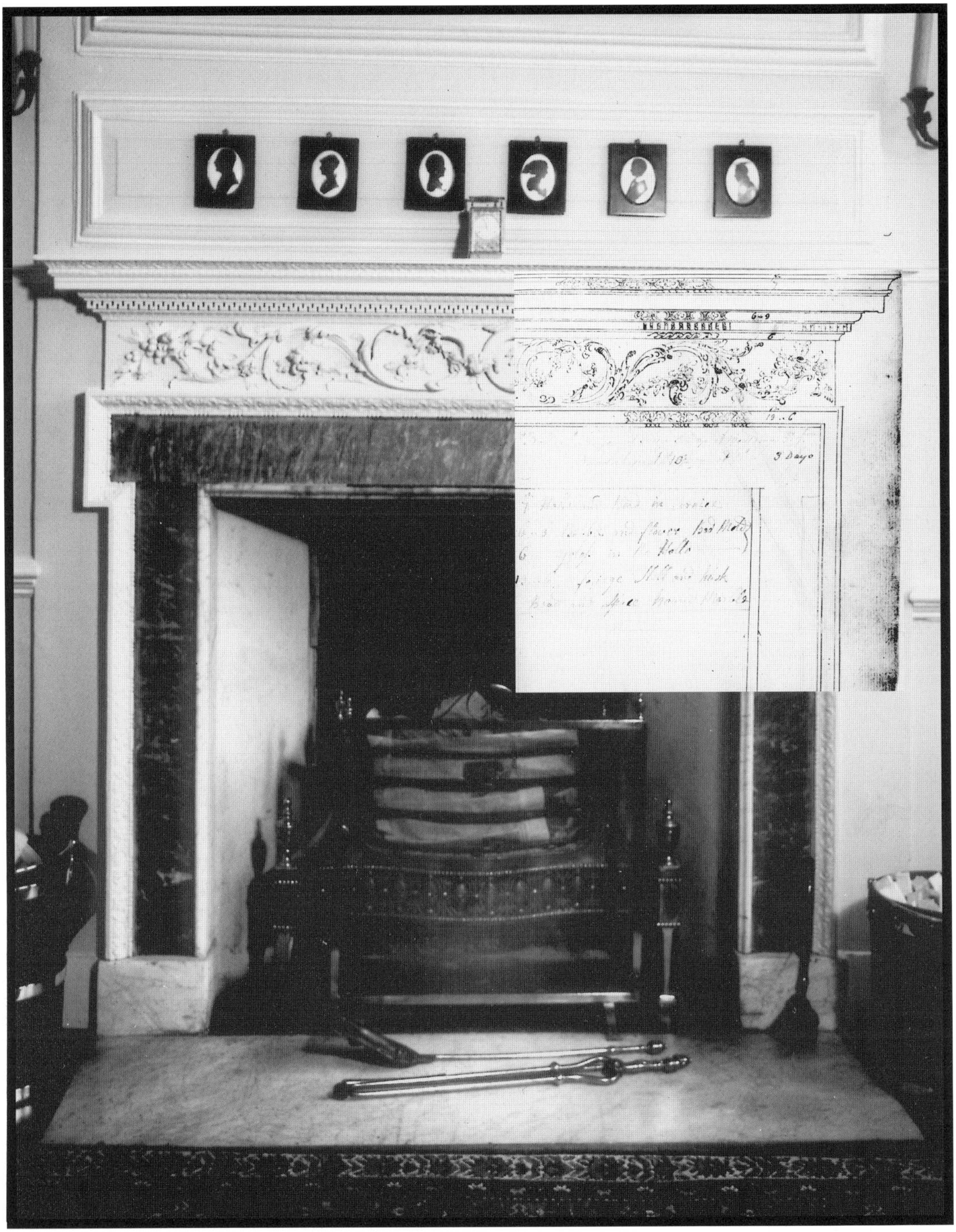

Chimney freeze for the Bishops Room Croft.

28

Facsimile of

The Drawing Book
of
Thomas Farnolls Pritchard

AIA1

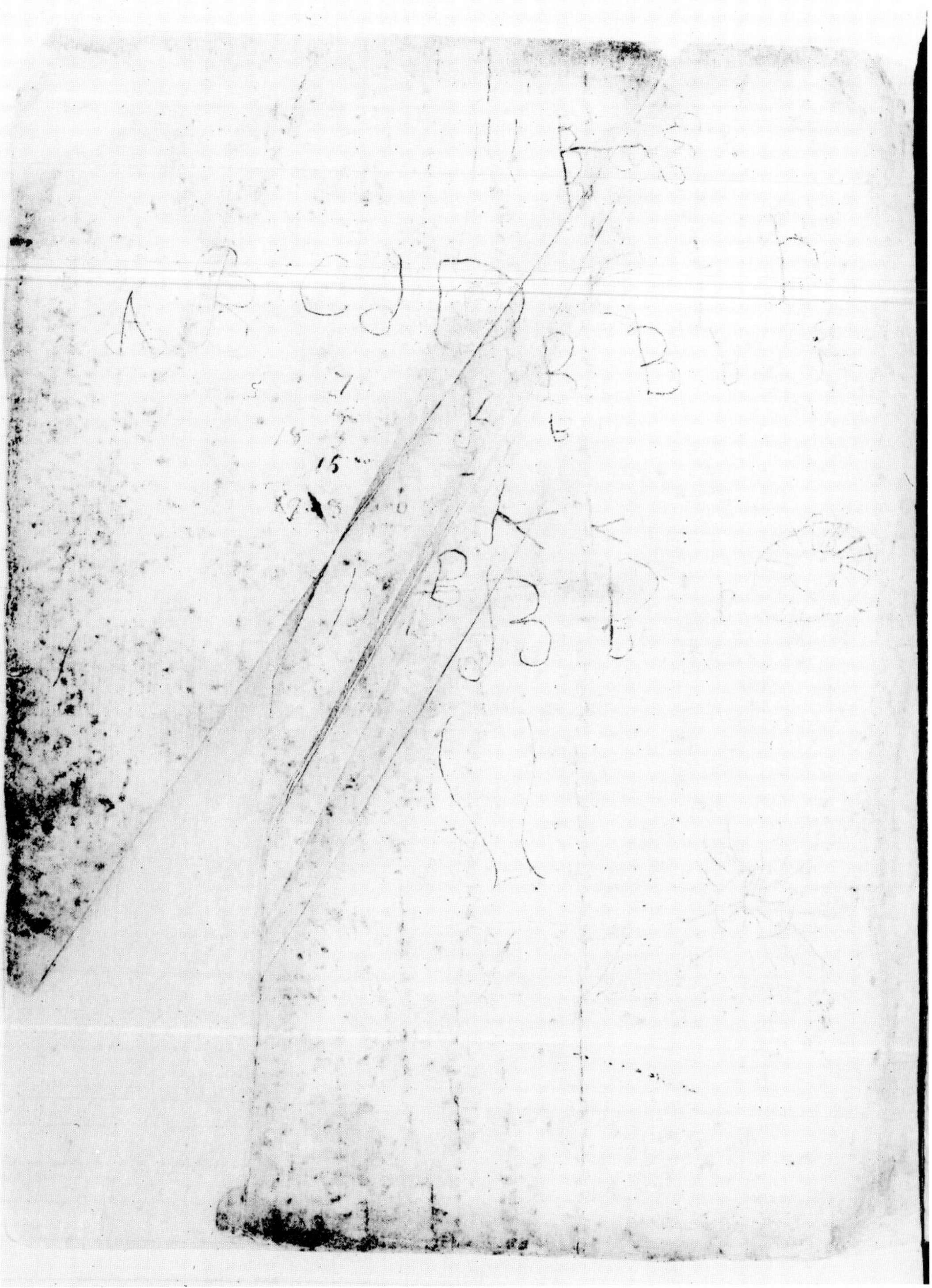

PAGE MISSING FROM THE DRAWING BOOK

AIA2 (small strip only)

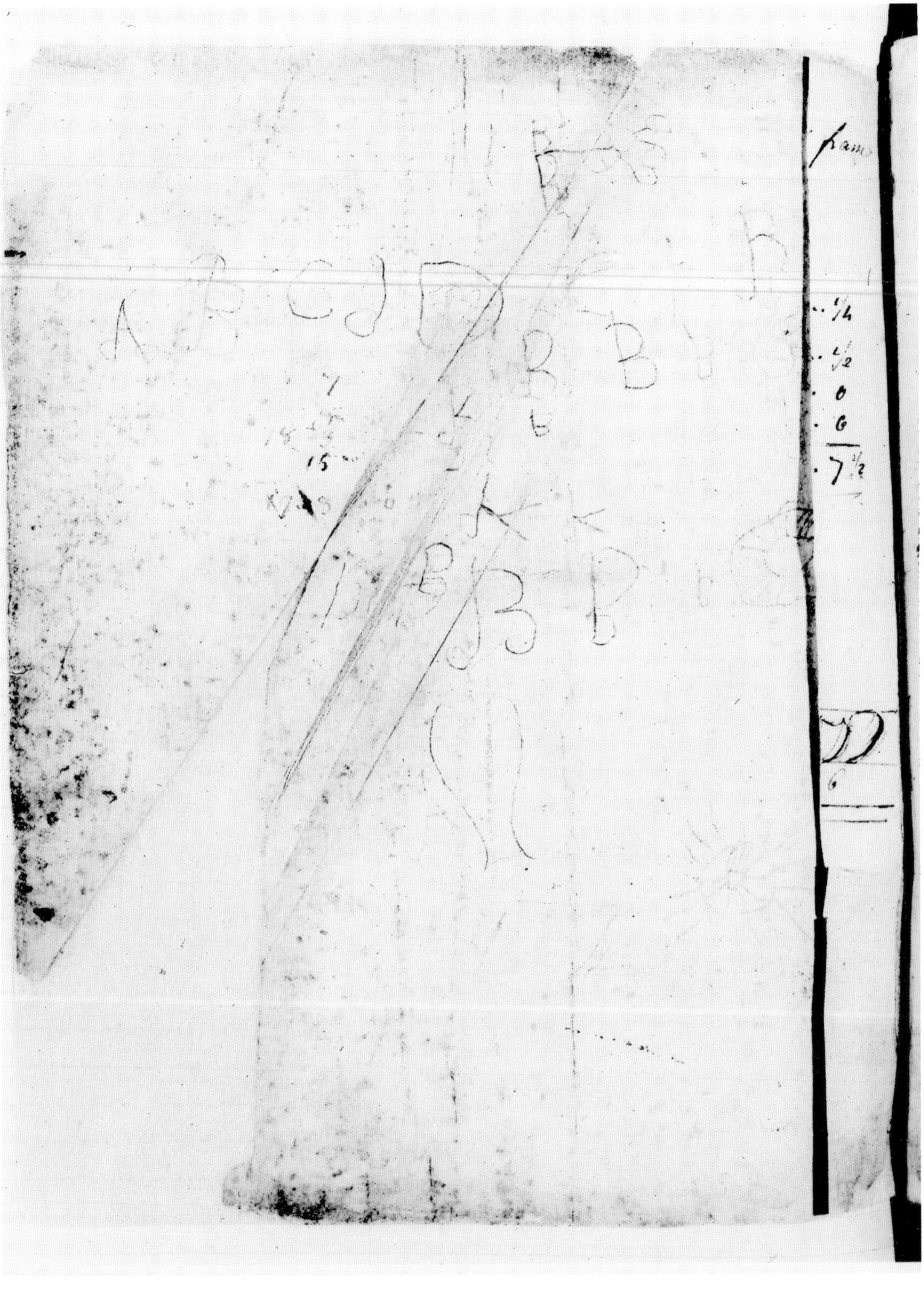

AIA3

AIA4

Time on the Liberary Chimney frame for Prof.

Nelson			Vanderhagen		
Sepbr	14	1 .. 5 . 0	Sepbr	14	1 . 0 . 0
	21	6 . 0 .. 0		21	2 .. 5 .. 0
	28	6 .. 0 . 0		28	5 . 2 . 0

AIA5

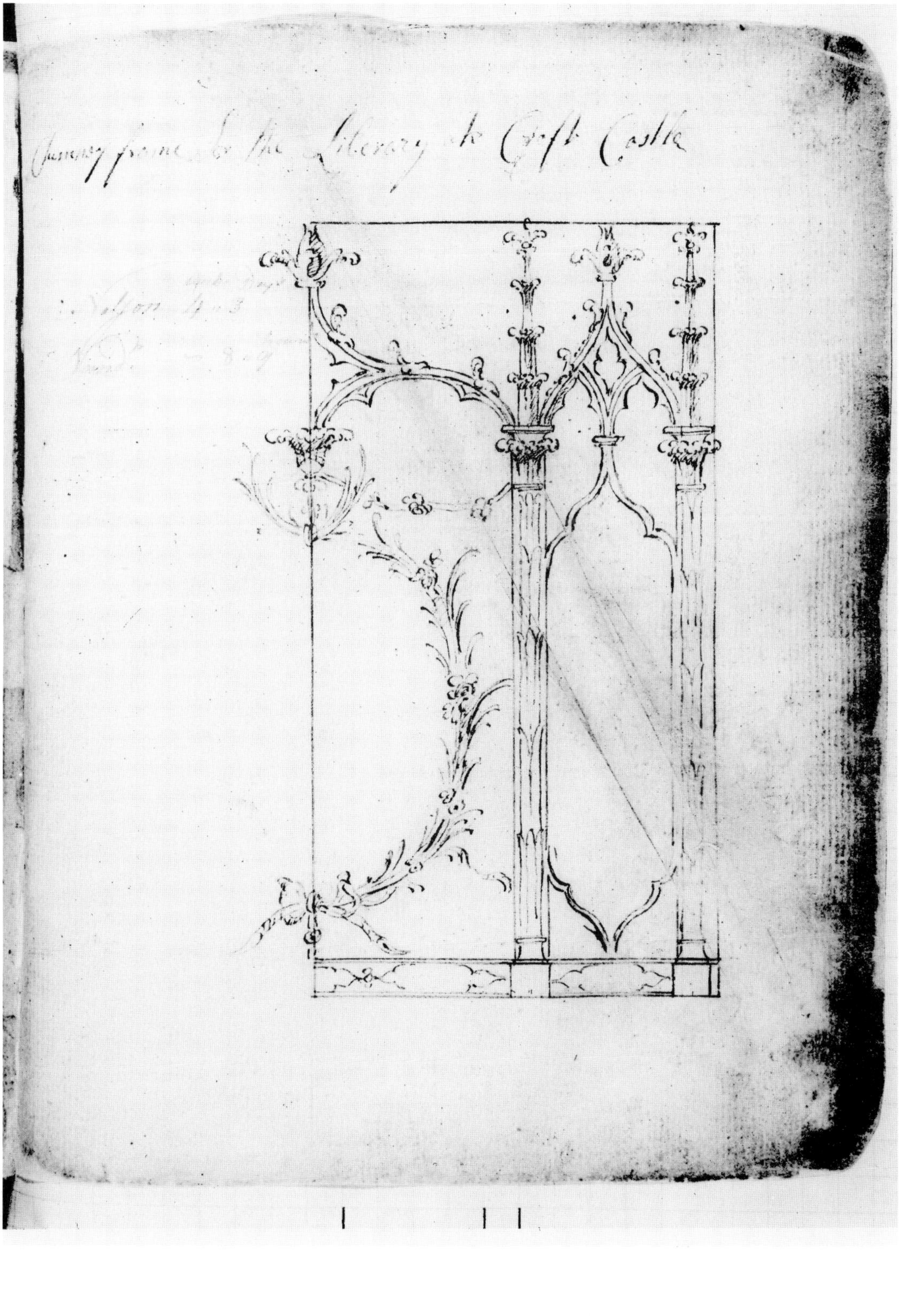

AIA6

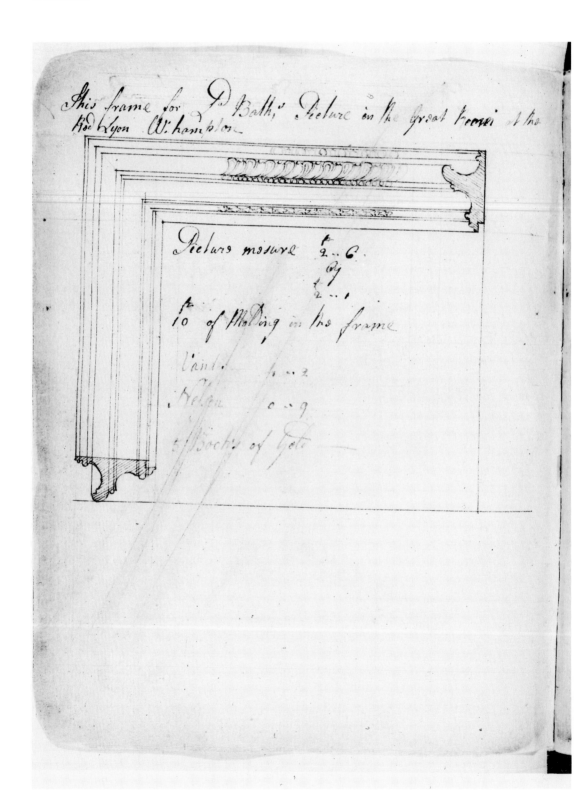

This frame for Ld Bath's Picture in the Great Room at the Red Lyon W: hampton

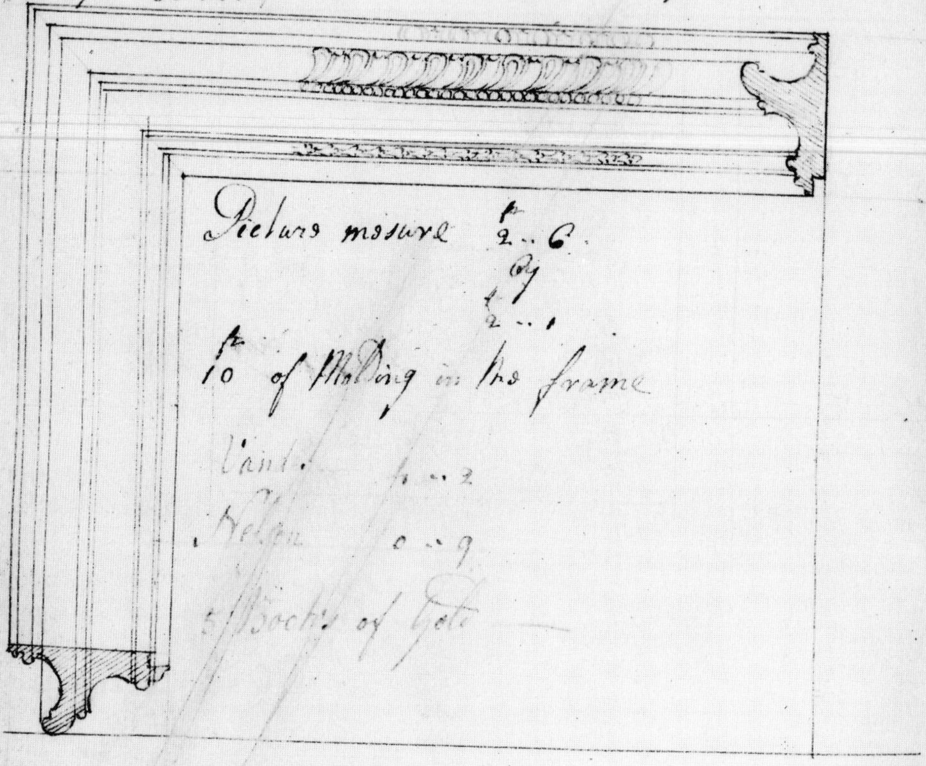

AIA7

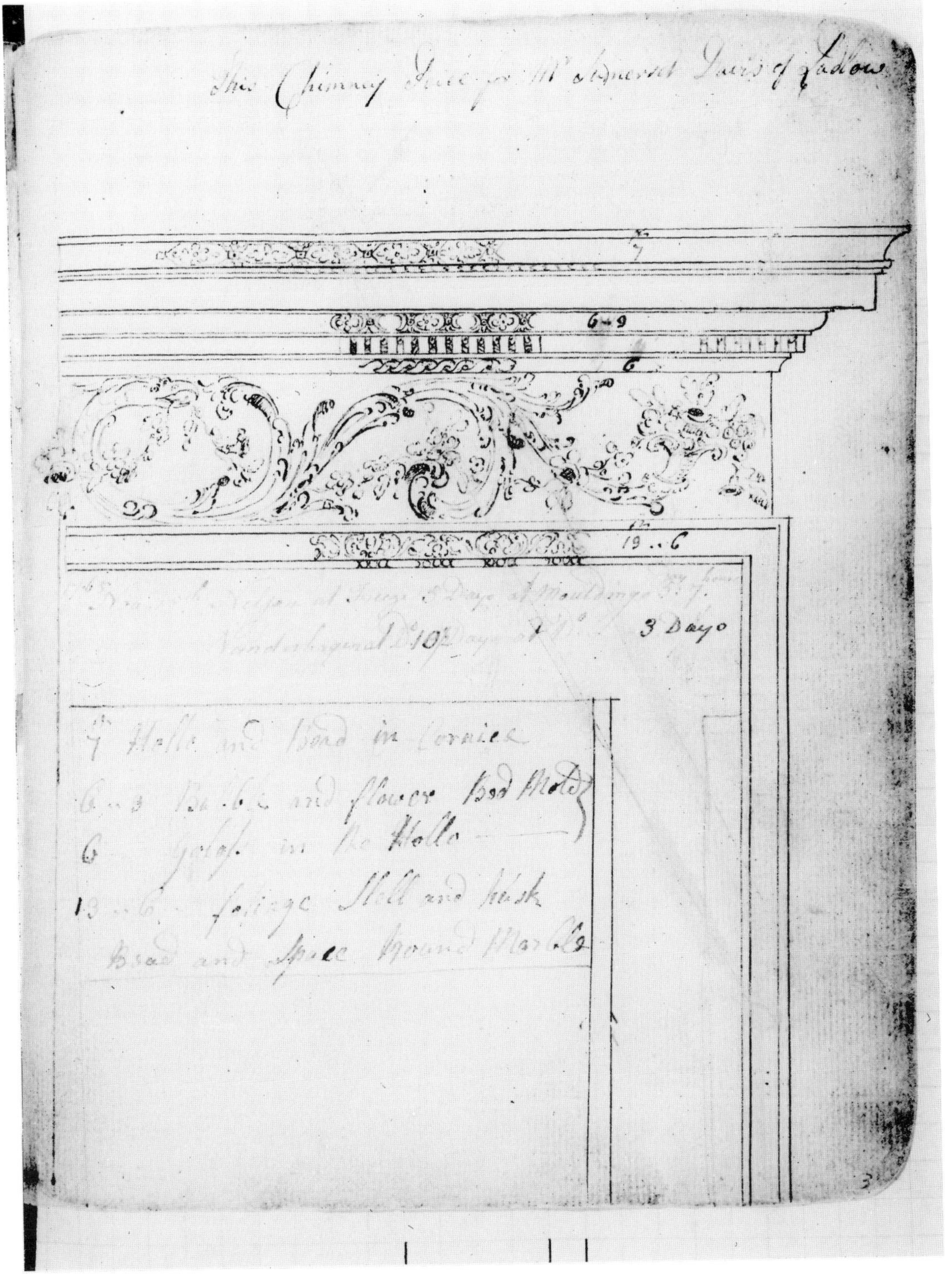

6..9
6
19 .. 6
3 Days
7 Hollo and Bead in Cornice
6 .. 3 Bead and flower Bed Mold
6 in the Hollo
13 .. 6 and Husk
Bead and Spire Round Marble

AIA8

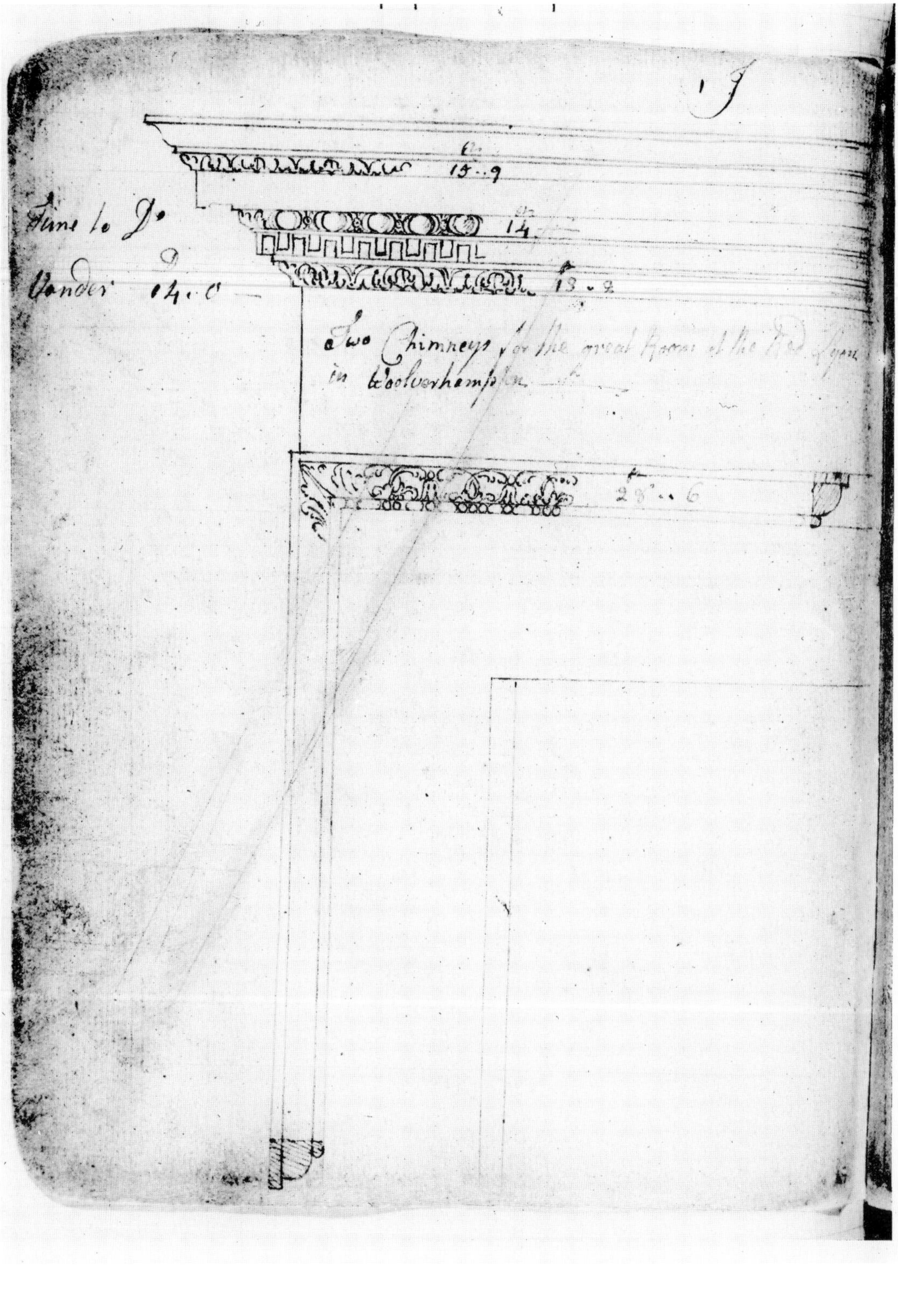
15..9
14
13..2
Vander 14.0
Two Chimneys for the great Room at the Red Lyon
in Woolverhampton
28..6

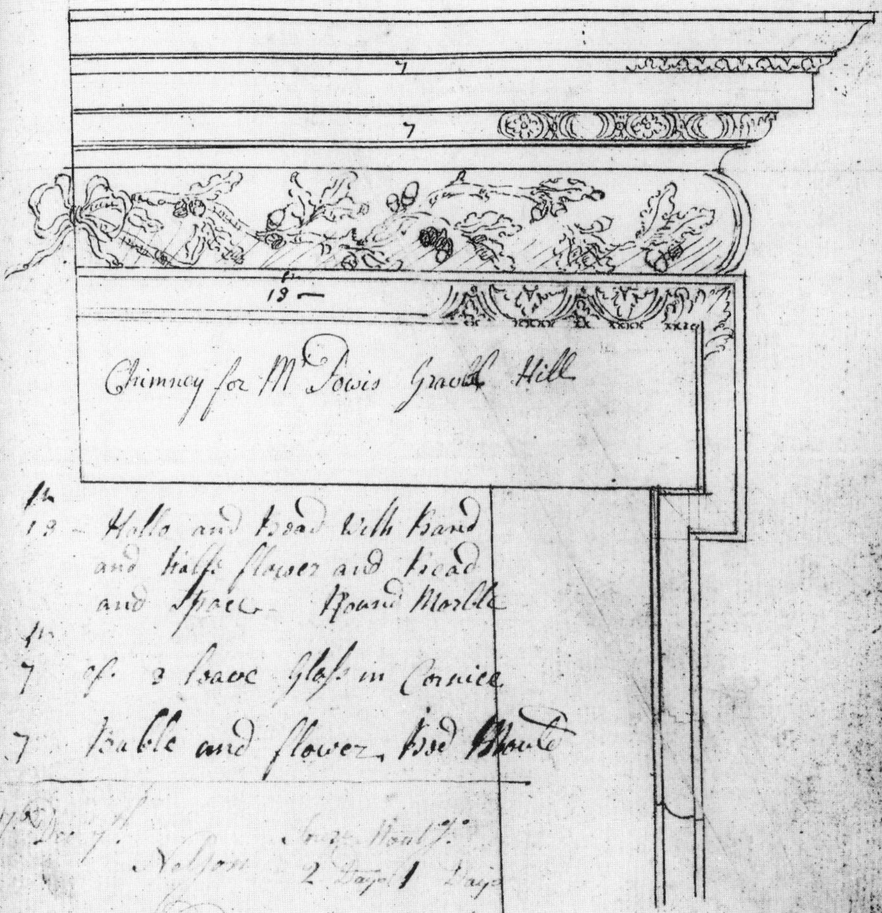

ft
13 – Hollo and bead with band and half flower and bead and space – Round Marble
ft
7 of 3 leave Glass in Cornice
7 Bable and flower Bed Moulde

7th Dec 71 Sm Mould
Nelson 2 Days 1 Days
Vanderhagen 3 Days ft 2 Hours

AIA10, top A, down to bottom D.

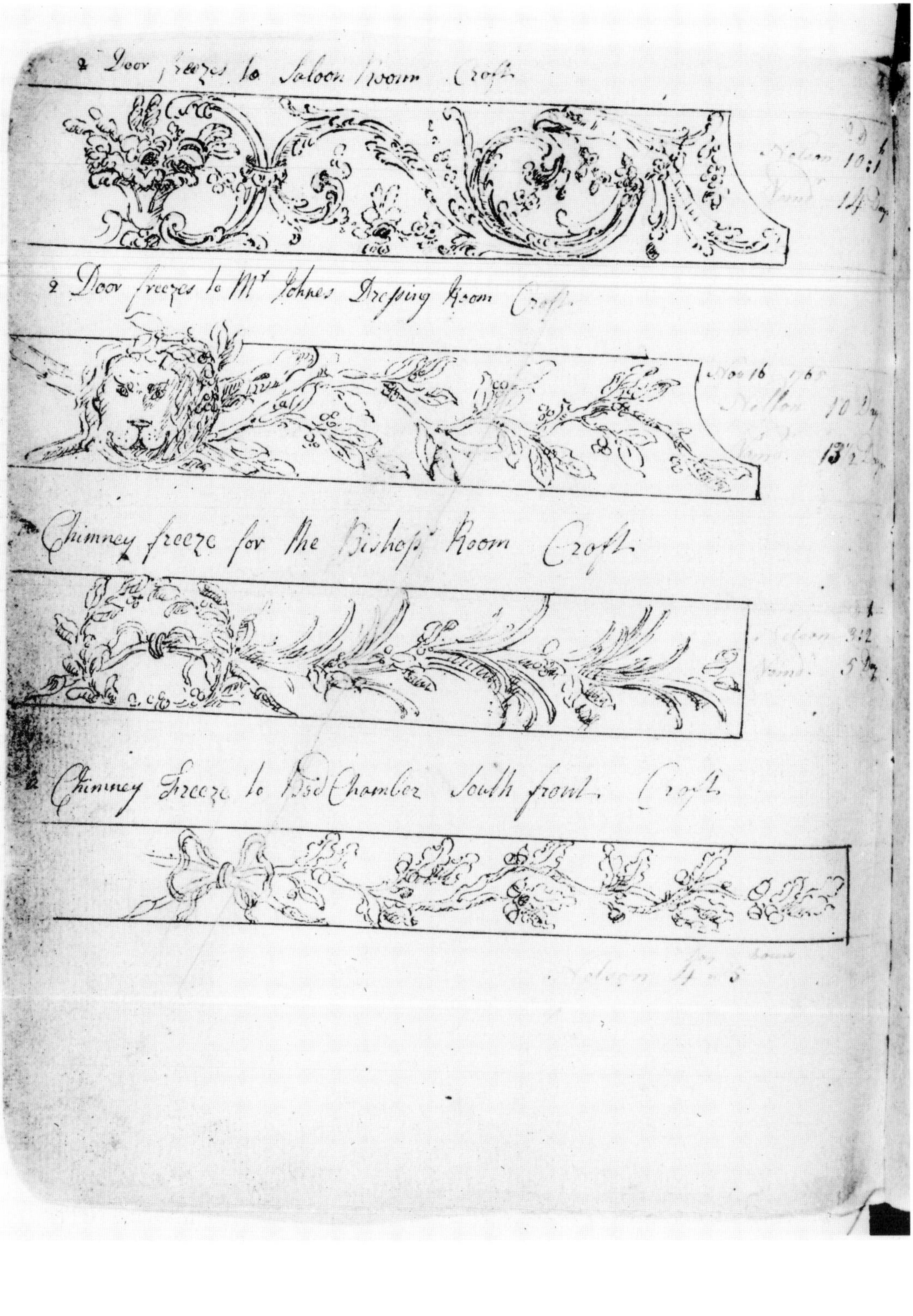

left A, right B, **AIA11**

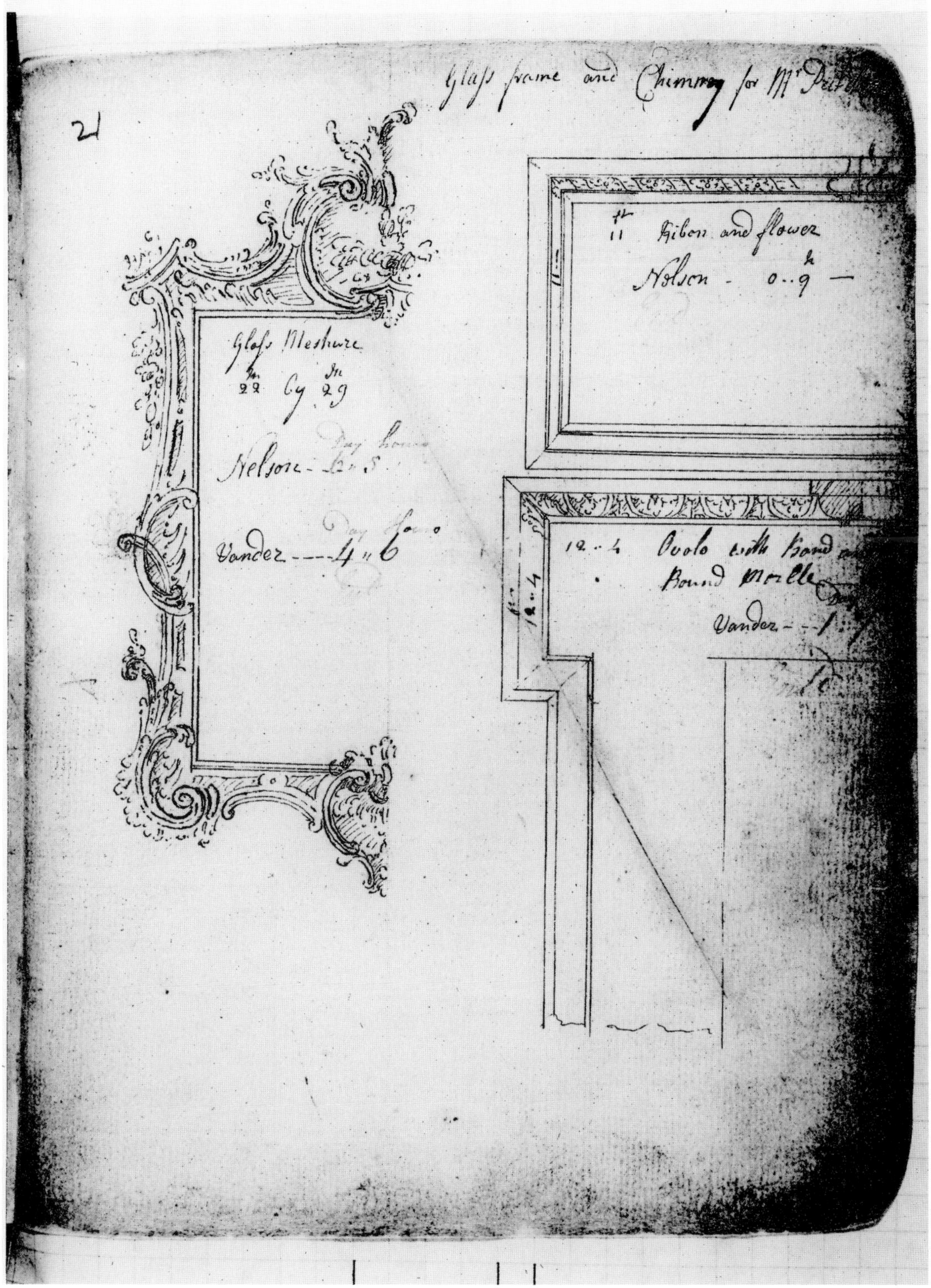

AIA12, top A, centre B and bottom C.

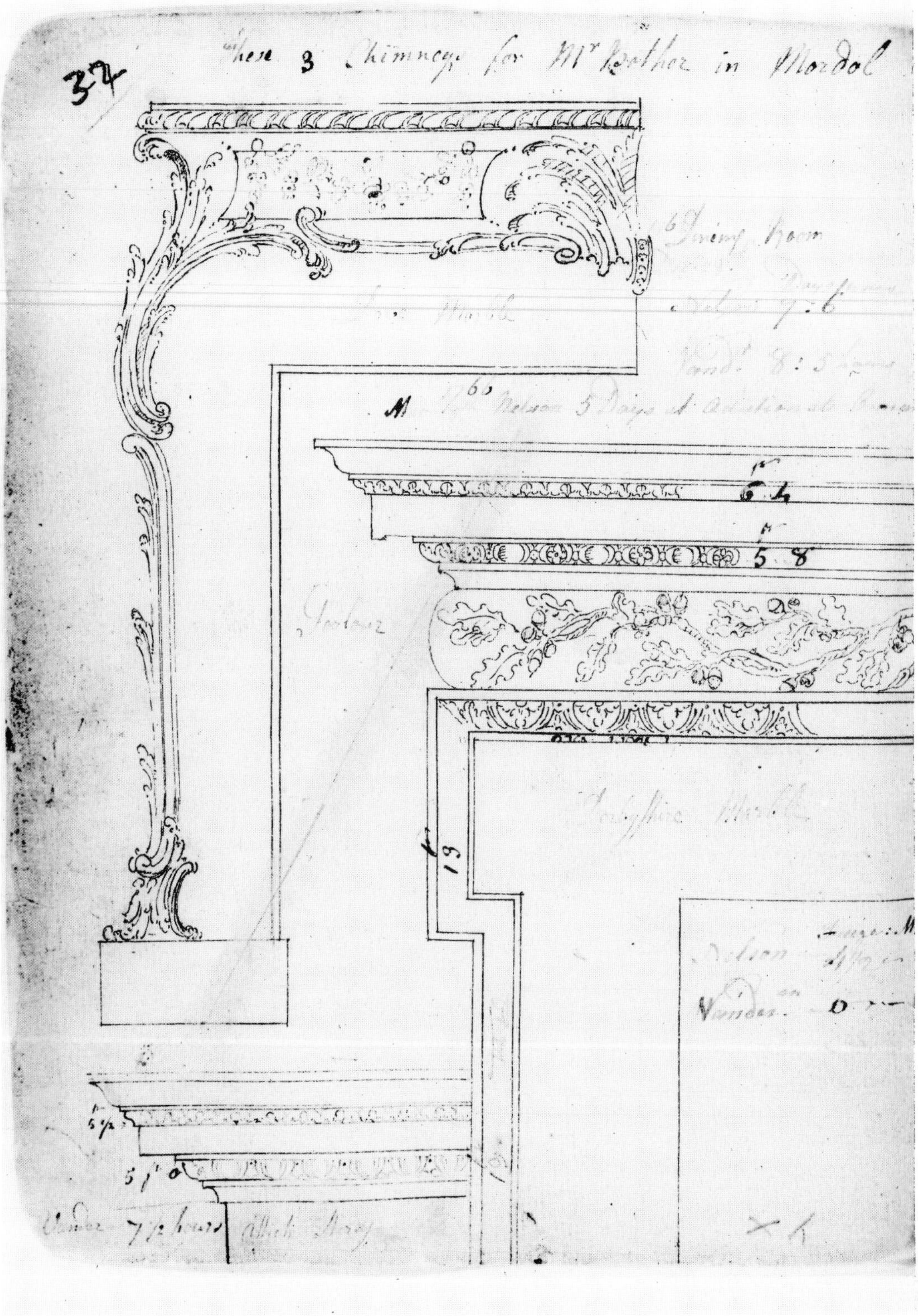

top A, bottom B, AIA13

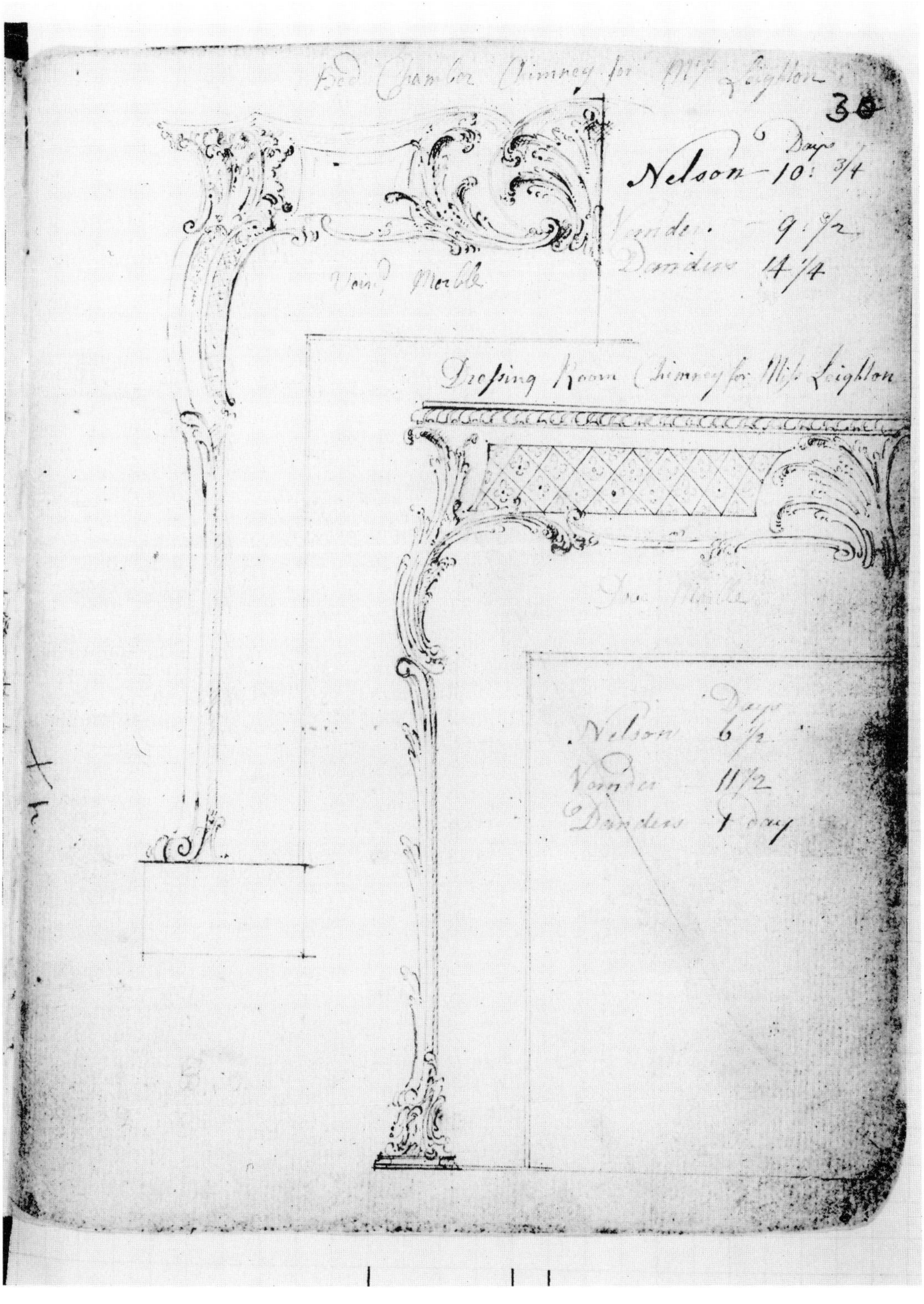

AIA14

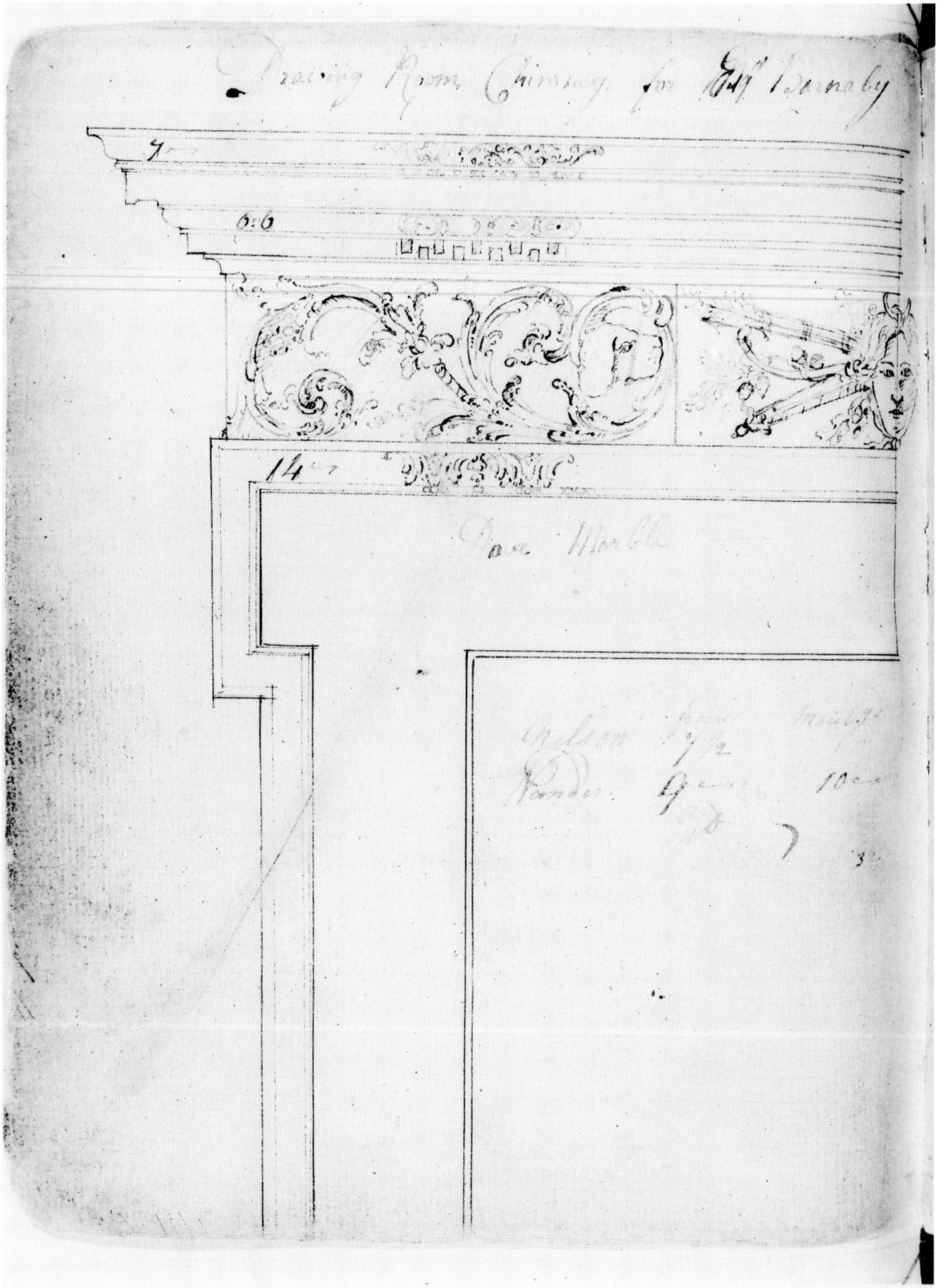

Drawing Room Chimney for Esqr Barnaby
7
6:6
14
Dove Marble
Nelson
Vander
7 1/2
9
10
7

top left A, bottom left B, top right C, and bottom right D. **AIA15**

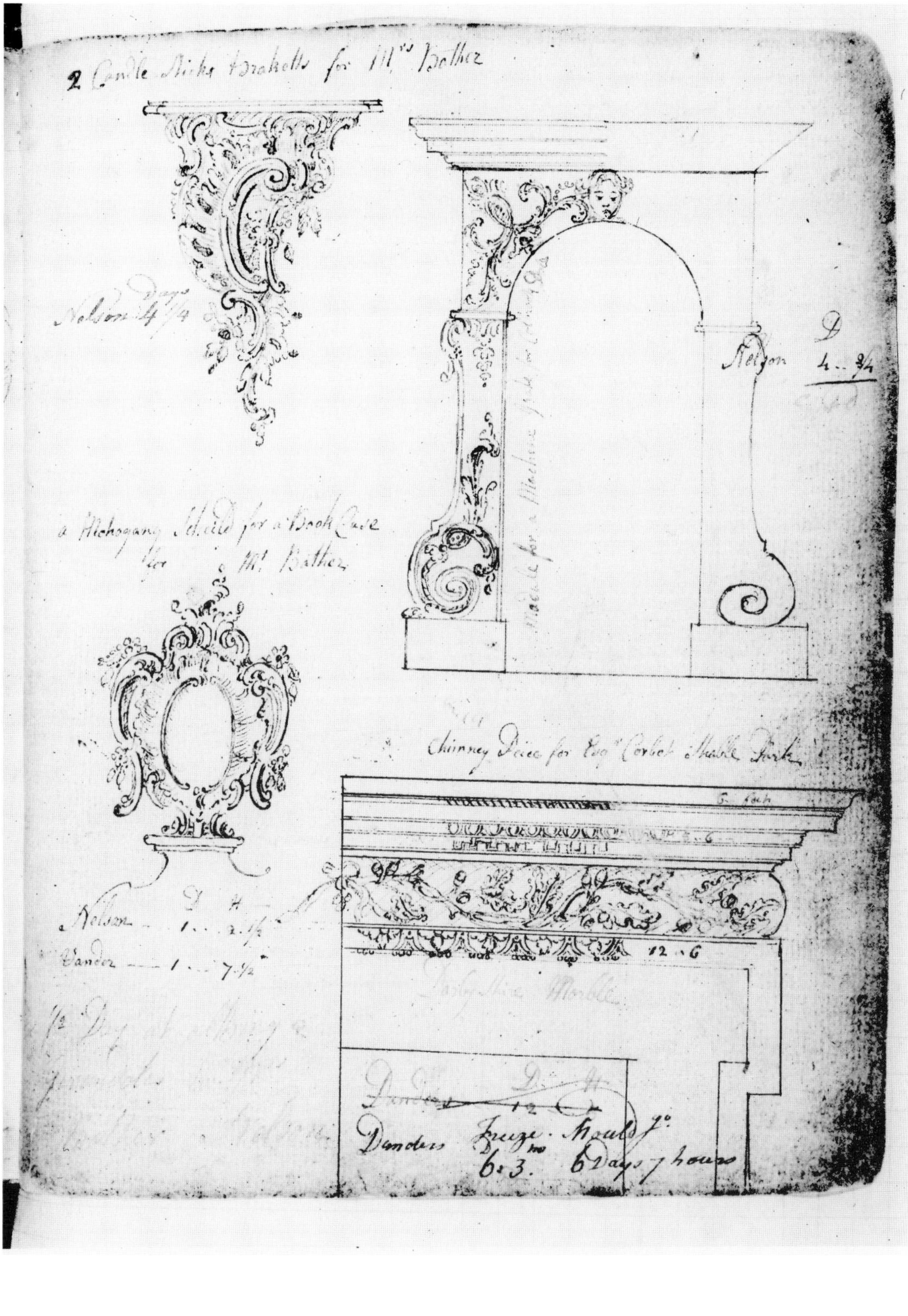

AIA16, top A, bottom B.

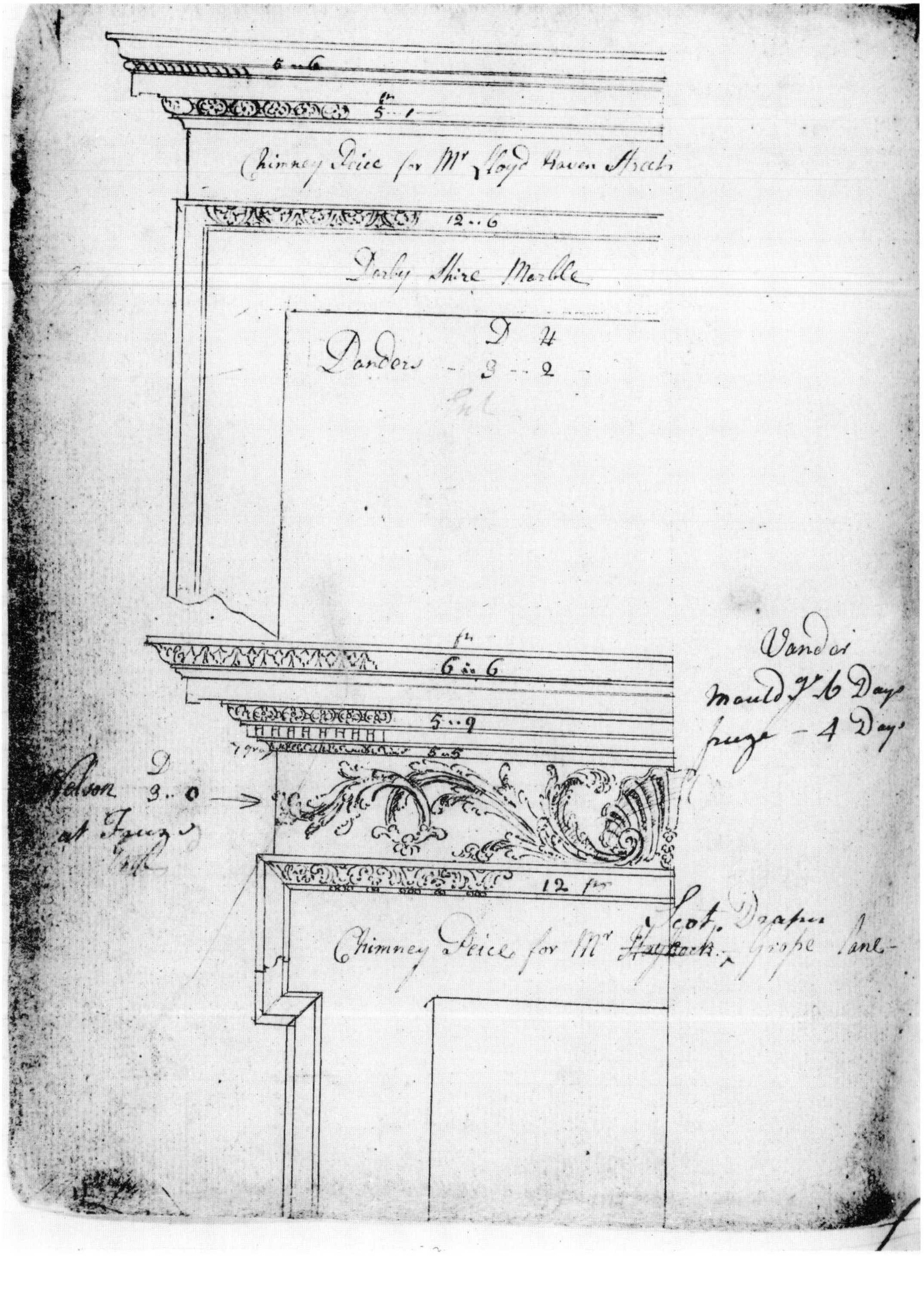

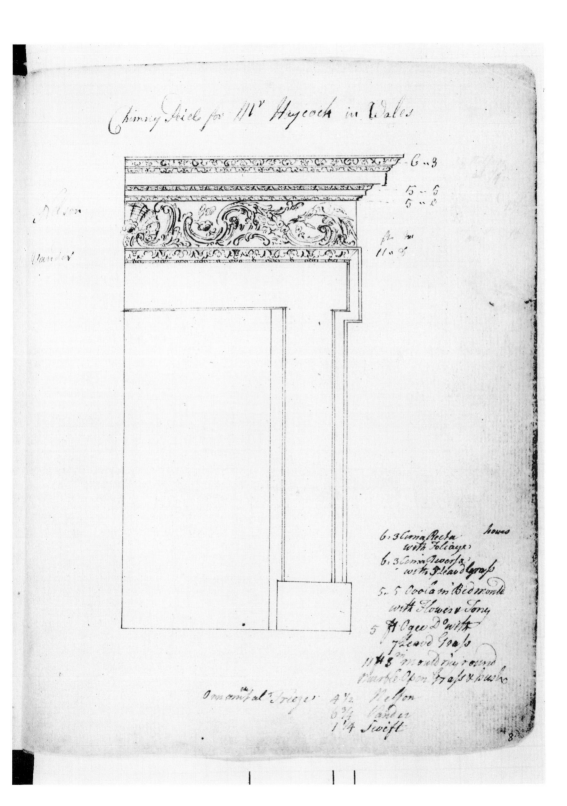

Chimney Piece for M[r] Heycock in Wales

Nelson

Vander

6 : 3 Cima Recta with Foliage — Howes

6 : 3 Cima Reversa with 3 leav'd Grass

5 „ 5 Ovolo in Bed mould with Flowers & Tong

5 ft Ogee D° with 7 leav'd Grass

11 ft 8 in moulding round Marble Open Grass & husk

Ornamental Frieze 4½ Nelson

6¾ Vander

1¼ Swift

AIA18

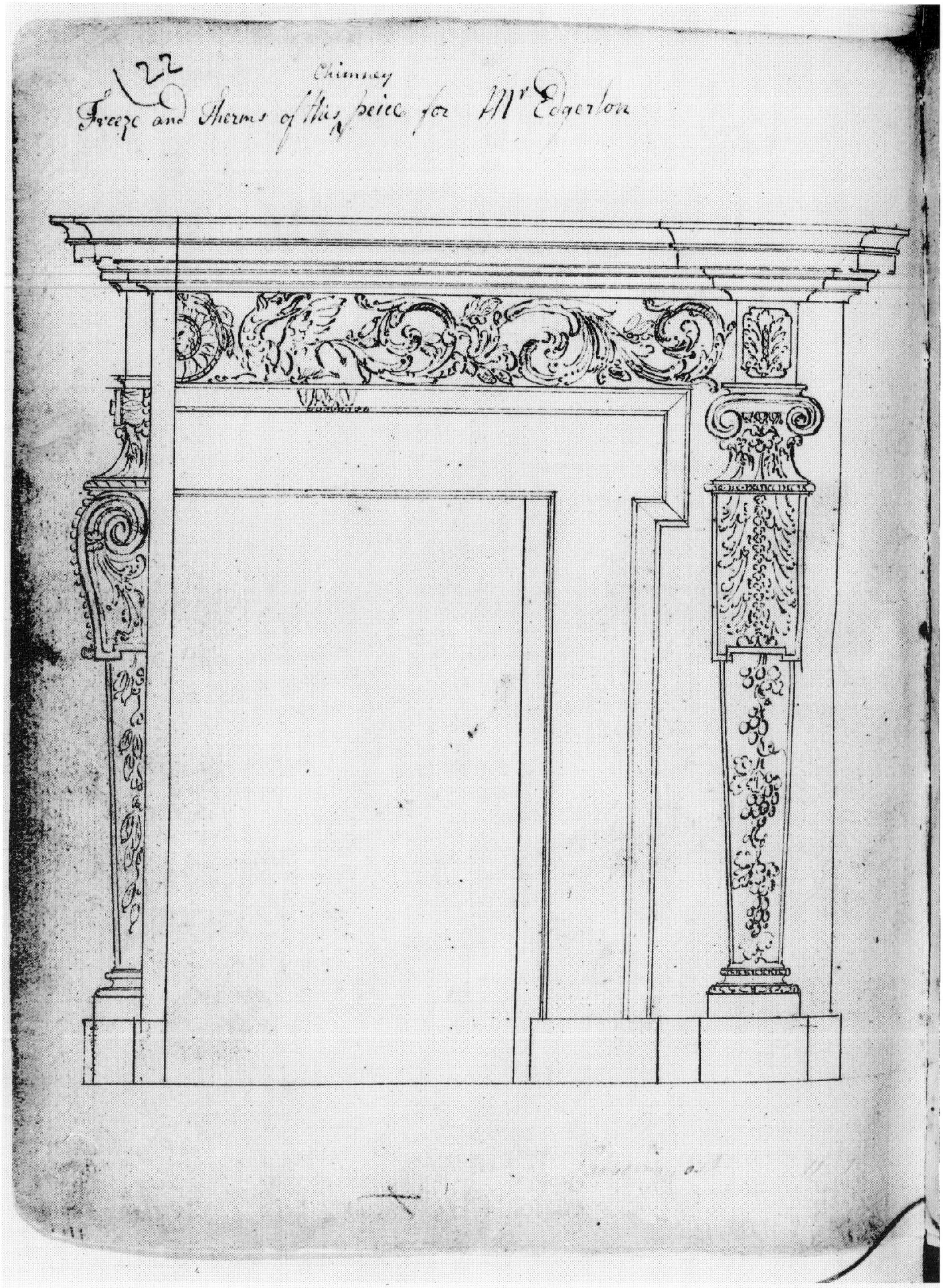
22
Chimney
Freeze and Therms of this peice for Mr Edgerton

(2

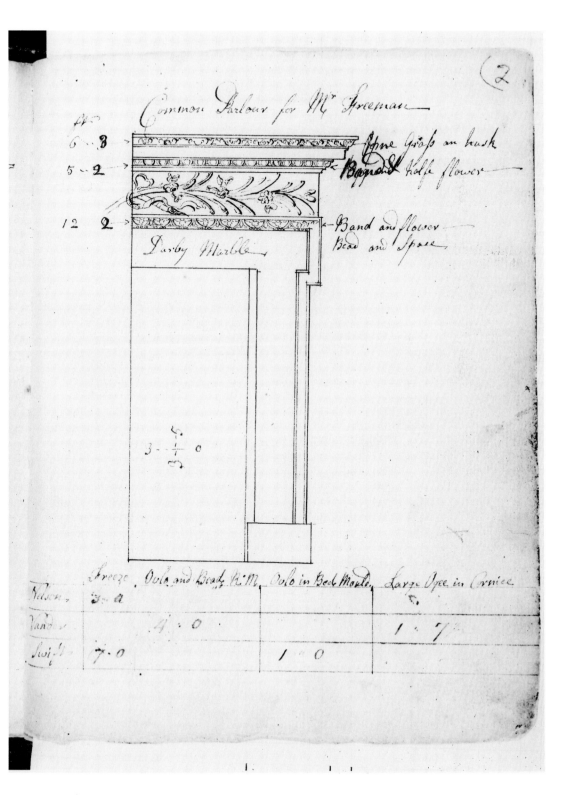

Common Parlour for Mr Freeman

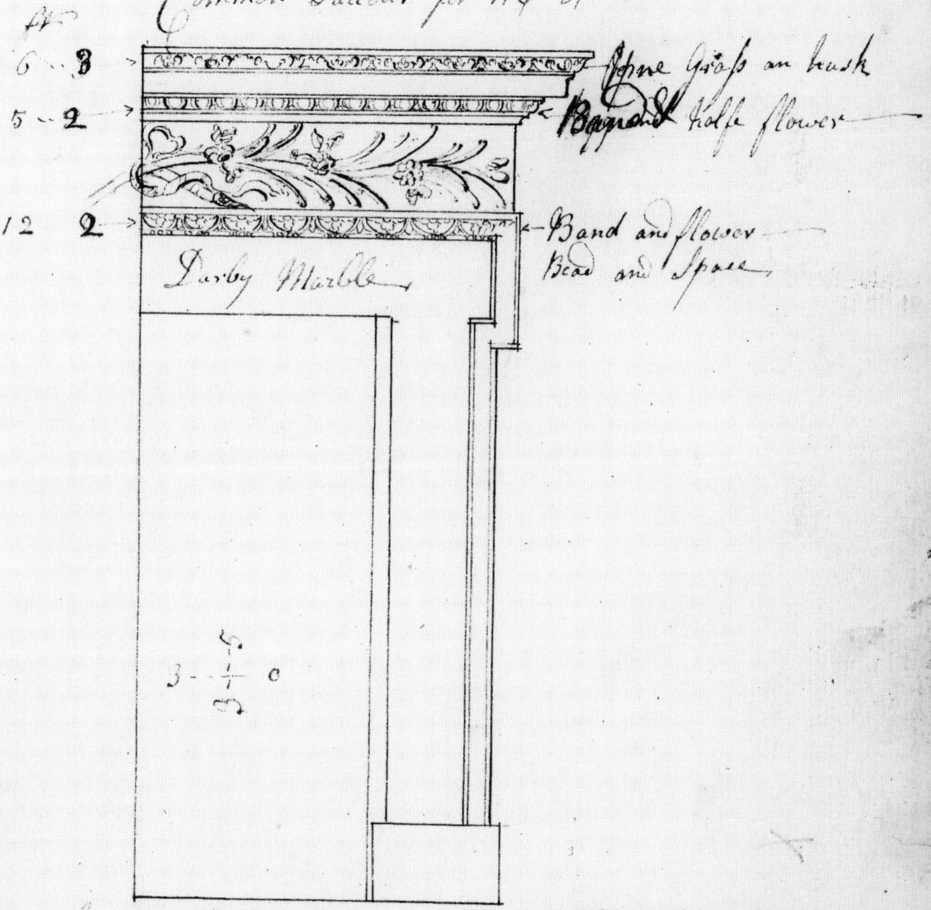

	Freeze	Ovolo and Bead R.M.	Ovolo in Bed Mould	Large Ogee in Cornice
Nelson	3 · 0			
Vander		4 · 0		1 · 7
Swift	7 · 0		1 · 0	

AIA20

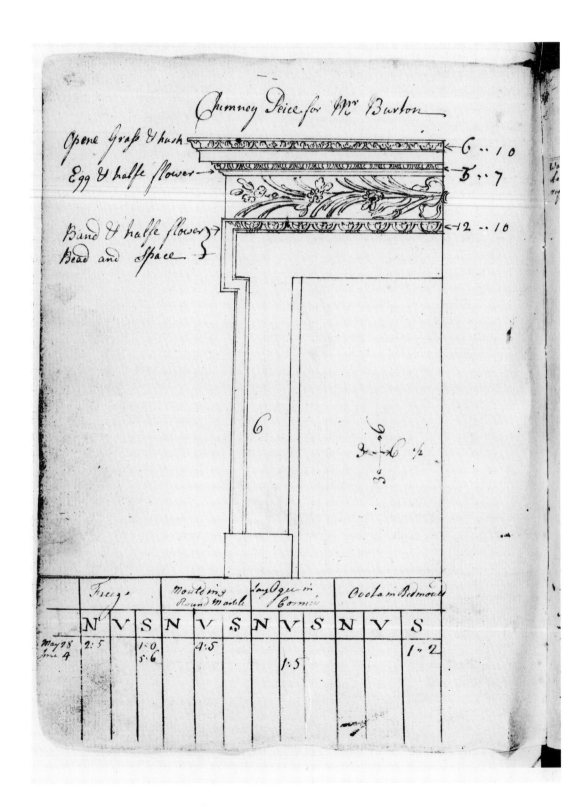

Chimney Peice for Mr Burton

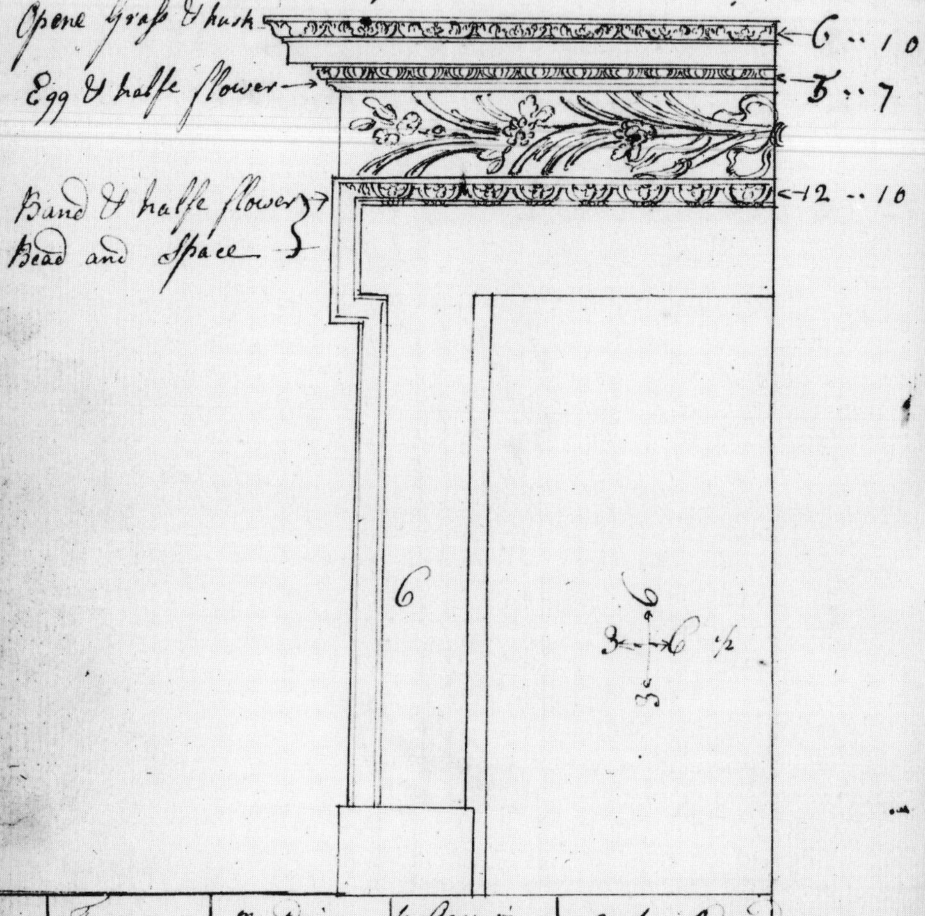

	Freeze			Moulding Round Marble			Lay Ogee in Cornice			Oocta in Bedmould		
	N	V	S	N	V	S	N	V	S	N	V	S
May 18	2:5		1:0		4:5							1:2
June 4			5:6					1:5				

French Marble Mr Freemans Chamber

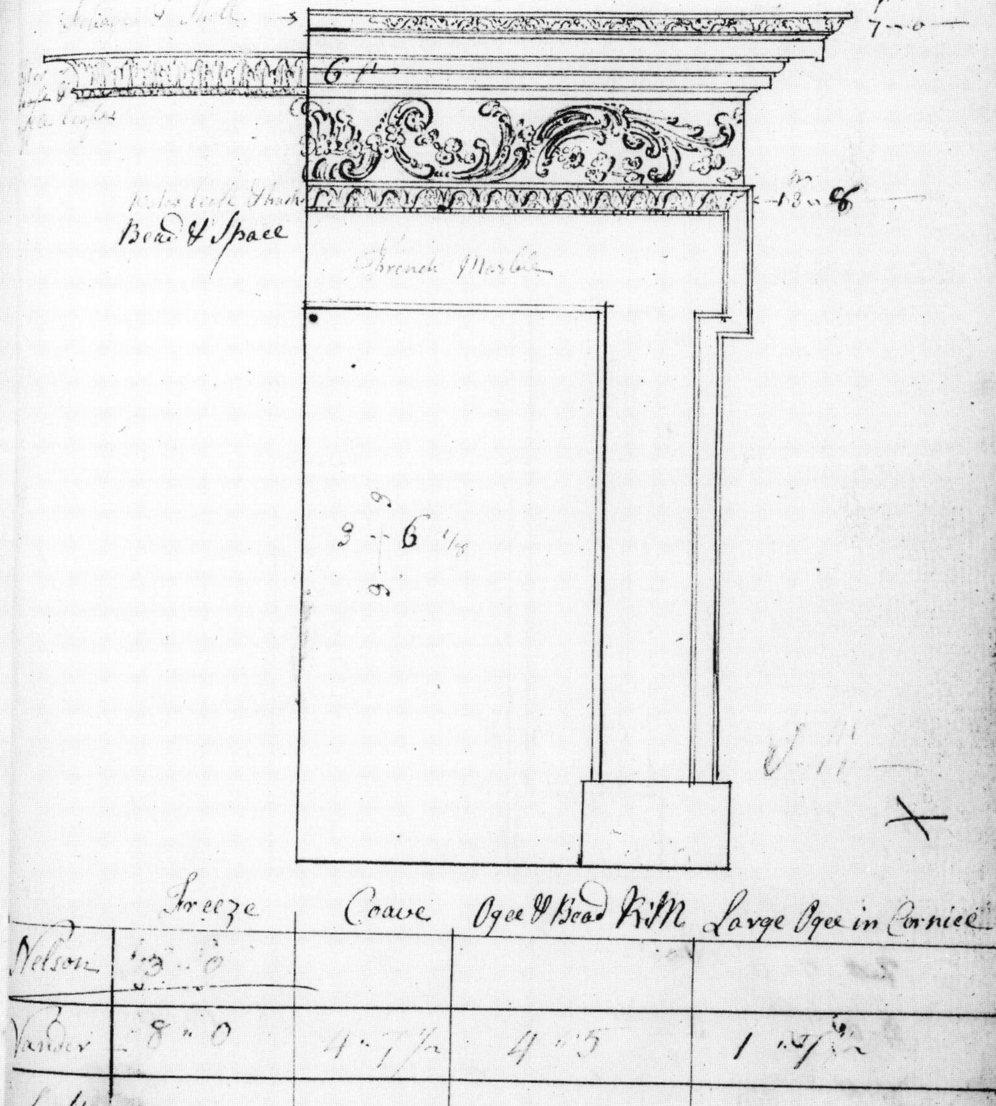

	Freeze	Coave	Ogee & Bead R.M	Large Ogee in Cornice
Nelson	3 . 0			
Vander	8 " 0	4 . 7 1/2	4 . 5	1 . 3 1/2
Swift				

AIA22

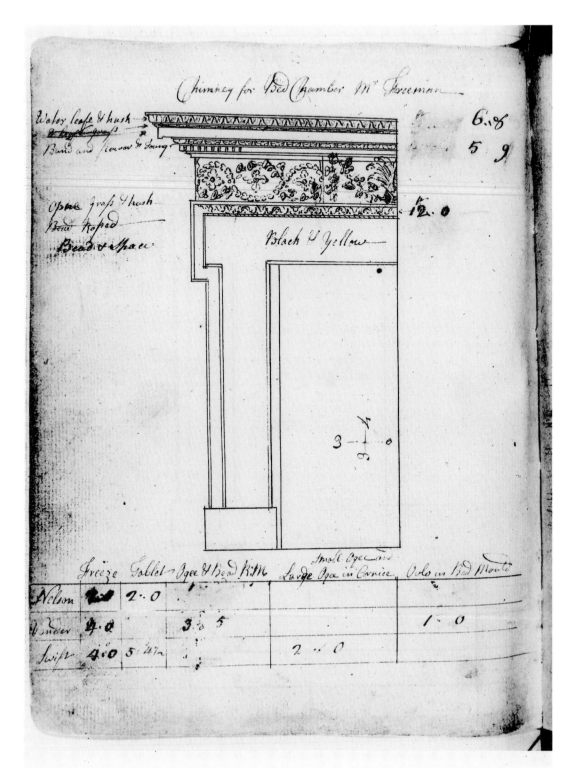

Chimney for Bed Chamber Mr Freeman

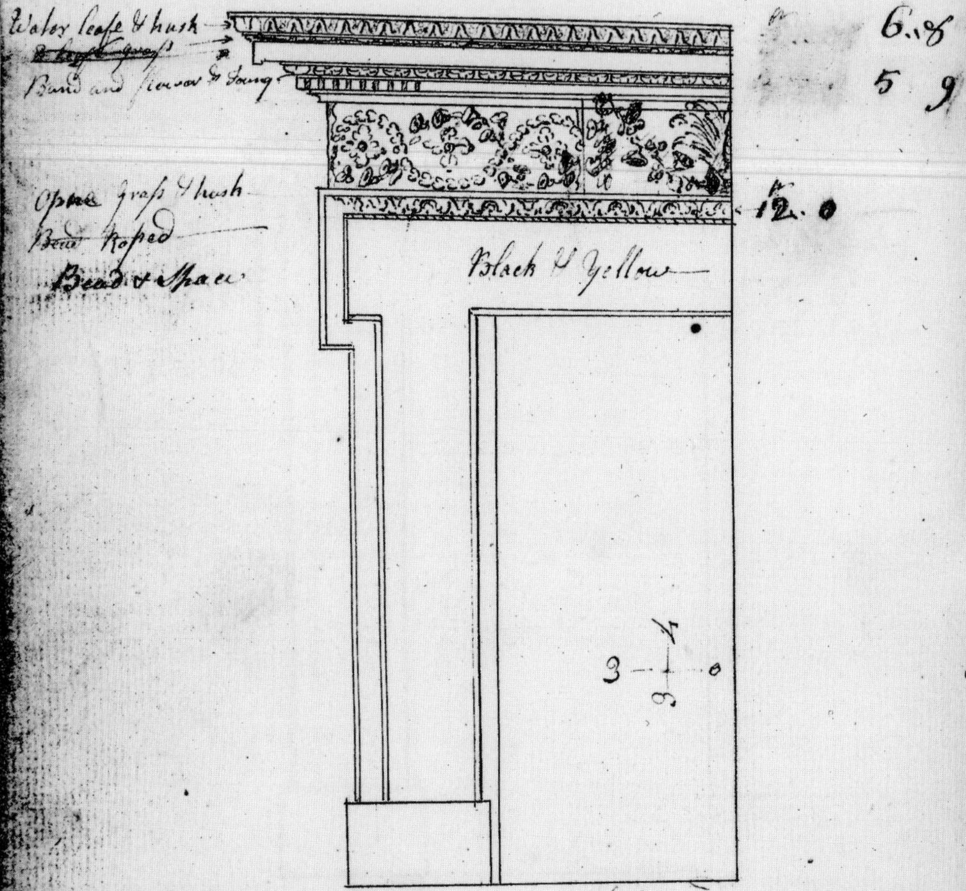

	Freeze	Tablet	Ogee & Bead R.M	Small Ogee and Large Ogee in Cornice	Ovolo in Bed Moulds
Nelson	[illegible]	2..0			
Vander	4.0		3..5		1..0
Swift	4.0	5..4½		2..0	

AIA23

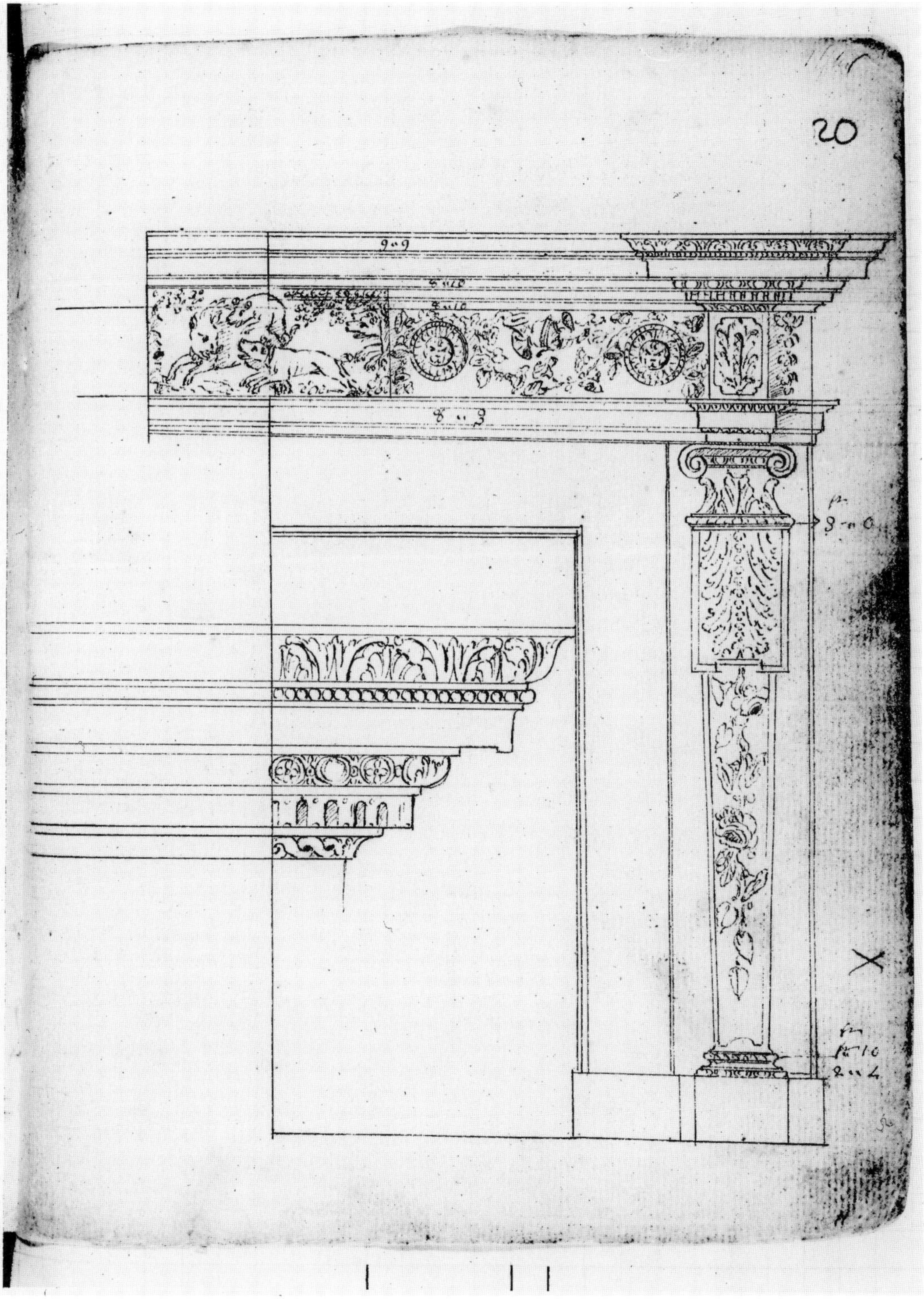

AIA24

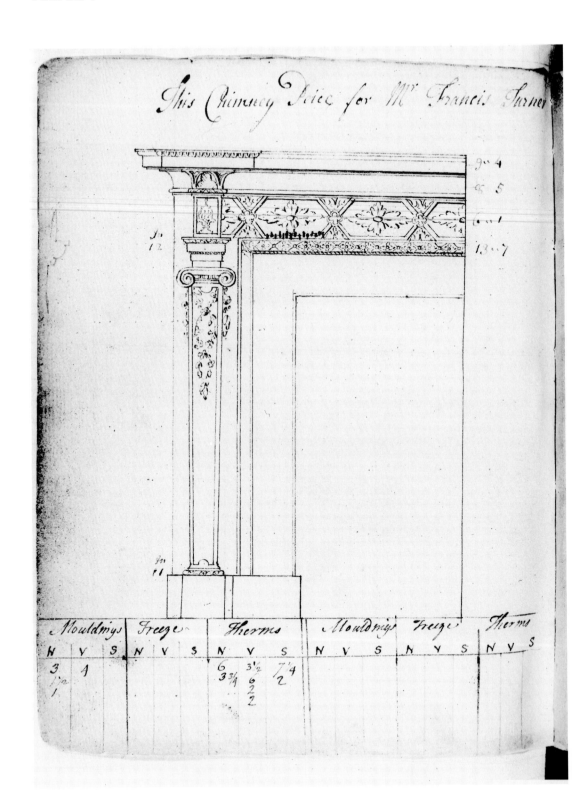

This Chimney Peice for Mr Francis Turner

Mouldings			Freeze			Therms			Mouldings			Freeze			Therms		
N	V	S	N	V	S	N	V	S	N	V	S	N	V	S	N	V	S
3	4					6	3 1/2	7 1/4									
1/2						3 3/4	6	2									
1							2										
							2										

AIA25

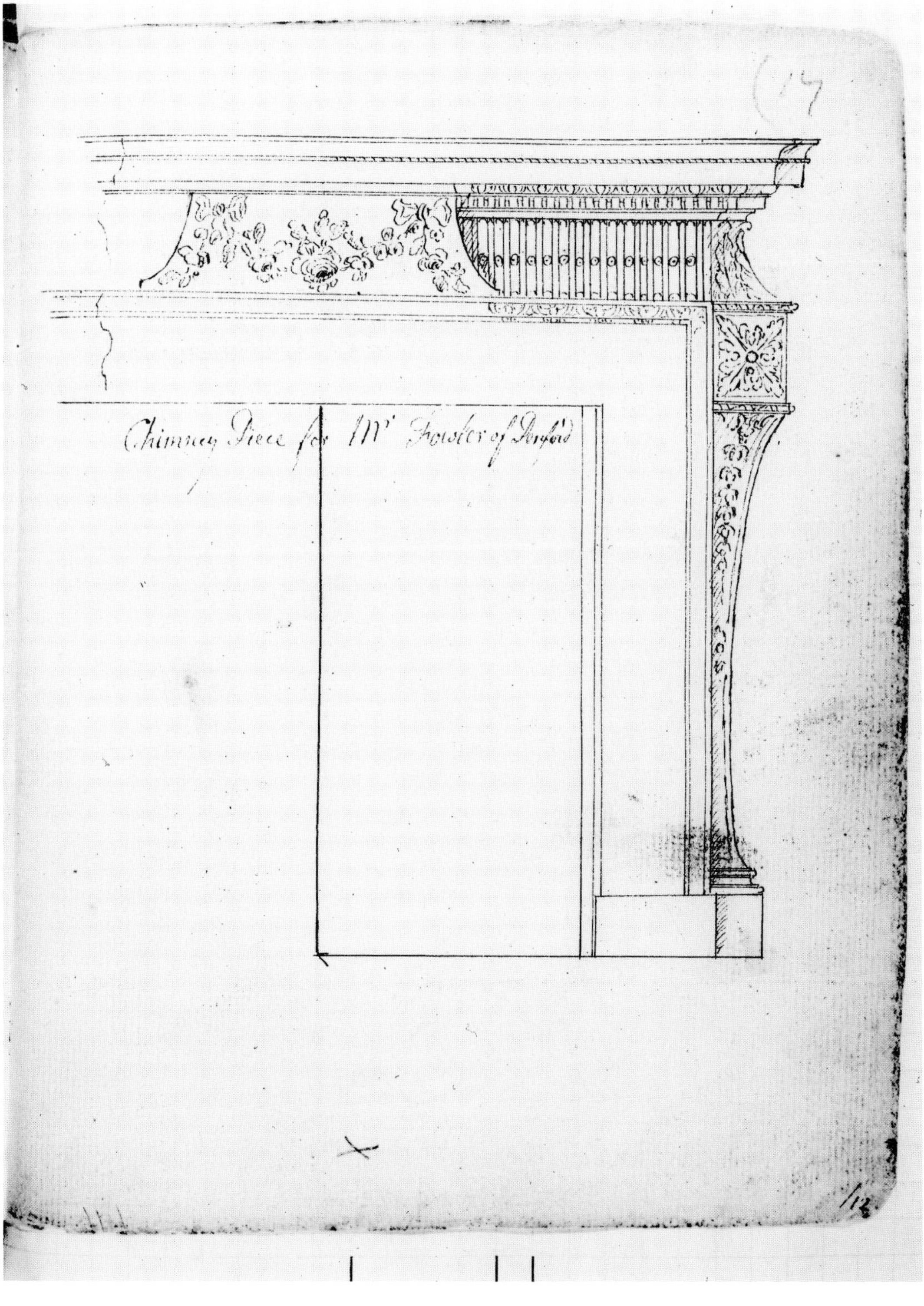

AIA26

116

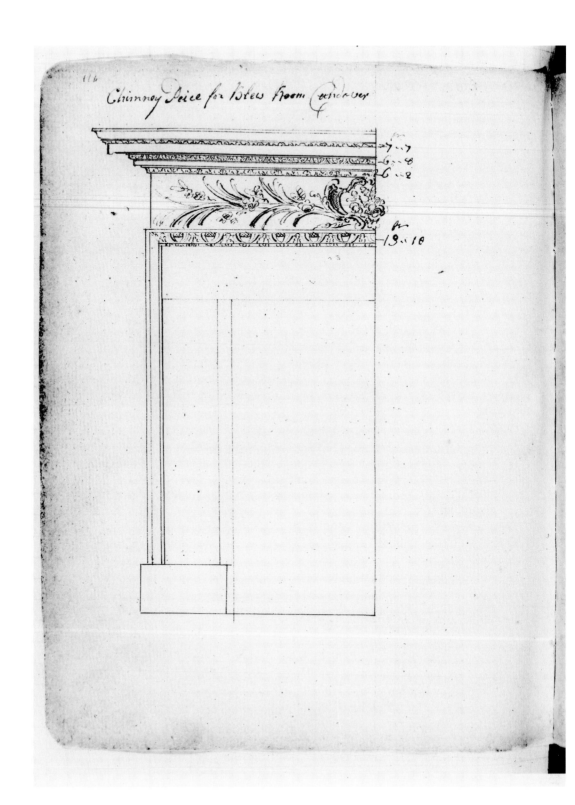

Chimney Peice for Blew Room Candover

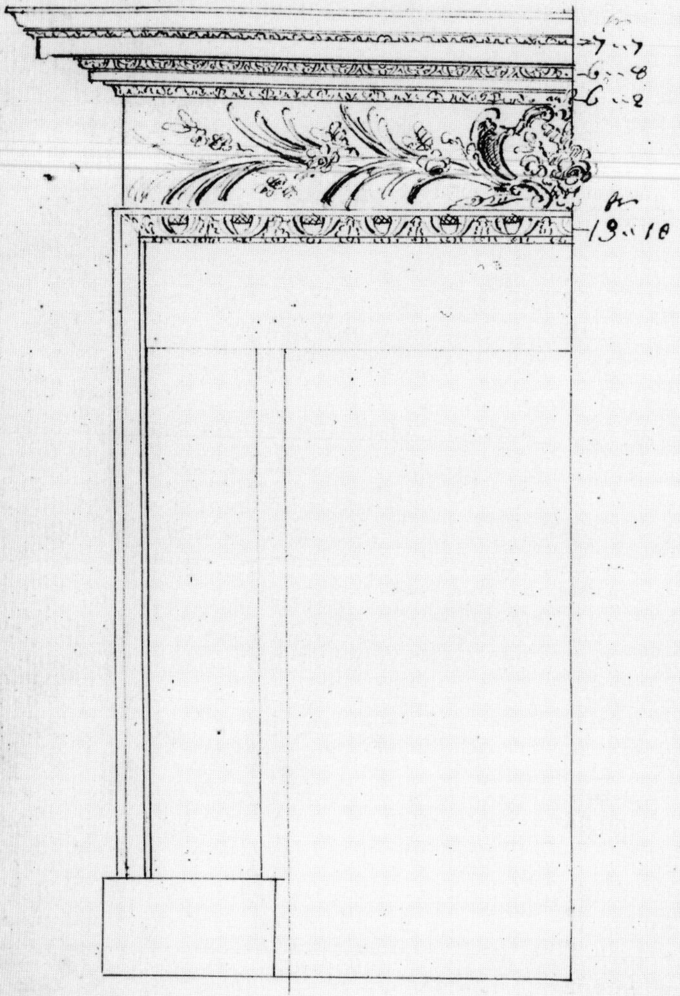

AIA27

Common Parlour Hon.ble Mr Hadley

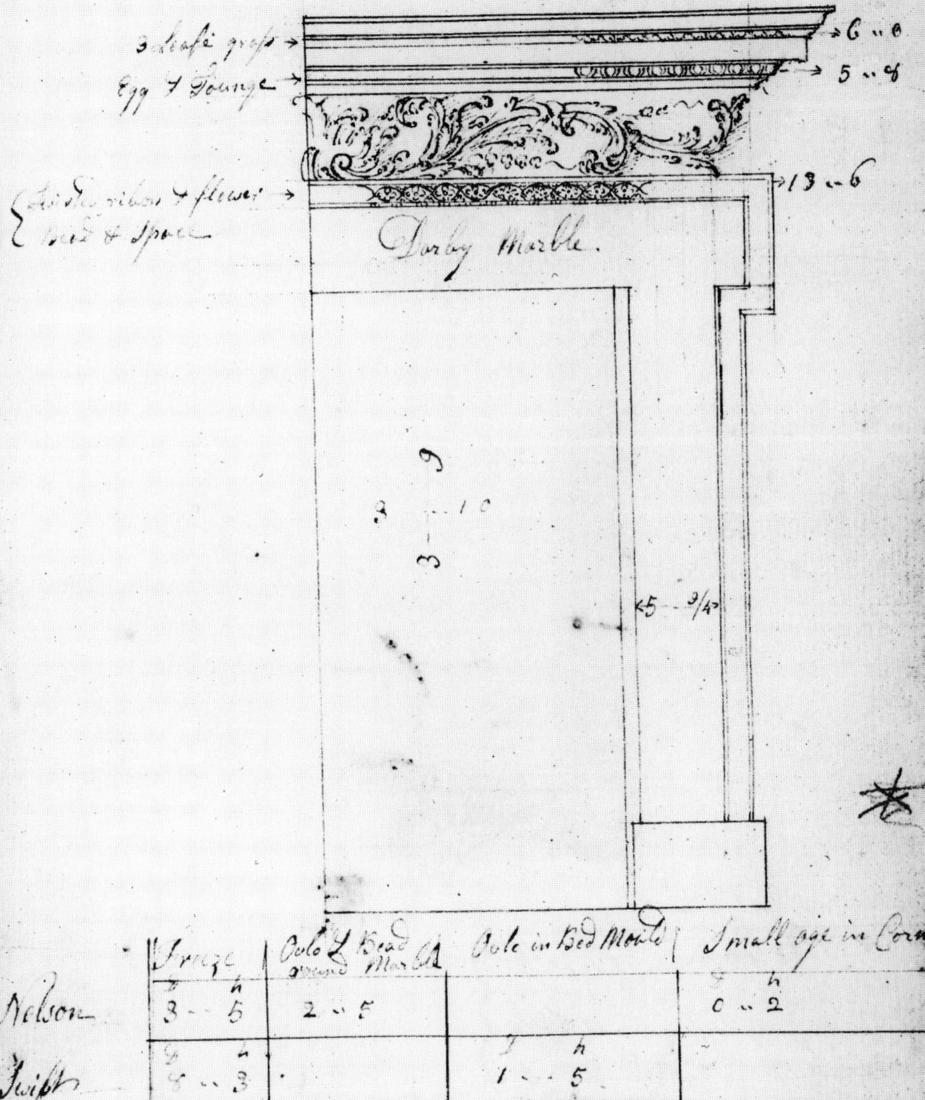

	Freeze	Ovolo & Bead round Marble	Ovolo in Bed Mould	Small egg in Corn
	d h			d h
Nelson	3 .. 5	2 .. 5		0 .. 2
	d h		d h	
Swift	8 .. 3		1 .. 5	

AIA28

3 111

2 Frames for Shell pieces for Mr Fowler of Alcham
Deliverd May the 15th 1765

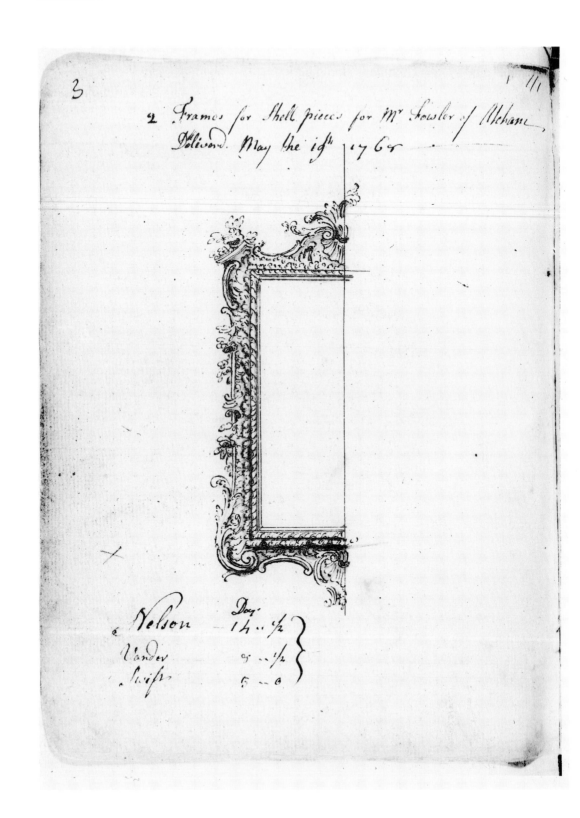

	Day
Nelson	14 .. 1/2
Vander	5 .. 1/2
Swift	5 .. 0

4

Drawing Room Chimney – Esqr Maney

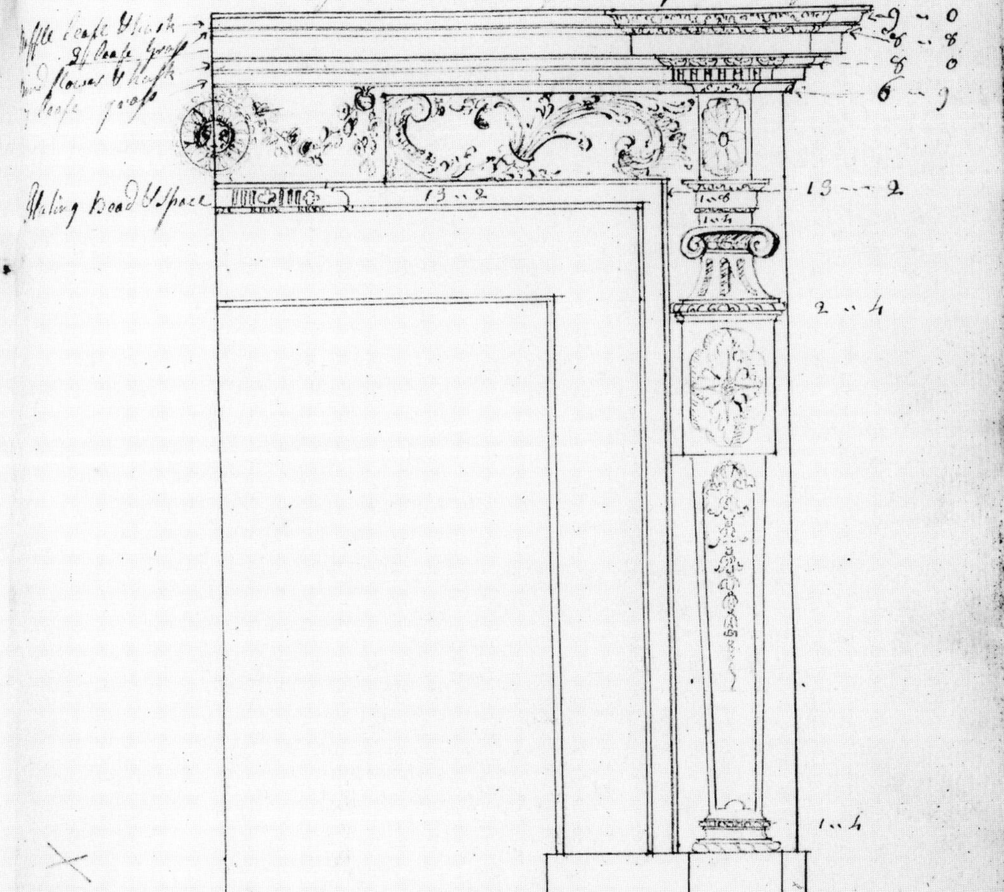

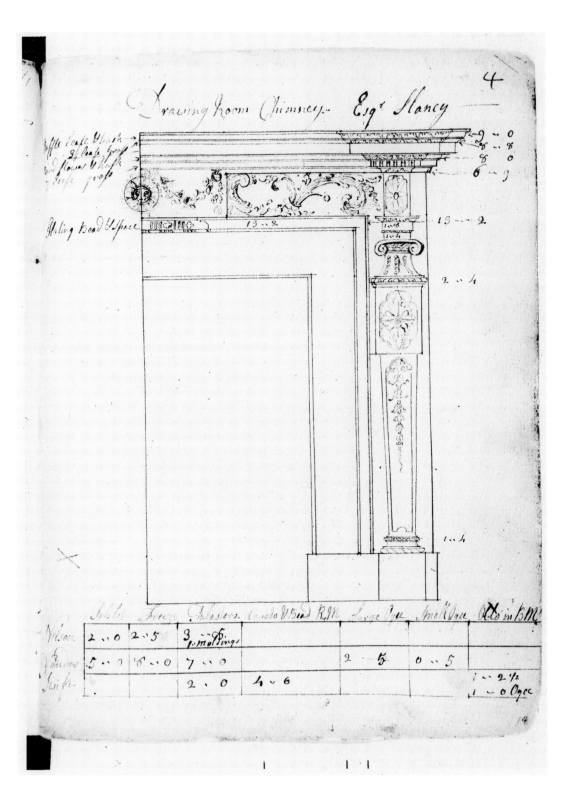

	Tablet	Freeze	Pilasters.	Cavetto & Bead R.M.	Large Ogee	Small Ogee	Ditto in B.M.
Wilson	2 .. 0	2 .. 5	3 .. 6 p. moldings				
Vander	5 .. 0	8 .. 0	7 .. 0		2 .. 5	0 .. 5	
Swift			2 . 0	4 . 6			1 .. 2½ 1 .. 0 Ogee

14

AIA30

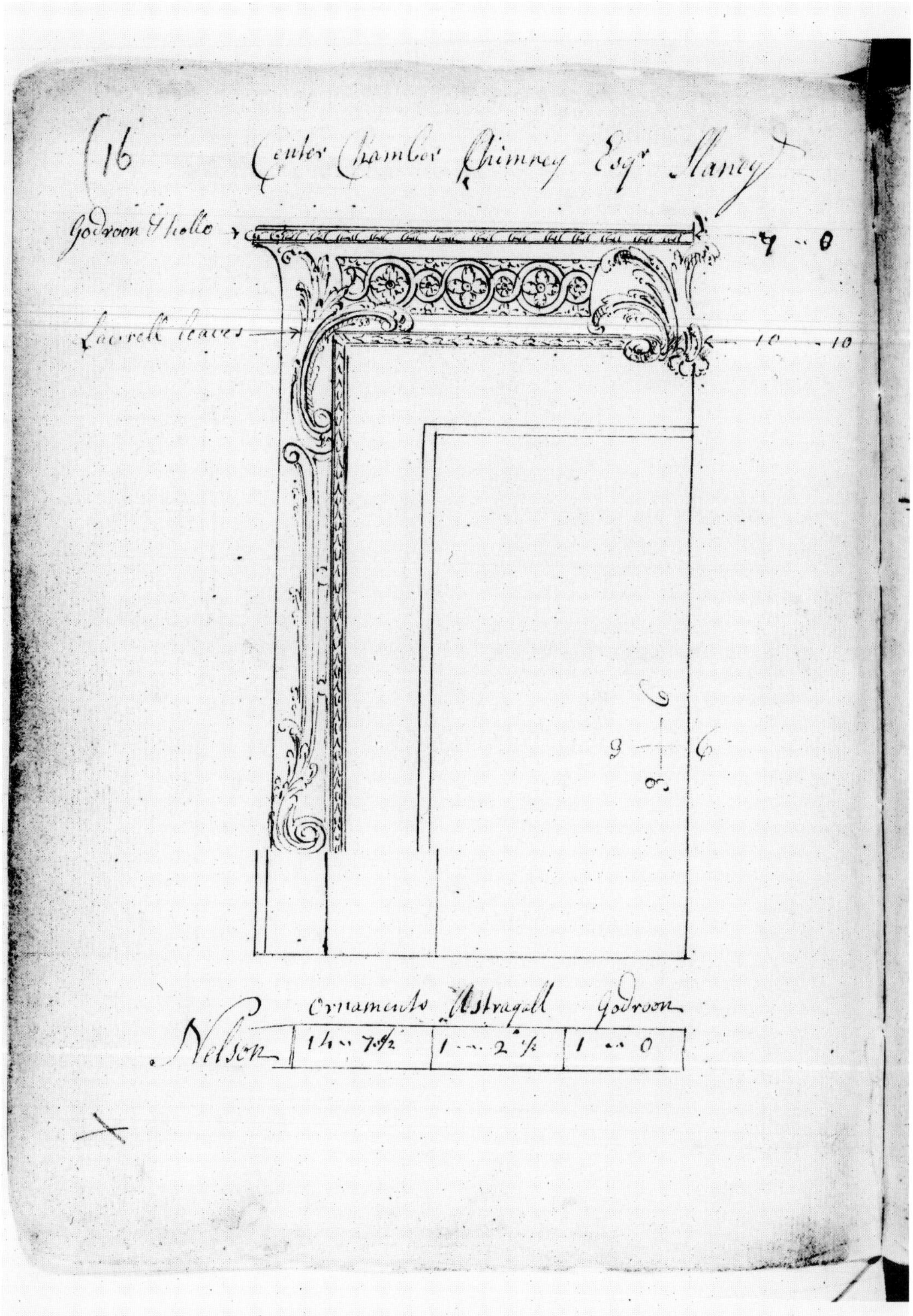
16
Center Chamber Chimney Esqr Maney
Godroon & hollo
7 .. 0
Laurell leaves
10 .. 10
Ornaments Astragall Godroon
Nelson 14 .. 7½ 1 .. 2½ 1 .. 0

top A, bottom B, AIA31

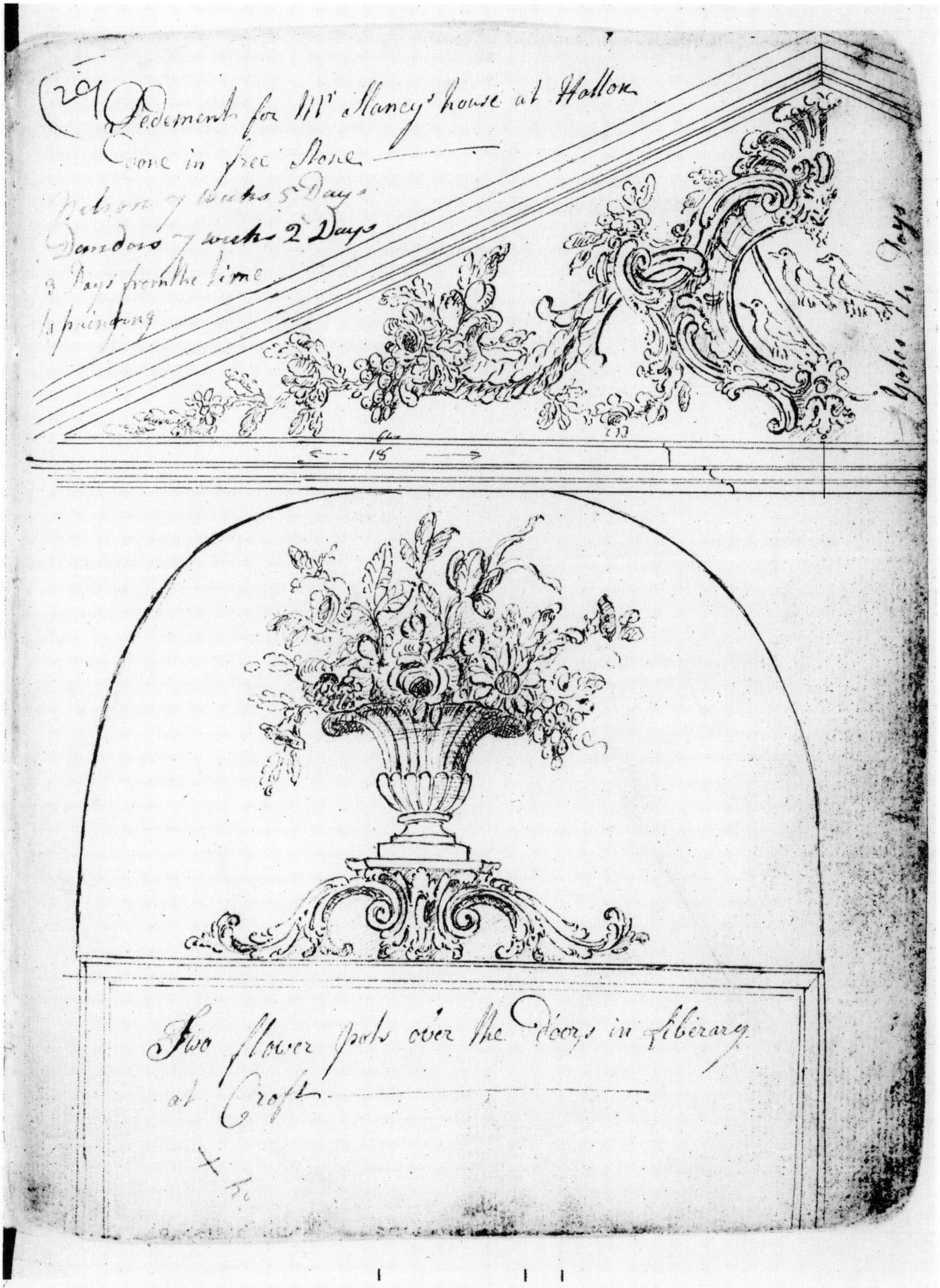

AIA32

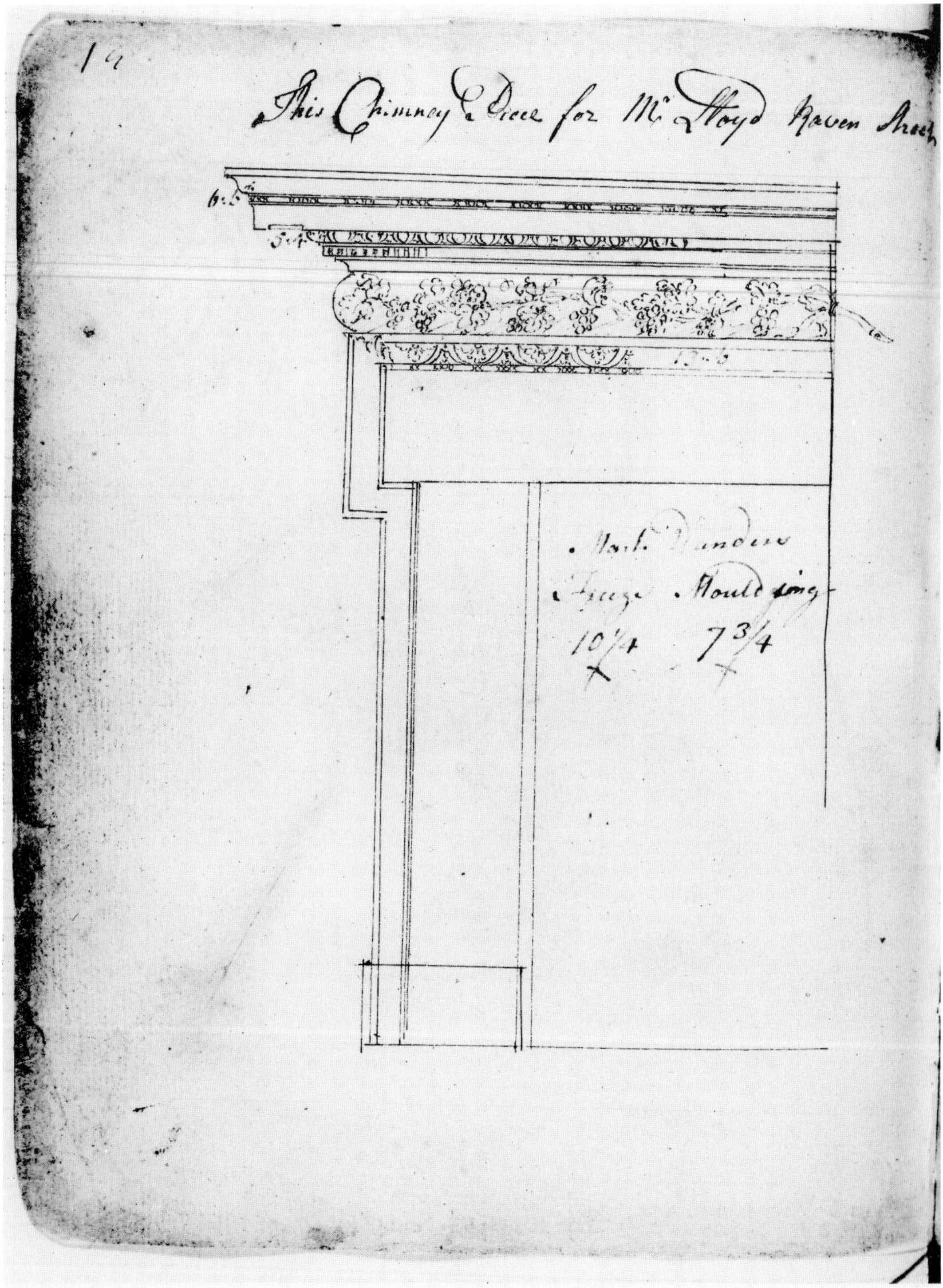

14
This Chimney Piece for Mr Lloyd Raven Street
6.5
5.4
Marb. Dundee
Freeze Moulding
10/4 7 3/4

(11 Chimney Piece in Freestone for Esqr Smith Candover

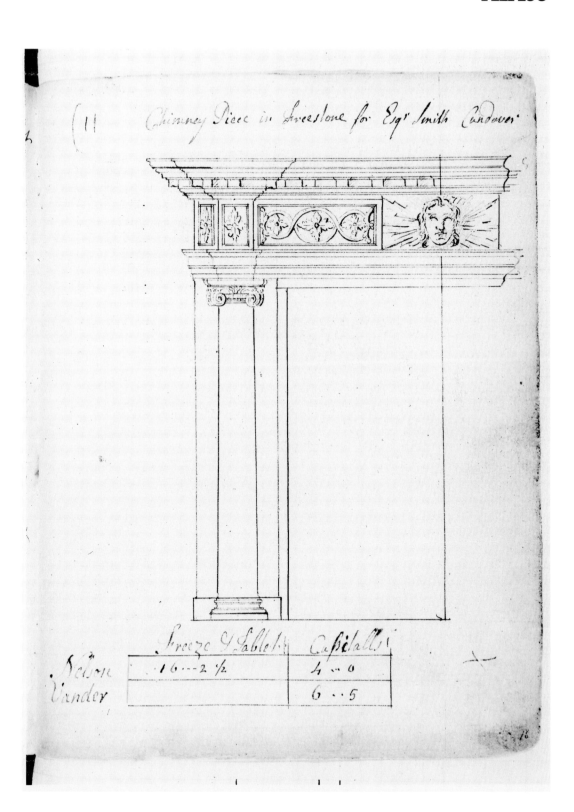

	Freeze & Tablet	Capitalls
Nelson	16 ... 2 ½	4 .. 0
Vander		6 .. 5

AIA34

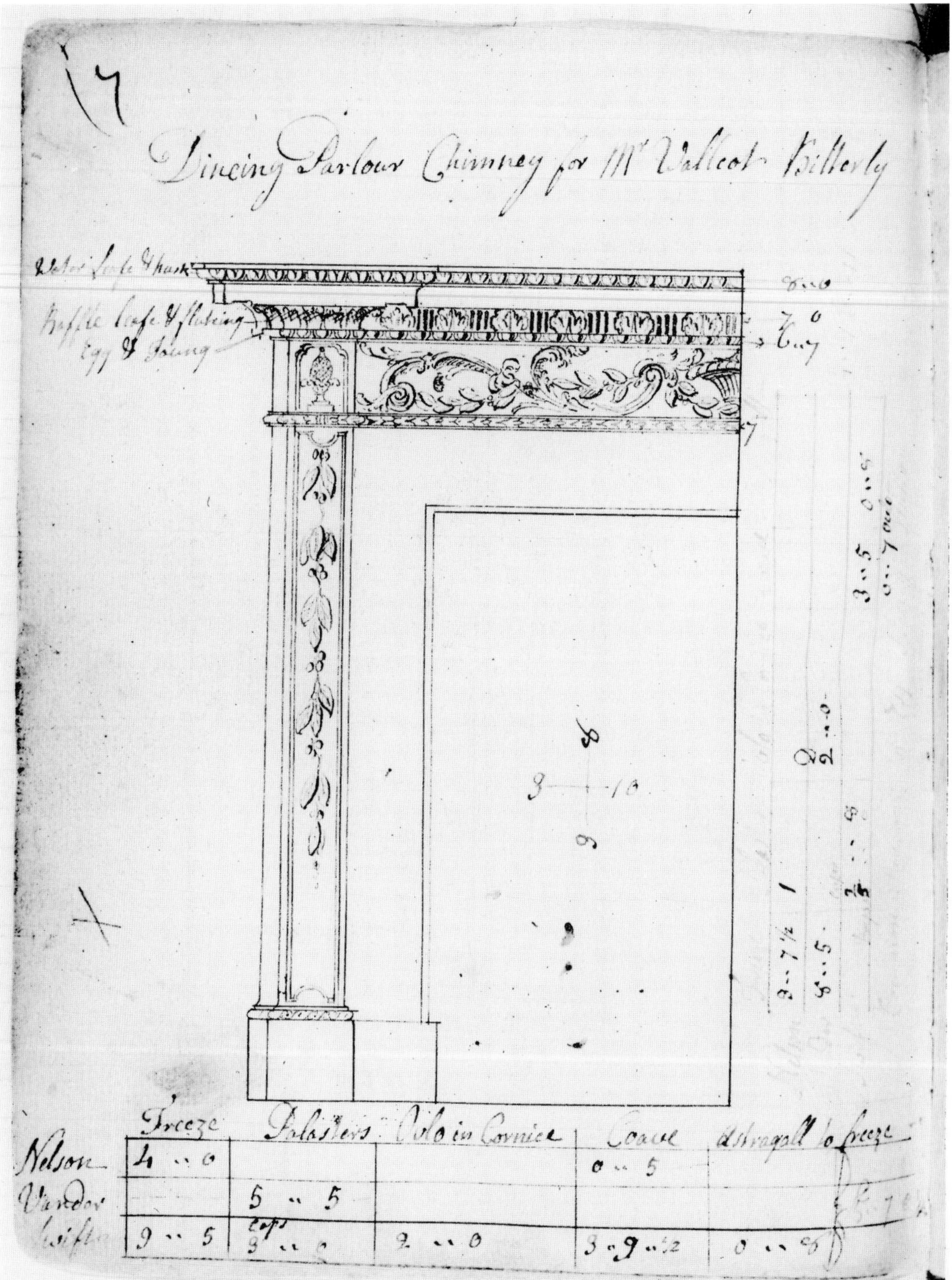
Dineing Parlour Chimney for Mr Wallcot Billerly
Ruffle Leafe & fluteing
Egg & Tong
Freeze
Palasters
Ovolo in Cornice
Coave
Astragall to freeze
Nelson
Vandor
Swift
4 .. 0
0 .. 5
5 .. 5
9 .. 5
caps
2 .. 0
0 .. 8

Best
~~Ye~~ parlour Chimney for the Honor.ble Mr. Harley 8

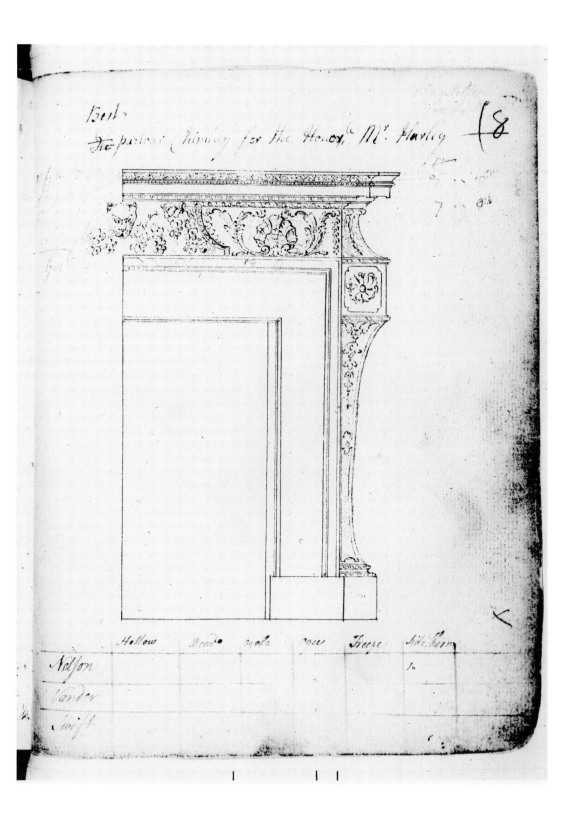

	Hollow	Bead	Ovolo	Ogee	Freeze	Side Term
Nelson						1
Vander						
Swift						

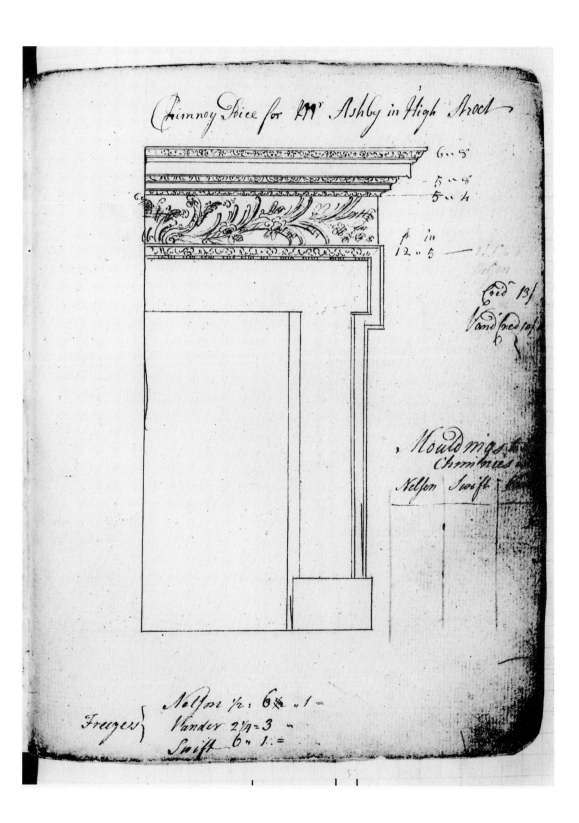

Chimney Peice for Mr Ashby in High Street

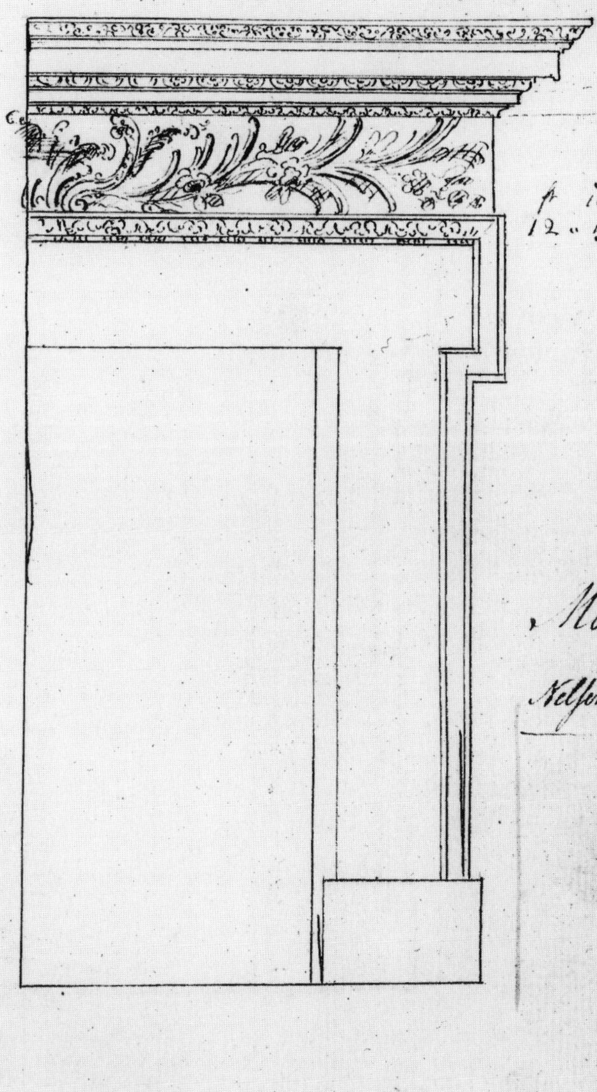

6 .. 8
5 .. 8
5 .. 4

ft in
12 .. 5

Cred 13/
Vand fred 10/6

Mouldings to Chimnies

Nelson Swift

Freezes } Nelson 1/2 : 6 .. 1 =
Vander 2 1/4 = 3 =
Swift 6 .. 1 =

AIA37

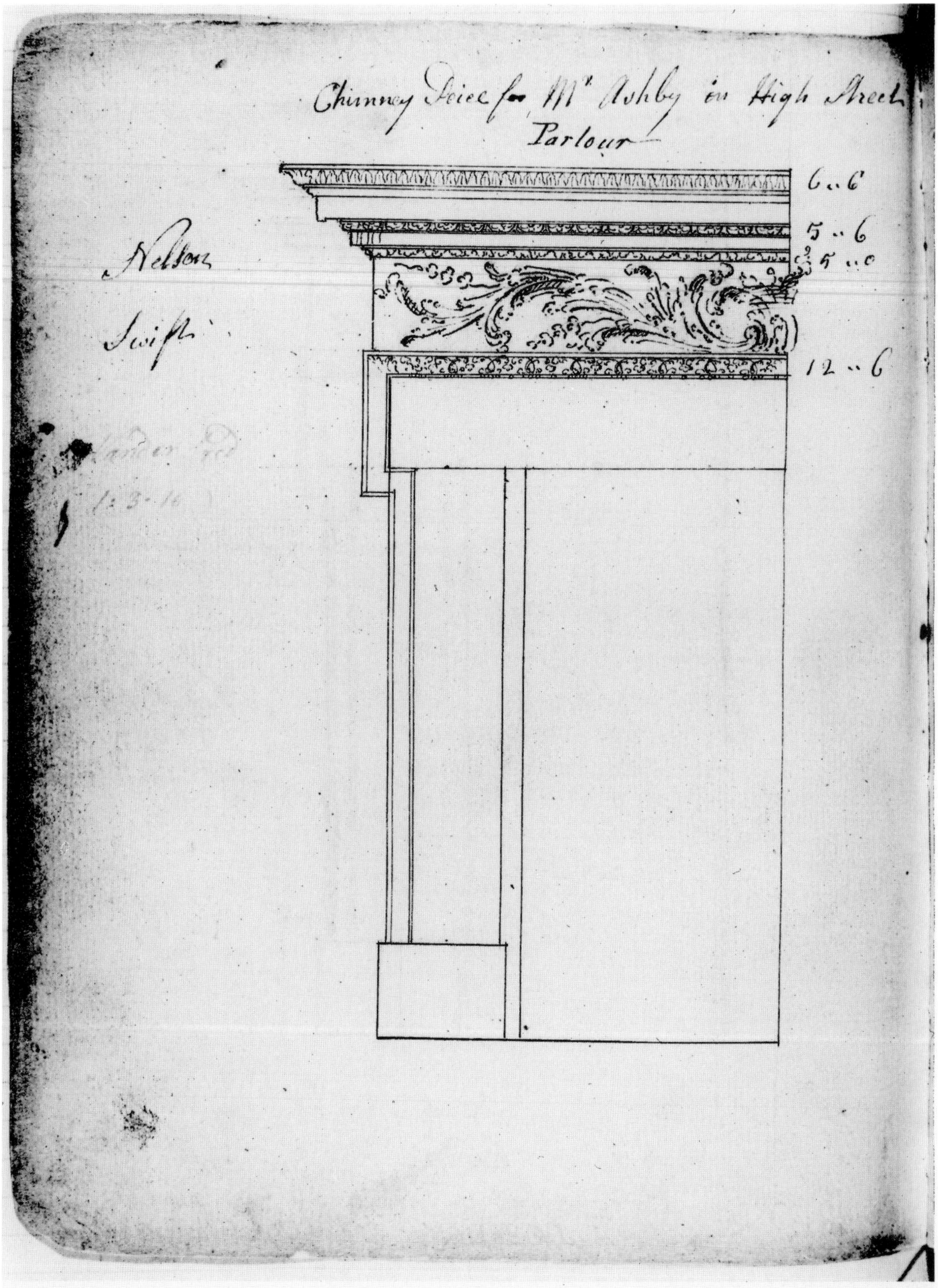

Chimney Peice for Mr. Ashby in High Street
Parlour
6..6
5..6
5..0
12..6
Nelson
Swift

AIA38

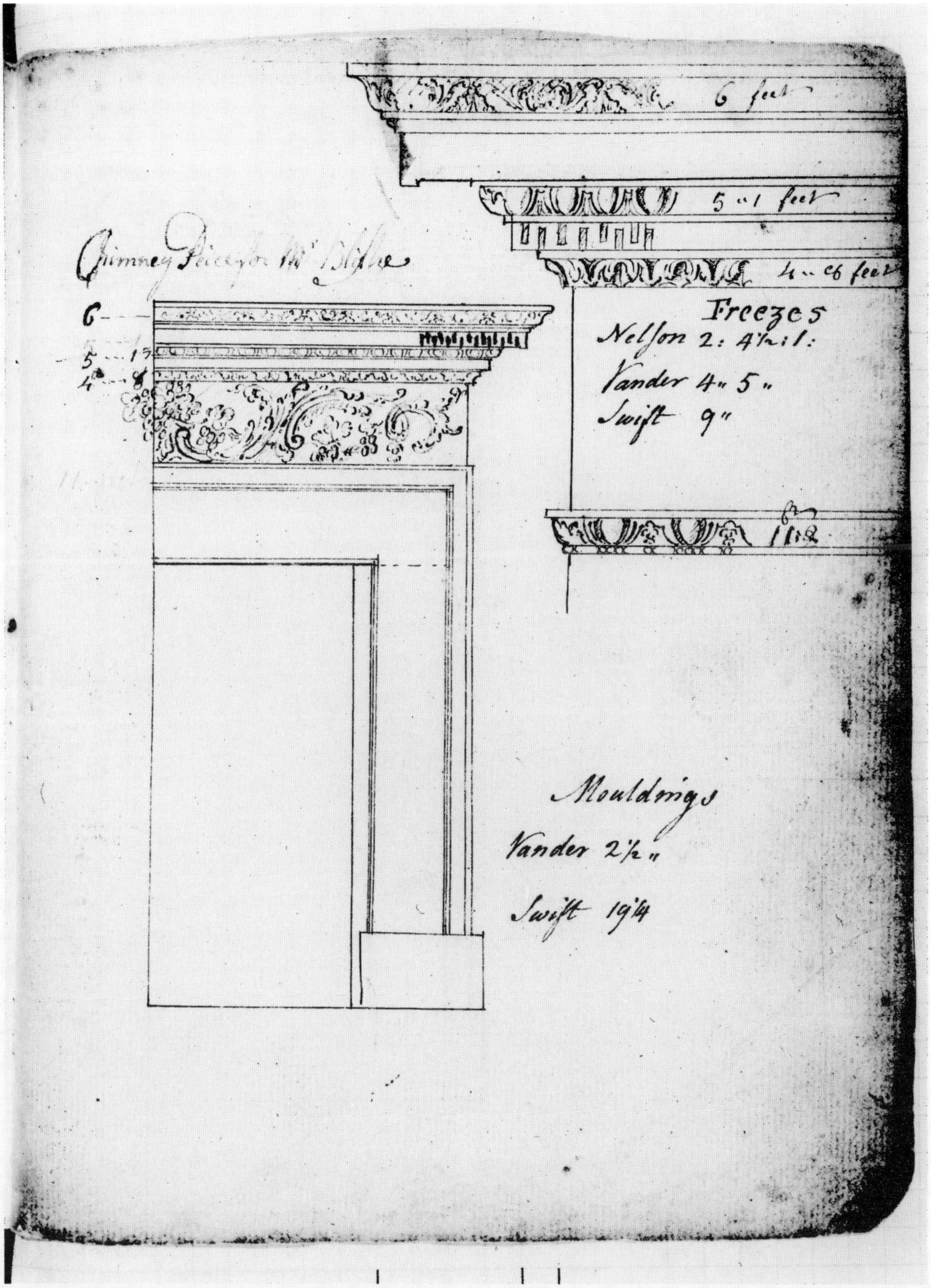
6 feet
5 .. 1 feet
Chimney Peice for Mr Blythe
Freezes
Nelson 2: 4½: 1:
Vander 4" 5"
Swift 9"
Mouldings
Vander 2½"
Swift 1¼

AIA39

6"10
6-10 Not Enrich'd
5-10
Bed Chamber Chimny
Chimny Peice for Mr Blythe
13 feet

Chimney Peice for Samuel Egerton Esq[r]

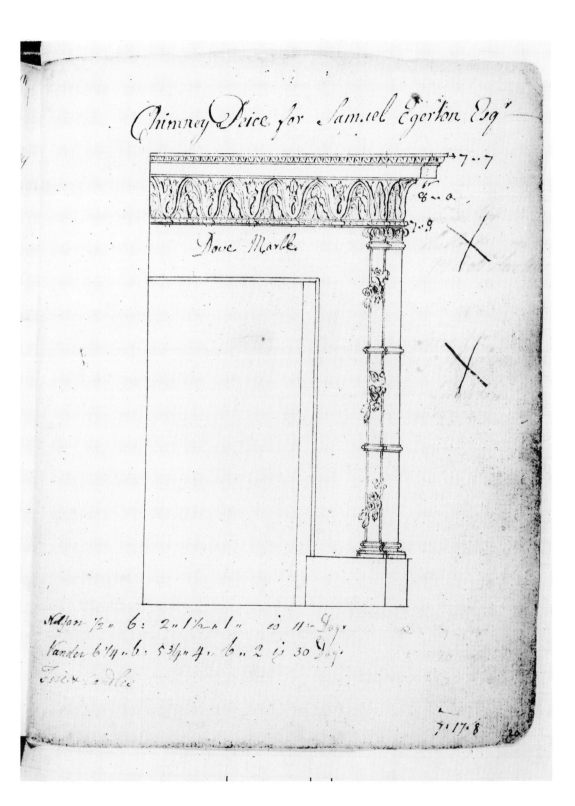

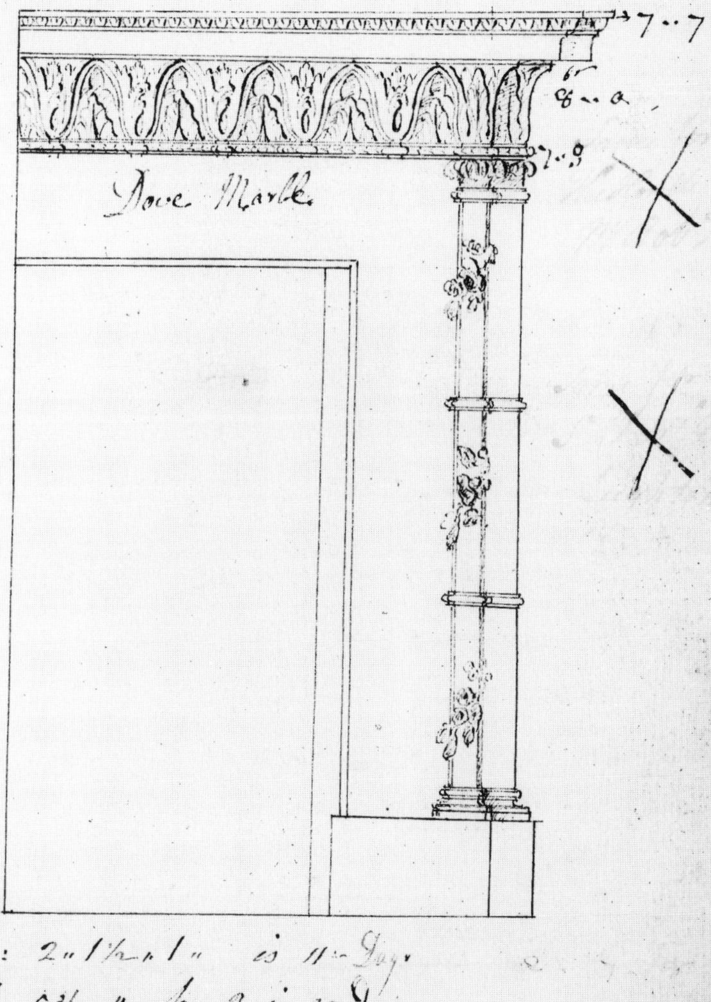

Nelson 1/2 .. 6 : 2 .. 1 1/2 .. 1 .. is 11 - Day.
Vander 6 1/4 .. 6 . 5 3/4 .. 4 .. 6 .. 2 is 30 Day.
Fire & Candles

7 . 17 . 8

AIA41

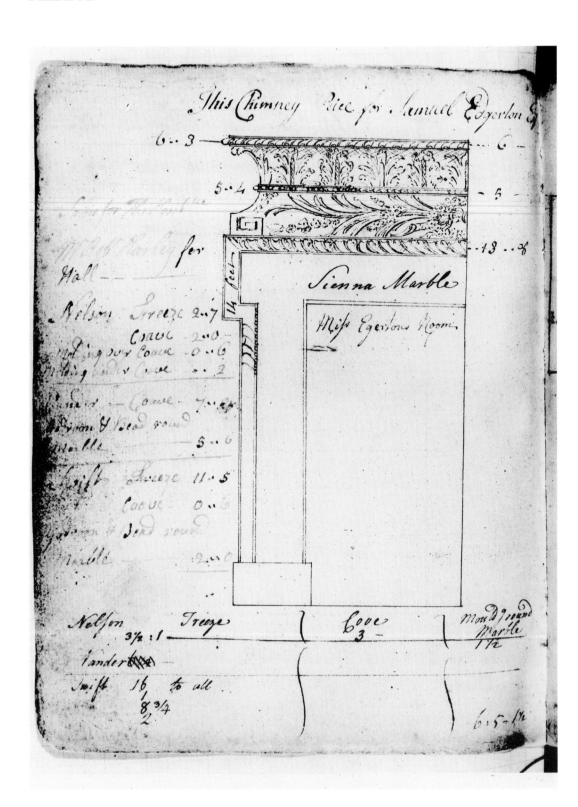

This Chimney Piece for Samuel Egerton Esq

Same for the [illegible] the

Mr [illegible] Harley for

Hall — —

Nelson Freeze 2 .. 7

Cove 2 .. 0

Molding over Cove 0 .. 6

Molding under Cove .. 2

[illegible] — Cove 7 .. [illegible]

Groom & Bead round

Marble 5 .. 6

Swift Freeze 11 .. 5

Cove 0 .. 6

Groom & Bead round

Marble 2 .. 0

	Freeze	Cove	Mould round Marble
Nelson	3½ : 1	3 —	1½
Vander[illegible] —			
Swift	16 to all 1 8 ¾ 2		6 : 5 - 1½

23 Stair Case Bracket in Oak - Esqr Slaney

	£	s
Nelson	4	5
Swift	14	0

AIA43

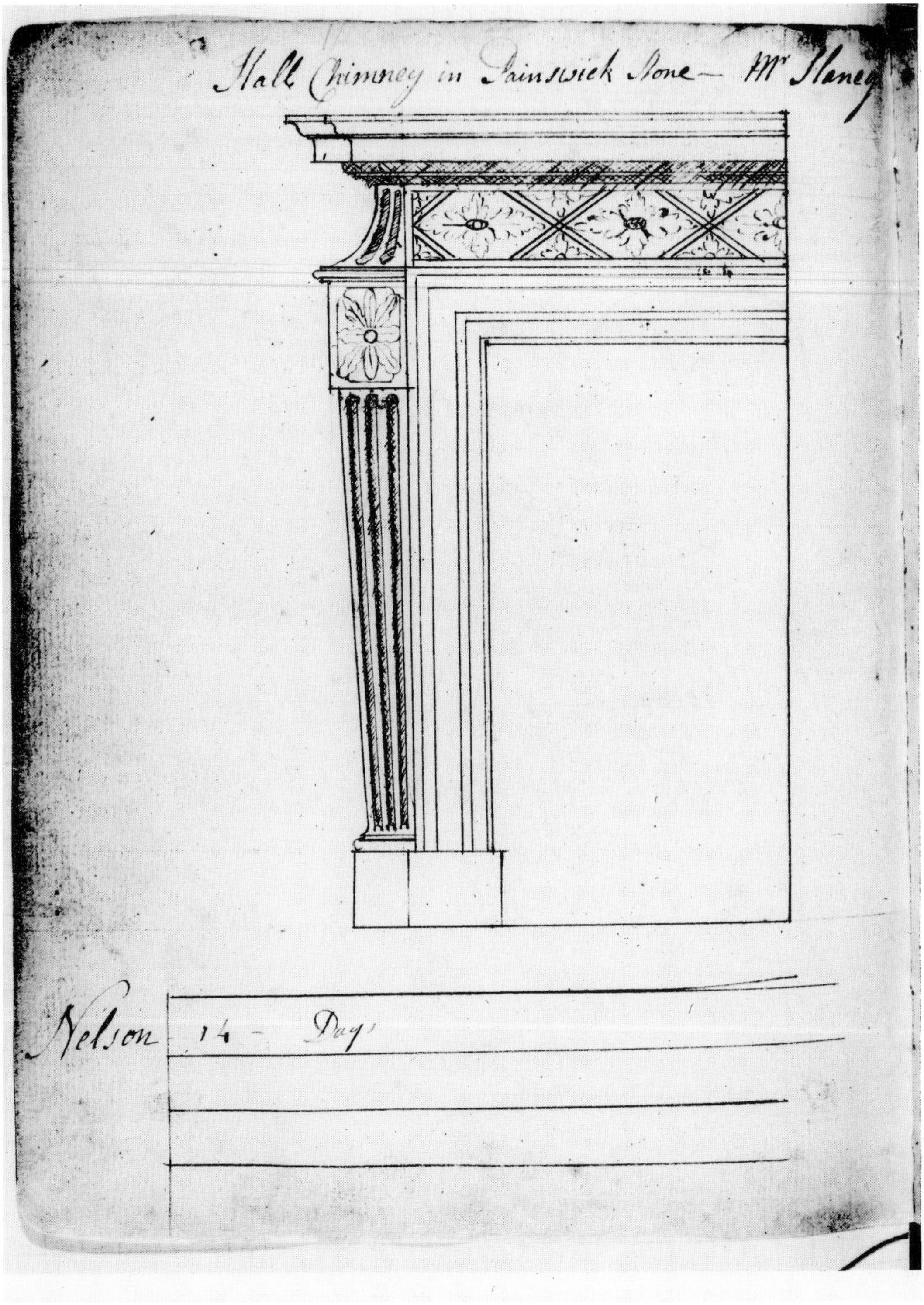
Hall Chimney in Painswick Stone — Mr Slaney
Nelson 14 - Days

top A, bottom B, **AIA44**

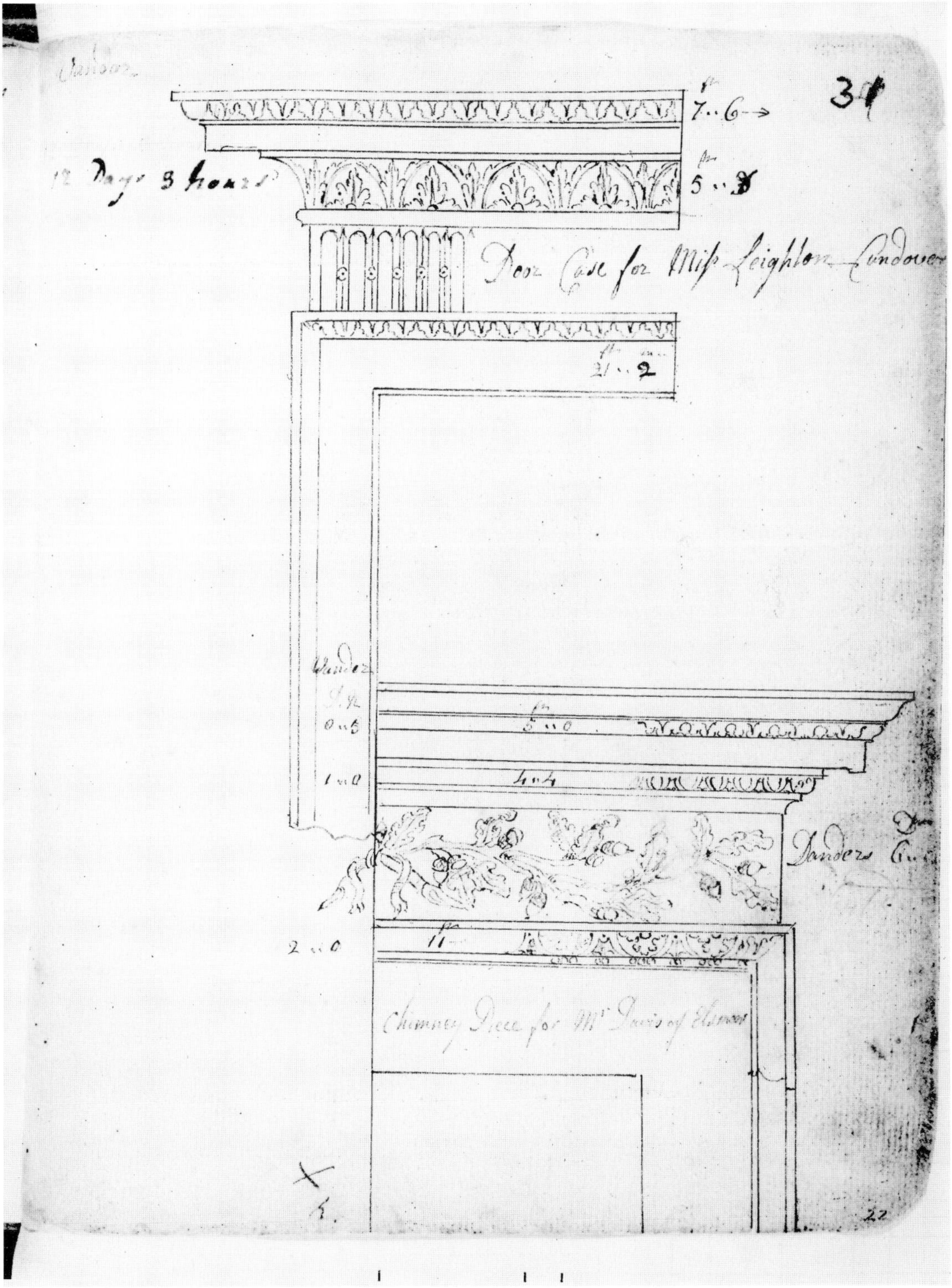

AIA45

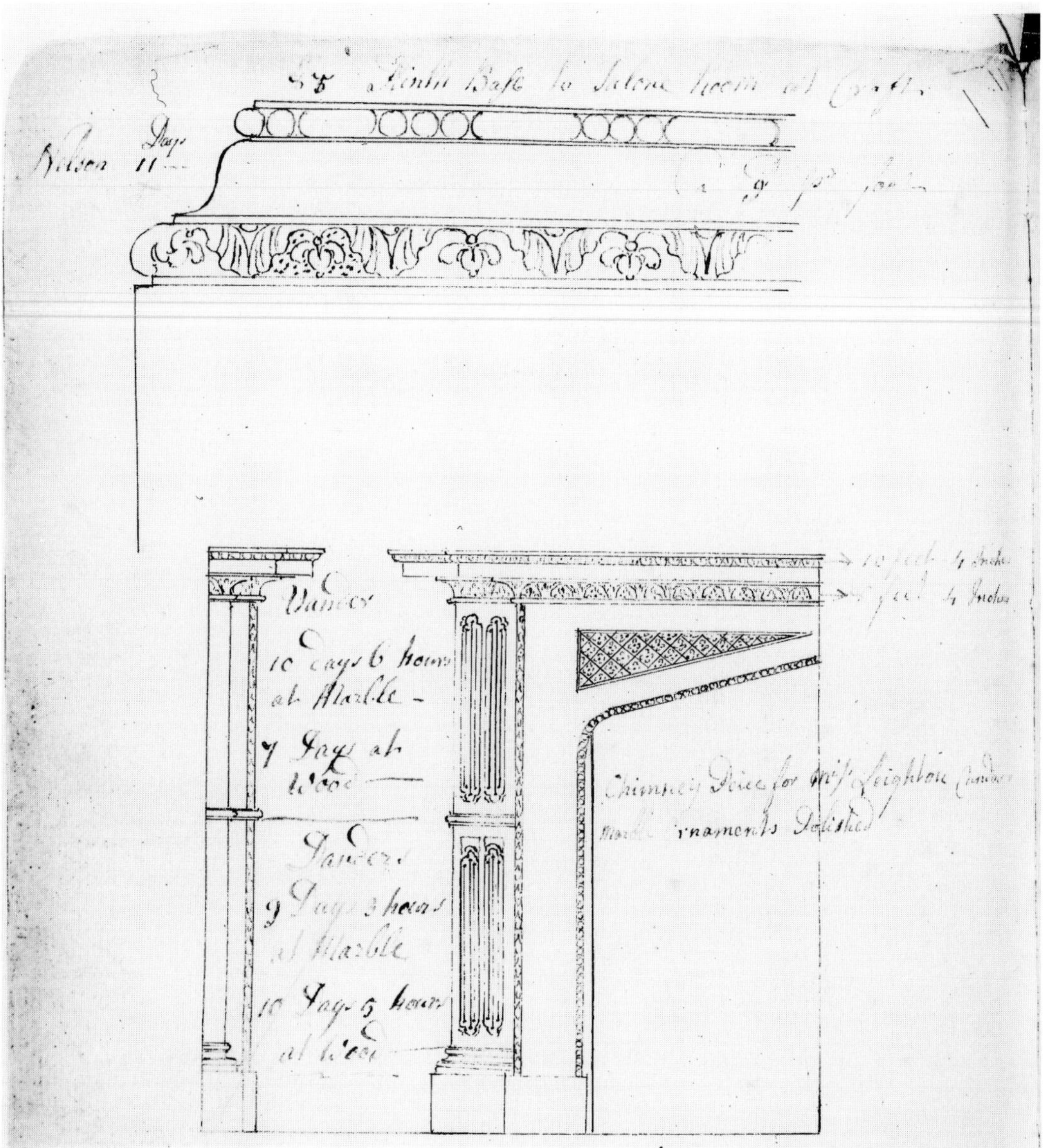

Days
11
10 Days 6 hours
at Marble
7 Days at
Wood
9 Days 3 hours
at Marble
10 Days 5 hours
at Wood
Chimney Piece for

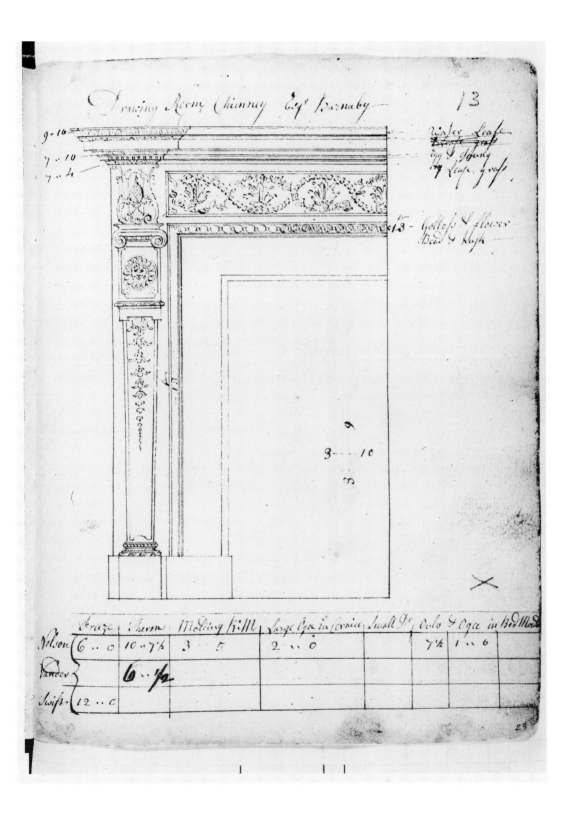

Draing Room Chimney Esqr Barnaby — 13

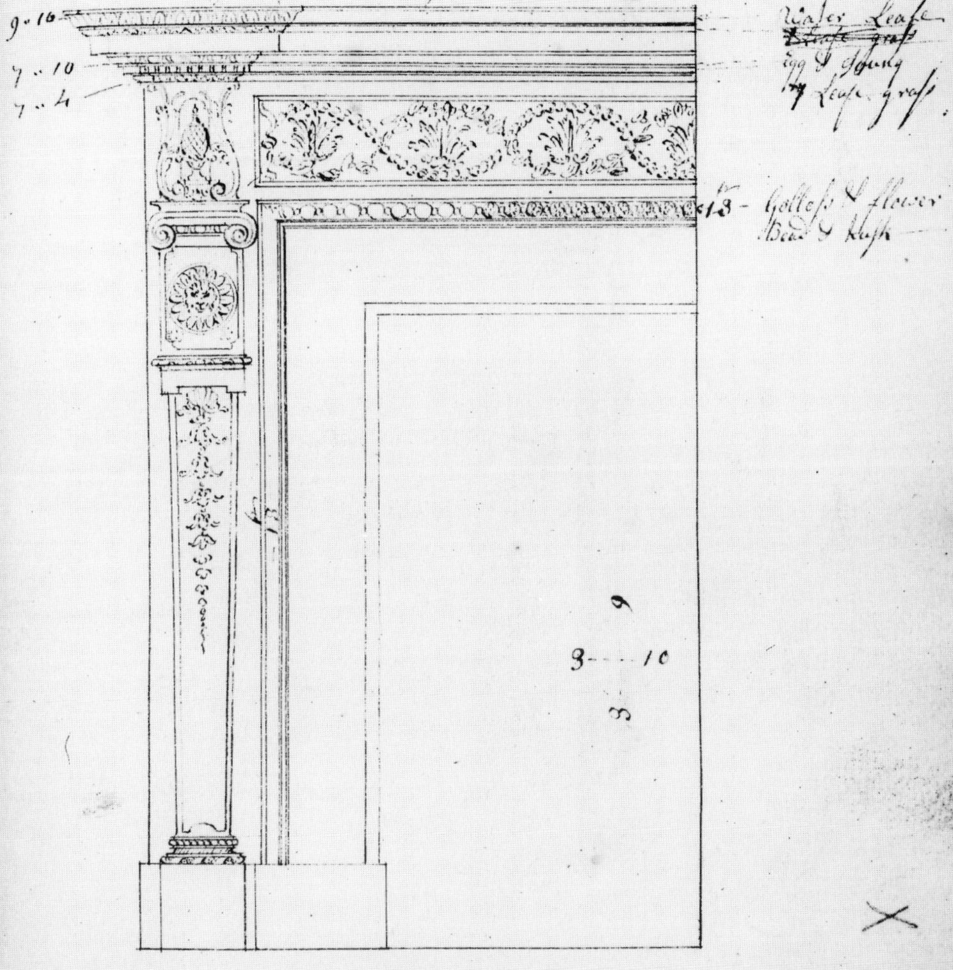

	Freaze	Therms	Molding R^d M	Large Ogee in Cornice	Small D^o	Ovolo	& Ogee in	Bed Mould
Nelson	6 .. 0	10 .. 7½	3 .. 5	2 .. 0		7½	1 .. 6	
Vander		6 .. ½						
Swift	12 .. 0							

AIA47

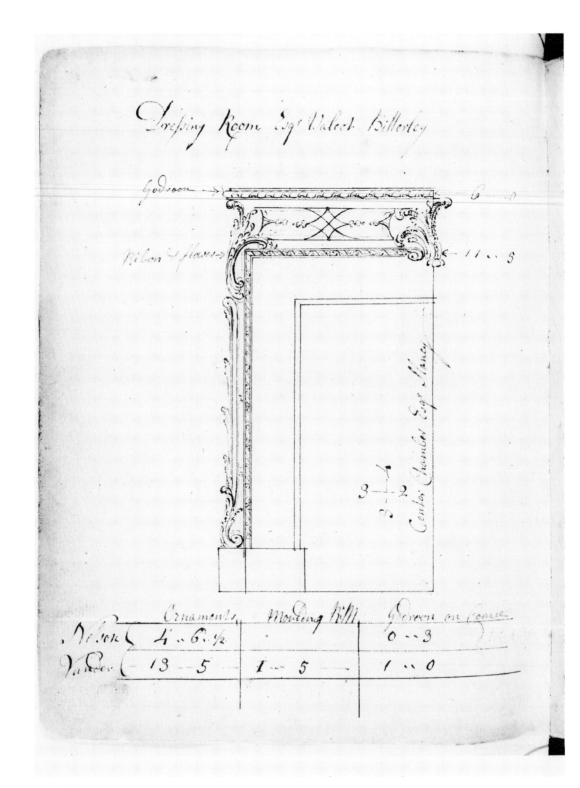

Dressing Room Esqr Walcot Bitterley

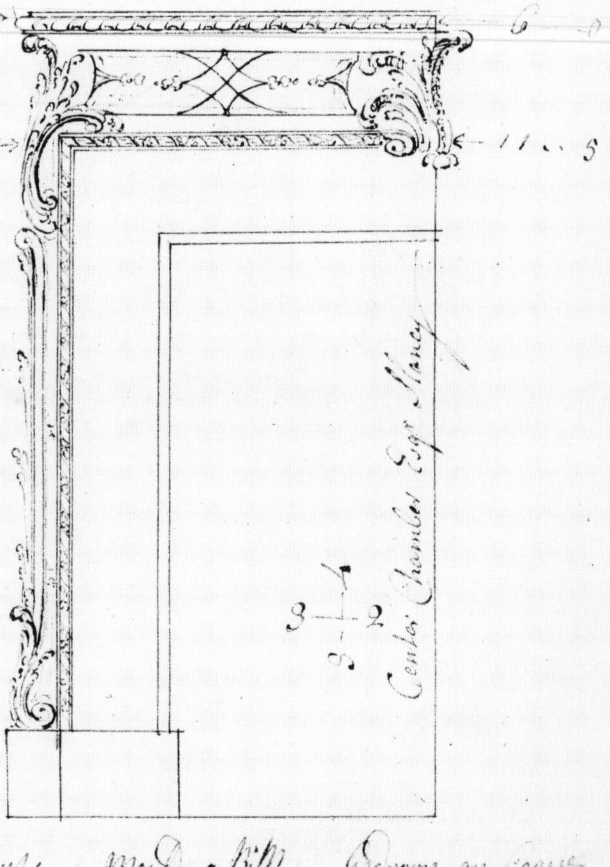

	Ornaments	Moulding W.M	Godroon on Course
Nelson	4 .. 6 .. ½		0 .. 3
Vander	13 .. 5	1 .. 5	1 .. 0

R . I . P
S.R EDWARD BLOUNT/
Jasper

AIA49 top A, bottom B.

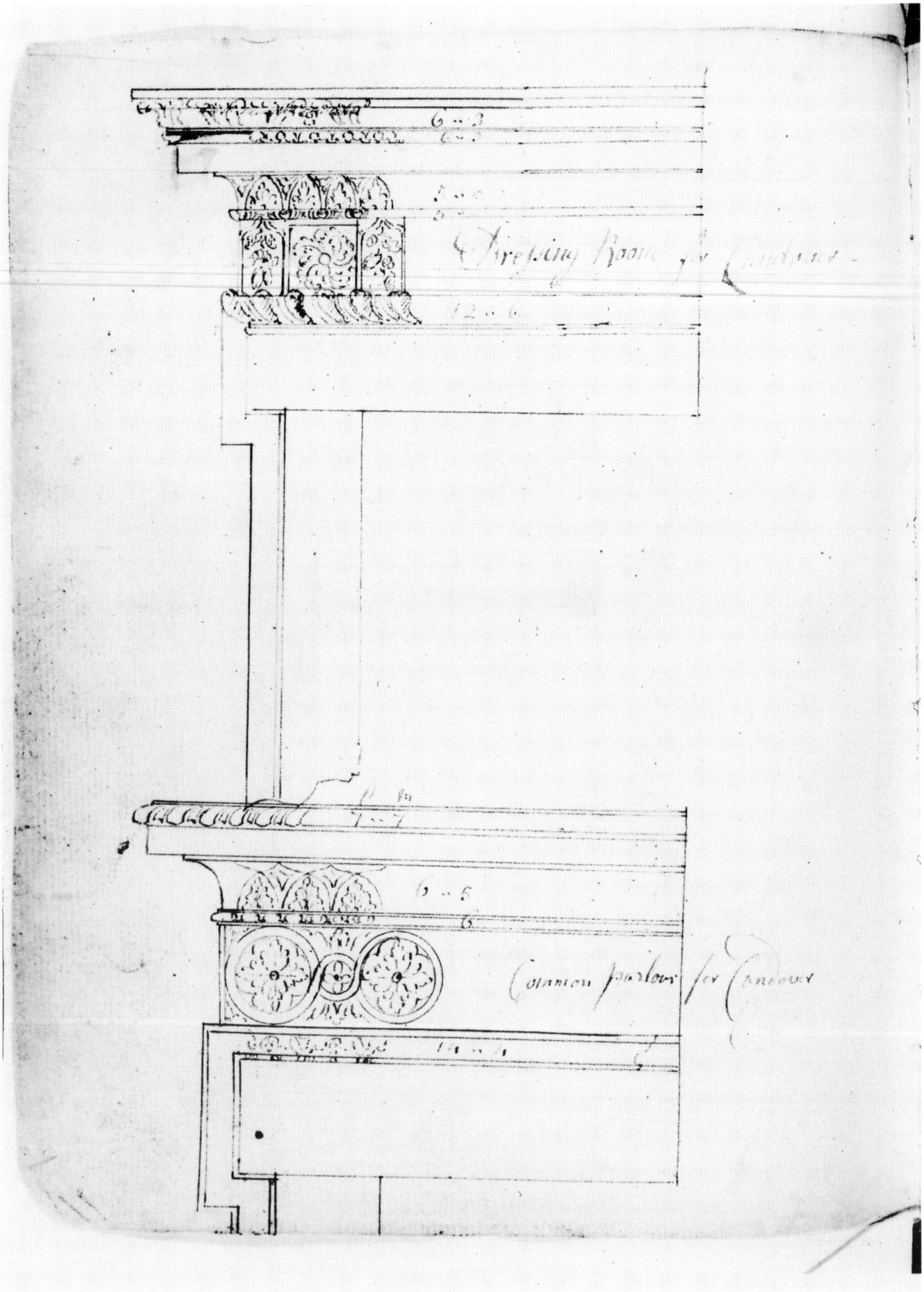

AIA50

AIA51

AIA52

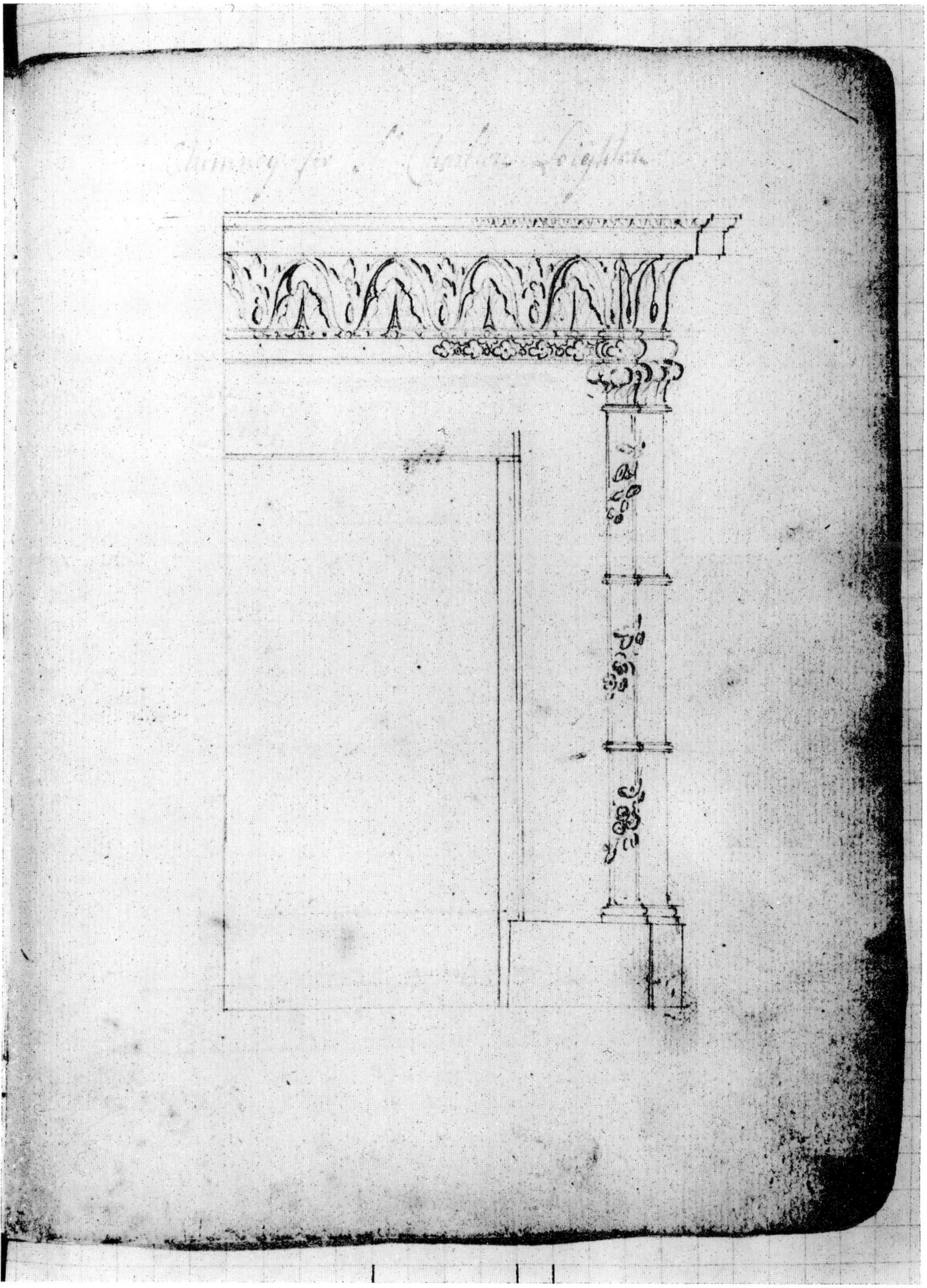

AIA53

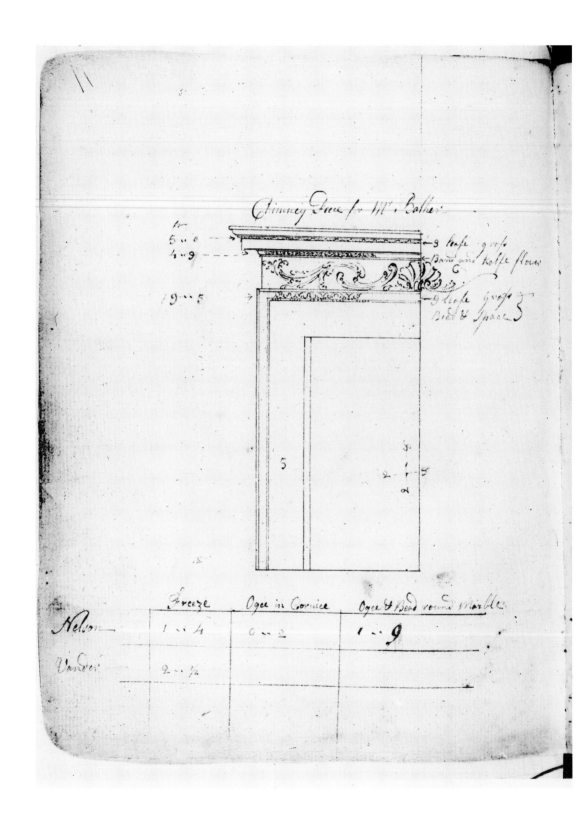

Chimney Piece for Mr. Bather

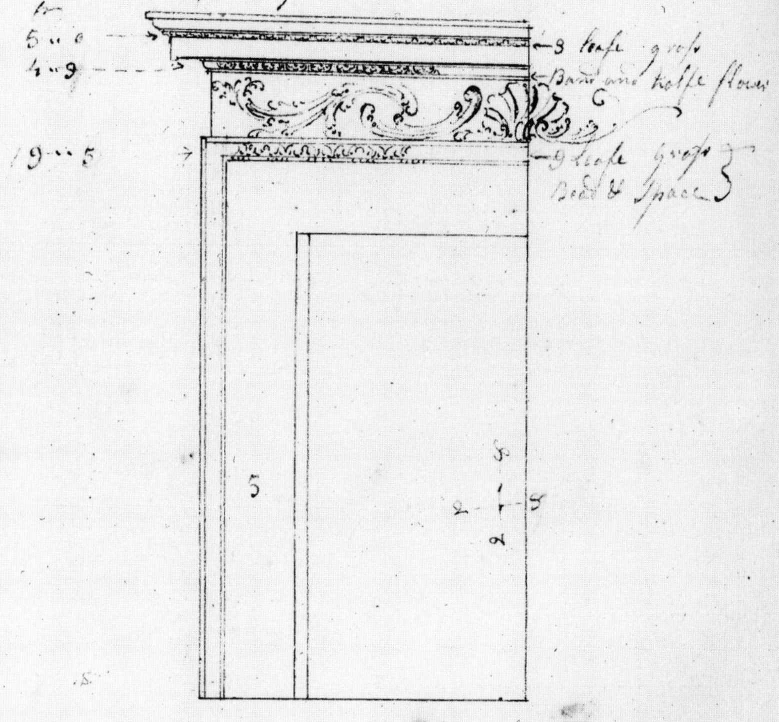

	Freeze	Ogee in Cornice	Ogee & Bead round Marble
Nelson	1 .. 4	0 .. 2	1 .. 9
Vander	2 .. ½		

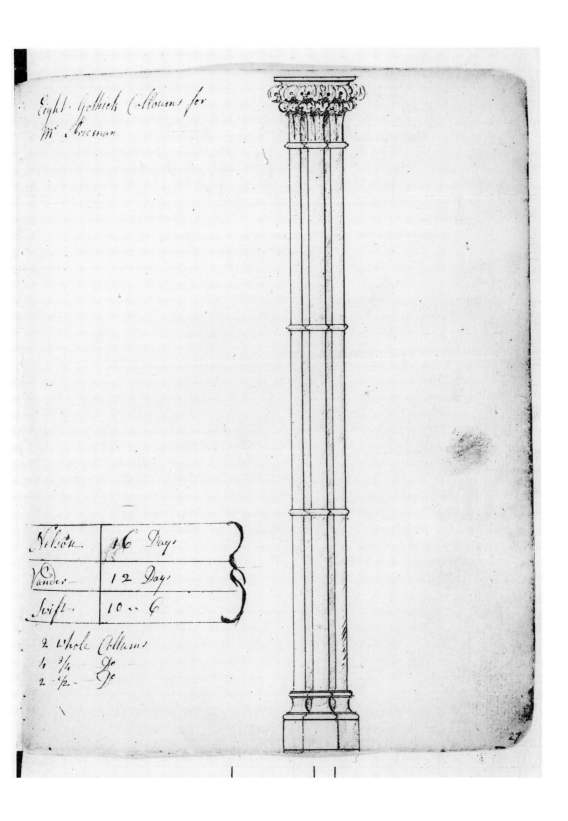

Eight Gothick Colloums for
Mr Freeman

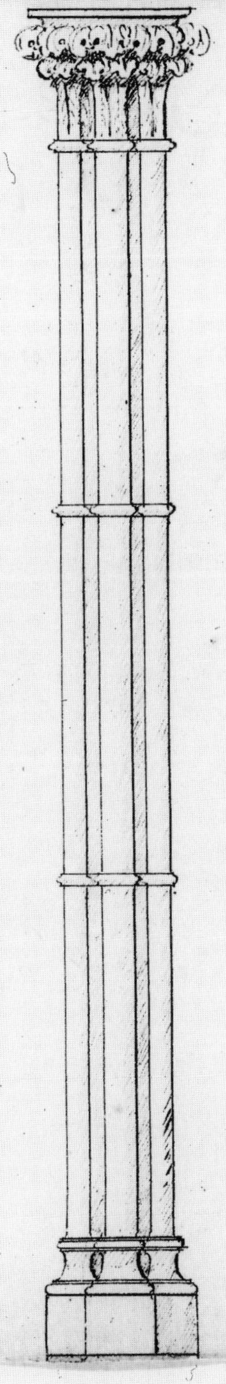

Nelson	16 Days	}
Vander	12 Days	}
Swift	10 .. 6	}

2 Whole Collums
4 3/4 Do
2 1/2 Do

AIA55

Three frames in Burnished Gold for a Dessert Table Mr Lee

	d	h	
Nelson	3 ..	5	4 Bookes of Gold
Vandox	14 ..	0	

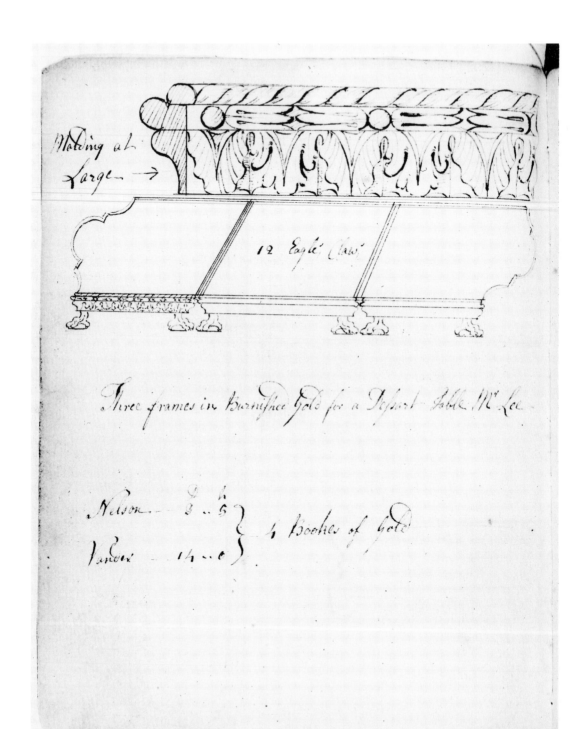

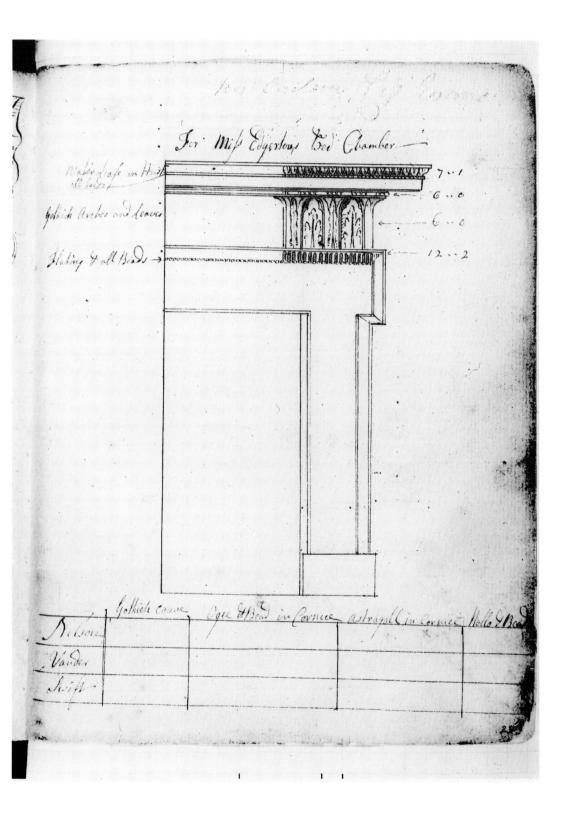

For Miss Edgertons Bed Chamber

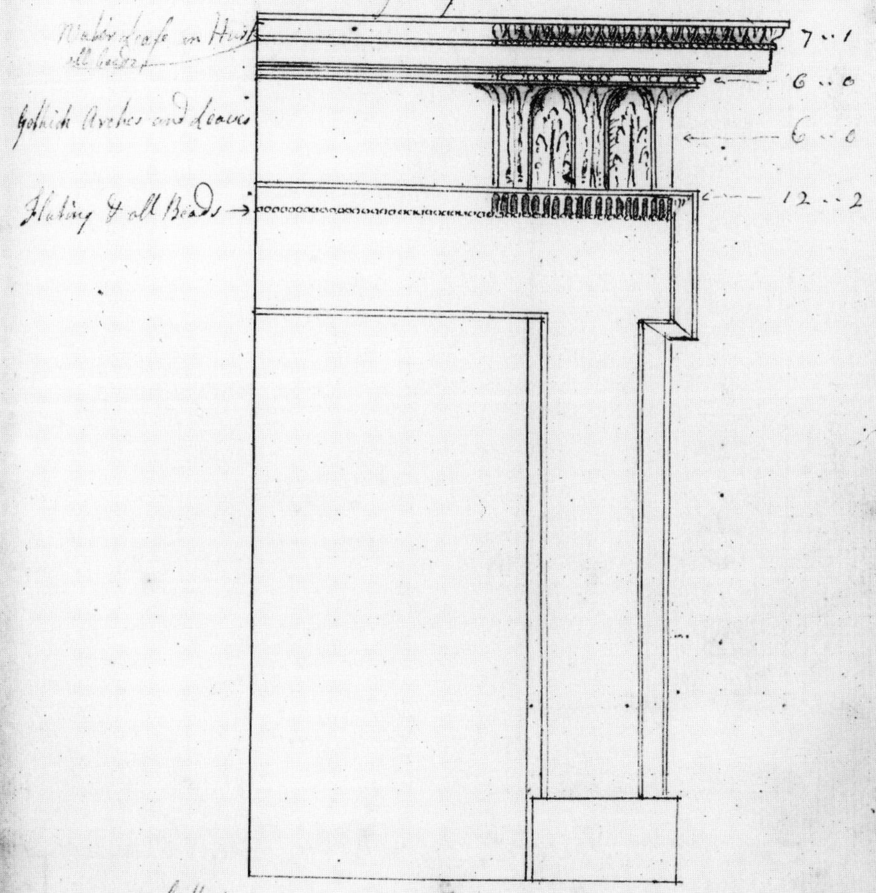

	Gothick Cove	Ogee & Bead in Cornice	astragall in Cornice	Hollo & Bead
Nelson				
Vander				
Swift				

AIA57

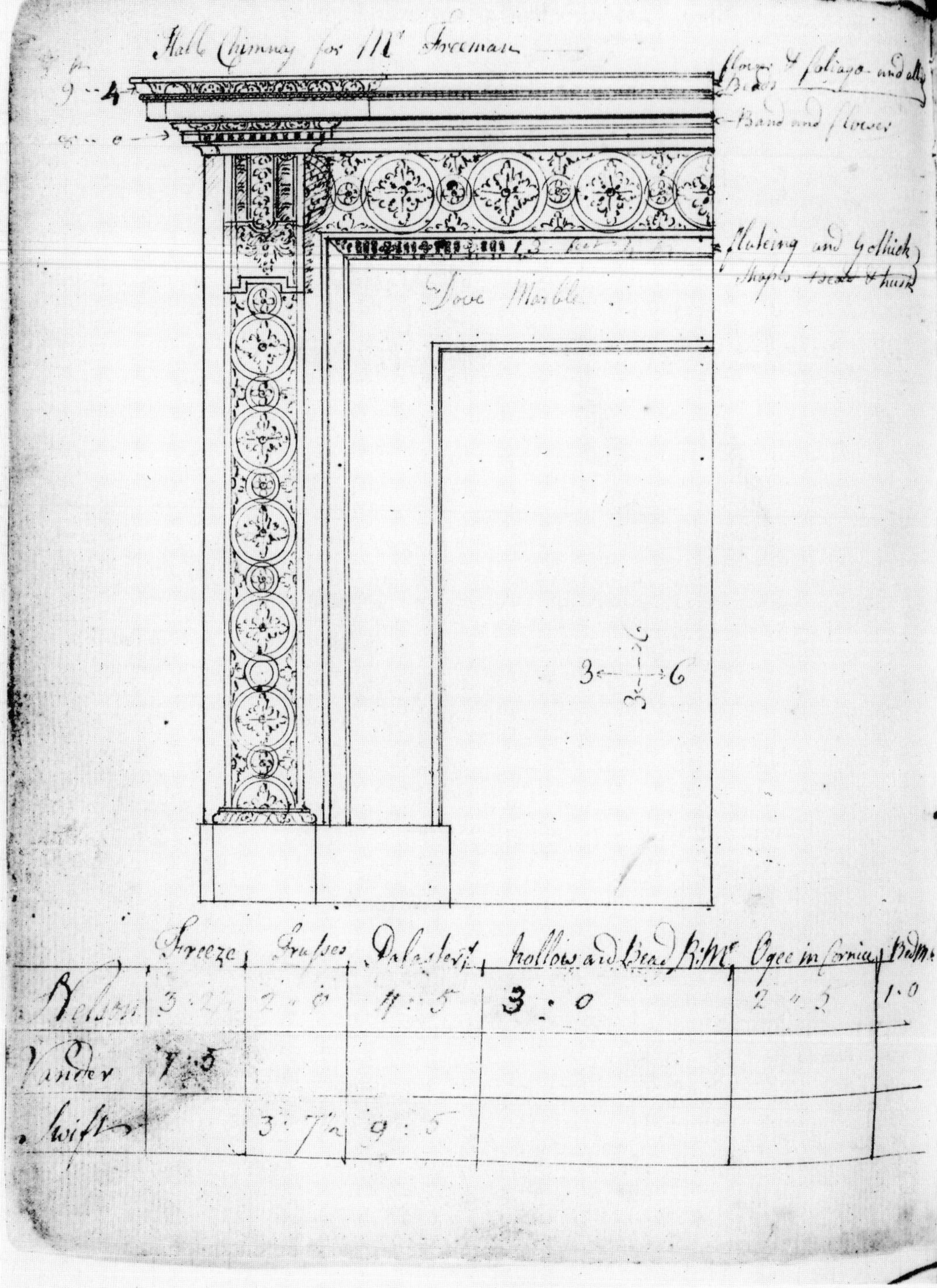

	Freeze	Trusses	Pilasters	hollow and Bead R.M.	Ogee in Cornice	Bd M.
Nelson	3 : 2½	2 : 6	11 : 5	3 : 0	2 : 2	1 : 0
Vander	7 : 5					
Swift		3 : 7½	9 : 5			

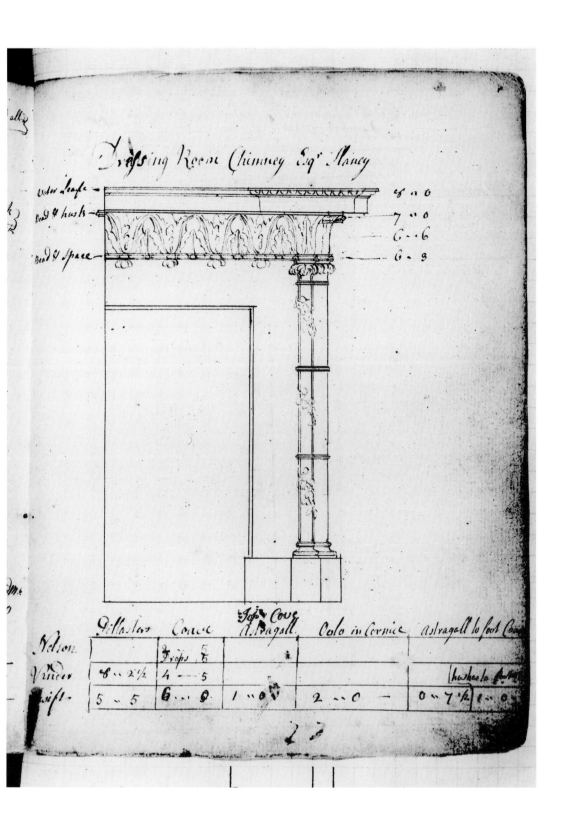

Dressing Room Chimney Esqr Maney

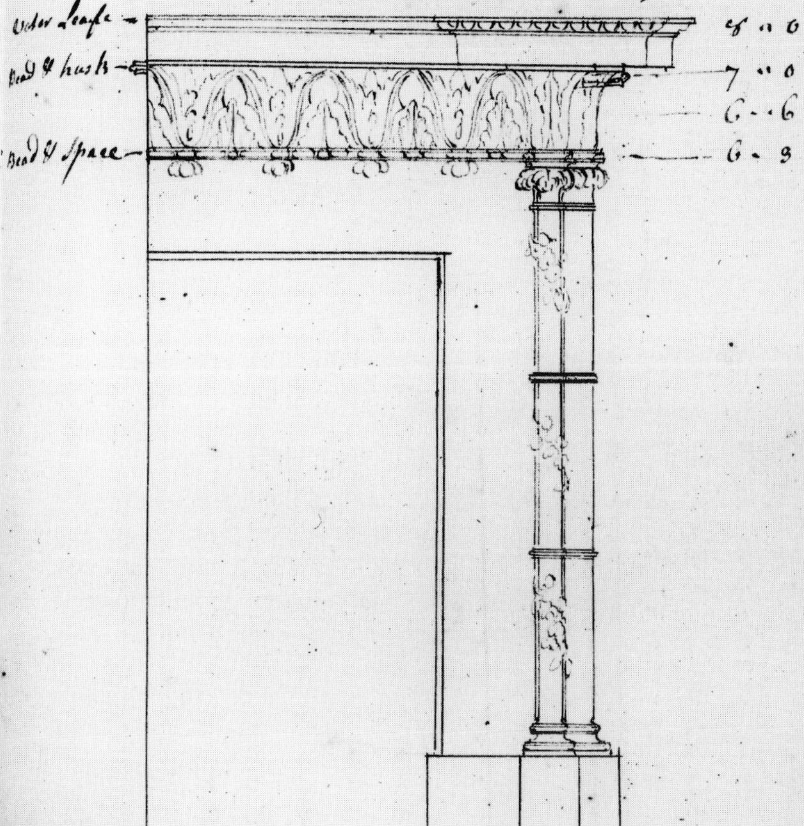

	Pillaster	Conce	Top Cove Astragall	Oolo in Cornice	Astragall to foot Co	
Nelson		2 5 Drops 5				
Vineer	8 .. 2½	4 — 5			hushes to foot	
Swift	5 .. 5	6 .. 0	1 .. 0	2 .. 0 —	0 .. 7½	1 .. 0

AIA59

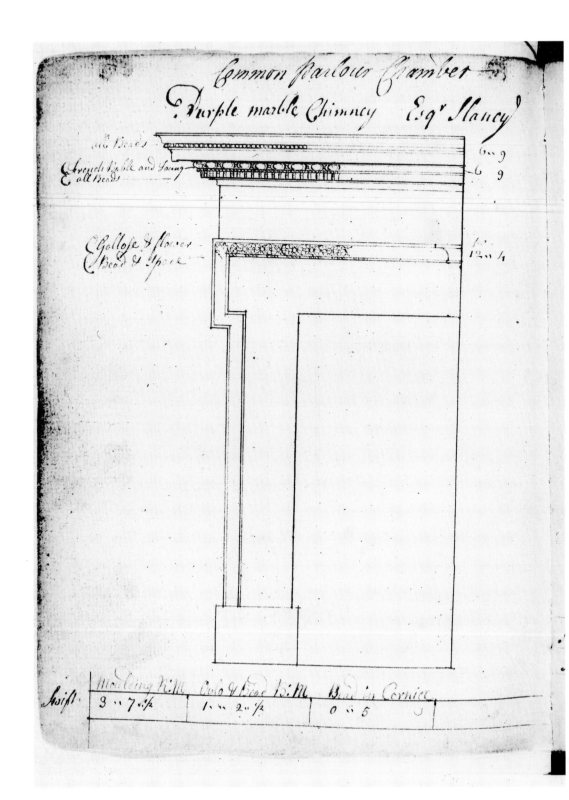

Common Parlour Chamber

Purple marble Chimney Esqr Slancy

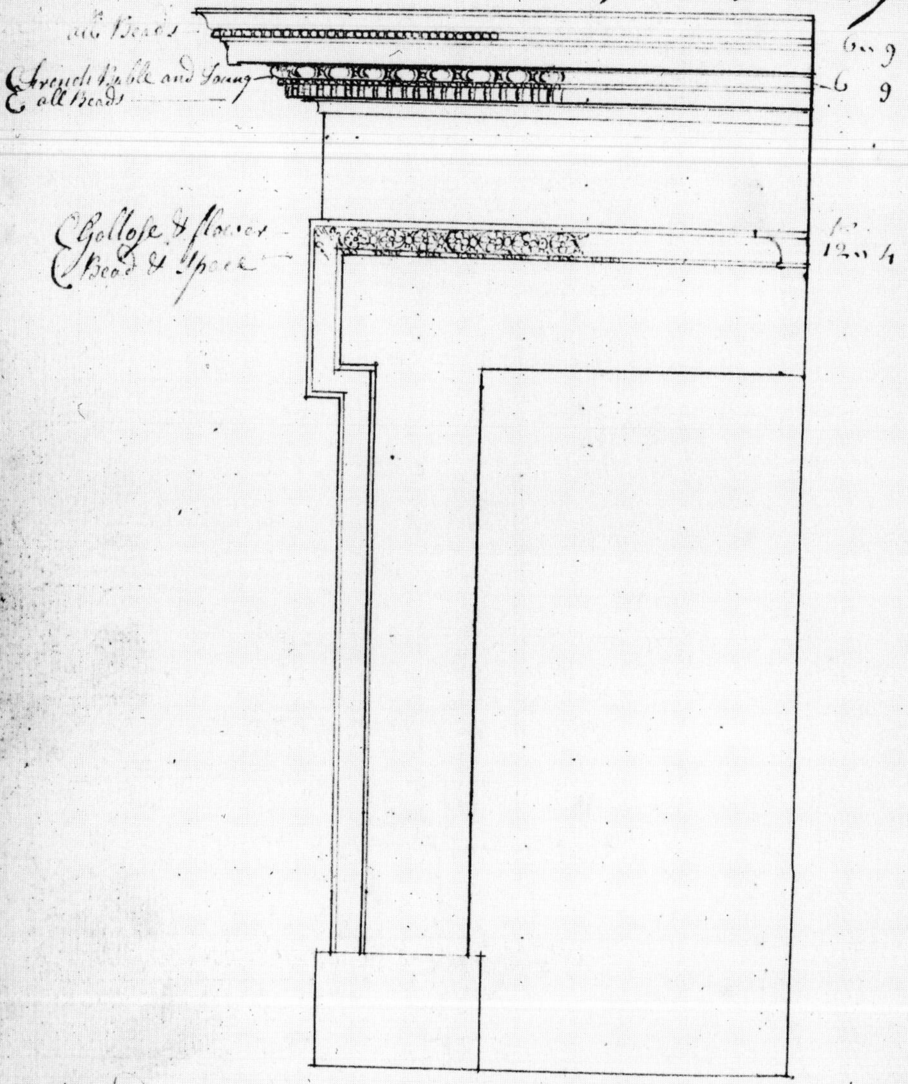

	Moulding R:M	Ovlo & Bead B:M	Bead in Cornice
Swift	3 .. 7 .. ½	1 .. 2 .. ½	0 .. 5

AIA60

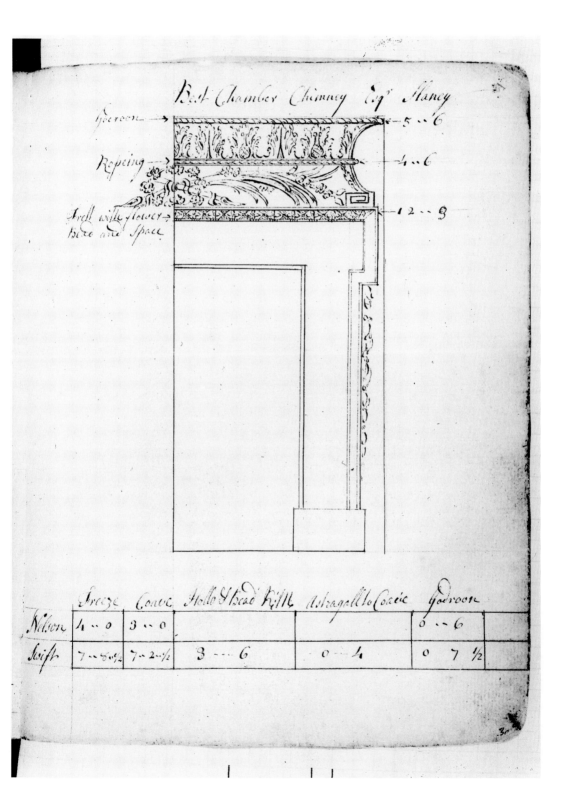

Best Chamber Chimney Esqr Staney

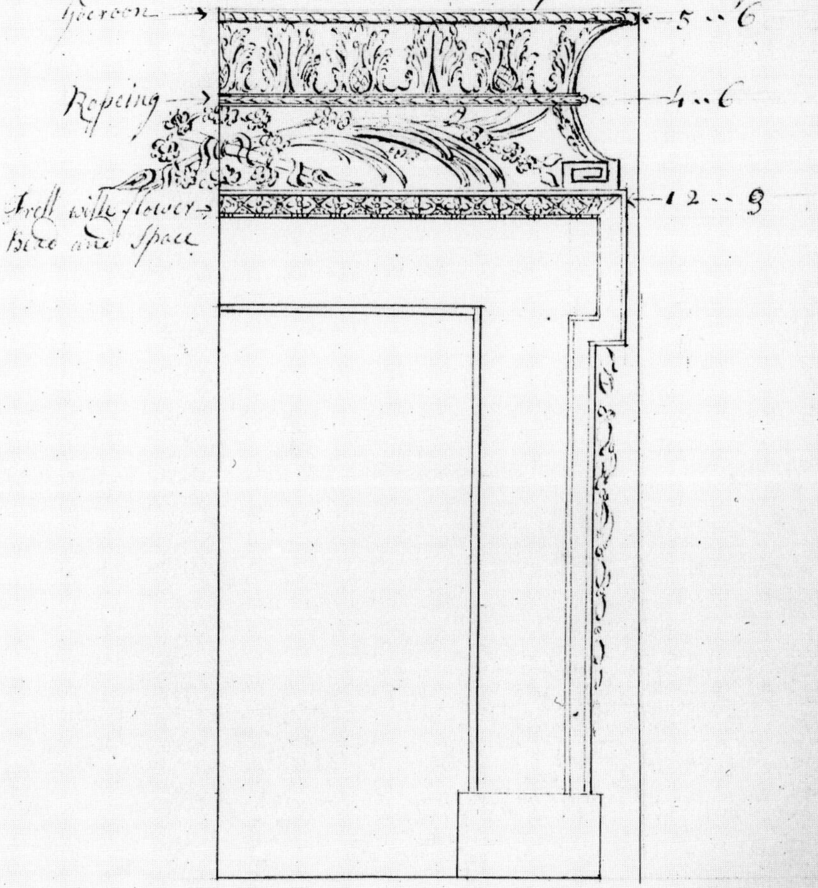

	Freeze	Coave	Hollo & Bead Kill	Astragall to Coave	Godroon	
Nelson	4 .. 0	3 .. 0			0 .. 6	
Swift	7 .. 8 .. ½	7 .. 2 .. ½	3 ... 6	0 .. 4	0 7 ½	

AIA61

	W	D	H	
Nelson	0	4	5	Freeze to Esqr Burnaby
Swift	2	1	0	
Vander	0	2	0	

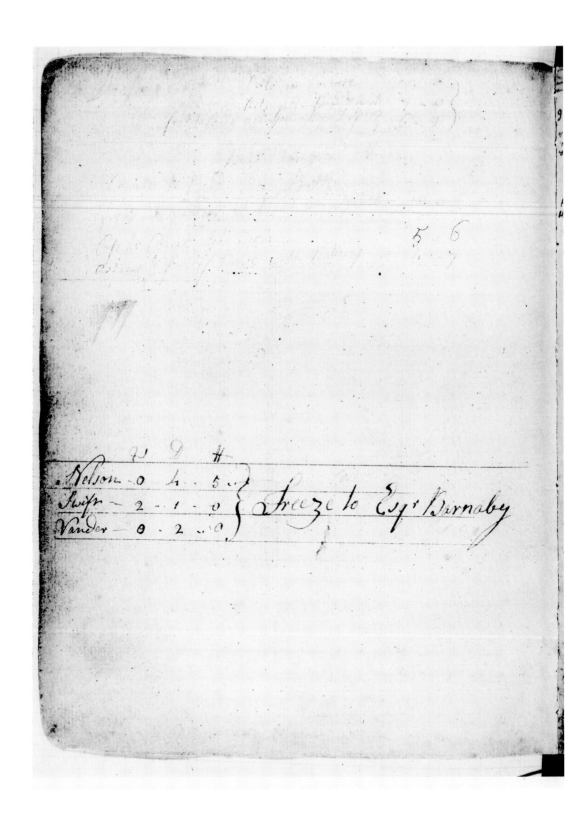

Dining Parlour Chimney for Esqr Slaney

	Tablet	Freeze	Pillasters (1 moldings)	Trusses	Coave	3 members	Mold BM	Cornice Covetto & Beads
Nelson	6..0	4..5	7..7½	2..0	2..0	—		2..5
Vander	12..0	11..0	6..0 0..5 Mol	3..0	3..0	—	6..0	
Swift			10..2½	3..5	1..3	—		

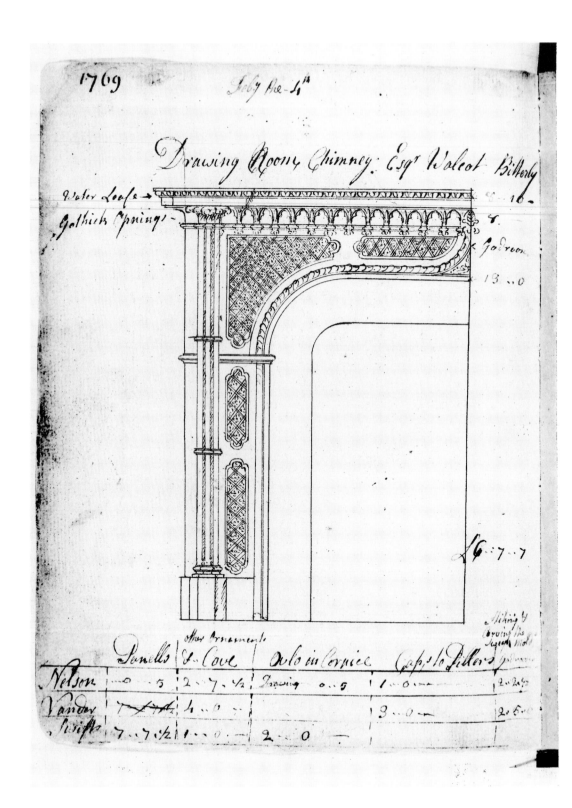

1769 Feby the 4th

Drawing Room Chimney: Esqr Walcot Bitterly

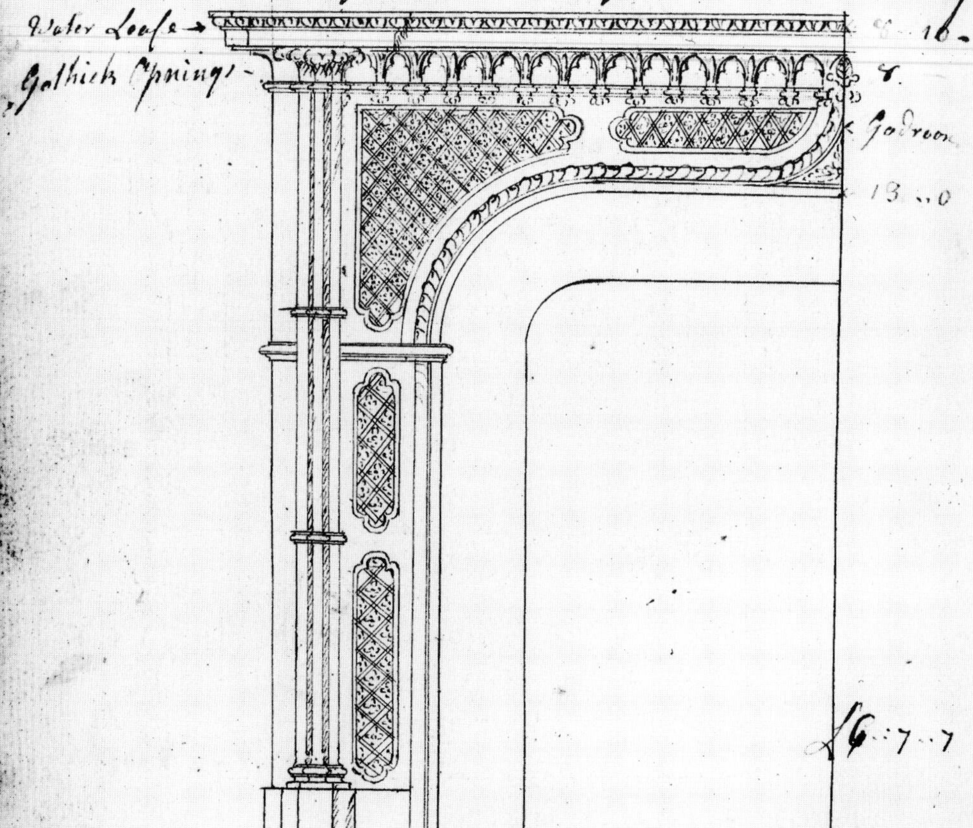

	Panells	other Ornaments & Cove	Ovlo in Cornice	Caps to Pillers	Miking & Carving the [illegible] Mold Gadroon
Nelson	..0..5	2..7..½	Drawing 0..5	1..0..	2..2..½
Vander	~~7..7..7½~~	4..0..		3..0..	2..5..0
Swifts	7..7..½	1..0..	2..0..		

AIA64

Jany the 28th 1769 (18

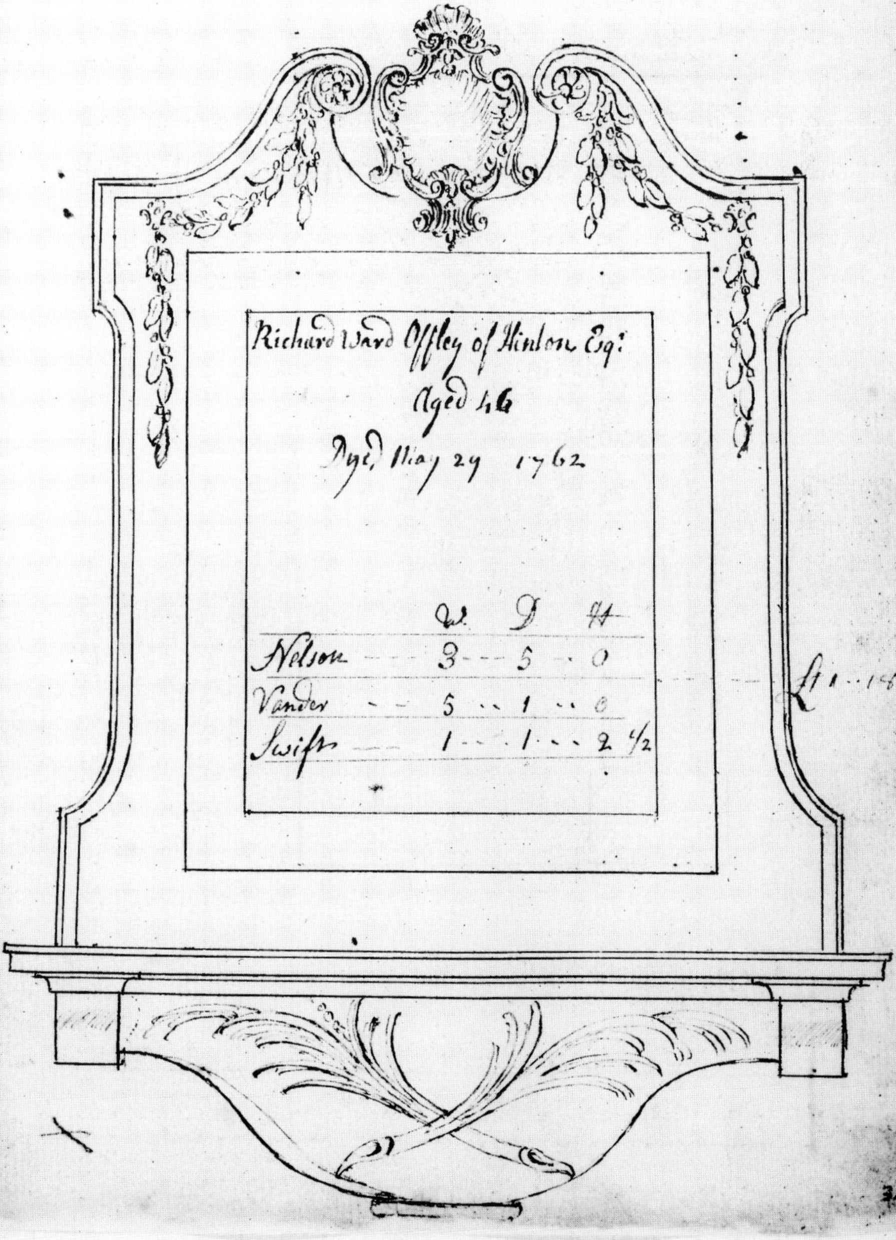

£1..18..8

32

AIA65

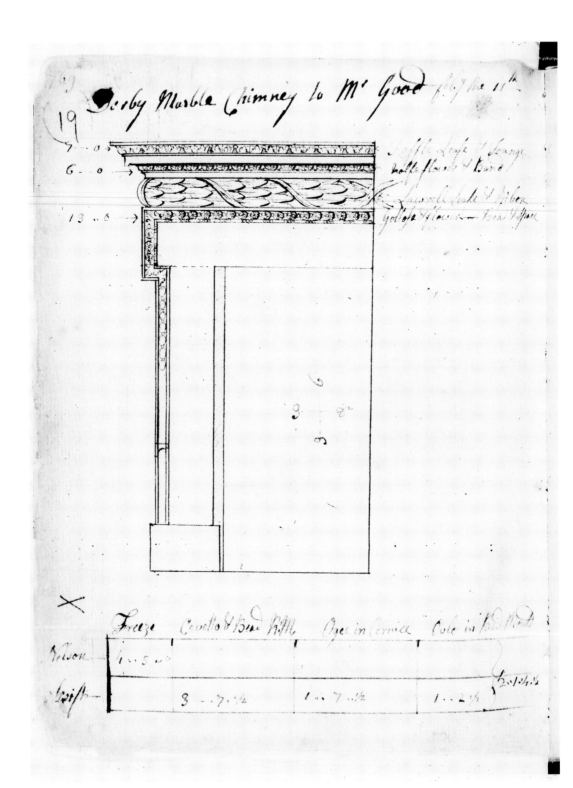

19 Derby Marble Chimney to Mr Good feby the 11th

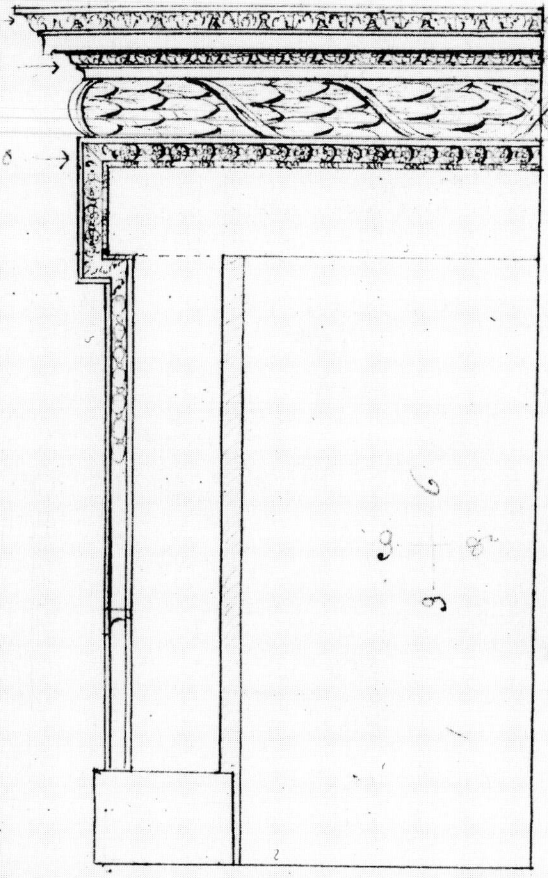

X

	Freeze	Cavetto & Bed Md	Ogee in Cornice	Ovle in Bed Mould	
Nelson	4 .. 5 .. 0				2 .. 14 .. ½
Griffith		3 .. 7 .. ½	1 .. 7 .. ½	1 .. 2 ½	

AIA66

Dining Parlour Chimney — Henrey Powys Esq the Abby

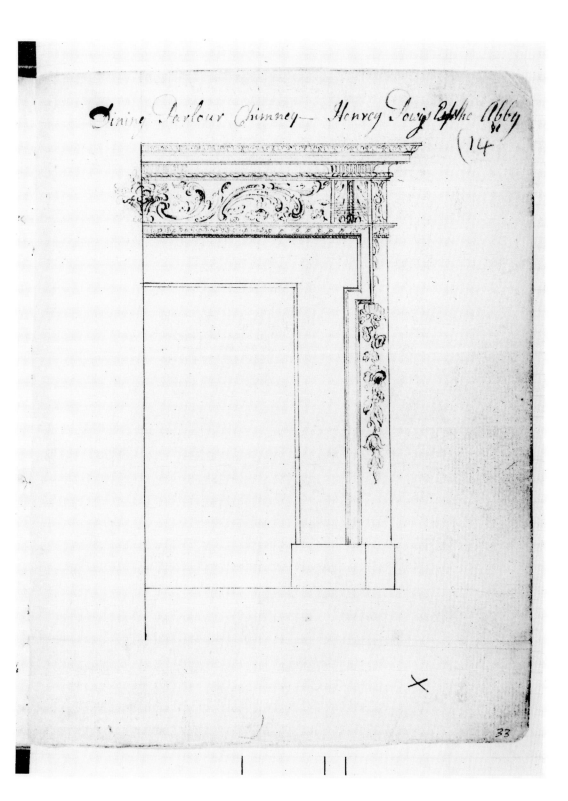

(14 30

AIA67

Design of a Chimney -- Henry Dawkins Esqr the [illegible]
Alcove Bedchamber.

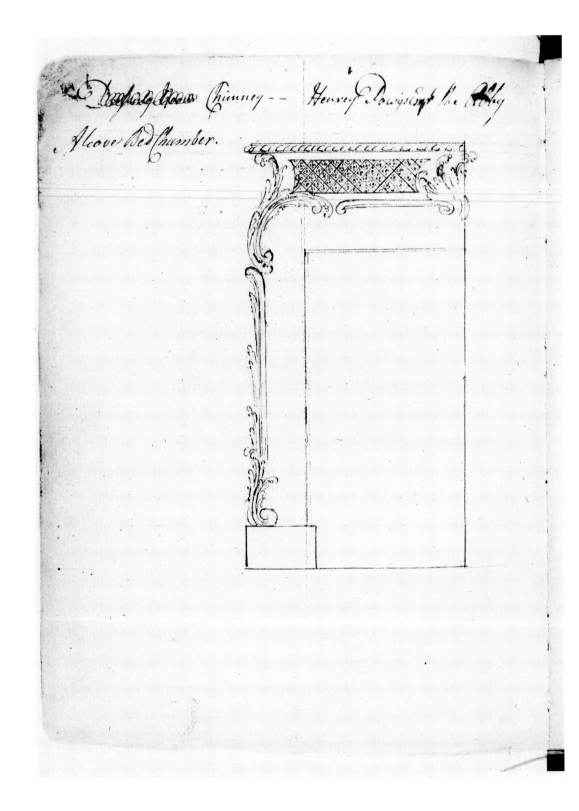

AIA68

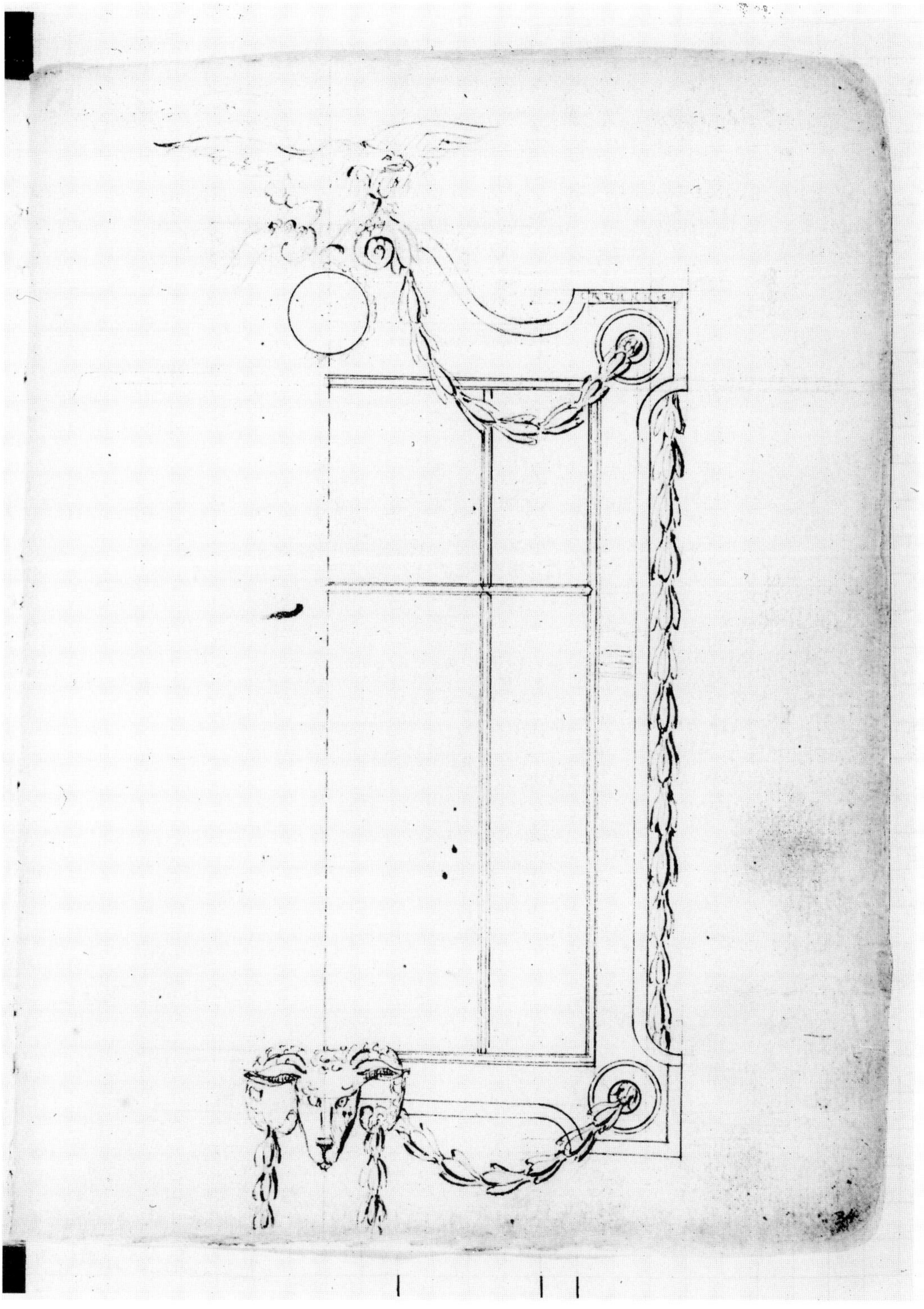

AIA69

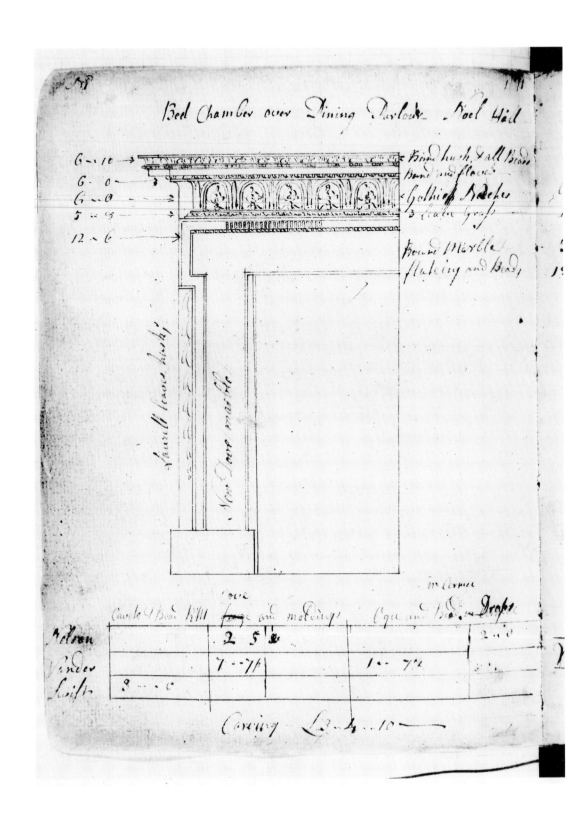

Bed Chamber over Dining Parlour Noel Hall

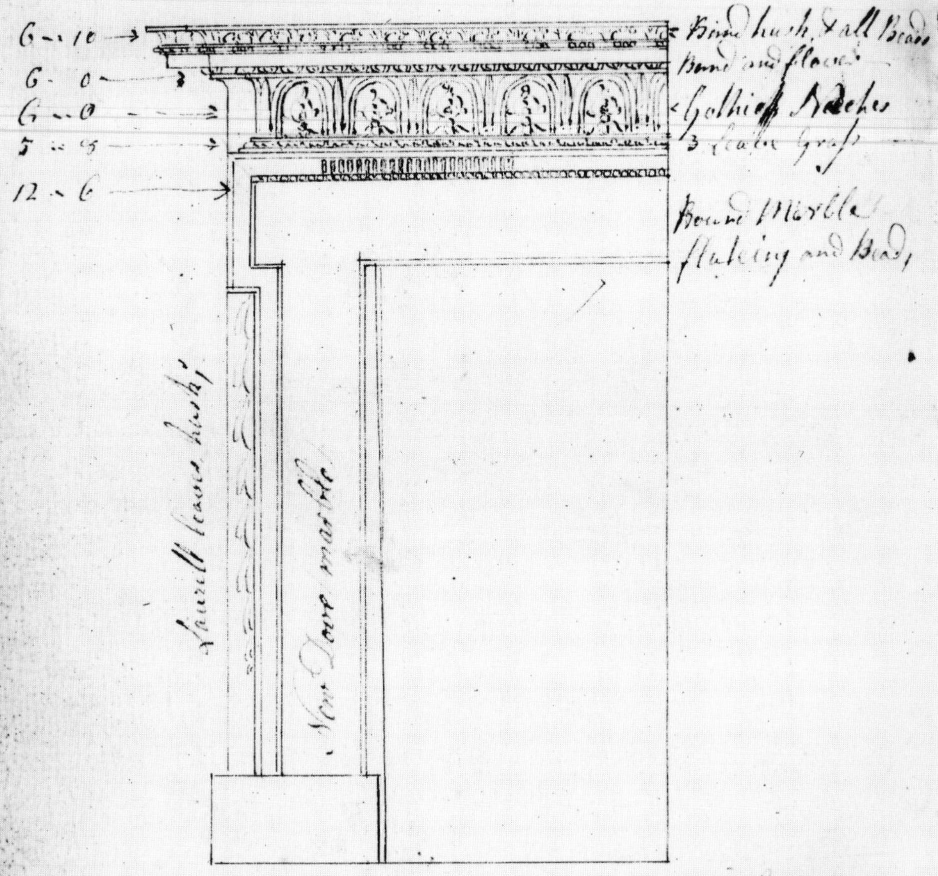

	Cavetto & Bead Fillet	Cove and molding		Ogee and Bead in Cornice	Drops
Nelson		2 5			2 .. 0
Vander		7 .. 7½		1 .. 7½	
Smith	3 .. 0				

Carving £3 .. 4 .. 10

Right hand Chamber over Hall Abel Hill Esq
Same as Mr Tomkins

Nelson	Tablets	2 .. 2½
	Freeze	2 .. 5
	Ovolo in Cornice	1 .. 5
Vander	Tablets	6 .. 0
Swift	freeze	8 .. 0
	Cove	2 .. 0
	Ovolo and bead R:M	3 .. 7½

done with frett flower &
raffle flower bead & space

Abram bead all beads and ogee in bed mould & leave gross | Carving £1 .. 15 .. 5½

AIA75

Chamber Over Drawing Room — Rich[d] Hill Esq[r]

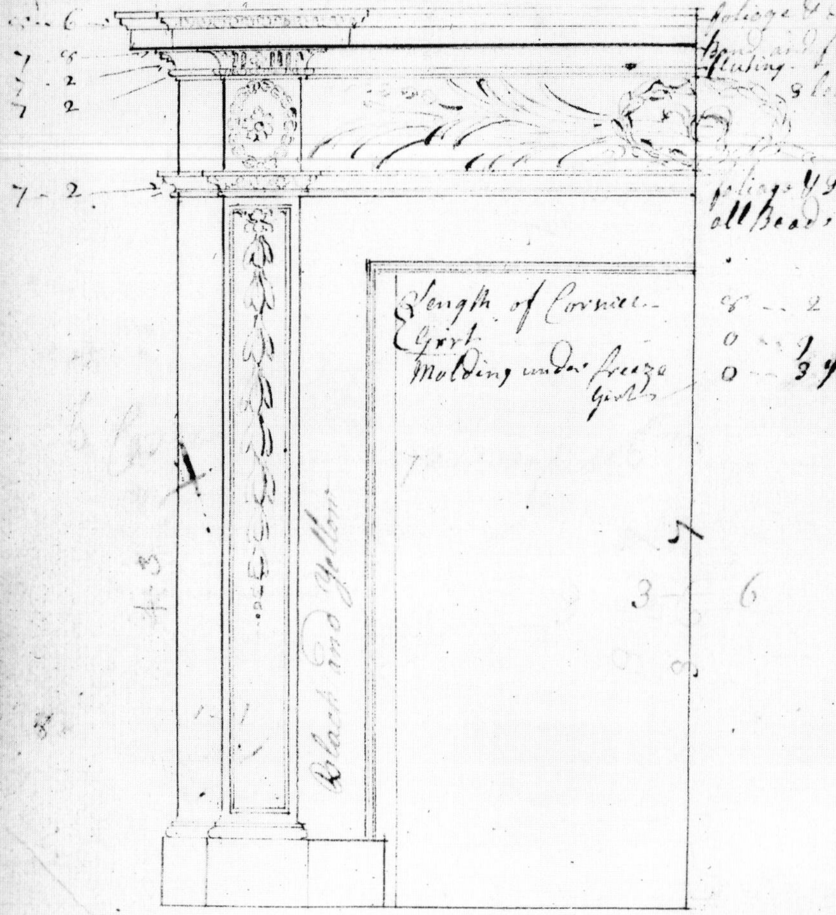

	Freeze	Pilaster	Cove	Pelm in B.M	Ogee in Cornice	under freeze Ogee & Bead
Patron	2 .. 5	4 5				
Vandew		3 .. 7½		ogee to Cove		
Swift	6 .. 7½		2 0	1 .. 2½ 6	1 .. 7½	2 .. 0

Carving £ 5 – 12 – 11 ½

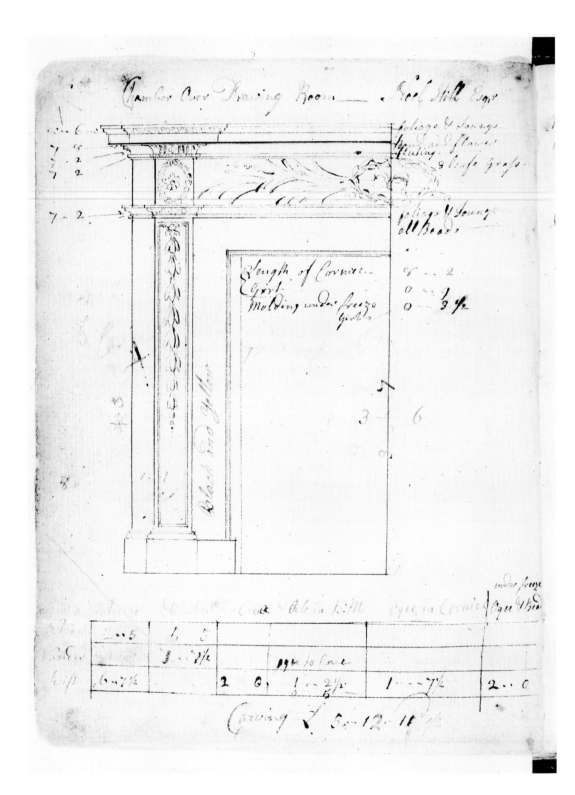

No. 5

Chimney Peice for Sir Joins

Eight Rooms Chamber of Noel Hill

~~Noel Hill~~

Raffle Leafe Carving

all round

fluting

13 Leafe grass

Eagle & Beads in space

ft	in
7 ..	0
6 ..	4
6 ..	0
6 ..	0

(10

13 .. 10

The Same for Noel Hill Esqr

N	Tablet	2 .. 2½
	freeze	2 .. 3
	Ovolo in Cornice	1 .. 3
V	Tablet	6 .. 0

S	freeze	8 .. 0
	Cove	2 .. 0
	Hall Rill	8 .. 7½

	Tablet	Freeze	moulding Rill	Egg in Cornice	Cove	Bead and Egg in Rill
Wilson	2 7½	3 0	1 .5			
Swift		8 0		2 0		
Vander	6 ½	1 .5	4 7½		2 0	1 .. 0

Carving £5 .. 19 : 11

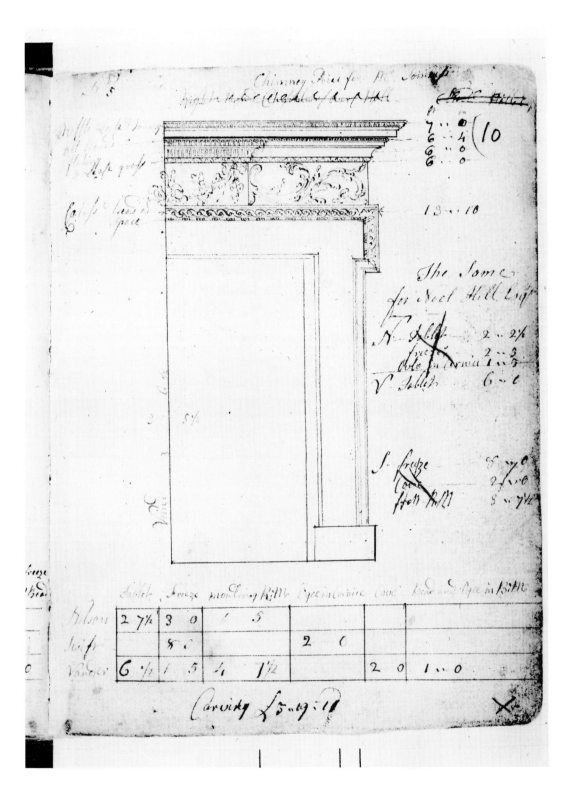

AIA77

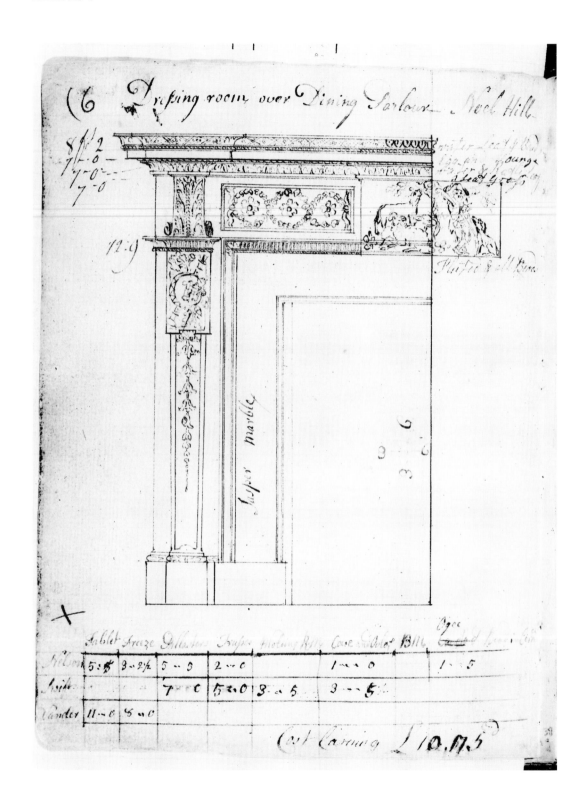

(6 Dressing room over Dining Parlour — Noel Hill

	Tablet	Freeze	Pillasters	Trusses	Molding R.M.	Cove and Volut	B.M.	Ogee
Nelson	5:5	3-2½	5-0	2-0		1-0		1-5
Smith			7-0	5-0	3-5	3-5		
Vander	11-0	8-0						

Cost Carving £10.17.5

(12) 1759

John Marble Chimney Price for Mr Yool Feby the 18th

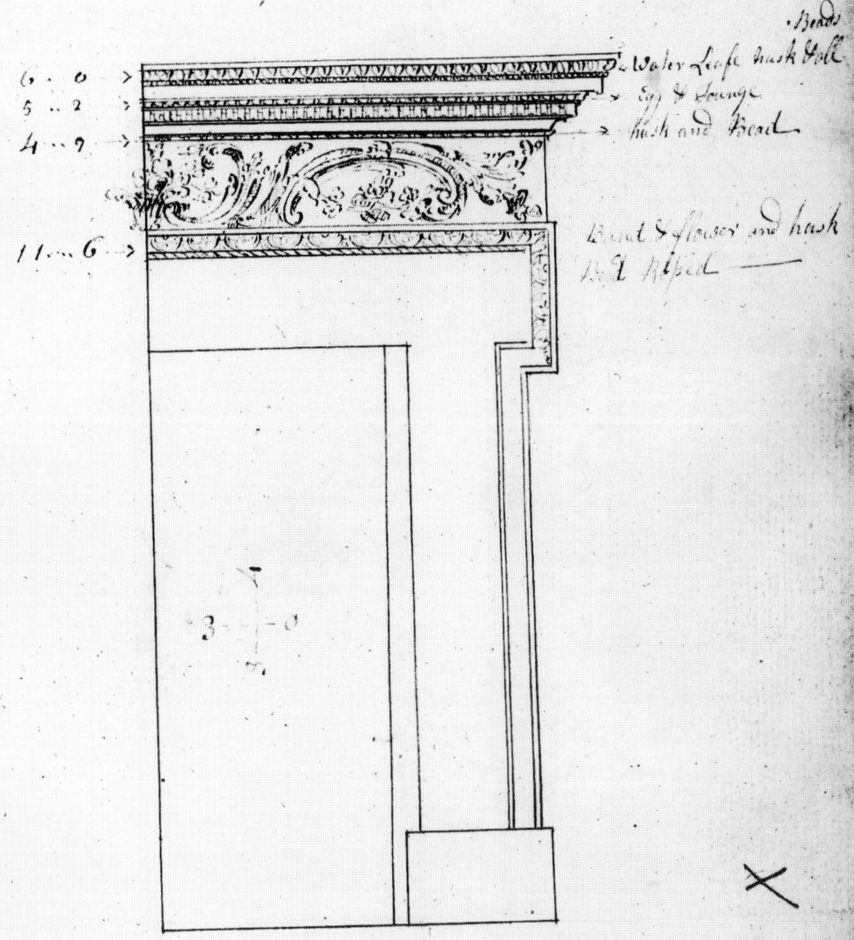

	Freeze	Ovlo & Bead Rd Mc	Ovlo & Bead Cornice	Ovlo Bed Mould	Astragall Do
Nelson	4 .. 5		1 .. 2 . ½	0 .. 3	0 .. 2 ½
Vander	10 .. 5				
Swift		4 .. 0			

AIA79

1769 44 Vello   111

Chimney Piece for Mr. Wilkinson Feb. 1 Cornice   5

Foliage Bead & Space

Band and flower

5 leafe grass

Covetto and Bead

Round Merlle

fluted and all Beads

5 10

4 10

4 10

12 6

Nelson		4 - 7½	0 - 5 -	
Swift	4 - 0	[illegible]	[illegible] 0	
Vander		2 - 5	0 5	1 - 7½
	Hollo & Bead R.M.	Cove	Ogee and Ovolo Cove	Ogee and Bead Cornice

AIA80

Chimney for Ric^d Corbet Esqr Highhatton

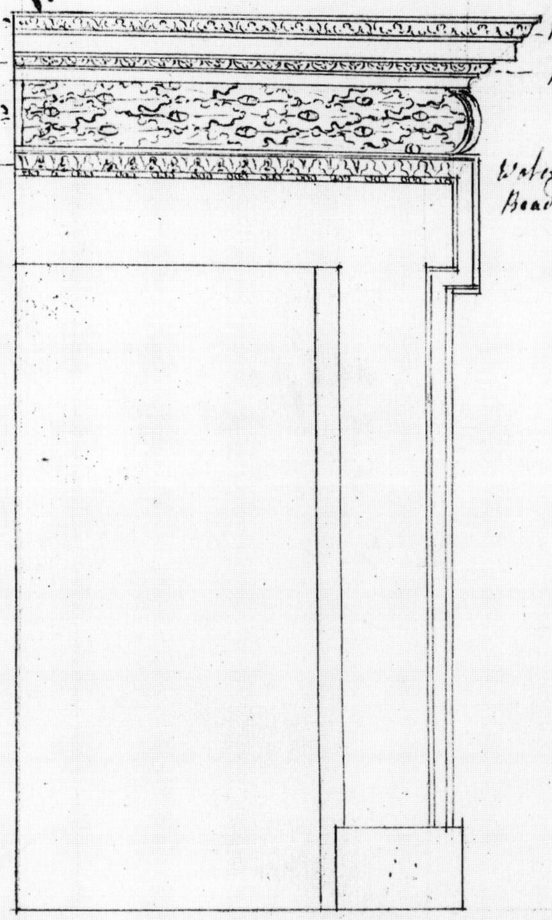

	freeze	Ogee in Cornice	Ovolo in Bed Mould	Ovolo & Bead	Round Marble
Nelson	2 .. 0	1 .. 2½	0 .. 7½	2 .. 5	
Vander	5 .. 0				£ 2 .. 6 . 6
Swift					

AIA81

Glass frame Mr Walcot. Betterley
in Burnish gold

N — 10 .. 0
V — 37 .. ½
S . 2 .. 0

} 12 Books gold

AIA82

(9

41

AIA83

An Account of Time in the

Side Bracketts				Sheild and Ribbon				Laurells			
Nelson	Land	Swift	Dandes	N	Y	S	D	N	Y	S	D
Leidger				Impost				Vase			

Wilton Monument

	Cherubs Heads				Trusses				Side palms				palms on pedestal			
Days	N	V	S	D	N	V	S	D	N	V	S	D	N	V	S	D
5=																
6=																
18=									6							

Festoon Truss

AIA85

2 frames for Ld Palmerston

AIA86